THE RISE OF CHICAGO'S BLACK METROPOLIS, 1920–1929

THE NEW BLACK STUDIES SERIES

Edited by Darlene Clark Hine and Dwight A. McBride

A list of books in the series appears at the end of this book.

The Rise of Chicago's Black Metropolis, 1920–1929

CHRISTOPHER ROBERT REED

UNIVERSITY OF ILLINOIS PRESS
URBANA, CHICAGO, AND SPRINGFIELD

Manufactured in the United States of America
C 5 4 3 2 1
∞ This book is printed on acid-free paper.

Library of Congress Cataloging-in-Publication Data
Reed, Christopher Robert.
The Rise of Chicago's Black Metropolis, 1920–1929 /
Christopher Robert Reed.
p. cm. — (The new Black studies series)
Includes bibliographical references and index.
ISBN-13: 978-0-252-03623-1 (hardcover : acid-free paper)
ISBN-10: 0-252-03623-9 (hardcover : acid-free paper)
1. African Americans—Illinois—Chicago—History—20th century.
2. Chicago (Ill.)—History—20th century.
I. Title.
F548.9.N4R445 2011
305.896'073077311—dc22 2010046046

CONTENTS

ACKNOWLEDGMENTS

At the end of the twentieth century, I began the daunting task of constructing a one-hundred year history of African America settlement that began during the nineteenth century, along with an exploration of this population's contributions to the growth and development of Chicago. Along this tortuous path, I was aided by many persons and institutions through which personal contact the sharing of information and interpretation of thought and actions became the norm. The family historian of the Hall (Rev. Abram and Joanna) family, Mrs. Jeanne Boger Jones of Grand Rapids, Michigan, led the way into understanding how the trove represented in family histories provided insight into the "interior history" of black Chicago. In addition, Mrs. Elizabeth Mitcham Butler of the Mitcham family and Mrs. Libby Davis Topps of the Davis family, both of Chicago, rendered valuable assistance in discerning those essential elements in African American life needed to understand what W. E. B. Du Bois wrote of in The Souls of Black Folk as the "meanings of their lives." Moreover, Doris Saunders of Jackson, Mississippi and Chicago shared her insight on African American polite society generally as well as about specific individuals. Jeff Ball of Chicago, a relative of the late Third Ward alderman Robert R. Jackson, proved a persistent witness to his relative's accomplishments and contributions. The Rev. Leon Scott of historic Berean Baptist Church joined with the Revs. James and Corliss Moody of Quinn Chapel AME Church in showing the way toward appreciating the significance of religion in the lives of Chicago's black population.

Scholarly advice flowed as readers of this manuscript in its roughest form braved the author's sometimes complex, often confusing, concepts and interpretations and rendered their valued criticisms and suggestions. Dean Lynn Y. Weiner of Roosevelt University and Pia Hunter of the University of Illinois at Chicago volunteered first and stayed the course to their credit and benefit. They were joined in this effort by Marionette Catherine Phelps who has proved a faithful and insightful reviewer. Moreover, Professors Clovis Semmes, Robert T. Starks, and Robert Howard, all members of the Black Chicago History Forum, demonstrated that organization's valuable role as they provided insight and clarifications on key historical events in Chicago history. The late Dempsey Travis, one of the key contributors to modern black Chicago history, banker Billy Williams and businessman James O'Neal helped the author sort out many questions that arose about banking and business that appear in chapter 3.

Acknowledgment must be accorded the staffs at the Harold Washington Library Center of the Chicago Public Library for their professional approach to scholarly research over many years. Their ranks included Theresa Yoder and Majag Walsh in Special Collections, Warren Watson and George Tibbits in the Reference Division, and Ronisha Epps and Claudia Armstrong in Microfilms. I am compelled to extend special recognition to Curator Robert Miller, Archivist Michael Flug and Beverly Cook at the Vivian G. Harsh Research Center of Afro-American History and Literature at the Chicago Public Library's Carter G. Woodson Regional Library. This dynamic trio always stood ready to assist in mining the Harsh Collection's many treasures, especially within the famed Illinois Writers Project. At the offices the Chicago Landmarks Commission, where the author serves as a member, Brian Goeken, Lisa Willis, Susan E. Perry, Terry Tatum, Eleanor Gorski and Beth Johnson provided needed assistance through their informed knowledge of Chicago's architecture and design. Chicago's extensive repositories of knowledge—the Newberry Library, the University of Chicago and Northwestern University—always opened their doors with staff support that was cordial and informed. Librarian Pia Hunter, assisted by microfilm technicians April Pittman and Delores Thomas, at the main library at the University of Illinois at Chicago gave generously of skills as this project proceeded. Thanks go out to Leroy Kennedy and Christopher Stewart at the Illinois Institute of Technology for their participation in searching out and providing visual evidence of black Chicago's rise.

Lastly, at my alma mater, Roosevelt University, I received continuous technical assistance from Helen Taylor, Dayne Agnew, Cheryl Williams-Sledge, Jaime Reyes, Vincent Perkins, Bernard Turner, Heidi Foster, Mary Foster, Chris Mich, Lynnett Davis and Michael Ensdorf as well as printing assistance from Wayne Magnus and Richard Woodfolk.

The editorial and marketing staffs at the University of Illinois Press encouraged the production of this book, so loud huzzahs go out to acquisitions editor Joan Catapano along with Jennifer Clark and Ann Beardsley. The entire Reed family that includes my wife, Marva, children, and grandchildren contributed in various ways as well to what exists in the end as a personal salute to courageous and productive Chicagoans of the 1920s.

Introduction

> What a change ten years has wrought in the affairs of our people! . . . The changes wrought seem almost revolutionary and not a gradual and continual change in the regular or evolutionary course of affairs.
>
> —Joseph [D.] Bibb, 1929

For over a half century, perhaps the best scholarly work exploring African American life in large, industrialized, northern cities with expanding populations has been St. Clair Drake and Horace R. Cayton's *Black Metropolis: A Study of Negro Life in a Northern City* (1945). This tome's value to scholarship over the years extended beyond its use as a sociological tool to become a reference and model in related fields. Moreover, its appearance as a major reference in historical studies has been just as widespread, and many of its assumptions have become pervasive in historical interpretation. The study, in particular, examined the important role in understanding the migrant as it clarified the positive (as well as the negative) role any sojourner could have on northern city life as the forces of urbanism reciprocally molded his or her new experiences and worldview.

As a document originally meant to examine the underlying causes of juvenile delinquency, it delved extensively into areas that required greater attention than that given by the myriad researchers who scoured Chicago's South Side during the decades of the 1930s and 1940s. This valued exploration, sometimes an excursion taken by strangers into African American life, took place amid the ruins of the Great Depression and advent of global conflagration. As a consequence, it reflected conditions during these times rather than that of the 1920s, America's "Age of Prosperity," or "Jazz Age," or "New Negro" period. Significantly, had the research been conducted earlier and contemporaneously during the third decade of the new century, it would have encountered a local black mind-set endeavoring ideologically to bring a dream of near independence into the realm of actuality. A major event had transpired, and yet, over a very short period of time, its impact on black life seemed to be obscured by the equally dramatic events that followed in its wake.

The sheer enormity of the data collected for *Black Metropolis* as well as the broad scope of the study's parameters meant that it covered a huge tract of physical and human landscapes. For some aspects of life, short shrift seemed to have been accorded politics, civic and community activism, banking and other financial activities, general business operations, the myriad dimensions of the culture, and the disparate shades of religion and worship. Methodology and conceptualization beyond that employed in sociology seemed more appropriate to understanding this community of hundreds of thousands of persons with as many different and interesting stories to investigate and tell. Acknowledging this need, the rigor of historical examination with its emphases on change over time, historicity, multiple causation, and evidentiary substantiation held the probability that a different perspective on what transpired between the years 1920 through 1929 was apparent.

Under historical scrutiny, it appeared that growing African American control over the political economy of Chicago's Black Belt somewhat confirmed the reality of the Black Metropolis's triumphant emergence. Yale-trained newspaper editor Joseph D. Bibb of the *Chicago Whip*, as one example, became thoroughly convinced that what he was witnessing represented a transformation in virtually all aspects of life in nothing short of revolutionary change.[1] He had indeed witnessed the decade-long metamorphosis of blacks from being a population with a presence that was barely discernible into one that gained recognition from the dynamics of its political and economic leaderships, the entry of its massive working class into the city's industrial labor force, and the enormity of its territorial expansion. Among the necessary conditions for this remarkable change had been a massive increase in population, a rising racial consciousness affecting and unifying all classes of African American society, a level of racial solidarity that bonded a community's thinking into a unified thrust, and a conscious desire for spatial hegemony—manifesting itself in the appearance of the Black Metropolis.

Documentation supporting the historical perspective revealed that African Americans were well aware of complex and interrelated global, national, and local forces at work, so they conceived—as did other ethnic groups in their distinct enclaves—that they could control the vast, expanding district blacks occupied on Chicago's Near South Side. Polonia was created by the Poles, Andersonville by the Swedes, and Chinatown by the Chinese, along with Little Italy, Greektown, and the Old Jewish Colony surrounding Maxwell Street. Contextually, creation of the Black Metropolis, as consistent with *imperium in imperio*, a city within a city, seemed less bizarre as a phase of separate development apart from mainstream American life preparatory to gaining a future acceptance.

Although a historical sketch (in part I) preceded the body of the sociological results presented in the body of *Black Metropolis*, a formal history examining businesses as part of an institutional structure, the role of a professional class, religion and the church, and political organization was never undertaken. This work, *The Rise of Chicago's Black Metropolis, 1920–1929*, at long last presents the contributing factors that produced the contemporarily recognized dynamism of the period as well as the many impediments encountered. Hindsight produced one view of life in this vibrant area of settlement, one that was not yet the "ghetto" that future historians in the 1960s would envision and write about, and that later saw the human and physical landscapes as quite dysfunctional. Absent was a tone of optimism in the pages of *Black Metropolis*. Yet—from the vibrancy of the numerous jazz and blues clubs to the energy of consumerism found along the State Street commercial corridor to the rise of a near independent, brawny political submachine of the Republican Party—hope, proverbially, seemed to spring eternal during this short span of time.

Temporally, the advent of the twentieth century brought the promise of a new day in which the racial progress of the African Americans of Chicago would be measured in tangible advancement in the quality of their lives—in employment, housing, education, and personal freedom from police and civilian harassment. Relegated to the service and domestic sectors of the city's economy as well as excluded residentially from large portions of the city, African Americans refused to accommodate themselves permanently to a second-class status. The tone Booker T. Washington assumed while in the city confirmed this. In 1910, before a large gathering of interested listeners, he exclaimed almost with defiance, "You meet severe competition here in Chicago and you have to take care of your bodies if you are not going to fail. . . . I have recently been in southern Europe, where the people talk slow, and walk slow, and work slow. Why, we can keep up with those white people easily. But here in Chicago it is different. You can't keep up with this northern white man I find up here so easily. He walks fast, and talks fast, and he works fast."[2] Washington's call for an energized drive toward competition with whites on their own terms proved compelling to many black Chicagoans and made him a favorite among this group, along with W. E. B. Du Bois, who advocated full citizenship rights on an immediate basis. Both leaders, as outside observers, perceived that among the people of the South Side a spirit, or ethos, existed that would propel them forward at such a pace that it would resemble their being in the center of a whirlwind. Or, as E. Franklin Frazier described it in his encounter with this force in the 1920s, "a whirl of life."

Encouragement from outside the city notwithstanding, local initiative set the parameters for progress. As early as 1905, Robert S. Abbott started a news sheet that would revolutionize black publishing and the presentation of news, affecting the thinking and behavior of African Americans nationally. That same year, Robert Motts opened his Pekin Theater, which he claimed was the first "Colored owned and operated" theater in the country. This venue offered acts from vaudeville to elocution to dance to semiserious dramatization.

By 1908, successful real estate promoter Jesse Binga embarked on his banking career with the inauguration of black financial operations at his Binga Bank on South State Street. Three years later, a business transplant from Kansas City, Missouri, arrived in Chicago to open his Overton Hygienic Company to exploit a larger market for women's beauty aids. The peripatetic W. E. B. Du Bois noticed what his friends and racial compatriots in Chicago were accomplishing and saw fit to feature them in his September 1915 issue of the *Crisis*. What those persons who possessed the mind-set of the New Negro envisioned as reality appeared similarly in the perceptive eyes and acute mind of W. E. B. Du Bois. In its essence, this ideal evinced vitality and paralleled the national mood for progress. Consistent with his policy in presenting a different African American population and city in the NAACP's house organ, the *Crisis*, Du Bois used the September 1915 issue to focus on black Chicago, the host of a half-century celebration of emancipation. The watchword of the pictorial and narrative essay centered on human dynamism. The Harvard-trained social scientist declared, "As compared with other cities Colored Chicago is noted for its push and independence, its political aggressiveness and its large number of middle class working people who are doing well." He also observed of the inhabitants that "out of the mass of Colored folk in Chicago have risen members of distinguished people who have who have made their mark in city life and even the life of the nation quite independent of their race or color."[3]

Over the short span of four years beginning in 1916 and extending through 1919, several momentous events—global war, interregional migration, internal and external group assimilations, and race riot—influenced life in Chicago and defined it for decades and generations to come. As a result, a new phase in African American city living dawned as these events embraced as well as affected change. First, the United States witnessed the birth of a global conflict in August 1914, originating in Europe with an influence over all aspects of life for every segment of the American citizenry to some extent. Patriotism and xenophobic hysteria enveloped thinking and behavior, carrying them to an extreme level of intensity. At the same time, the buildup of a half century's black martial ardor found its outlet in a limited military expedition into Mexico in 1916 by members of the 8th Infantry Regiment of the Illinois National Guard, the nation's sole black-led military unit. As the federally redesignated 370th Regiment, the all–African American officers' corps led these men into combat in Europe by 1918.

At that time, the movement of over 51,000 able-bodied young, African American men and women from the southeastern United States' "Black Belt" region had already begun into Chicago. Their arrival, especially into the South Side's Black Belt district, provided an unanticipated body of workers that, along with African Americans already in residence, constituted the city's first black industrial proletariat. Composed mainly of the rural unskilled, their ranks also contained a smattering of urbanized, skilled, and professional groups, along with some children. As part of the epochal Great Migration, "The mass migration which began in 1916 represented the transfer of a large population from participation in a caste-system to participation in a social order characterized by greater social mobility, less economic subordination, and a system of ideas which did not sanction the 'fixing' of the Negroes' status. Such a system reconditioned them, and they, in turn, modified it (*in tandem with the existing residential population*)" [emphasis added].[4] Indeed, the dynamic impact of this newest wave of migrants overshadowed the forgotten phenomenon of *melding*, or internal assimilation into the African American population already in place.[5]

Although Pullman porters in the service sector had previously constituted 20 percent of the male workforce and proved a dominant social force in black Chicago, in this succeeding period of history, this cluster of packinghouse workers expanded to comprise 25 percent of that constituency in the industrial arena. Conflict in the ranks of labor—coupled with contention over housing, recreation space, and rising black political power—contributed to the infamous race rioting of July and August 1919. African American resolve and resistance to discrimination, threats, harassment, and murder stiffened in the aftermath of this social disaster.

Phenomenally, according to Drake and Cayton, "the Black Belt became the Black Metropolis in the twenty years between the close of the First World War and the beginning of the second. . . . [Here] the dream of the Black Metropolis [evolved]. . . . To some the dream was inspiring. To many it was a makeshift dream, a substitute for the American Dream of complete integration into American life. . . . To some . . . the dream seemed a fraud and a delusion."[6] The halcyon days of the 1920s represented a time when black racial consciousness and the positive manifestations of racial solidarity reached their apex in black Chicago. In a complete lack of contradiction, both a perceived and an actual Black Metropolis evolved but with a longevity as a viable institutional reality in the latter case that extended only through the decade. The fulfillment of this "Dream of the Black Metropolis" represented a successful culmination in pursuit of an intended consequence. In a deliberate, formulated manner, African Americans who supported this ideal amassed capital, recruited professionals to constitute an infrastructure, persuaded the various classes to lend their support, discarded old notions of negativism, started and expanded businesses, and supported this territorial concept through an extraordinary political organization.

Although the success of the Black Metropolis rested heavily on the continued expansion of the African American political economy of the South Side, at the beginning of the decade it benefitted directly from the post-wartime boom. The marvel of this situation existed in the ability of African Americans to position themselves to take advantage of opportunities that circumstances presented despite the many obstacles they encountered. Although African Americans could not be credited with molding the overall economic conditions that made the Black Metropolis a reality, they surely could be recognized for their power of motivation, will, foresight, and perseverance in their perception of the possible. Here was ample proof that a required mentality intersecting with advantageous conditions could produce salutary results. The New Negro possessed that mindset and Chicago provided the venue.

* * *

Organizationally, although the importance of material factors affecting historical change were undeniable, the inner workings of the political economy of the 1920s were intricately linked to the demographic changes, emerging social structure, level of racial consciousness, cultural and aesthetic expressions, and religious practices and activities of this pivotal period in Chicago's history. Chapter 1 focuses on demographics and the thinking accompanying expansion of this population, while chapter 2 explores the intricacies of the first discernible class structure that conformed to normative standards of socioeconomic status in the city's history.

The relationships, dynamics, and complexities making up and driving the political economy were fully apparent as political progress accompanied and complemented economic growth. With new political influence and the vestiges of real power benefitting both the legitimate business world as well as the underground economy, the Black Belt of racial isolation transformed itself into the Black Metropolis of manifested racial progress.

Within the economic sphere, new African American businesses were organized and revitalized in various areas ranging from the financial to retail to service to light manufacturing. Meanwhile, older ones grew and prospered. As to its economic foundation, its financial strength rested heavily on the continuing maturation of its banks, the vitality of the real estate market, and the expansion and success of its smaller business enterprises. Critically, although there was growth, widespread, highly tangible economic development was missing and identified this phase of African American business evolution as incipient. Chapter 3 examines business activities while chapter 4 provides insight into the status of labor from which the foundation of consumerism emanated. If political successes and business gains represented tangible evidence of progress toward some semblance of independence, the status of labor proved the Achilles' heel of African American society. High levels of unemployment due to fluctuations in the economic system remained as much of a problem as underemployment based on racial discrimination. And without a mass base of consuming workers, the foundation of the Black Metropolis remained vulnerable to dissolution.

The decade witnessed a dual black presence beyond tokenism in the chambers of the Chicago City Council as well as possessing the nation's sole black voice in the U.S. Congress. Further, the Illinois Senate, the Illinois Commerce Commission, the Cook County Municipal Court, and the Chicago Library Board accommodated a new African American membership. Among white racists, Chicago's City Hall even derisively carried the label of being "Uncle Tom's Cabin" because of extensive black employment and a small black decision-making capability. Chapter 5 explores this occurrence. With foci on economically regenerative politics and robust economics as integral features of the bedrock foundation for the heralded Black Metropolis, chapter 5 also explores the nexus of politics and nonpolitical economic protest, along with this pivotal relationship to the economic fabric of black Chicago in business, labor, associational linkages, the professions, and the underground economy.

The longevity of the Black Metropolis was short-lived, mostly attributable to a countervailing movement in both politics and economics that became apparent between 1926 and 1929. While the independent political leadership of Edward H. Wright was amassing influence and power until his last and most independent stratagem failed in 1926, white Chicago simultaneously began to infuse the South Side economic structure with massive amounts of capital manifested through business ventures that shifted the epicenter of African American business interest away from 35th Street and farther southward to 47th Street. Accompanying this shift was a decline in the black retail trade as well as a surge in unemployment that was mounting as early as 1926.

For a group relying on the spiritual core of its culture to allow transcendence over mundane adversities, the roles of religion and accompanying church life in the modern age remained one of the major wellsprings of black agency. It was within these spheres that E. Franklin Frazier observed a type of religious freedom and expression that permeated the African American class and cultural spectrum. Blacks attended religious services and practiced a variety of beliefs that ranged from Christian Science teaching to genuine Islam to elevated Baha'ism to black Judaism to various esoteric strains of Christianity.[7] Chapter 6 covers this transformation, which also witnessed the city's black clergy bridging the constitutional gap between church and state in a most dramatic fashion.[8]

Cultural and recreational activities certainly added to the whirl of life, giving rise to the reputation of Chicago as a "swinging town." From choral music to jazz to early blues, the city's reputation as a music magnet and incubator for innovation grew. The cultural undergirding that made the Jazz Age what it was is discussed in chapter 7. The performing arts—which included instrumental music, choral music, and individual vocal presentations—dominated creative performance in Chicago. Mastery of the voice heard in sopranos, tenors, baritones, and basses accompanied widespread mastery of the piano. As a result, highly skilled musicians abounded. In the second decade of the century, ragtime, blues, and jazz emerged. Black groups performed throughout the city in concert halls such as the downtown district's Orchestra Hall and Auditorium Theater, in South Side churches, and in the private homes of wealthy whites on the North Side. Notable among choral groups was the Chicago Umbrian Glee Club. As a sign of advanced African American organization, by 1915, an All Colored Composers conference opened on April 23 of that year.

The visual arts of painting and sculpture found some African Americans students studying at the Art Institute of Chicago. Notable among their ranks were William Eduardo Scott, who arrived in the city in 1904 to study artistic techniques and whose productive years of creating masterpieces in churches (Providence Baptist, Pilgrim Baptist), schools (Lane Technical High School), and other buildings spanned several decades and past the 1930s. Archie Motley Sr. started his study and work that led him to create his famous night scenes. Creatively, the works of Charles Dawson would follow, as would those of William Farrow.

The literary arts encompassing drama, poetry, fiction, criticism, and scholarship (including newspaper journalism, such as that which appeared in the pages of the *Chicago Defender*) had begun to flourish earlier in the century. As early as 1900, poets such as Fenton Johnson contributed creative progress in writing that was to slowly evolve into the Black Chicago Literary Renaissance of the later 1930s.[9] By 1914, the National Association of Negro Authors and Writers had organized and held a conference to assess the state of the group and to plan greater advances in the future. The year 1915 brought yet another meeting of its members in Chicago.

* * *

Black Chicago was fortunate to have amidst its ranks as local eyes, ears, and voices a group of academically trained activists who also participated experientially and reported dispassionately on what transpired in the Black Metropolis. Scholarship benefitted especially from the presence and written accounts of contemporaries Charles S. Johnson and E. Franklin Frazier, who took note of the dynamics and distinctive flavor of life apparent in Chicago's South Side neighborhoods. These influential agents illuminated occurrences, structures, and processes present in a cohesive community as African Americans sought control of this space to the fullest extent possible. Consequently, what Berkeley historian Leon F. Litwack referred to as interior history gained an unusual authenticity as well as gave a more poignant meaning to African American life. In addition, even with a meager literary tradition on black Chicago, its ethos and pathos was captured nonetheless by nonfictional and fictional accounts of life published widely in mainstream publications from the pens of Langston Hughes, Richard Wright, and Gwendolyn Brooks, along with peripheral accounts in James T. Farrell's *Studs Lonigan: A Trilogy*. Along with increased coverage in the *Chicago Tribune* and the *Chicago Daily News*, the reporting of the *Chicago Defender* was peaking in its broad coverage of various aspects of black life.

Periodization encapsulating the third decade of the twentieth century allowed a focus to be placed on the uniqueness of this span of time in American history and in black Chicago history. Moreover, the comprehensive scope of the historical Black Metropolis accommodated the interweaving of the dynamic social forces in such a fashion as to demonstrate that correlations clearly existed between politics, labor and work, business, religion, cultural activities, protest advocacy, and militant and revolutionary activism.

CHAPTER 1

Demography and Ethos

> Much is said of the "New Negro," we haven't seen such a critter, just the same old tinted individual, roused into self-consciousness, awakened to his own possibilities, with stiffened backbone, and new ambitions, new desires, new hopes for the future.
>
> —*Chicago Defender*, 1920

> He is a new type of Homo sapiens psychologically. . . . He has no narrow religious creed, supports human principles instead of race prejudice, ignores the unfounded flattery heaped upon the Negro, does not boast, but achieves [and] has a scientific mind. . . . He does not seek philanthropy but an opportunity.
>
> —Frederick H. H. Robb on the New Negro, 1927

> It is the whirl of life that goes on in the "Black Belt" that one thinks of when he talks of the Negro community.
>
> —E. F. Frazier, *Opportunity*, 1929

The Jazz Age was a national period filled with anxieties resulting from the unsettling pursuit of world peace, labor and racial unrest, anticipated economic recession, and a besieged value system. Within the South Side black community, a new sentiment prevailed so it was also the age of the "New Negro." Prohibition challenged the imagination of those who wished to imbibe in violation of the law, leading to highly organized criminal efforts and the creation of an underworld government of sorts. The whirl of life to which Frazier referred could well have been the sound of arriving migrants, whose movement was constant throughout the decade.

The remarkable demographic increase in the African American population of Chicago between 1910 and 1920 of 148.5 percent, and specifically between 1916 and 1919 of 86 percent, was matched in significance by the increase in population from 109,458 persons in 1920 to 233,903 persons in 1930. In and of itself, Jazz Era migration represented an increase of 114 percent over the decade of the twenties. Whenever a demographic milepost was reached during the twentieth century, it now indicated an almost automatic increase. Despite reductions in the labor force as part of a national recession at war's end, it appeared to be the beginning of what Dickens would describe as "the best of times."

For 1920, when the population climbed to 109,458, the percentage of African Americans constituted 4.1 percent of the city's total makeup. The next year, 1921, a time of discouraging economic conditions and labor discord, the black population climbed to include 121,902 persons as the magnetism of life in Chicago continued to beckon to black southerners. By 1923, the increase resulted in a mass of 146,791 old and new black residents. Some black newcomers expressed a sentiment that Chicago offered them a hope not to be found elsewhere or under any other circumstances. One man responded resolutely when confronted with high joblessness in Chicago, "I also know that there is no work in Mississippi, and I had rather be out of work in Chicago than out of work in Mississippi."[1]

Heading toward mid-decade, the surge of migrants continued, and by 1927, a head count around the city in all three of the major geographical divisions found 196,569 persons of African descent in residence. With the possible influence of the devastating flooding that occurred in the Lower Mississippi Valley, this out-migration just might well account for the next federal census year of 1930 showing an astronomical climb of African Americans to 233,903 persons. The phenomenon of black population doubling between 1910 and 1920 seemed to be nearly replicating the pattern again between 1920 and 1930.[2] The demographic growth of the Black Metropolis rested firmly on the continuous in-migration of primarily adults from the South—not only from the plantations of the Deep South and small towns but also cities such as Birmingham, New Orleans, Atlanta, and Mobile. The one set of characteristics they possessed in common was, as Congregationalist minister Rev. Harold M. Kingsley described these new residents, they were just as "divergent, vivid and compelling, as any other group or all groups."[3]

* * *

In-migration brought some important and many more obscure arrivals. Among their ranks were professionals, members of the laboring class, refugees carrying the scars of experience with racial violence, and persons filled with wanderlust. Dr. Calvin Paul Davis and his family fled the terror of the rioter and lynch mob in Longview, Texas, arriving in 1920 and reestablishing himself in the medical field. Also from violence-prone Texas, the eight-member family of Scott and Violet Arthur from Paris, Texas, fled the terror of murder and sexual assault against their immediate family members during the summer of 1920. After hiding from vengeance-filled mobs, they finally were able to leave the southwest and arrived in Chicago on August 30, 1920. Another member of Dempsey J. Travis's family left Georgia for Chicago and work at the stockyards. Steelworker Alex W. Walker, both a refugee and fugitive from the Atlanta riot of 1906, arrived from Birmingham's steel mills with his wife, Julia, in 1921.[4] Attorney Oscar C. Brown, a World War I veteran from Edwards, Mississippi, and graduate of Howard University, joined his brother in the practice of law in 1925. Another traveler from Mississippi named

Richard Wright took the place of the original sojourner from Georgia, Rev. Richard R. Wright Jr., and also left his indelible imprint on this city's life.[5]

Meantime, two individuals destined to contribute to the most influential intellectual wave of thought in sociology during the twentieth century arrived on the campus of the University of Chicago to pursue graduate study. Charles S. Johnson began work as assistant researcher for the monumental study conducted under the auspices of the Chicago Commission on Race Relations in the aftermath of the Chicago riot of 1919. In June 1927, E. Franklin Frazier followed in Johnson's wake, beginning two full years of doctoral-level research and study with the faculty of the famed "Chicago School." The thirty-three-year-old Frazier was making his reappearance in the city after a four-year hiatus following summer graduate courses in 1923.[6]

In a metropolis that swelled with pride for its military traditions, the black military veteran still remained another important element in the ranks of this growing demographic with the exception that he was younger, more assertive, and sometimes more aggressive than his Civil War and Spanish American War counterparts. Collectively these veterans numbered in the hundreds and expanded their individual and overall influence formidably. These men returned from combat in Europe in 1919 with honors and a rugged determination to change race relations in the city and the nation. Within their officers' ranks were exceptional men whose names filled business, political, civic, religious, and fraternal lists as leaders of various spheres in black society—Earl B. Dickerson, William Levi Dawson, William Warfield, Oscar C. Brown Sr., Rev. William Braddan, Franklin A. Denison, and others. Within the ranks of the enlisted men, a similar determination to progress prevailed, one extending far beyond the racist limits set upon them when they left for war and "to make the world safe for democracy." Not all belonged to Old Eighth that had fought as the 370th Infantry Regiment in France; many had served in the famed and decorated 365th Infantry as well as other units. As New Negroes they shaped a transformed way of thinking about themselves, the obstacles they encountered, and solutions that exceeded their parents' and grandparents' wildest imaginings.

* * *

Fortunately for later generations, the character of this ever-expanding mass of humanity was explored during 1927–1928 in the exhaustive work of renowned sociologist E. Franklin Frazier, who penetratingly examined all dimensions of group life through data for the census year 1920, along with acute observation and normal interpersonal contacts. Frazier's contribution on family life as it existed in its various dimensions of class, occupation, age, residence, and marital status throughout the city resulted in his first tome, *The Negro Family in Chicago*, published shortly after the decade ended.[7] He further expanded his work beyond Chicago into other northern cities and published *The Negro Family in the United*

States in 1939. Both as a detached scholar mingling freely among the populace and as a participant-observer, Frazier matched the perceptive abilities of University of Chicago scholars who preceded him—Monroe Nathan Work, Richard R. Wright Jr., and Charles S. Johnson. While studying the history of the formation of the black community (but not a ghetto) with its many complexities, a valuable and more accurate history of a socially and economically differentiated group within a community was being uncovered, although its internal dynamics were generally overlooked in the latter part of the twentieth century.[8]

Family life and structure was a good case in point. In his study *The Black Family in Slavery and Freedom*, historian Herbert G. Gutman established that the social integrity of the family unit was underestimated and underrated, pointing to greater community stability in the historical past. Using his New York City data, he concluded that the two-headed family structure still predominated up to and beyond the influence of the Great Migration. By extrapolation, he extended his postulation to the entire North and that would have included Chicago.[9] Interestingly enough, Frazier proved one-half century earlier that the two-head household existed in Chicago as a normative model with variations within the total based on income and class. His overall conclusion from examination of the data was that the black family had, indeed, become "progressively stable" in the North in the one or two generations after emancipation.[10]

Distribution by age revealed that the black population in all areas of Chicago was predominantly an adult population and one that was represented almost equally by gender. Frazier acutely used the "zones of settlement," or an ecological model, made popular at the University of Chicago that consisted of dividing the typical northern city into concentric circles of living instead of a static "ghetto." New patterns of life were revealed that advanced understanding of the dynamics of black life undergoing urbanization. This breakthrough moved beyond acceptance of statistical generalizations offered without an explanation to acknowledging variations within a given population. Social researcher Irene Graham wrote, "in spite of the fact that in 1920 the Negro population was still very largely composed of migrants, we find that only 8.3 per cent of the units making up the households had no real family group as a nucleus. And even of this 8.3 per cent, such groups as grandparents and grandchildren actually represent a family relationship, although not technically so."[11]

Different patterns ensued in family formation and with influence over marriage rates and marital arrangements. Just like Chicago historian Timuel D. Black Jr., future magistrate Earl Strayhorn arrived in 1924 in the company of his parents and with a sibling.[12] In contrast, some family groups split in the South only to reconstitute in the North. This was the experience of future businessman George Johnson, who arrived in the city in the company of his eighteen-year-old mother and two other siblings. With two sisters and two brothers already in Chicago, his mother heeded the opportunity for improvement and traveled to Chicago's South Side with her three youngsters in 1929. She had been unable to convince her husband to accompany her because of a fear of the North implanted in his mind by manipulative whites. Dauntlessly, and only looking forward, Mrs. Johnson secured work within two weeks of her arrival, joining the service sector of the labor force and proceeding on her way to independence.[13] One of the most famous photographs associated with black migration (that of the Arthur family of Paris, Texas) and to the Great Migration, 1916–1918, is really one that belongs to the 1920s.

The legacy of family disorganization that had marked slavery days plagued the newcomers to Chicago as they transplanted their habits to this new locale.[14] However, low fertility rates noted in 1920 and again in 1928 contributed to this condition as well.[15] Frazier, in describing the presence of the very young within the black Chicago population in 1929 (that is, persons under fifteen years of age), referred to the population as exemplifying "a migrant group without many children." He further compared it to the European immigrant groups and found the circumstances as to childbearing between the groups quite comparable.[16] In his comprehensive study of the evolution of the African American family in Chicago, he found that "sixty per cent of employed male heads of households were without dependent children."[17] So, black Chicago remained an adult-oriented society in 1920 with a limited proportion of children both within the recently arrived group and the clusters of persons of lengthier residence. Combined, the number of children reached 20 percent of the total black population of 108,000.[18]

With Frazier using fifteen years of age as his cutoff for the youthful phase of life, the farther south one proceeded along the State Street axis, the higher the percentage of children under fifteen, with the poorest area nearest the downtown business district as an exception.[19]

The opportunity to attend school in an integrated setting with equal standards and resources had been another appealing aspect of life for African American families whenever the period they decided to journey north. By the end of this decade, 14,000 African American youngsters were attending neighborhood schools.[20] Their experiences, however, on both social and educational levels were not always pleasant, as they faced discrimination based on white assumptions of intellectual inferiority related to their race, their status as migrants, and their having southern backgrounds.[21] The presence of these children in large numbers in the schools became an incentive to many white parents to move away from what was becoming an ever-expanding, black, South Side community.[22]

Consistent with the growing problem for all groups in urban living during this period, the number of children under fourteen years of age (the legal age of consent until 1925 when it was raised to sixteen years) without supervision and protection increased. Although various religious bodies established supervisory facilities for children, white Protestant institutions routinely rejected the admission of African Americans. With the number of African American dependent children in particular increasing after 1916, the two facilities expressively designed to care for them—the Amanda Smith Home for Girls and the Louise Manual Training School for Colored Boys—closed in 1919 and 1920, respectively.[23] With neither home nor friendly institution to accommodate their needs, the more estranged youth either became permanent denizens of the streets or rebellious and placed in reform school facilities.[24] Overall, the condition of the black family had improved only slightly when evaluated through the lenses of marriage rates, general dissolutions involving male desertion, divorces, single parenting, and juvenile delinquency rates.

School-age children represented only one end of the spectrum of youth, however. The presence in the population of infants (under one year of age) remained constant along the State Street axis, with a slight increase in their ranks as one moved south of 39th Street where better housing existed. All in all, this age cohort represented approximately 3 to 5 percent of the population.[25]

While the young experienced their bitter taste of the world from their end of the age spectrum, another group of black notables who experienced the last throes of the Civil War as very young children or the earliest phase of the emancipation were advancing toward their last days on earth. A number of persons over sixty years of age and who were familiar with the slave experience through their slave parents or slave infancy filled the demographic pool also. Their days were numbered, and death came to S. Laing Williams before the end of the year in 1921, Frank L. Gillespie (May 1925), Dr. Charles E. Bentley (October 1929), Daniel Jackson (May 1929), and Mrs. Irene Goins (May 1929). Significantly these were the people who formed the backbone of the elite and the solid middle class. The older persons had influence over the lifestyles of the collective nature of the group in a manner similar to economic forces at work in the city. Frazier wrote of the latter when he analyzed the reasons behind family disruption.[26]

With the passing of these leaders, a new coterie of leaders was coming into its own based on wealth accumulation and personal merit. However, the shape of the society they would lead was undergoing transformation due to economic depression and war. Loss of status and income awaited the professionals in medicine and law, while unionized and skilled workers, along with members of the underground economy and the underworld, could look forward to such an improvement in their socioeconomic status that they entered the post–World War I era as members of the segmented middle class.

Ethos: New Negro Thinking

No more auspicious time presented itself for the emergence of another phase of a perpetually transformative group mentality than a period of rapid social change nationally. No more auspicious place existed than the burgeoning northern American cities of the postwar era. In Chicago, America's second city, the New Negro personality of the 1920s bloomed and grew enormously in terms of an expanded African American worldview, expectations, and accomplishments. As both an internal and external manifestation of a changing racial outlook, a look at the various elements within the collective mind-set of Chicago African Americans offers the best medium for understanding what transpired during the 1920s.

The African American consciousness was constantly being raised with its self-perpetuating sense of self-awareness. It was the collective mind-set of the group, first independently and voluntarily fixing its place in the universe—or at least in America's multiracial society—and then transcending chronological age or generational status to constitute its evolved, shared, twentieth-century attitudes. During the second decade of the century, the thinking and motivation of Chicago's African Americans encapsulated a philosophy that rejected a long-held view of what was possible to achieve in a racially charged, yet fluid, society while guaranteeing the course of its probability through self-actualization. It was a place in the eyes of one young migrant girl where a person had "a chance"—a chance to dream and bring that dream to fruition.[27] Now, a heightened self-confidence encouraged African Americans to examine and criticize themselves through self-analysis and reflection without fear of racial self-incrimination. Displaying expectations that existed widely across the spectrum from the conventional to the hoped for, from politics to business to civil rights and public image, they also manifested themselves in modern spheres of entrepreneurship and finance; in aviation with the successes of aviatrix Bessie Coleman and youthful aviation enthusiast Harold Hurd; in architecture with the design contributions of Charles S. Duke and William T. Bailey; in academics with Charles S. Johnson and E. Franklin Frazier; and in sports with the basketball "phenoms" in the Forty Club Five and later the Savoy Big Five. Convincingly, the New Negro phenomenon changed the way the African American viewed himself as well as how others did.

Late in the 1910s, the perpetual search for the proper group labeling—Negro, Colored, Afro-American, or whatever—developed into almost an ideological crusade. The name "Ethiopian" was now added to the controversy.[28] Unwilling to adhere to guidelines involving racial protocol set outside of the group's emerging new foci, black ideological development continued its transformation. Racial self-identification fell under this overwhelming influence. It reached a point at which the two leading news journals—Robert S. Abbott's *Chicago Defender* and Anthony Overton's *Half-Century Magazine*—promoted the redefinition of the race's name, or label. Discarding "Negro," "Colored," "African," and "Afro-American," the publishers recommended and then unilaterally began using the terms "Race" and "Libranians" respectively. The *Defender* explained its nomenclatural shift thus: "The constant play on the word Negro has made us a marked people. It keeps us a thing set apart, separate, distinct, different. It makes us something to be shunned, despised, condemned. . . . The injury done us comes a matter of evil suggestion, and is almost irreparable. We become subjects of table and fireside discussion. Over the morning coffee women and little children hear a recital of all the vices charged to us and learn to associate them with our color."[29] For the *Half-Century Magazine*, a new name was a necessity, explaining its position in these terms:

> There are a number of synonymous terms applied to our people in America that are so decidedly distasteful. So objectionable are some of these that for a number of years the thinking members of the race have been searching diligently for a name by which the race shall be known. . . . The first of our race in the United States were brought from that section of the west coast of Africa, just beyond the Gold Coast (now Ghana), that lies about four hundred miles east of the country now known as Liberia. At that time the country was unnamed; then why not give to that section of the country from which our ancestors came, the name Librania and designate the descendants of those who came from that section . . . as Libranians.[30]

The most nationalistic organization of the period, the Universal Negro Improvement Association (UNIA) and African Communities League, however, preferred to continue to use the racial designation of "Negro." In its commitment to worldwide, mass-level, black advancement, the UNIA earned and assumed a posture of authority and leadership. War in Europe between the imperial powers of Germany, Great Britain, and France, all African colonizers, meant the involvement of black colonial troops from such colonies as Morocco, Algeria, and Senegal—in particular, the latter two nations. Readers of the *Chicago Defender* were well aware of black participation and bravery, and this served to raise the interest in Pan-Africanism. As the UNIA's president, Hon. Marcus M. Garvey, explained its nomenclatural position, the word *Negro* worked just fine:

> The custom of these anthropologists is: whenever a black man, whether he be Moroccan, Algerian, Senegalese or what not, accomplishes anything of importance, he is no longer a Negro. The question therefore, suggests itself, "Who and what is a Negro?" The answer is, "a Negro is a person of dark complexion or race, who has not accomplished anything and to whom others are not obligated for any useful service." . . . Let us not be flattered by white anthropologists and statesmen, who, from time to time, because of our success here, there or anywhere, try to make out that we are no longer members of the Negro race. If we were Negroes when we were down under the heel of oppression then we will be Negroes when we are up and liberated from such thralldom.[31]

Just as the language of racial self-identification showed variations on how African Americans envisioned themselves in a nation where the common identity of *American* should have been available, the language of interracial contact assumed an ominous tone. It seemed reflective of the war but its use would extend decades beyond the war. Blacks were accorded none of the dignity expected of humans describing fellow humans when military and animalistic terms were put in use.

African Americans moving into new neighborhoods became *invasions*, blacks moving to newer residences in families or in small groups became a *swarm* or a *horde*, their arrival was an *influx*, and attacks on them were delineated by the cowardly act of anonymous *bombings*. The very use of racial label *Negroes* when hardly necessary for clarification seemed to distinguish these Americans as apart from all others.

As to New Negro thinking involving any incipient or evolving militancy, perspective dictates relevance of this assessment. To be sure, both contemporary and present data substantiate the existence of militancy among recently arrived and acculturating West Africans from the seventeenth century through the conclusion of the Civil War. In Chicago, in pursuit of group affirmation, advancement, and hegemony, that militancy existed on a continuum, thereby placing the germ of the mentality of the 1920s as being preexistent rather than not unforeseen.

The origins and conditions that contributed to this new sentiment are somewhat well known. *The Negro in Chicago* placed it partially at the end of the First World War and the influence of returning troops.[32] As described by African American intellectual Alain Locke, a Harvard graduate and Rhodes scholar, this incipient mind-set had its locus in "the younger generation [that] is vibrant with a new psychology; the new spirit is awake[ning] in the masses [too, as both transform] what has been a perennial problem into the progressive phases of contemporary life." Locke added, "For generations in the mind of America, the Negro has been more of a formula than a human being—a something to be argued about, condemned, or defended." Further, he said, "With this renewed self-respect and self-dependence, the life of the Negro community is bound to enter a new dynamic phase, the buoyancy from within compensating for whatever pressure there may be of conditions from without . . . [even] the migrant masses, shifting from countryside to city, hurdle[d] several generations of experience at a leap."[33]

Within the Black Metropolis and elsewhere in the city wherever African Americans resided, a new sentiment prevailed: The whirl of life manifested itself in the mind and spirit as well as the body. Throughout America, the Jazz Age was also the age of the New Negro whose origins had been noticeable in the previous decade. And who was this "New Negro," this racial creature with indomitable resolve and titanic abilities? The *Chicago Defender* offered one explanation in 1920: "Much is said of the 'New Negro,' we haven't seen such a critter, just the same old tinted individual, roused into self-consciousness, awakened to his own possibilities, with stiffened backbone, and new ambitions, new desires, new hopes for the future."[34] This assessment coincided with the emerging, perceptive view of Frederick H. H. Robb, the Northwestern University law school student who was president of the Washington Intercollegiate Club. As Robb wrote of their view, which contrasted greatly with that of the previous generation, this New Negro was presented as "a new type of Homo sapiens psychologically. He believes in preparation, in himself, in fighting but not merely by petitions, orating, and delegations, but in using the courts to insist on his civil rights [as well as] the effective, intelligent use of the ballot to oust those who would disgrace the race. . . . He has no narrow religious creed, supports human principles instead of race prejudice, ignores the unfounded flattery heaped upon the Negro, does not boast, but achieves [and] has a scientific mind. . . . He does not seek philanthropy but an opportunity."[35]

As explored by Robb, the new decade exposed the public to the New Negro mind-set, which featured a psychological dimension that was keeping pace with a national trend to embrace the modernization of America. As to the intellectual undergirding of this New Negro thought, neither Charles S. Johnson nor E. Franklin Frazier was impressed with black Chicago's collective mental acuity. In black Chicago, "the direction of her energies [gravitates] towards practical accomplishments."[36] Rather than being socially isolated, Frazier and his wife had contact with black Chicagoans in many cultural and supposed intellectual settings, so Frazier's assessment was especially condemnatory and resented locally.

In the metaphysical world, the New Negro showed a willingness to move beyond the strict confines of the established religions, but in complete contradistinction at times to the desire of the recently arrived working- and lower-class migrant to enjoy a folk-based religion steeped in spiritualism and emotionalism. Depending on the circumstances, the latter two expressions had their place also in the New Negro's pattern of worship. Frazier noted aptly that black Chicago was exhibiting a progressive trait in that it "had no narrow religious creed" and that this was manifested in an increase in the number of Baha'ists and members of the Christian Science belief.[37] Interest in the higher-status Episcopal, Presbyterian, and Congregational churches grew likewise as observed by Yale-trained Congregationalist minister Rev. Harold M. Kingsley. As for the fate of denominationalism, under pressures from "the demands of the New Negro," at least twelve ministers, including AME Revs. William D. Cook and M. C. Wright at Bethel and St. Stephen, respectively, broke with creed and tradition in rejecting their church structures and the accompanying bureaucracies to form independent community churches that were open to all believers.[38]

Supportive of the basic principles of humanity, the New Negro embraced interracial contact, transcended the manifestations of race prejudice he or she encountered, eschewed racial hatred or any resort to revenge, and moved beyond an appeal to white charity in favor of black self-reliance. Black talent pursued various administrative responsibilities that were challenging, such as in the leaderships of the Chicago NAACP and Chicago Urban League. Once in office, these New Negro types steered a course toward eventual organizational successes in a manner that escaped their white predecessors. This transfer of power along lines of merit rather than white privilege was exemplified by the early 1930s in the Chicago NAACP with a shift in racial leadership and greater relevance in its programming initiated in the mid-1920s. Dr. Midian O. Bousfield's and attorney Earl B. Dickerson's rise in the hierarchy of the Chicago Urban League represented the culmination of the same pattern within another decade.

Robb also spoke of greater self-reliance when he explored the extent to which the New Negro "does not seek philanthropy but an opportunity (and accepts the challenge of northern competition from whites)." Robb defined the New Negro's thinking on the subject of accomplishment as one that ignored any unfounded flattery heaped upon African Americans unless it was earned. Rewards for mediocrity were to be rejected as substitutes for real achievement. The young student continued, "the New Negro does not boast, but achieves [and] has a scientific mind." Whether it was Charles Pierce in the classroom explaining intricate theories in physics, Lloyd Augustus Hall in a corporate chemistry laboratory, the chemists of Overton Hygienic Company, Paul E. Johnson producing therapeutic electric lamps, or Dr. Julian Lewis of the University of Chicago Medical School working in the pathology lab, the New Negro proved conclusively that he possessed a mind for science.

While supposedly eschewing a tendency to boast, Frazier noticed that as the decade progressed, black Chicago assumed a sense of its importance to national black life and had the temerity (in the scholar's eyes) to challenge New York's Harlem's claim to the mantle of African American cultural hegemony, even without a literati or an intellectual base. Frazier observed the following:

> Ever since Harlem won the reputation for being the Mecca of the New Negro, the Negro Community in Chicago has been very conscious of its place in Negro life. Lately because of this quickened consciousness the leaders among Chicago Negroes have bestirred themselves to make the American public cognizant of their contributions to, and place in, Negro life in America. The feeling of rivalry between Harlem and Chicago has caused each to cast uncomplimentary epithets at the other. New York has charged Chicago Negroes with being a group of money getters, without any sense for the finer things of life; while Chicago has retorted that the "homeless ones" of New York float in the clouds of spirit without any sound economic basis for their culture.[39]

The 1925 assessment of New Negro thinking from Robert W. Bagnall, the director of branches for the national NAACP network, observed that the changed psychology of the Negro avoided paternalism.[40] This theme would be picked up by the Brotherhood of Sleeping Car Porters in its struggle to gain popular support for its cause in a city beholden to the corporate charity of the Pullman Company.

Further, since New Negro sentiment crossed gender lines, the *Messenger* could write of a "New Woman." Correct for all times, the *Messenger* included women into the category of "New Negroes." In its lead editorial for July 1923, the magazine wrote:

> Yes, she has arrived. Like her white sister, she is the product of profound and vital changes in our economic mechanism, wrought mainly by the World War and its aftermath. Along the entire gamut of social, economic and political attitudes, the New Negro Woman has effected a revolutionary orientation. In politics, business

and labor, in the professions, church and education, in science, art and literature, the New Negro Woman, with her head held erect and spirit undaunted is resolutely marching forward, ever conscious of her historical and noble mission of doing her bit toward the liberation of her people in particular and the human race in general. Upon her shoulders rests the big task to create and keep alive, in the breast of black men, a holy and consuming passion to break with the slave traditions of the past; to spurn and overcome the fatal, insidious inferiority complex of the present, which, like Banquo's Ghost, bobs up ever and anon, to arrest the progress of the New Negro Manhood; and to fight with increasing vigor, with dauntless courage, unrelenting zeal and intelligent vision for the attainment of the stature of a *full man*, a free race and a new world.[41]

Of this group, the names of social workers Irene McCoy Gaines and Lillian Proctor Falls, librarian Vivian G. Harsh, educator Maudelle Bousfield, minister Mary Evans, and community organizer Annie Oliver immediately emerged. This "New Negro Woman" followed progressive and courageous types personified in the earlier thinking and action of Fannie Barrier Williams, Ida B. Wells-Barnett, Irene Goins, Dr. Fannie Emanuel, Ada S. McKinley, and Elizabeth Lindsay Davis.

Generational lines were broached also. This was reflected in the scrutiny of E. Franklin Frazier, who was well aware of the transition. He wrote, "The younger generation throws off the shackles of ignorance, poverty and dirt and catches a new vision of higher things in the achievements of those at the top."[42] Among the more "radical" circles of thought, its members were "eager to press every force available into such labors as the organization of the Pullman porters, development of educational facilities, free clinics, political betterment and everything that will improve racial opportunities."[43] In Chicago, it meant that Milton P. Webster, whose youthful energies and imagination were stirred by the martial greatness of Illinois's 8th Regiment, would lead the effort locally in Chicago to build the Brotherhood of Sleeping Car Porters into black America's first trade union.[44]

The antithesis of this new mood in black Chicago existed in the mind of newcomer Richard Wright immediately upon his arrival in the city. Both his inability and reluctance to make new acquaintances and embrace the vitality of the Black Metropolis were recorded in his own hand.[45] He continually exhibited a suspicion about the motivations and intents of others, which appeared to have been the result of his dysfunctional childhood in the South. Only with his departure from this country would he recover somewhat psychologically from his deeply ingrained hurt and sense of alienation.

The New Negro and the Black Metropolis

When the New Negro expressed his or her interest in race advancement, it was manifested through individual assertiveness as well as black institutional development. Black Chicago relished the possibility of a Black Metropolis. In a plain sense, a new reality had already been struck. George F. Robinson Jr. described in 1929 that "this rapidly increased Negro population forms a virtual city within a city,"[46] and within this milieu the New Negro mentality reached its apogee. According to Drake and Cayton, this transformation of mind over space took place between the two world wars as "the Black Belt became Black Metropolis."[47] Frazier saw the influence of mentality in the pervasive, raised racial consciousness of the African American, and Johnson wrote that "Chicago is in more than one sense the Colored capital and in every sense the top of the world for the bruised, crushed, and thwarted manhood of the South."

Historical circumstance played its part. A generation removed in time, scholarly examination by historian August Meier found migration, the wartime experience of sanctioned violence, the incidence of domestic self-defense, and socioeconomic class and cultural evolution as the main contributors to the development of a new way of thinking.[48] Historian Allan H. Spear talked of a "'New Negro' [who] emerge[d]—proud, defiant and racially militant,"—signaling to many the beginning of a newer phase in black personality development.[49] Missing in later scholarship was an appreciation of black thought on control over space or territory, such as that exhibited in the creation of the Black Metropolis as a conscious effort. To an equal extent, a local historical figure played his part. Recognition of the legacy of the city's founder, Jean Baptiste Pointe Du Sable (De Saible), reached a high point during this decade.[50]

The oldest Negro became a source of inspiration to the New Negro. Cultification enveloped thinking among all strata—the upper class, the middle and middling classes, and the working class—and in all spheres of life, from the political to the economic to the cultural and aesthetic. From the De Saible Club of the Men's Division of the Chicago Urban League organized by physician Arthur G. Falls to the predominantly female De Saible Memorial Society to the Colored Citizens World's Fair Citizens Committee led by schoolteacher Mrs. Annie Oliver, Du Sable's persona assumed the center of attention and became the focus of adulation. What the antebellum, Civil War, Great Fire, and Reconstruction Era experiences had been to the Old Settlers, recognition of a real or fictive linkage to Du Sable was to the New Negro of the 1920s.

Frazier wrote:

> Because Chicago has not attained the cosmopolitan character of New York and has not lost many of the features of smaller cities, she represents more nearly the pattern of Negro life at large in America. Chicago has drawn in the plantations of the lower South for her population more than New York whereas the latter has in her population a larger proportion of the eastern Seaboard. A trip on a local elevated train from the Chicago Loop will not only make visible in the types of houses along the route the different strata of the population, but those who get off at the stations are living documents of the different sections of the population they represent. Yet within this diversity there is a certain unity

> expressed in a community consciousness that is lacking in the cosmopolitan life of New York. In the first place, the Negro Community in Chicago has a tradition extending back to 1790 when Jean Baptiste Point de Saible, a San Domingan Negro, built a rude hut on the north bank of the Chicago River. *Although no historical connection between this first settler and the present Negro group can be established, it is of paramount importance in making the community conscious of a history in the growth of the city.* The recent successful struggle of the Negro group for some recognition of the first settler in the form of an appropriation by the city for a monument is significant of the increasing consciousness of its unity.[51] [emphasis added]

Whereas Du Sable's legacy earned a popular acceptance and had a racial hero's appeal to all African Americans, it also freed blacks from a cumbersome rigidity associated with entrenched tradition that might need change. All were, in effect, Du Sable's children and equal beneficiaries. As for ancestry and the southern plantation tradition, Johnson wrote as to why it could be both discounted and discarded: "There were 182,274 Negroes in Illinois in 1920 of whom 109,594 lived in Chicago and all but 20,000 of the rest in six other of the State's 930 municipalities. And of these, 182,274 or seventy-six percent are migrants. That is why one hears so little of family trees and ancestry. For the State, and even more Chicago, is a composite picture of the Negro population of every southern state in the Mississippi Valley. Twenty-three thousand from Tennessee, thirteen thousand from Alabama, nineteen thousand from Mississippi—this is Colored Chicago—the dream city—city of the dreadful night!"[52]

The Great Migration of 1916–1918 brought over 50,000 energetic southern workers to the city, mostly young people without children but pregnant with hopes of asserting themselves to their fullest potential. They melded with the resident population into a consolidated group. Importantly, the martial spirit of an emerging people, experientially confident that they had proven themselves capable of protecting themselves and their interests during the race riot of 1919, shaped their thinking about themselves forever. In addition, the adulation accorded the military cohort's extensive service in France during the First World War inspired residents to new heights of pride, feeding their self-esteem. The triumphant return of its black soldiers to the city in May 1919 had mesmerized a predominantly white downtown throng as much as it did the African Americans present. The emergence as the 8th Regiment Armory on Forest Avenue (later renamed Giles in honor of a war hero who fell in France) as the place linking circumstance, mind-set, and venue represented another manifestation of increased awareness and presence. It appeared as though every event of major importance was held in this sacred space on the South Side.

As to the pervasiveness of the New Negro mentality that swept broadly through the ideological camps, it favored no one belief system in particular but rather strengthened the ranks of the Universal Negro Improvement Association just as it also stimulated the Chicago NAACP to finally reach a level of organizational efficiency in program, fund-raising, and membership. In response to being asked what had been wrong with operations and governance of the branch in Chicago, from the association's New York headquarters, Robert W. Bagnall, the director of branches, confided to the incoming president, Dr. Carl G. Roberts, "The Association in Chicago has so long been regarded as an organization dominated by whites and a few Colored individuals that it will take some time to educate public opinion to the realization that it is an organization of the people. . . . Since the World War, there has been a revolutionary change in the psychology of the Negro. He now will work with whites or permit them to work with him; but he resents it when they work for him—he being their ward. He wants to control to a large degree, his own affairs. In other words, his racial conscience has been greatly developed."[53] Bagnall had written perceptively with an awareness of the influence of New Negro thinking, stating not only the obvious but also remarks that have to be considered prophetic.

This was the type of thinking that fueled the concept of the Black Metropolis, the ethnic dream of *imperio in imperium*, which reigned supreme during this decade. The conversion of concept into actuality was muddled because of its complex nature. Drake and Cayton clearly distinguished the multifaceted character of this concept: "To some the dream was inspiring. To many it was a mistake, a substitute for the real American Dream of complete integration into American life. To some . . . the dream seemed a fraud and a delusion. . . . To others, the development of a greater Black Metropolis was a tactical maneuver within the framework of a broad strategy for complete equality."[54]

Importantly, to a significant numbers of blacks, the dream was also viewed as an end in itself. The end in question encompassed recognition of one's worth by those already enjoying the American Dream while living in the mainstream, and it involved enjoying the benefits of racial equality. From pulpits, through the press, and over business counters, the message permeated the Black Metropolis. Up and down the class pyramid, across the social spectrum, African Americans delighted in the notion of their controlling a city within a city—the Black Metropolis. And it did not matter that other groups in the city controlled districts and enclaves, namely the Italians, the Chinese, the Jews, the Greeks, the Swedes, the Germans, and the Poles. African Americans wanted this domination over space and culture because it satisfied their cultural needs to experience a glimpse or taste of "home" every day of their lives. Moreover, it did not matter that it was fundamentally illusory. In a world where they were denied so much because of racism and impoverishment, the means, abilities, and resources to satisfy their dreams gained even greater currency. Thorstein Veblen's admonition against conspicuous consumption meant little to an individual or group that had worked so hard for so long for so little at the end of the long workday. Materialistic and idealistic enjoyments had their places and roles to play.

It was in this light that the black Chicago relished the idea of establishing a Black Metropolis. The difficulties of transforming this concept or dream into a reality presented themselves in various complexities. Implementing a black version of *imperium in imperio* appeared feasible given the circumstances of the 1920s to other pragmatic African Americans to whom racial equality was a pipe dream. A segment of blacks believed that they could remain free of white interference and still live their lives to the fullest extent possible despite the ubiquity of racial constraints. This interpretation was apt to be used incorrectly by the masses who severely misapplied the principles of the late Booker T. Washington as well as those of Marcus Garvey's American phase of his UNIA plan for the redemption of Africa and African communities everywhere in the world.

Although the Black Metropolis concept was not totally—or for that matter, actually—nationalistic, the concept shared some of the same strains of separate development under black control and therefore was anathema to many racial egalitarians who believed in interracial cooperation. Just as significantly, the dream represented a way out from racial dependence and racist humiliation. Although it was impossible for any group to live independently of others in urban America, the world of American racism distorted the American Dream so much that it essentially took on surreal qualities. The emergence of this fantasy, which was contradictory to white racial supremacy, seemed reasonable to some blacks.

One conventional element in African American thinking posited the idea that the mentality of the residents of the Black Metropolis centered on the dichotomy of localized black culture versus a white, American, mainstream wave of thought. "All of Bronzeville's standards of appraisal are conditioned by the way Negro-white relations are organized."[55] Its opposite was biculturalism, which posited that a mixed African-based, southern slave-folk culture existed, according to historian Herbert Gutman, alongside an attempt to emulate Anglo-American culture.[56] This pattern of thinking was persuasive, as the argument had been made for over one-half century, but no allowance was made for aspects of African American agency or any other form of new thinking, such as that exhibited by the New Negroes. Reiterating Robert Bagnall's analysis is necessary to clarify the issue.[57] This accounted for the slow response of blacks to the NAACP appeal and strategy for change.

The changing mind and mood of the Black Metropolis had not escaped the attention of Charles S. Johnson and E. Franklin Frazier. The former sarcastically evaluated the nature of the situation in 1923 and found that "the frontier mind [in the Black Metropolis] is too suspiciously sentimental about the virtues of mother wit [common sense] and too brutally contemptuous of [modern, racially pluralistic] culture."[58] Prophetically, his evaluation predated the observations of Bagnall by two years. At the end of the decade, Johnson's colleague Frazier wrote that "the Negro community in Chicago has been very conscious of its place in Negro life. Lately because of this quickened consciousness the leaders among Chicago Negroes have bestirred themselves to make the American public cognizant of their contributions to, and place in, Negro life in America."[59] What these two scholars recognized in its incipient form, but failed fully to appreciate, was the maturation of a people who were progressing systematically beyond the psychological dependence on whites for leadership imposed upon them by their parents and grandparents. Furthermore, many African Americans sought affirmation of their dreams for a better life through the pursuit of equality of opportunity rather than social equality. The latter aspiration seemed too distant, and in actuality, only appeared real in the activism of the 1950s and 1960s.

At the same time, the Dream of a Black Metropolis seemed useful as a means to an end, especially for many in the equal rights movement. So application of the dream was especially beneficial to understanding the Chicago NAACP and the equal rights movement as it helped the NAACP in realizing its organizational, programmatic, and ideological goals. However, for avid egalitarians this meant a breach in prospective bettering of race relations and these were too valuable to be threatened. The dream, therefore, was a nightmare to Dr. Bentley and to the rising New Negro leader within the Chicago NAACP movement A. C. MacNeal, both staunch egalitarians.

The dream was more palatable to Dr. George Cleveland Hall and another up-and-coming New Negro, postal worker Archie L. Weaver, who saw it as a tactic of significant use. Hall reasoned, like his late intimate friend and former patient Booker T. Washington, that the road to recognition and respect in America would come through visible manifestations of competence and competitive demonstrations of worth. Either asking for or demanding the equality associated with recognition and respect would inevitably prove futile. Only by combining these two qualities could an individual or group achieve the goal of finding happiness.

Black Humanity's Landscape: Residential Patterns

With national, postwar prosperity, the decade of the 1920s heralded the debut of the Black Metropolis, the attempt by blacks to build a self-contained city within the city of Chicago. This dream of a district controlled by the members of the same ethnic, racial, or religious group persisted for generations in Chicago history. Basically it was an attempt of persons of immigrant experience to recreate a new home as part of their diaspora. This spirit of independence was as much an integral part of the African American sense of being as any other group's. When the notion of recreating the essence of a distant homeland far away from past familiar spaces is applied to African Americans, it was treated as illusory. Yet the city's North Side was filled with successful attempts at relocation of native populations. The Polish community re-created Poland diaspora in Polonia along the Near North Side's Milwaukee Avenue. Farther along Milwaukee Avenue to the northwest lived the Germans. The Swedes concentrated even farther north around Lawrence Avenue and Ashland in Andersonville. The Chinese did likewise in Chinatown, which had been relocated by the city southward to the area south of 22nd Street and along Wentworth Avenue,adjoining the soon-to-be-designated Black Belt. The various groups from the Italian peninsula and Sicily lived in "Little Italy" on the city's North Side and West Side. In all of these enclaves, the character of a community's housing represented a residential haven, a sign of group consciousness, an indicator of its status and being, and even an enduring economic investment for family or profit-making ventures, such as banks.

As African Americans developed a greater sense of their demographic strength and an awareness of their need to control their living space, the logical consequence was acceptance of residential succession as perhaps a positive good. Scoffed at by some but endorsed by many more, the dream of building on the imprint of the Black Belt, a Black Metropolis, a black city within a city, seemed feasible and grew to rest on the potential of a solid political and economic base. According to Frazier, the movement of African Americans southward away from the central business district, Chicago's Loop, occurred as part of normal progression in any city's pattern of natural growth.[60]

As many opportunities as Chicago offered, it paradoxically withdrew just as many because of entrenched racism. For example, blacks were excluded from a citywide movement to expand housing opportunities and construct bungalows for the working classes. Bungalows were reasonably priced for the weekly budgets of the white industrial worker who toiled in the city's immense network of steel mills, foundries, factories, and packinghouses. This housing matched the times and population in that it was inexpensive and "the workingman's answer to the single-family comforts of suburban life at a practical city price."[61]

What black Chicago on the South Side needed most, improvement in its housing stock, was not forthcoming. So the enclave that welcomed writer Richard Wright's eyes in 1927 proved anything but attractive. "My first glimpse of the flat black stretches of Chicago depressed and dismayed me, mocked all my fantasies. Chicago seemed an unreal city whose mythical houses were built of slabs of black coal wreathed in palls of gray smoke, houses whose foundations were sinking slowly into the dank prairie. Flashes of steam showed intermittently on the wide horizon, gleaming translucently in the winter sun."[62] These early glimpses of Chicago were recognizable as those seen from a train travelling up from the South on the Illinois Central Railroad tracks past the steel district where few African Americans lived. Where Wright would have detrained would have been in Central Station on the south edge of the Loop at Roosevelt Road. From there he saw another Chicago, for as he looked back the downtown section he saw "towering buildings of steel and stone." As he travelled on a streetcar heading southward along State Street, the complementary exciting and congested Black Metropolis came into full view. This Chicago had its problems in housing along with bright spots in the Overton Building and the theaters, and would soon feature the magnificent Binga Arcade.

No matter the obstacles, the size and territorial dimensions of black Chicago grew through the years. With his usual acuity, Frazier recorded his observations and conclusions of the occurrences that took on the properties of both phenomenon and process. As to the Black Metropolis, "Its expansion over a vast territory as the population increased has fitted into the general pattern of urban growth and, at the same time, has been similar to the movement of other racial and migrant groups in the city. The growth of the *community* has been more than an addition of numbers. There has been a selection and segregation of economic and cultural groups which has determined the social structure of the community"[63] [emphasis added]. This community, *not a ghetto* in any general sense except in its aging, deteriorating housing stock, continued to expand, with diverse opinions as to whether it was rapid enough to accommodate its growing population needs in terms of good housing in healthy circumstances. In this action, it continued the phenomenon of residential elasticity so common to hopeful blacks and worried whites. Frazier made note of this dispersed population in 1919, writing that "like most American cities, the Negro group is not completely segregated from the white community."[64] *Daily News* journalist Carroll Binder even wrote of the existence of a housing glut by 1927 that demonstrated that property ownership had outstripped both demand and the resources of the population to attain its affordability.[65]

The family of future Chicago public schools educator Madeline Robinson, born in 1906, moved to 5440 South Dearborn as part of a wave of upwardly mobile African Americans who pushed the boundaries of the American Dream outward and beyond any arbitrary limits set by whites. They were citizens who acted as independent citizenry had since the founding of the Republic. Their movement was southward, however, instead of westward, along the State Street axis. In their movement they showed how tenuous the concept of an expanding black ghetto was, since their standard of living and values were anything but mainstream. They constituted Chicagoans who were, if anything, expanding the boundaries of a community of kindred souls. For young Madeline, who dreamed of facilitating the introduction of a better world through education, it provided her with the opportunity to learn and develop her intellectual skills for a future productive, professional career in teaching.

Meanwhile, the families of future poetess Gwendolyn Brooks and novelist Richard Wright experienced the process of melding firsthand. According to Brooks, when it came time for her family to move within the expanding district, "They naturally gravitated toward a community of friends from familiar surroundings, or 'down home.'"[66] In addition, when not in direct contact, they gradually established linkages, as occurred with Wright and several of his playmates and schoolmates from Mississippi. The Black Metropolis took on a spatial configuration resembling no known geometric shape because it was constantly expanding. One portion was the area designated by academics during the 1930s as the Douglas community area, which extended from 22nd Street to 35th Street and Federal Street east to Lake Michigan. While blacks lived in most parts of this section of the city, clusters of whites remained for many years, especially along the lakefront near 35th Street. Also attracted to the area, Alderman Louis B. Anderson decided to build his lifelong dream home in this area in 1922 at 3800 South Calumet Avenue, which was nearly one-half mile east of the State Street corridor. Designed in colonial revival style by the architectural firm of Michaelsen and Rognstad, the firm that had designed the Metropolitan Community Church at 41st and Grand Boulevard (South Parkway), the home stood prominently on the southwest corner as a symbol of African American progress and upward mobility.[67]

But along the State Street corridor and to the west, a mix of multistory commercial structures was found, with housing or office space on the second level and retail space at street elevation. Also sitting on these narrow lots were two- and two-and-one-half-story frame houses with gable roofs looking somewhat familiar (to rural southerners) as well as some two-story brick houses on equally narrow lots. Charles S. Johnson wrote lyrically of this area as encompassing nineteen blocks where 92,000 people lived, "nauseated by the stench of the stockyards on the west and revived again by the refreshing breezes of Lake Michigan on the east."[68]

Adjacent to the south, the Grand Boulevard community area was undergoing a complexion change, from 32 percent black in 1920 to 95 percent black by 1930; and, even farther southward, the Washington Park community area was transforming from 15 percent to 92 percent black by 1930. The continued movement of the black population southward continued until the Grand Boulevard mansions south of 47th Street were being purchased (where, for example, the famous Hollywood-bound comedic Marx Brothers had lived) and enveloped by African American residents. This shift was significant as it indicated once again the elasticity of the boundaries of the Black Metropolis.

Grand Boulevard as a thoroughfare was transformed into South Parkway by 1925 as the former thoroughfare was widened northward between 35th and 24th Streets to conform more to the configuration of the former Grand Boulevard's service parkways and wide grassy dividers as well as to connect with South Lake Shore Drive. The new South Parkway's physical transformation extended the continuous verdant attractiveness of the community from 51st Street to 24th Street, but at the same time exacerbated the sense that a class divide existed between the residents of the South Parkway District[69] and the residents of the adjacent old Black Belt. It did not have to, but did, alter perceptions since separate clusters of residents who shared common values now were obvious. Many people in the old Black Belt referred to those living east of the State Street corridor as strivers whose values regarding public deportment, upkeep of property, education, and the need for public order reflected those of the fleeing white, middle-class citizens who never took time to recognize intragroup differences among blacks and cross-group similarities between whites and blacks.

* * *

Whatever the possibilities of intergroup cooperation and amiability, white opposition grew so intense, unrelenting, and well organized that no accommodation was to be reached. Disparate white homeowner groups united to formulate a strategy to curtail housing opportunities for blacks and keep their neighborhoods racially pure, as they saw it. The Hyde Park and Kenwood Property Owners' Association, the Grand Boulevard Property Owners' Association, the Park Manor and Wakeford Improvement Associations, and others eventually came to rely on the use of the restrictive covenant, a legally binding agreement between white neighbors designed to exclude blacks from their neighborhoods. The impetus came in 1926 as the U.S. Supreme Court reversed its position of six decades on fair housing with its decision in *Corrigan v. Buckley* that upheld the legality of racially restrictive agreements. The day of the restrictive covenant had dawned.

The restrictive covenant—a written, contractual agreement that excluded blacks or any other group deemed undesirable from residency—became the preferred device of various white neighborhood associations. It first appeared in Chicago in 1927. Although "the operation of covenants began relatively late in Chicago [as opposed to other northern cities], they [covenants] were organized in large numbers and received immediate acceptance. In the two years between 1927 and 1929, two fifths of the covenants located in Chicago's South Side were enacted."[70] In the Englewood section of the city, evidence of its use was seen in the concern shown by the national office of the NAACP in 1929, although it could have been in existence at least two years earlier.

The Hyde Park and Kenwood areas enforced housing segregation at an invisible dividing line between the black and white communities at Cottage Grove Avenue (which was exactly one mile east of State Street). The residents of Hyde Park and Kenwood had traditionally opposed the movement of blacks into their area and, as early as 1908, the wealthiest residents established the Hyde Park Improvement Protective Club to keep the area as free of blacks as possible. Blacks who already lived there as homeowners or renters were encouraged to sell or surrender their leases.[71] By 1918 the Hyde Park Property Owners Association was actively trying to keep the area all white, indicating the area evidently was covered by covenants before the Depression decade.

From the legal to the illegal, from white flight to secretive exclusionary agreements (preceding the formal, legal restrictive covenants) to bombings, any means at the disposal or in the imagination of white bigots were utilized. Since black bankers also engaged heavily in real estate dealings, Jesse Binga's home and holdings at 5922 South Parkway and 4724 South State Street, as well as those of the

Woodfolk Bank at 4732 South Calumet, were targeted.[72] By 1927, Carroll Binder, a staff writer for the *Chicago Daily News*, observed black residential expansion in a different light. Binder analyzed:

> In the final analysis, however, the new status of the Negro in metropolitan Chicago had been achieved by his own economic, political and personal power. The Colored man refused to be confined within a ghetto defined by his white neighbors and he defied all the economic and social pressure supplied to keep him there. He demonstrated that he had the money to invade territory once monopolized by whites and the courage to stay there in the face of bombs which wrecked his homes, churches and business places. . . . Negroes are therefore to be found in almost all parts of the city. Being among the most gregarious of the races the Negro chooses to dwell in colonies but the boundaries of his colonies are so far-flung that he cannot absorb all the property which white vendors thrust upon him.[73]

As African Americans exercised their rights as citizens to enjoy freedom of movement and the right to live where their incomes allowed, they met white opposition of a nature that was reminiscent of the authoritarianism recently defeated in Europe in 1918. African American movement into attractive residential neighborhoods that were dominated by white homeowners were considered "invasions," or they were conceived as episodes of aggressive racial takeovers as Caucasians moved in fright or hostility. Meanwhile, as reported in the *Illinois Crime Survey*, the area or district of the Black Belt "has become quite as rigidly a designated area for Negroes as if it had been provided by law."[74]

Consistent with the illogic of American race protocol, a violent phase in the crisis in housing appeared. Using dynamite bombs with impunity, as evidenced by the fact that no bombers were ever apprehended and no public disgust was ever evinced, white attempts to intimidate blacks were doomed to failure by the indomitability of the African American spirit to persist in enjoying their right regardless of the circumstances. Jesse Binga's property was bombed six times yet he refused to ever move and eventually won his right to reside where he and his wife wished. His response to a reported decision to leave his home met with this retort: "Statements relative to my moving are all false . . . I will not run. The [honor of the] race is at stake and not myself. If they can make me move they will have accomplished much of their aim because they can say, 'We made Jesse Binga move; certainly you'll have to move' to all of the rest. If they can make the leaders move, what show [or example] will the small buyers have?"[75]

* * *

Yet unabated violence in white neighborhoods directed against African Americans purchasing homes and negotiating rentals led the latter to organize for purposes of self-defense in January 1920. The Protective Circle of Chicago represented organizationally the vehicle for the coordinated, black legal response to the absence of effective municipal action from either the Chicago Police Department or the Cook County State Attorney's office. As an *ad hoc* civil rights group aimed at securing justice in the courts, on the streets, and inside the safety of the homes of African Americans who wished to purchase property where their money would take them, it seemed a reasonable response before the decades of concerted federal intervention. The group's constitution called for a "commit[ment] solely to the policy of offsetting and suppressing in every legitimate and legal way lawlessness that has recently been evidenced in intimidation, bombing, threatening and coercion of Colored and white citizens of Chicago."

One especially aggrieved citizen was banker Jesse Binga who sought assistance when his home in the Washington Park community was regularly being bombed. At that time, the Chicago NAACP lent no support locally as an organized entity because of its national office's involvements in the Elaine, Arkansas, riot defense and other crises around the nation. However, the kingmaker of the Chicago NAACP, Dr. Charles E. Bentley, did serve on the executive committee and A. C. MacNeal directed a key committee. At the decade's end, the national NAACP asked Binga to take out a life membership in order to help finance exposure of restrictive covenants in the nearby Englewood district, unbeknownst to these egalitarians in the East that Binga had suffered through numerous bombings ten years previously when he lived east of the Englewood area in the Washington Park community.[76]

Collectively, black Chicagoans looked for leadership and solutions within their own local community. The solution came in the resulting organization of the Protective Circle, to which the various business, civic, military, fraternal, religious, and political leaderships belonged. Rev. John W. Robinson of the St. Mark's Methodist Episcopal Church was president of the group. Engineer Charles S. Duke served in the office of secretary; business titan Anthony Overton appropriately held the position of treasurer. Oscar De Priest's Unity Hall political headquarters at 3140 South Indiana Avenue doubled as the Protective Circle's command center.

These were individuals accustomed to organizational work, so they planned an internal structure composed of four essential committees. These included investigation, headed by the Chicago NAACP's A. C. MacNeal, who was invigorated by the ongoing riot defense; publicity, with Nahum Daniel Brascher, editor-in-chief of the Associated Negro Press, informing the public of the circle's purpose and progress; legal defense, featuring De Priest in the unlikely role of law interpreter; and propaganda, headed by group's most victimized member, Jesse Binga, whose home and office had been bombed on several occasions. The founder of the Douglass National Bank in 1922, P. W. Chavers, probably would have belonged also since his property at 4722 South Calumet was bombed with all the doors locked to prevent tenants from escaping the blast. Massive meetings were planned for at least six locations at the most heavily attended churches, including Olivet, with its over 10,000-member congregation.[77]

Meanwhile, accommodating the housing needs of a diverse black community stretching throughout the city required resources and financing. Although there was some building on the South Side, the story that Robert R. Taylor of 1950s public housing fame built individual homes on Chicago's South Side as he did in Alabama was reported inaccurately by journalist Roi Ottley a generation later.[78] Over on the West Side, master carpenter and home builder Jesse Johnson did construct houses made of wood for prospective black homeowners.

The relationship between housing and class structure has long been used by historians and social scientists as an indicator of the status of the African Americans in U. S. society. More recently over the last two generations, it has appeared as a device to explain the existence of the "ghetto," that measure of how far blacks have or have not progressed as citizens. In a parallel vein, evolution within the black class structure did not escape the perceptive senses of merchant prince Julius Rosenwald. Rising African American earning power and increased consumption accordingly affected housing needs. As one of the nation's astute business leaders, Rosenwald demonstrated that the time was right for pursuing this market with vigor.

So one very bright spot appeared late in the decade back on the South Side: Julius Rosenwald reconsidered his abandoned 1918 plan to build affordable housing for middle-class blacks. He now invested in a monumental project to provide residential units in an apartment complex covering one square city block at Wabash to Michigan, and 46th and 47th Streets. Known as the Michigan Avenue Garden Apartments (or the Rosenwald Building), the philanthropic Rosenwald set out to break the myth that African Americans were poor risks and therefore irresponsible tenants. Knowing that a housing shortage for lower-middle-class and working-class families persisted in the Black Metropolis, the philanthropist proposed and built 421 units at $2.7 million, anticipating an annual profit of 6 percent. Once built and occupied, Rosenwald made his profit, and with the cooperation of good tenants and an efficient, no-nonsense, African American manager named Robert R. Taylor (the son of Tuskegee Institute's chief architectural teacher Robert Rochon Taylor), dispelled the myth of black neglect of property and recklessness. Rosenwald was quoted expressing his satisfaction with the venture a year after its opening. "By the results I do not have in mind primarily the financial side, important and desirable as that is, but more particularly the fine type of tenants . . . filling the building. Those living in our apartments have proven that the Negro is a law abiding citizen and desirable tenant. In doing so they have added to the prestige of their race and have tended to encourage the investment of money in kindred projects."[79]

When the complex opened in 1929, the five-story building featured eight entrances and thirty-eight separate stairwells (and no corridors) every 100 feet for every two or three apartments for privacy. There were no elevators, which helped lower construction costs, but tenants were provided with an interior, two-acre landscaped courtyard for their enjoyment. A nursery and youth center for children to play was built across the street on the complex's Wabash Avenue side. Rental units featured three-, four-, and five-room floor plans, which attracted Joe Louis and other high-profile tenants through the years. For maximum shopping convenience, fourteen storefronts on the 47th Street side provided space for local black businessmen, along with enterprising white establishments such as Walgreen's. Just how perceptive Julius Rosenwald was about the evolving class structure of the Black Metropolis is a subject explored in greater detail in the following chapter.

CHAPTER 2

"The Whirl of Life"

The Social Structure

> The social order which the race riot shattered temporarily was a remarkably fluid one, but there were certain fixed points in "social space" which were stable enough to maintain their existence . . . [Set within the larger urban world was a 'Negro world.'].
>
> —St. Clair Drake, *Churches and Voluntary Associations*, 1940

The whirl of life that E. Franklin Frazier observed contemporarily might have been the synergy generated by the various social classes in their collective pursuit of racial progress and the enjoyment of living, the latter quality well noted in a group that learned to laugh and smile despite adversities. For the first time in the history of Chicago, African Americans separated into noticeably distinct groups based on the amount of wealth they possessed and how closely they associated with others with the same level of material resources and interests. St. Clair Drake in *Churches and Voluntary Associations* recognized it a decade later, observing that "the social order which the race riot shattered temporarily was a remarkably fluid one, but there were certain fixed points in 'social space' which were stable enough to maintain their existence." Among the fixed points were the statuses held by the nineteenth century's African American elite, which included Drs. Daniel Hale Williams and Charles E. Bentley. At the other end of the spectrum were the Civil War families who suffered economically for decades after the war. In the divide between these social poles was an expanding middle that quickly formed into discrete social units nurtured by the external arrival and local emergence of professionals, semiprofessionals, and persons without credentials but with aspirations imitative of that status.

The character of African American social stratification during the Jazz Age relied on the sociological observations of emerging giants in their field—Johnson, Frazier, Drake and Cayton, and Oliver Cromwell Cox—who had studied sociology at one of America's most prestigious institutions of higher learning, the University of Chicago.[1] Lying dormant at the same time as scholarly monuments to both contradiction and substantiation were records suitably characterized as historical, indicating that the semblance as well as the partial substance of a *normative* class structure based on wealth production and self-identification as a class had appeared during that same period. So even without definite standards of ancestry and culture, reasonably absent for a migrant group in a city rebuilt over the last fifty years, a bona fide upper class appeared during this decade. St. Clair Drake's depiction of a triple-layered society shaped by cultural influences—the refined, the respectables, and the riff-raff—in the late nineteenth and earliest portion of the twentieth century had been transformed by economic forces and influences into a modern pyramidal structure containing several distinct segments. Black Chicago now contained a very small but distinguishable upper class, large segments within the broad middle classes, enormous laboring classes including industrial and service sector workers, and an underclass.

The Elite or Upper Class

With an eye to New York City's 300-year-old social fabric that was less fluid, Charles S. Johnson had written of black Chicago that "the social set is still a bit promiscuous—vague and uncertain, lacking definite standards of ancestry and culture and even wealth—a sort of one big union."[2] E. Franklin Frazier commented in following years that "among the upper classes who consider themselves the most emancipated of the Negro group" a type of religious freedom existed that found them attending Christian Scientist churches and a Baha'i temple. Of importance here was Frazier's partial recognition of the existence of an intricate class structure with an easily distinguishable upper class. Wealth began to appear and assume the same importance in class standing that it did in mainstream America. Composed of persons possessing noticeable to immense wealth and a consciousness of their position in the modern industrial, cosmopolitan setting of Chicago, the members of this elite owned and managed businesses, chose housing commensurate with their status, consumed their disposable income with conspicuous delight, engaged in civic activities, and socially acted as a group apart from other segments of their racial cohort to which they traditionally held their primary social allegiance. They could never, however, have considered themselves aristocrats in any sense of the word.[3] They lived foremost as rich people, with an awareness that they also carried the designation among whites of being indisputably, and just primarily Colored, or Negroes. Yet a major disparity in wealth and social linkages between and within the black and white worlds prevented the parallel development of a consistent set of standards for membership. More of an overlap occurred within the ranks of the upper classes than would be recognized in white society, businessmen with formal educational training intermingling with the professionally trained from some of the nation's most prestigious universities.

The names of Mr. and Mrs. Robert S. Abbott, Mr. and Mrs. Jesse Binga, Mr. and Mrs. Anthony Overton, Dr. and Mrs. Charles E. Bentley, Dr. Midian and Maudelle Bousfield, attorney Edward H. and Mrs. Morris, Dr. and Mrs. A. Wilberforce Williams, Dr. George Cleveland Hall and Mrs. Theodosia Hall, Dr. and Mrs. U. G. Dailey, Mr. and Mrs. Frank Gillespie, and others led the list of persons comprising this class. More important than Southern ties to an antebellum white aristocracy that had held its ancestors as chattel, validation in Chicago from the white world appeared in the 1917, 1926, and 1931 editions of the mainstream directory of established Chicago's upper crust, *Who's Who in Chicago and Vicinity*, edited by Albert Nelson Marquis. As an authority on status, it was the source to which Dr. Spencer C. Dickerson directed an interviewer before he consented to begin his interview.[4] For this decade, Marquis's *Who's Who in Chicago and Vicinity* listed Robert S. Abbott, Dr. Charles E. Bentley, Jesse Binga, Edward H. Morris, Anthony Overton, Dr. A. W. Williams, and Dr. Daniel Hale Williams as persons of societal significance.

Wealth production and the manner of its accumulation, of course, became the essence of upper-class standing as the various social groups in black Chicago fit comfortably into a discernible class structure consistent with American standards. The designation of "millionaire" was heard with a frequency unimagined in previous periods. Most importantly, its use was closer to reality than fiction and illusion. The successful businesses of Robert S. Abbott, Jesse Binga, and Anthony Overton, along with the lucrative professional activities of Drs. Charles E. Bentley, Midian O. Bousfield, A. Wilberforce Williams, U. G. Dailey, Carl G. Roberts, Herbert Turner, and others, were illustrative of their having attained a level of economic stability commensurate with that of other Americans. Carter G. Woodson found that, among all of the professions, physicians in large cities did especially well.[5]

Civic involvement, moreover, reflected an individual's social position in mainstream Chicago, and participation limited to the affairs of the Black Metropolis was too provincial for the overseers of black Chicago's destiny. A twelve-person interracial Chicago Commission on Race Relations convened to oversee an investigation into the causes and future solutions to the race riot. Within the Riot Commission, representatives of the upper class came from law, in attorney Edward H. Morris; commerce, in publisher Robert S. Abbott; and medicine, in Dr. George Cleveland Hall.[6] Other members of the upper class were added because of their respectability and acceptance to the white establishment. These persons included Rev. Lacey K. Williams, realtor Jackson, and politician Adelbert Roberts. Fannie Barrier Williams's membership in the Chicago Woman's Club illustrated an anomaly in that she and her husband, S. Laing Williams, never accumulated the wealth or professional credentials expected of her white counterparts. Membership on the boards of the Chicago branch and national directorate of the NAACP and on the Chicago Urban League likewise qualified. The Chicago Urban League was evaluated by circumspect establishment whites at the headquarters of "A Century of Progress," the 1933 World's Fair executive body, as "an organization of the better class of Colored people in Chicago."[7] Along the same lines of civic service, they formed the core of a legitimate civic infrastructure far in advance of the civil rights decade of the 1960s through memberships in the Protective Circle, the World's Fair Colored Citizens Council, the Chicago Urban League, and the Chicago NAACP.[8]

Another dimension of upper-class belonging involved the close association with upper-class whites, the movers and shakers of the city who constituted the civic leadership, or establishment. Highly visible were Dr. George Cleveland Hall., Robert S. Abbott, and Dr. Charles E. Bentley, the latter whose role with the Chicago NAACP warrants examination.[9] At the same time, there emerged a complementary sociocultural grouping self-defined as "Colored Society," or what today we would refer to as "Black Society." Its members considered themselves a part of the social aristocracy or "upper 10 percent." Appearing regularly in the pages of the Saturday *Chicago Defender* and the Sunday *Chicago Bee*, they entertained, danced, feasted, traveled, recreated, and partook of myriad social activities as they sought to make known their respectability and sense of socially arriving. They lived lifestyles of leisure and enjoyment that extended beyond the previous standards of owning a tuxedo and a décolleté evening gown, accompanied by a self-perception of elevated status.

Unlike the black lifestyles of the nineteenth and early twentieth centuries, social differences were more evident now when living a life amidst a population possessing wealth, moderate income, and decent income, along with those facing economic struggle and deprivation. Stratification along lines seen in mainstream American society had become established in black Chicago. This conclusion is at variance with a number of sociological descriptions presented by active researchers during the 1920s, 1930s, and 1940s in the works of Charles S. Johnson, E. Franklin Frazier, St. Clair Drake, and Horace R. Cayton. One answer for the discrepancies lay in the use of research methods, the significance placed by the historian on her or his tools of time and change, and the complications placed on analysis by the designation within the African American population of its own version of stratified rankings. The period of time that a study was conducted, and completed, played a major role in depicting life as it existed in another temporal setting. For instance, Charles S. Johnson's depiction of black social organization as "a bit promiscuous—vague and uncertain, lacking definite standards" reflected his impressive scholarship in *The Negro in Chicago* (1922) with its emphasis on the adjustments and maladjustments of the newly arrived southern migrant. Interestingly, Johnson overlooked the existence of, for example, African American male leaders who sat on the Chicago Commission on Race Relations based on his own civic merits.

At the end of the decade, Frazier additionally talked of the competitive *nouveaux riches* without likewise accounting for an extant social structure with a history of evolving class differentiation. Although these *nouveaux riches* lacked the highest educational exposure, they possessed immense measures of initiative and creativity as evidenced by their laying the economic, political, and social foundations from which migrants of the Great Migration, previous waves of migration, and persons experiencing the riot of 1919 would benefit. By 1929, Frazier talked of a major social shift in the Black Metropolis that he attributed to the Great Migration, writing, "The old equilibrium was destroyed." This theme was adopted by Drake and Cayton a decade later, leading them to conceptualize about the rise of a new class structure within black Chicago by the beginning of the 1920s.[10]

No explanation as to the identities of this new leadership was given, possibly because none could be presented without personal or knowledgeable and direct contact with the peers of this group. Finally, when *Black Metropolis* appeared in print in 1945 after the devastation of the Great Depression and at the end of the Second World War, it presented a picture of a society that had undergone transformation of immense proportions without accounting for the changes in the *status quo ante bellum*. In writing that the upper class of the 1940s "rose to power during the Twenties, displacing an older status group—the pre Great Migration upper class," history was effectively rewritten without proper historical documentation.[11] Historical evidence confirmed that well-to-do medical figures Drs. Charles E. Bentley and George Cleveland Hall, along with Anthony Overton, Robert S. Abbott, Jesse Binga, Edward H. Morris, and many others, came into prominence during the pre-Migration period and remained in power until their deaths in the early 1930s or shortly thereafter.

The challenge presented from studies written *outside* the field of history necessitates the demand from *within* for an exploration of the story that is supportable by written evidence and acute memory. Consistent with this demand, when dealing with a normative American class structure, are the proofs of meeting the criteria associated with it—recognizable wealth production from business and professional standing, civic involvement in both the affairs of mainstream Chicago and Black Metropolis, philanthropy, place of residence and social commitments—that form the perimeters of belonging and social arrival. Closely associated with this group based on their cultural and social standing were persons whose presence from the early twentieth century led some observers to place them in the purported upper class. Their lack of wealth showed otherwise, yet their social standing posed a problem in classification. This group included Dr. Daniel Hale and Alice Williams, S. Laing and Fannie Barrier Williams, and Ferdinand L. and Ida B. Barnett. E. Franklin Frazier further complicated the issue by including among the ranks of the upper class the following groups: "Physicians, dentists, lawyers, artists, school teachers, entrepreneurs, business executives, social workers."[12]

Documenting the existence and emergence of this class structure were three members of the upper tier of the middling class who performed the functions of, respectively, master of protocol at most of the major social gatherings of the upper class, chronicler of the family histories of the upper class and claimants to Old Settler status, and chronicler and Chicago historian on African American past and contemporary achievements.[13] These men were Julius Avendorph, Franklyn Henderson, and Frederick H. H. Robb, respectively. Avendorph, although serving as a personal messenger to members of the white upper class, acted with regularity as master of ceremonies for decades at upper-class and mixed-social-class events.[14] Franklyn Henderson was a member of the old-line, nineteenth-century Atkinson family and committed himself to diligently collecting and preserving photographs and memorabilia of the past century's notables and popular individuals in early black society.[15] Robb, while a law student at Northwestern University, distinguished himself as the interpreter of black Chicago progress up to this time, along with being the compiler of the composite, data-filled yearbooks for 1927 and 1929, *The Negro in Chicago*.

Examination of the life and social lifestyle of the well-known and popularly recognized publisher Robert S. Abbott seems to be an excellent starting point for entry into the world of the upper class. Abbott's lifestyle exemplified the ultimate in the upper-class experience. He lived lavishly, as he was acclaimed as extremely wealthy, and definitely became a millionaire during this period.[16] After his success as a publisher, which launched him into a stratospheric realm among African Americans nationally, he cast himself as a patron of the arts, a sphere in which he encouraged the city's young literati—black and white Americans, Haitian, Chinese, and African—into his homes to stimulate thought and writing. While his first home was in a middle-class neighborhood on Champlain Avenue, the second of these homes stood prominently (and does to this day) as a mansion on elegant, patronage-rich Grand Boulevard (4742, now Dr. Martin Luther King Jr. Drive)[17].

The Abbott mansion on South Parkway was situated in the Grand Boulevard community, the scene for decades of some of Chicago's most beautiful homes and mansions. His home was a sumptuous structure designed in the Queen Anne style and described as "baronial." Abbott purchased the structure for $50,000. His biographer Ottley described it thus: "Ivy-covered, three-story, red brick mansion trimmed in white stone and it was constructed of white stone and contained 14 rooms." The interior featured a "24-carat gold-plated dining set, deep-piled Chinese rugs, pieces of Hepplewhite [furniture], a billiard table, and an ebony-finished Mandarin living room set imported directly from China—as well as beautiful linen, china services and paintings."[18] Important visitors to town resided during their stays with the Abbotts. For example, when Nolle R. Smith of the territory of Hawaii was elected to the Fifth District representing Honolulu in the state legislature and made his stateside tour, once in Chicago he resided with the Abbotts.[19] Even after Abbott and his first wife divorced, he remained in the mansion and entertained as a society leader was expected to do. His World's Fair grand soiree in the next decade was one that attracted nearly every person of social and civic prominence in the Black Metropolis (as well as Jane Addams, Amelia Sears, Elbridge Bancroft Pierce, and Dr. Robert Maynard Hutchins, president of the University of Chicago), indicating that his social status remained high.[20]

Abbott's choice of wives showed an indulgence common to aging wealthy men in that he chose two "trophy wives" to wear the mantle of Mrs. Robert S. Abbott. Both were widows and much younger than he, with Helen Thornton, his first wife, being age twenty to his near fifty years upon their marriage in 1918. This union ended tumultuously in divorce in 1933. His second wife was Edna Denison, who at forty-three years of age to his sixty-six years in 1934 joined him in a union that lasted until his death in 1940. Abbott sought women of culture and personal attractiveness, but in what was peculiar to him and to meet his psychological needs, they had to be fair-skinned women with a Caucasian appearance. Critics called him "color struck" in this regard. His disappointing experiences with African American women led him to doubt that any worthy and truly cultured black women existed.[21] Much like Othello, it was a fatal flaw because he could never be sure his wives loved him for his strengths and inner qualities or because of his wealth and social influence. He was exceedingly conscious of his skin color, and this concern evolved into a fixation, making him the butt of jokes about his color obsession throughout his life.[22]

When Drake and Cayton published their findings and those of their fellow University of Chicago researchers in 1945, they found that unlike conditions in the South and Washington, D.C., skin color played a limited role in determining social status, especially that of the upper class.[23] On the other hand, Frazier found a positive correlation between skin complexion, occupational success, and residential tranquility the farther a Chicagoan moved southward along the South State Street axis.[24] Whatever the level of color snobbery in black Chicago, it surely affected Abbott adversely, indelibly scarring his social life and a chance for happiness.

Socialite Gerri Major's firsthand account of life within black society revealed an awareness and often adherence to following the internal color line.[25] Being "light, bright, or damn near white" was credited with elevating a number of persons into the ranks of the upper class.[26] During this decade, a pattern somewhat similar to the eastern seaboard cities' blue vein society rule seems to have held a grip on all social contacts from marriageable mates to friendships to club memberships. Major remembered well who married whom and under what circumstances. Another element gained in importance in Chicago though: Midwestern geographical location played its part as "the further one comes west the more emphasis is put on the amount of money one has."[27]

Although Abbott the philistine was neither an intellectual nor considered himself one; like many men of wealth who developed an interest in the *beaux arts*, he mastered the knack of promoting himself in the educational sphere into the realm of the seemingly real. Abbott took pride in having received two honorary LLDs, the first from Morris Brown University in 1923 and the second from Wilberforce University the following year.[28] Abbott's education had been completed at Hampton Institute in Virginia and Kent College of Law in Chicago. Had he fathered children, he no doubt would have guaranteed them an opportunity to avail themselves of the best education possible. Since he did not, he bestowed his interest in his nieces and nephews—Ethel, Flaurience, Mildred, Frederick, John, and Whittier Sengstacke—whom he hoped would carry his dreams into immortality. Each had an opportunity at a first-rate education in colleges and universities of their choice.[29]

Always the immaculate dresser and with his requirement for personal acceptance, Abbott was often seen in formal attire when it was not necessarily appropriate.[30] For example, his visits to the Chicago Opera House were more for show than artistic enjoyment. In an age when the average person depended on four-legged horse power and carriages, and the combustion engine had extended its competition with Ford's novel car models, Abbott's pea green Rolls Royce quite frequently carried the newspaper magnate and his wife to the doors of the Chicago Civic Opera building where he pretended to enjoy the music. Likewise, he maintained memberships in the Art Institute of Chicago, the Chicago Historical Society, and the Association for the Study of Negro Life and History in order to establish his credentials as one appreciative of the fine arts. The nouveau patron then started *Abbott's Monthly* in 1927 (which survived the Depression years until 1933) and contemplated publishing *Reflexus* (Reflects Us).

Travel being the habit of the enlightened and wealthy, he and his wife sojourned to Brazil in 1923 and completed that ritual by writing a ten-part series on his trip that informally gained support for, but neither merited nor won, Spingarn Award recognition. Evaluation of the series was that it was too "observant and not critical" enough for formal consideration, failing to reach a level of acceptable, high-quality nonfiction. He continued his travels to and through Europe and made the Grand Tour through the Renaissance countries, Greece, and Egypt that European royalty and their social pretenders completed. One especially positive result of his journey to Paris was his induction into the Institut Littéraire et Artistique de France.[31] Wishing to connect with his German family roots, he sent his relatives to visit the Sengstacke family until the rise of Nazism.

Robert S. Abbott had his faults as he satisfied his own ego needs, but he sincerely cared about others as shown through his charity and involvement in civil rights. Surprisingly missing from his biography by Ottley is mention of *Defender* charities, which through Abbott's efforts sponsored the annual Bud Billiken Day Parade for children beginning in 1929. His civic involvements further included active membership on several biracial bodies of high influence. These were the Executive Board of the Chicago NAACP, the Board of Directors of the Chicago Urban League, and the Chicago Commission on Race Relations. Having established himself professionally beyond the confines of the Black Belt, he was one of two African Americans to receive an invitation to join the initial investors of "A Century of Progress" (the Chicago World's Fair scheduled to be held in 1933). Later, when other African Americans committed $25.00 in pledges to keep Provident Hospital open, Abbott doubled the amount of his donation, contributing $50.00.[32]

Banker Jesse Binga and his wife, Eudora, lived at 3324 South Vernon Avenue until 1919 when they moved to 5722 South Parkway in a racially hostile, white neighborhood. His South Parkway abode was a spacious, but not architecturally impressive, two-and-one-half-level red brick dwelling. Located across from verdant Washington Park in the community of the same name, it was immediately south of the Grand Boulevard community in the Black Metropolis and across from the spacious city park originally designed by Frederick Law Olmsted and Calvin Vaux, and completed by Horace W. S. Cleveland. One would imagine that Binga's ownership of the two large, majestic, gray-stoned, six-unit apartment buildings on either side of his home reflected not only his defiance of unfriendly neighbors but also was meant as a display of his economic power. His unwelcomed presence seemed significant enough for it to enter the writings of Irish American writer James T. Farrell in his *Studs Lonigan: A Trilogy*.[33]

Now, in 1920 at fifty-five years of age, he acquired the image of a cranky autocrat although he personally greeted customers daily at the bank's door with a greeting aimed at ensuring confidence in the bank and its operations and its leadership. To some members of the downtown banking crowd, he was "a man of pleasing personality, and somewhat above the average of his race in culture."[34] Others in the Loop who were less charitable and less gracious considered him anything but a bona fide banker. W. E. B. Du Bois explained the variance in perception as he considered Binga as "self-assertive and the type of man the downtown bankers wanted to fail."[35] To the persons with whom he came into daily contact on the South Side, he was an exceedingly difficult man to understand and to relate to on any level, personal or business. His no-nonsense response resonated with egotism, coarseness, and a lack of congeniality. Binga was aware of this criticism and had a ready response: "Lots of people criticize me. They don't like my methods and they offer me suggestions. I always tell them: Jesse Binga knows what he is doing and he's doing it like Jesse Binga wants it done."[36] This confidence in self was further reflected in the pride he had in his personal achievements and in his family's accomplishments, past and present. Binga wrote to his first cousin's son during the latter's college years in Richmond, Virginia, that he wished him well and that he would "do honor to the name of 'Binga.'"[37]

Socially, the Bingas' Christmas Ball was a "cultured person's" delight to attend, if one was fortunate enough to get an invitation. "He regarded this as the social event of the season; none other counted."[38] And just enough of the right people were invited to satisfy Mrs. Binga's need to repay her social obligations. The most authoritative historian on black Chicago society described Mrs. Binga as looking "like a caricature" but possibly the first African American "to stay at the Plaza [Hotel] in New York." Her husband fared better, being depicted as "a distinguished looking gentleman . . . [and a man who] could probably have chosen anyone he wanted."[39] The Bingas' guest list for their Christmas party of 1922 included Mr. and Mrs. Robert S. Abbott, Dr. and Mrs. Julian Lewis (Anthony Overton's son-in-law and daughter), attorney and Mrs. Richard Hill (another Overton son-in-law and daughter), and enough of the social luminaries of the African American community to easily identity who had arrived in high society and who had not. The black-owned Vincennes Hotel hosted the event, which was considered the biggest society affair among leading African Americans.[40]

Although society writer Gerri Major assessed the Bingas as less than completely sociable and not on any socialite's "A list," Major's requirement that providing accommodations to prominent people indicated that this standard of importance was met.[41] Earlier, the Bingas had entertained Lavinia Jones, the daughter of black Chicago's previous leading and wealthiest couple, John and Mary Jones, in the old Binga home at 3324 South Vernon in 1913. In this decade, the Binga home was the site of many elegant affairs and even space on their front porch was a valued place to occupy.[42] The couple's ages might have played a part in their overall sociability as they had reached their sixties by mid-decade, a time when the bodily constitution grows weary of strenuous activity and the exertion required in entertaining. Another factor could be that Binga's formal educational training purportedly consisted of having completed high school in Detroit, and conceivably this might explain part of his social aloofness in a city filling up with self-confident, college-trained individuals.[43]

The philanthropic impulse was not lost on the Bingas, as their charitable interests included providing college tuition for young people to attend Fisk University, the University of Chicago, and the Chicago Music College, as well as for the necessities for desperate families in need of respite from their rental obligations. Following the Bingas' Christmas party for members of their social set, Mrs. Binga regularly held her annual party for the children of the South Side. As a matter of fact, she held two separate parties for the children: One children's party benefitted children of the Bingas' faith who attended St. Elizabeth Catholic Church; another was held for the Protestant children whose parents attended the scores of Protestant churches throughout the South Side.[44] Perhaps the leadership Mrs. Binga rendered in behalf of the Salvation Army doughnut drive of 1927, which included the Black Metropolis, for the first time demonstrated conclusively her citywide status as a civic figure.[45]

Demonstrating somewhat of an appreciation of high culture, the Bingas commissioned professional artists to complete portraitures for their home. They then proceeded to commission noted muralist and portraitist William Edouard Scott to produce a mural for the Binga State Bank at the newly built Binga Arcade located on the northwest corner of State and 35th Streets.[46] Scott possibly was the portraitist who also produced the Bingas' likenesses on canvas that hung in their home. "Although she was a lover of home, Mrs. Binga traveled extensively and ha[d] visited the principal cities of Europe. Abroad, she gathered a collection of art works."[47]

Binga's appearance in the May 8, 1927, issue of the *Chicago Tribune* worked wonders in heightening the level of his respectability in both the city in general and on the South Side. Significantly, whenever the *Chicago Tribune* made reference to Binga, and that occurred on several occasions, it was always in regard to his status as a man of prominence within the business world.[48]

Among the medical practitioners, Dr. George Cleveland Hall rose in prominence during this decade. He assisted historian Carter G. Woodson in organizing the first modern body to scientifically study the life and culture of people of African descent. Aptly named the Association for the Study of Negro Life and History at its birth in 1915,[49] Hall served as president of its Chicago branch once it was established as a permanent organization. He also was vice president of Provident Hospital until he later assumed the presidency; active with the Chicago Urban League, the Chicago NAACP, the Wabash YMCA, and the National Negro Business League; a member in 1925 of the Chicago Public Library Board and in 1926 of the Municipal Voters' League (a predominantly white civic association that evaluated the qualifications of prospective members of the Chicago City Council and the courts);[50] and he also sat on the Chicago Commission on Race Relations.

Professionally, Hall expanded his Provident ties to gain affiliation with the Chicago Medical College. Social antagonism between Dr. Daniel Hale Williams and his wife, Alice, and the Halls, George Cleveland and his wife, Theodosia, had reached fever pitch in earlier decades, with the feud causing a chasm in social affairs apparently greater than the supposed Washington–Du Bois conflict. Both men, interestingly enough, were friends of the Tuskegeean. At the heart of the conflict was Williams's challenge to Hall's medical credentials and the former's later attempt to keep Hall off the board of Provident Hospital. Other dimensions involved the inability of the two wives to mesh socially and supposedly a clash over skin color and cultural deportment. According to social chronicler Gerri Major, on one occasion early in the new century, immediately upon Mrs. Williams's arrival at a gathering, Mrs. Hall's presence caused the former to turn around and leave without taking time to sit.[51] Yet if Williams's biographer, Helen Buckler, found that Mrs. Hall received harsh treatment on that occasion, the former women's editor of the *Chicago Whip*, Mrs. Lovelynn Evans, remembered a different scenario as unfolding by the postwar years. This one had Mrs. Hall emerging as a major social force in black society with her approval as essential to social acceptability.[52] This prominence in social standing coincided with her husband's ascension in medical and civic circles.

Dr. George Cleveland Hall lived through the entirety of the decade, even enjoying a two-month cruise and vacation to the Bahamas, Panama, and South America in 1929. He was accompanied by rising medical star Dr. Herbert Turner on what probably amounted to an attempt to restore his health[53] before he passed away in 1931. Previous to the time of Hall's death, he had persuaded Julius Rosenwald to provide financing for the first public library facility in the Black Metropolis community. Competition during this period for both funding and municipal approval of facilities was intense, so the planned construction represented a major step forward educationally for the entire South Side. Located on the southeast corner of 48th Street and Michigan Avenue, the structure was designed in the Italian Renaissance style and cost $200,000. The Chicago Library Board, to which Hall belonged, named the structure after Hall subsequent to his death and the building's completion.

Two political figures rose to such a high stature as to warrant recognition as being part of the upper class. Edward H. Wright, with credentials in law, government, politics, and the civic realm, was also an individual who amassed a considerable fortune. His influence and power over the totality of activities in the Black Metropolis were likewise so considerable as to qualify him for this designation. His listing in *Who's Who in Colored America* confirmed socially his national standing. His ally in Republican politics, Major Robert "Fighting Bob" Jackson, alderman of the Third Ward, held governmental, political, military, business, civil rights, and social credentials that easily qualified him for inclusion in this group. Jackson's financial operations enabled him to amass considerable wealth and his prolific social affiliations provided him access to and recognition within an immense social network of prominent persons nationally. He also won a place in *Who's Who in Colored America*.[54] These two political leaders served as honorary pallbearers at the funeral of businessman Frank. L. Gillespie in 1925, upon whose death his earthly abode at 4524 Grand Boulevard (South Parkway) was referred to as a "palatial home."[55]

Likewise, two ministers were held in high esteem by blacks and recognized by whites as having civic prominence. Rev. Lacey Kirk Williams of the Olivet Baptist Church gained enough recognition as a civic leader to be invited to give his editorial opinion in the *Chicago Tribune* on the place of African Americans in the city's life at the decade's end.[56] Rev. Williams was cited for his civic standing and "his genius [which] is primarily that of an organizer. . . . He has a staff of over 20 people, six of whom are assistant pastors, who in turn are associated with tens of volunteer workers. This largest Protestant church in the world is large not only in members but in its constructive ministry."[57] Rev. Archibald J. Carey Sr. of Quinn Chapel AME Church was installed as a bishop of the AME Church in 1920 with wide-ranging responsibilities and powers in Chicago, the Midwest, and Canada. While his political involvements negatively affected his status as a clergyman and civic leader, his ability to balance his entry into Caesar's world (the domain of unrestrained quests for power) with ecclesiastical effectiveness, good deeds in the community, and many supportive friends elevated his prestige overall.[58] Rev. Carey's critics pointed to his heavy involvement in politics and his "most powerful machine which functions like a rock crusher."[59]

The geographical dimensions of African American residency in a city where housing restrictions based on race reached exasperating levels revealed interesting patterns. The emergence of black residency along South Parkway as a preferred location indicated the physical distance African American life had traveled.[60] It was described thus: "Stately masonry residences in the Romanesque Revival architectural style line[d] the boulevard."[61] As a matter of fact, the physical distance between the socially fading and physically deteriorating Stroll on State Street and palatial, tree-lined Grand Boulevard (redesignated as South Parkway in 1925) amounted to a scant half mile. Representative of the elasticity of the Black Metropolis's boundaries, the social distance between the two thoroughfares, on the other hand, represented the leap from sportsmen's pleasure and notoriety to bourgeois respectability. Beyond the leap in space, the new accent in residential living over residing where the pursuit of pure commercial gain dominated—for example, in the State Street/Dearborn Avenue corridor—demonstrated how far black Chicago had evolved in terms of developing a formal class structure. Future State Representative Corneal Davis and his new wife arrived in the Douglas community area and unknowingly had moved into an architecturally significant area on Calumet Avenue when, as he described the area, "it was just turning black. . . . It was white then. All down in there in fact it was white, all the way down to 18th St., Prairie Avenue and Calumet Avenue. All the way down to 18th St. was white. It was old Chicago and your blue bloods lived in there—over in there, especially on Michigan Ave."[62] When, in 1929, the *Opportunity* magazine sought to present a visualization of how well the new, prosperous, sophisticated Negro lived to the rest of black America, the photograph snapped was that of South Parkway. It contained homes that outshone the housing designated by E. Franklin Frazier as being located within an upper-class cluster the same year.

The demographics changed just as the decade did. Both the wealthy and the middle-class white Anglo-Saxon Protestant (WASP), German American, Jewish, and Irish American residents moved away, and in their place flowed in the ambitious African American professionals, along with semiprofessionals and the striving, upper-stratum members of the working class. Among the latter was the extended family of former Kentuckians Walter and Melinda Dee Green, who lived at 3159 South Parkway. Farther south along the thoroughfare was the migrant family of Dr. Calvin Paul Davis, his wife, and one-year-old Libby from Longview, Texas. The Davises arrived in the city in 1920 following the horrific 1919 race riot in Longview. They moved once before moving into 447 East 48th Place, where they became the first African Americans to reside on the block. Their arrival was neither heralded nor opposed.[63] In 1923, Lloyd G. Wheeler III, namesake and grandson of the legendary businessman of the John Jones–Lloyd G. Wheeler merchant tailoring enterprise, returned to the city with his mother and siblings from Urbana-Champaign following his father's death several years previously. They were fortunate to find housing in the Grand Boulevard community and moved there in proximity to the Davises. They resided in this community for six years, but their stay in this predominantly white neighborhood was made negotiable as long they neither revealed their racial identity to neighbors nor attracted any attention to their presence by entertaining their fellow co-racialists. It was a case of rarely being seen or noticed, and definitely never being heard. Subsequently, they experienced no overt difficulties, but by 1929 they tired of this situation and moved farther south into a predominantly middle-class African American neighborhood.[64] Dr. and Mrs. George Cleveland Hall represented another example of this residential mobility, living at 3249 S. Wabash Avenue while he maintained offices one block away at 3102 S. State Street in 1913. By May 1914, however, the Halls had moved to 3408 South Parkway where they lived until street widening forced them to move again to a home located one block south, onto the elegant former Grand Boulevard (now renamed South Parkway).[65]

From its northern end at 31st Street to its southern extreme at 51st Street at the foot of Washington Park (that verdant expanse built in the image of the Parisian park system and New York's Central Park) stood the boundaries where black residency was not allowable under the racial restraints of the infamous restrictive covenants. Still, to live on South Parkway was to reside on the street that superseded Dearborn Avenue and its adjoining streets as the most fashionable black thoroughfare in Chicago.[66] So, in defiance of white resistance, blacks moved steadily southward.

Male society club life revolved around memberships in the Boulé (which was national and ultraexclusive) and locally in the Appomattox, Assembly, Snakes, and original Frogs clubs. The Boulé purportedly exemplified the best in male social organization, being a part of the coast-to-coast network of emerging branches in Sigma Pi Phi, originating in Philadelphia. Its founder, Dr. Henry E. Minton, emphasized that wealth alone could not guarantee membership. Victorian virtues and qualities such as "education, respectability, and congeniality" were essential. Minton lived briefly in Chicago and once here recruited physicians and dentists into its ranks. Its highly exclusive membership included Drs. Daniel Hale Williams and Charles E. Bentley at its founding as the organization's first branch outside Philadelphia in 1907. Dr. George Cleveland Hall had been repeatedly rejected because of a lack of positive votes.[67] By the 1920s, engineer Charles S. Duke and attorney Robert A. J. Shaw, captain of the 370th in France, also belonged to this elite group.[68]

Unlike the Boulé, the Assembly was a local institution and purportedly exemplified the second best in male social organization. It apparently was the second of two clubs mentioned by Frazier "which had maintained their integrity for two decades [and] comprised the social-elite."[69] Led by a governing committee of twenty-five, membership in the Assembly was open to any male engaged in a legitimate enterprise and upon the recommendation of a sitting member. Their annual dances were "never featured in the *Defender* although [Abbott] belong[ed] to the club." As a further note to exclusivity, a club member explained, "We have never had a publicity agent. We give the dances among ourselves and let it go at that. . . . At the closed dances, worthwhile out-of-town visitors are permitted."[70]

Occupationally, the absence of Pullman porters or red caps in upper-class social clubs, with the exception of five men who were also college graduates, indicated a case of occupational exclusivity, however.[71] According to Dr. Spencer C. Dickerson in 1938, even a postal employee meeting acceptable standards could join the Assembly, although this sounded more like retrospective egalitarian theory than it did social reality, given the social climbing underway. Other major clubs such as the Original Forty Club had not reached their social maturation and were just positioning themselves to enable elevation of their members in status. The club had formed around 1915 as the Forty Club with a middle-class to middling-class membership, and had reorganized under a state charter as the Original Forty Club of Chicago in July 1920. Over the years, its membership increased and its collective professional status rose as well. Earl B. Dickerson joined by 1925 and was followed by Dr. Leonidas Berry, the pioneer physician in the city in the use of the gastrointestinal endoscope.[72] On the horizon, elite standing beckoned, reflecting the accomplishments of its members.[73]

Among recent college graduates, the Washington Intercollegiate Club was coming of age as a feeder for individuals seeking high social status as it entered into its third decade. It now boasted of being the voice of hundreds of the city's black college students, both foreign and native-born. Its leader was Frederick H. H. Robb, a law student at Northwestern University and editor of an influential, two-volume compilation on African American economic, political, and social progress entitled *The Negro in Chicago* (1927 and 1929).

The Upper-Middle, Lower-Middle, and Middling Classes

A highly discernible, multitiered middle class existed as well by 1920. In its semblance as well as substance it assumed the forms of the center tier of a modified version of a *normative* class structure. Its features included occupation, wealth production, educational attainment, cultural interests, and character. According to E. Franklin Frazier, who during the 1920s was preparing a comprehensive study of classes among blacks in America, adoption of modern ideas in business and an embrace of basic capitalist values marked their progression. In their psychology toward life, "they have the same outlook on life as the middle class everywhere."[74] Its members were a set of future leaders in the making, contrary to the impressionistic assertion of Frazier that "This new class of professional and business men is setting the standards of behavior for the rest of the community."[75] As evidence of its complexity, the middle-class spectrum included prosperous smaller businesspersons, established politicians such as the aldermen and high-ranking party officials and appointees, along with professionals with less wealth than the members of the upper class and employed by others, such as teachers, civil servants, and other white-collar workers. Surprise at its emergence led the *Defender* to editorialize on the eve of a vaunted national conference of major African American organizations titled the Negro Sanhedrin: "Up to a few years ago a petty bourgeoisie [*sic*] was an unknown factor in [black] American life. Today it is a definite fact, with daily growing influence in commerce and politics."[76]

Black Chicago's professional men and women continued to play as vital a role in the political economy of the Black Metropolis as they did in the civic and social realms. They were concentrated in medicine, law, dentistry, nursing, architecture, education, and the sciences, and proved their competence by their adherence to national standards in place since the end of the nineteenth century. Emergence of African American national organizations aimed at maintaining standards and promoting the growth of African American practitioners served to enhance their professional abilities.[77]

Being a professional brought honor, respect, and sometimes envy from peers and less-privileged individuals. However, because of the economic conditions under which their patients, clients, and customers lived—deprivation related to post-wartime economic recession and lingering unemployment and underemployment—it meant limited income at times from those who could not pay fully or with regularity. According to Frazier, the ranks of the city's black professions grew with the migratory wave during the war years, and produced a newer, expanded class that vied for stability as a first step, then influence and power.[78] The Chicago NAACP attracted lawyers of the highest caliber, while black doctors garnered respect from the community also. Their stultified earnings, which reflected the low income level of the South and West Sides in general, constituted another matter altogether. In those instances where a physician's patient load was low or filled with poorly paying patients, maintaining a standard of living equal to a desirable higher status proved impossible.

Physicians appeared to have enjoyed a high status commensurate with upper-middle-class or lower-middle-class ranking. Dr. Ulysses G. Dailey, a protégé of Dr. Daniel Hale Williams as well as noted physician because of his surgical skills, identified closely with and supported the *beaux arts*. Possessing a University of Chicago or Northwestern University diploma elevated one's status immensely. This emphasis on occupational grouping and wealth accumulation is more consistent with Frazier's assessment on class structure than that of Drake and Cayton, who placed greater weight on the standards of behavior and "front," meaning outward appearance.

Retrospective insight by later analysts, both scholarly and lay, provided functional guidelines to understand the dynamics of this portion of the social structure. One especially usable description from Drake and Cayton placed this class "off from the lower [that is, working] class by a pattern of behavior expressed in stable family and associational relationships, in great concern with 'front' [public reputation and deportment]" and "respectability [high moral public and private standards]," and in a drive for "getting ahead." Organizationally, joining the right group became "the means by which middle-class people 'on the rise' come into contact with people 'above' them socially and by which mobile lower-class individuals can rise from the class below."[79]

Moreover, recognition that the upper-middle class differed from the lower-middle class can be seen in the exploration of the leading example of the former group, attorney Earl B. Dickerson. The grandson of slaves, Dickerson arrived in Chicago as an economically poor but intellectually endowed migrant from Canton, Mississippi, in 1907 at age sixteen. One of his most poignant memories was his being reared by his widowed mother, whom he accompanied as a youth on her rounds as a laundress. He never forgot this experience and dedicated his life to the social and racial betterment of all people. Dickerson entered the professional phase of his career as a fledgling lawyer with a degree from the University of Chicago in 1920, but with limited paths to occupational advancement despite a stellar academic record. While holding an undergraduate degree from the University of Illinois, he had taught at Tuskegee Institute for one year in 1913–1914. His two years of legal training at the University of Chicago were interrupted because of military service during the First World War. In service to the nation, he rose to the rank of first lieutenant in the 365th Infantry Division. Afterward he returned to Chicago to help found the American Legion and complete his rigorous law training. Upon graduation in 1920 as the first African American to receive the JD at the university, he naturally sought employment commensurate with his ambition and training, with the reality facing him that racism could immediately undercut his ability to advance in Chicago's legal circles. Opposition to Dickerson's hiring came immediately upon his being presented by Chicago NAACP president Judge Edward Osgood Brown to his law partners as an up-and-coming legal star. Unfortunately, they feared a loss of clients and Dickerson was rejected and left to accept the humiliation, which he did with great resolve.[80]

With one door shut in the white community, another one opened in the Black Belt. Opportunity came with the proposed formation of the all-black Liberty Life Insurance Company. Dickerson now had the opportunity to demonstrate his legal and administrative abilities, and he soon became the firm's legal counsel. It was he who drew up the company's papers of incorporation, and both economic and occupational security followed with Dickerson protecting the company's financial status during the Great Depression and assuming its presidency during the 1950s.[81] A heightened commitment during the 1910s to correct society's injustices also found Dickerson helping found the American Legion to protect the rights of returning servicemen, joining the Chicago NAACP in 1920 and chairing the Legal Redress Committee, then joining the Chicago Urban League in 1921 and later being inducted onto the board of directors, and finally helping to organize the National Bar Association.

Despite this rapid professional and civic advancement throughout the decade, Dickerson's class standing in 1920 was anything but secure. When he began his law practice in 1921, it was in the downtown offices he shared with the dean of black lawyers, Edward H. Morris, but not originally as part of his law firm. Subsequent success in court led to Morris inviting him to join the newly formed partnership of Morris, Cashin, and Dickerson. Nevertheless, Dickerson's maverick status as a Democrat and independent got him into trouble with Morris and a subsequent loss of a noted partnership.[82] Socially, Dickerson moved easily through various circles as a member of Kappa Alpha Psi fraternity, the Original Forty Club in 1925, and later the Boulé. He recalled that he knew many luminaries of the period, some (like Edward H. Wright and Frank L. Gillespie) better than others (such as Dr. Charles E. Bentley, S. Laing Williams, and Ida B. Wells-Barnett).[83] This was a clear indication of the generational gap and character of social relations that would separate this period and its social structure from the decades succeeding it up to the modern civil rights period. Most important to his social elevation was Dickerson's membership in the Chicago Urban League, followed four years later by ascension onto the board of directors in 1925. His political independence led him into the folds of the Democratic Party and charges of his being a traitor to his race by this affiliation. William L. Dawson, a Republican, used this charge extensively against Dickerson during the 1920s and 1930s.[84] Importantly, it likewise provided entrée into the party's inner circles in Illinois, which served him and Liberty Life Insurance Company well when the business faced its closing. At the decade's end, Dickerson had advanced in status to a secure position in the upper-middle class. By the end of the 1940s he would move into the upper class as one of the leading members of the black establishment. As evidence of his elevation in station, he could point to his having earned a million dollars.[85]

Dickerson's most active political opponent beginning in this decade was former Georgian William L. Dawson, who was born in 1886. Like Dickerson, the grandson of slaves, Dawson differed in that he had parents who possessed a *petite bourgeois* thirst for success for their children that reached fruition through their successes in later life in law and medicine. He arrived in Chicago around 1905 or 1906 after his graduation from the Albany, Georgia, Normal School in 1905. He attended and was graduated from Fisk University (with honors) in 1909. As an intellectually endowed migrant but one who was typically poor with "fifty cents in his pocket," he arrived in Chicago, which he envisioned as a place of great opportunity. Ambitious, he attended the Kent College of Law in 1915 at age twenty-nine and also interrupted his studies for military service. Although above the age for the military draft, he served in France in the Great War in which he likewise rose to the rank of first lieutenant in the 365th Infantry Division. Wounded in battle by both poison gas and shrapnel (the former left a mark on his temple and the latter affected his ability to raise his left arm any higher than his shoulder), neither broke his candor nor ambition.

In later years in the halls of the U.S. Congress, he pointedly remarked to segregationists who challenged blacks' claim to full citizenship rights, "That would have been a good joint if hospitalization had been available, and I had not been a Negro American." He would further challenge his white colleagues to vote to eliminate segregation and the denial of civil rights: "How long, how long, my conferees and gentlemen from the South, will you divide us Americans on account of color? Give us the test that you would apply to make anyone a full-fledged American, and by the living God, if it means death itself, I will pay it. But give it to me."[86]

William L. Dawson began this decade as a fledgling lawyer with a degree from Northwestern University (1920), whereupon like Dickerson he faced limited paths to occupational advancement because of the city's racial protocol. Dauntless and racially inspired, Dawson dared challenge the sitting white congressman, Martin B. Madden, in the 1928 primary at a time when the latter's popularity because of job procurement at the post office was at its highest. Dawson lost decisively.

The diversity of occupational pursuits remained a bright spot in the whirl of life in the Black Metropolis. William L. Dawson, for example, had only to look at his brother, the professionally respected Dr. Julian Dawson, a well-known surgeon in a field Dawson had once thought of entering, to gain inspiration.[87] The number of black physicians reached well over 150 practitioners by 1923–1924.[88] Meantime, the high status within the medical and dentist professions held for decades earlier in the century by Drs. Daniel Hale Williams and Charles E. Bentley was now being assumed by the likes of Dr. Julian Lewis, a son-in-law to Mr. and Mrs. Anthony Overton. Dr. Lewis was a graduate of the University of Illinois at Urbana, held a Phi Beta Kappa key, and became the first African American to join the medical faculty at the University of Chicago, entering in the area of pathology.

Vivian Gordon Harsh represented that strain of black Chicagoans with Old Settlers' credentials and a life's experience as a member of the middle class from birth. She was born in Chicago in 1890 to college-trained parents who arrived in the 1880s. Harsh received her education in the Chicago Public Schools, graduating from Wendell Phillips High School in 1908. The next year she became the first African American to be employed within the Chicago Public Library system and assumed clerical duties. Confident that she could carve her career path in library work, she enrolled at the Simmons College Library School in Boston and by the 1920s had received her degree in library science. In 1924 she became the first African American to become a branch librarian, serving on Chicago's predominantly white North Side. Harsh became active in the Association for the Study of Negro Life and History, which had its beginning in 1915 in Chicago, and thus combined a love of and commitment to her field with the concern for advancement of scholarship in black areas. With black political pressure being exerted on the library board by appointee Dr. George Cleveland Hall to begin library services in the Black Metropolis, coupled with Hall's influence with philanthropist Julius Rosenwald to finance a library on the South Side, Harsh's future took a major turn toward realization of a dream. She would introduce an entire community in need of enlightenment to the services of a first-class library with reading, learning, understanding, and access to critical thinking. In January 1932, the George Cleveland Hall branch of the Chicago Public Library opened with Vivian G. Harsh as head librarian and a bright future ahead for Bronzeville's inquisitive minds.[89]

Young medical professional Dr. Arthur G. Falls emerged at this time from professional training at Northwestern University's Medical School to assume a place in his field. Falls was a northerner who was born in 1907 in Chicago and reared in the racially integrated Englewood neighborhood, which was located west of the Black Metropolis. He was the son of a postal worker with an indomitable spirit to succeed who trained others who passed him by due to race. Dr. Falls's mother enjoyed one year of college, and his ambition, dreams, and thinking sprang from this household where a premium was placed on achievement as well as free and critical thinking. As a religiously motivated activist of Catholic upbringing, he dedicated his life to helping others who were less fortunate than himself in accordance with deep-rooted principles encompassing justice and egalitarianism.[90]

The professional classes, first in formation in Chicago by the 1880s and 1890s, and illustrated by the previous examples, only proliferated in size over time. In 1929, E. Franklin Frazier assessed its importance: "In order to serve the newly created as well as old wants of the Negro population a large group of professional men and women were attracted to the city. This group has become large enough to comprise a new leadership as well as a distinct class."[91] Frazier also wrote: "[It was] the largest number of successful young Negroes of any city in the country." From their ranks, civic leadership drew its strength.[92]

The legal profession had attracted African American men and women since the nineteenth century, with a small cadre expanding in the field. The reception the lawyers received from their communities, according to research conducted by Carter G. Woodson and his team, differed by region and city. One testimonial summarized the situation in Chicago: "In Chicago, all are treated as members of the bar and courtesies are mutual and where otherwise, Negro lawyers of caliber demand it."[93] By weight of numbers, the lawyers in Chicago reached at least 106 by 1927.[94] As to their civic service, they became noted for their volunteer service in behalf of guaranteeing citizenship rights, for example, through their service with the Chicago NAACP. From their ranks the first African American municipal judge would emerge, Albert B. George.[95] According to Gosnell writing specifically on Chicago, "the lawyers have been the most active in politics, both individually and as a group."[96] Yet, in addition to restrictions related to race, Charles S. Johnson wrote that black lawyers following the riot of 1919 were disparaged by whites as to their general abilities.[97]

The diversity of occupational pursuits in the Black Metropolis included architects, engineers, and designers, additional evidence of success within the American mainstream in spite of obstacles. One was Charles S. Duke, an architectural and structural engineer who drew "Plans and Estimates for Building Construction." Surveying the ranks of his peers, he deduced that their numbers seemed sufficient enough for him to plan an organization of engineers and architects.

An Alabama native with early Arkansas educational training, Charles S. Duke matriculated at Howard University in Washington, D.C., after attending the prestigious Phillips Exeter Academy from which he earned his AB degree in June 1924. "His service as an engineer has been with the Pennsylvania Railroad, the Missouri Pacific Railroad, the Chicago and Northwestern Railroad and the George W. Jackson, Inc., tunnel builders. . . . He was designing engineer in the Bridge Division of the City of Chicago. . . . In 1921, he was appointed member of the Chicago Zoning Commission where he gave special attention to zoning problems as they affected members of his race."[98] The following year he was registered as a licensed structural engineer with control over his own firm. In 1926, he was appointed by Democratic mayor William E. Dever to serve on the Chicago Housing Commission, a board that served as a precursor to future housing agencies concerned with the city's extant and future housing stock. Later Duke assumed the responsibility of replicating a Du Sable homestead in collaboration with the National De Saible Memorial Society at the Chicago World's Fair of 1933–1934.

Another architect, Walter T. Bailey, was born in downstate Illinois in Kewanee. He was a graduate of the University of Illinois at Urbana-Champaign in 1900 with a degree in the science of architecture. Bailey headed Tuskegee Institute's Architecture Department until 1913 when he moved to Memphis, where he opened his own office and began designing buildings throughout the South. The lure of success in Chicago found him residing here in the "City of Big Shoulders" in 1924. His first office was in the Overton Building one block north of the Pythian Building, where he assisted the Knights of Pythias in constructing their skyscraper. Bailey designed the National Pythian Temple located until 1980 at 3745 South State Street that was constructed at a cost of $850,000. Rising eight stories from the ground and covering a quarter of a city block, it was completed in 1928.[99] As the skyscraper nudged upward, the Knights were realizing their dream of prominence with a structure to match their national fraternal eminence. As a contemporary and professional collaborator of Duke, he planned the separate African American celebration of "A Century of Progress" for the city completely from a black perspective.[100]

At the other end of the spectrum of middle-class life were teachers, postal employees, skilled craftsmen, municipal workers, and others, all earning hefty enough salaries or wages allowing them to rent roomy apartments or rental homes. Home ownership often escaped them. With home ownership, however, the income from roomers, or lodgers, made the difference in maintaining possession of their property. For the next decade of the 1930s, Drake and Cayton were reporting that "Bronzeville tends to have middle class *buildings* in all areas, or a few middle class blocks here and there," but there was no middle class area such as whites had.[101] One such attempt at an enlarged residential haven emerged late in the decade.

By 1927 with the opening of the Michigan Avenue Garden Apartments (also known as the Rosenwald Apartments) located at 47th Street and Michigan Avenue, African Americans could secure clean, spacious, safe housing far enough away from the Black Belt to experience prestige among others of their economic group. Whether upper-middle class or lower-middle class, the ties of shared values bound these persons together.

There were blacks to be found in the chemical industry. In 1901, the possibilities of a career in chemical engineering had seemed anything but promising for any African American at the newly opened Armour Institute of Technology on the South Side. The thirst for knowledge and the ambition to match it nonetheless propelled Charles Pierce, a native of Texas, forward as he earned the institution's and nation's first degree in the field. Restricted by race and his dark brown complexion from a position in the industrial world, Pierce turned to education, teaching at Wendell Phillips and (the new) Du Sable High Schools.[102]

Lloyd Augustus Hall, the grandson of Chicago pioneers Rev. Abram and Isabel Hall, whose family had moved outside the city to the Fox River Valley midway through the nineteenth century, returned to Chicago in 1922 to further his career in the chemical industry; his fate was different. Hall had been well educated at Northwestern University where he had entered an important social network.[103] In the field of pharmaceutical (or food) chemistry, Hall moved upward from his position as chief chemist at the Boher Chemical Laboratory in 1922 to become president and director of a consulting laboratory, the Chemical Products Corporation. His specialty was innovative food production.[104] Having entered the field as an individual, Hall attempted to open it wider for other talented African Americans.[105]

Finance required accountants and others with skills in money management and financial planning. The managers of the Liberty Life and Victory Insurance Companies were persons of training, experience, and vision. Well-qualified cashiers were ready to assume these positions as soon as the Binga State and Douglass National Banks issued their call for professional assistance. Binga hired C. N. Langston, an Oberlin College graduate with twelve years of experience in a southern black bank.[106] The Douglass National Bank secured the services of Arthur J. Wilson, a certified public accountant educated at Northwestern University, the University of Illinois, and the University of Chicago. Wilson was the first African American to become a CPA in the state of Illinois, hold membership in the National Association of Cost Accountants along with the National Society of Industrial Engineers, and become licensed to practice before the U.S. Internal Revenue courts.[107]

In the primary and secondary educational levels, African Americans maintained their presence within the sphere of public education, and slowly were increasing it. Exemplary in this regard was Maudelle Bousfield, who became the first African American principal of a Chicago high school. Blacks continued to pressure the Chicago Board of Education for the opportunity to prove their leadership abilities. Perseverance was needed because the Chicago Public Schools did not relent in their racist practices until the principal's examination was opened in 1947, and then no more than two African Americans would find employment.

The dearth of leadership was proving severe because there were serious problems brewing with the advent of *de facto* segregation in the schools of the South Side. Moreover, the physical condition of the schools was deteriorating, the percentage of black children was beginning to reflect a transfer policy geared toward separating the races, and most importantly, the quality of education was slipping.[108] For Ida Mae Cress, who was a granddaughter of Civil War veteran Charles Griffin of the 29th Illinois and who graduated from Stephen Douglas Elementary in 1920, the quality was still maintained in that racially changing neighborhood, although the racial balance in her graduating class shifted to fifteen blacks and fifteen whites. She then was sent outside the district by her parents to avoid Wendell Phillips High School, and she subsequently attended the basically all-white Hyde Park High School.[109] Phillips was becoming an all-black school, although Alonzo Parham remembers that there was "a pretty good sprinkling of white kids."

Phillips had a sprinkling of black teachers as well, a rarity at the high school level in Chicago. Maudelle Bousfield was joined by Bishop Archibald J. Carey's daughter Annabelle and by Charles Pierce, the nation's first graduate in chemical engineering. Pierce's demand that all students adhere to high and rigorous standards convinced some poor-performing athletes and their coaches to avoid Pierce's classes. This matter was of little concern to young Mr. Alonzo Parham because of his ability to excel in academics. After graduation from Phillips, he entered West Point where he ran afoul of military racism.[110] Young Harold Hurd developed an interest in aviation, which led to his organizing an aviation club at Wendell Phillips, and later in life, helping train pilots at Tuskegee Institute during World War II.[111]

The importance of education as a means to social advancement as well as enlightenment was stressed by the Washington Intercollegiate Club, which boasted of being the voice of hundreds of the city's black college students. It saw its role as channeling the "talented tenth" into their future roles as leaders over black society. In 1927, these young persons with their sharp minds and nimble feet participated in a canvass of South Side neighborhoods to complete an employment survey conducted under the auspices of the Chicago Urban League. With an economic crisis looming, the object of their effort was to determine how stores were using black labor as they depended on black clientele to sustain their business operations.[112] Obviously, these data once evaluated would play an integral role in the end of the decade's decision to increase public pressure on local white businesses under the banner of the "Don't Spend Your Money Where You Can't Work" campaign, or "buying power" crusade.

In the sphere of higher education, black scholars of the period encountered no black faculty while studying at the University of Chicago. At the same time, the first African American to hold a professorship joined the faculty of the University of Chicago's Medical School in the mid-1920s in the person of Dr. Julian Lewis. He was admitted into the ranks of the faculty as assistant professor of pathology.

Just as the First World War had introduced the world to the airplane in military service during the modern age, its peacetime place was promoted by a woman flyer who captured black Chicago's and black America's heart. She was the diminutive, courageous Bessie Coleman, known affectionately among blacks as "Queen Bess." Former Texan Coleman wanted to fly, and with the backing of Robert S. Abbott and Jesse Binga, she traveled to France where a black person could learn the intricacies of flight. So fly she did after receiving her international pilot's license in France in 1921, becoming the first African American to achieve that distinction. Barnstorming followed, with her making appearances throughout America. Her tragic death while flying in 1926 served only to stimulate interest in flight.

* * *

Middle-class living revolved around a higher level of concern for the enjoyments of the material world and hedonistic pleasures. As reported in the society pages of the *Defender*, what would be considered mundane activities in the white world assumed out-of-proportion importance with notices of visits, illnesses, and parties dominating the weekly columns.[113] Belonging to social clubs played an important part of filling social life for these classes. The activities and camaraderie of the Forty Club and other social clubs and the fraternities fulfilled both the need to be a part of an acceptable group and complete the cycle of pleasurable living. Yet black Chicago never reached the level of social pretentiousness associated with the nation's capital. Langston Hughes criticized the pretentiousness of elite Washington, D.C., blacks—who were middle class, after all.[114] Chicago was democratic with all classes sharing the delights of choral music, blues, and jazz.

Recreational outlets such as the Idlewild Resort in Michigan provided summertime relief from the routine of big city living along with overcrowding and noise. Idlewild provided resort living across the economic spectrum—for the elite, the upper- and lower-middle classes, and some members of the working classes. Conspicuous consumption in dressing also assumed an important role for both the men and women. Yet clothing had to be considered tasteful, so examples such as the clothing lines presented by the *Half-Century Magazine* in its March 1920 issue served as models worthy of imitation.[115]

Church life revolved around social as much as spiritual foci, and each shared important parts of middle-class life. The old-line AME and Baptist churches catered to middle-class sensitivities as they continued their cross-class appeal to the lower class. Public decorum concerned this stratum and they sought influence over the Black Metropolis, as they wanted to remake the South Side in their own image. "Because the upper class and upper middle class control the press, the schools, and the pulpits of the larger churches, they are in a position to bombard the lower class with their conceptions of 'success,' 'correct behavior,' and 'morality'—which are in general the ideals of the white middle-class."[116] The pages of the *Half-Century Magazine* and the *Chicago Defender* served as bloody pulpits on morality just as the *Broad Ax* had done during the early twentieth century.

Military ardor had its role in middle-class purpose. Military service and the attendant organizations, like fraternal orders and fraternities, offered an elevation in status. World War I veterans joined the George O. Giles Post No. 1, an American Legion affiliate established in 1918 by attorney Earl B. Dickerson immediately following service in the European war. This activity continued a tradition begun with post–Civil War recognition of service and the formation of John Brown Post No. 50 as part of the Grand Army of the Republic. As the 8th Infantry Regiment continued its role as military protector of the nation both in peacetime and wartime during this decade, the attractiveness of a man's affiliation with this unit in the eyes of the civilian population enhanced the veteran's status in the Black Metropolis. Once the impressive statue to the 8th Regiment's valor rose triumphantly over South Parkway at 35th Street, every succeeding generation was to be left wondering, "Who were these men who earned such public distinction?"

The Middling Class of Pullman Porters and Postal Workers

Pullman porters and U.S. postal workers were two groups that fit comfortably into the indistinct category of belonging to a middling class, situated between the lower rung of the middle class and the upper echelon of the working class. These two sets of employees enjoyed a unique social status because their occupational duties carried an elevated status within the African American workforce, steady employment despite difficult times in the economy for most other workers, and wages that were reliable and *relatively* high for blacks. Further, each contained significant numbers of persons with educational accomplishments or at the least, high ambitions, which made them overeducated for their employment pursuits.[117] A number of porters had adopted a bourgeois attitude and set of values from association with some of the wealthiest whites in the nation, and this influenced both their thinking and lifestyles.[118] Recognized as stepping stones to future achievements, the occupations of these workers hovered somewhere in social prestige above the average working-class individual and around, if not equal to, the members of the lower-middle class. According to the research of E. Franklin

Frazier on the incidence of highest areas of home ownership, the farther south one moved along the State Street axis, the higher the number of homeowners. Both Pullman porters and postal workers figured prominently in this regard.[119] Lastly, each group produced its heroes for the public, though the porters had the advantage: In 1925, a porter named Daniels shut a door on scalding steam that was filling a car on a derailed train on one of the eastern lines. He fell unconscious after that scalding and died of his burns shortly thereafter.[120]

By the end of this decade, 9,000 men served in the employ of the Pullman Company as porters and dining car waiters nationally, and the 4,000 who lived in Chicago constituted 11 percent of the total black male workforce in Chicago.[121] Employment with the Pullman Company still appealed to African American males even after the rise of an industrial proletariat anchored by workers in the meatpacking and steel industries. Despite the rise of the industrial proletariat with impressive wage totals, the Pullman porters still maintained a higher social status by virtue of their place in black labor history, public and private deportment, personal style of living, and property ownership. As physically demanding as Pullman service was, along with its long hours and time away from home, working with the "Pullman" standard on one's cap offered an opportunity that was appealing during this decade. Then, there was the increase of black workers being hired at the Pullman car shops on the far South Side, located approximately eight or nine miles southeast of the heavily black populated portion of the city's South Side. Their numbers would reach 11 percent of the total Pullman Company labor force before 1927.[122]

In the opinion of one prospective porter, Sylvester Hicks, there was opportunity aplenty and he preferred the rails. Hicks had sampled various types of employment, serving eight months in the Pullman Company's Burnside Car shops followed by work with Armour and Company in the stockyards as a machine operator in the soap department. In a letter of recommendation, a former supervisor cited a litany of good character and work traits, including "honest[y], industrious[ness], faithful[ness] and [a] willing[ness] to work." The manager wrote, he "believes if he is able to secure a position with your firm that it will be an advancement to him in compensation and a better and cleaner job."[123] Indeed, earning a higher level of compensation in a safer, healthier setting made Pullman service appealing despite the attention that work and decent wages in the stockyards attracted.

The experience of Pullman service affected one of the Jones brothers of policy fame (the numbers racket) in the opposite way. During the 1920s, he tried his hand at running a taxi business, became disillusioned with that enterprise, and began working as a Pullman porter. "I began 'running on the road' and made about a hundred dollars a month. After I quit railroading—I didn't like being a porter—I went into the gambling business—race horses."[124] The ingredients of success in a person's life were fully outlined in this terse statement, indicative of ambition attainable only through self-employment and the amassing of wealth through one's own efforts in this case, even if illegal. This was Jesse Binga's story relived with the Pullman service in the middle, rising hopes and dashing them, yet never vanquishing the flame of ambition, only fueling it.

Facing a shortage of good and dependable workers during one summer crunch, the Pullman Company could display a sensitivity to personal failings if a prized employee found himself in trouble. One porter benefitted from this heightened understanding out in the West during 1926 where a construction boom proffered higher wages. Bending over backwards to accommodate the reinstatement of this worker after a successful court defense that included the following—[He has] "a quiet disposition, not of an aggressive type, [is] mild mannered, ha[s] a good appearance"—the porter received a second chance on the job.[125] Nonetheless, the issue of character remained a paramount consideration to the Pullman Company. Positive interviews, on-site housing inspections, and recommendations from employers, creditors, and family members continued to mark the basic requirement for employment with the company. Commonplace among the comments rendered were of this variety: "has always found him to be of good character, industrious, and bearing a good name in the community"; "at this address . . . everything appeared to be orderly and in a clean and tidy condition"; and, at a time when jobs were drying up through the South Side, the applicant "was very industrious, but he seemed to be unable to find a permanent position."[126]

When the new decade opened, organizing efforts by various factions continued within the ranks of the Pullman porters. Meanwhile, the number of black workers under the Pullman influence increased, with more young men joining the ranks of the porters traveling nationally, and at the Pullman shops at the southern end of Chicago, their number rose to 450 by 1920.[127] The dominant organizations included the Pullman Porter Benevolent Association, conceived in 1920 and functioning by February 1, 1921, with 10,000 members, and the Brotherhood of Sleeping Car Porters (BSCP) Protective Union.[128] Chicago's Milton P. Webster belonged to the former until 1925, at which time he became convinced that another, more militant, confrontational organization with a bolder approach would best serve the interests of the porters, and he then helped form the BSCP.

The most ambitious men continued to break away from the Pullman Company's hypnotic grip and seek success in other areas of endeavor. Lee Averett was one such person by this decade, when he pursued self-employment in the men's clothing business. His transformation was described in Frederick H. H. Robb's paean to African American individual and group progress: Once in Chicago, Averett worked as "a porter in a store. He tried this for a while and then decided he would try and run on the road as a Pullman Porter. He did for several years, being promoted to one of the best jobs on the road. He still was not satisfied, for he thought there was something he could do for himself, and perhaps for his fellow man."[129] Averett and his wife subsequently opened a single, small, men's repair and pressing service at 30th and State in 1922 that blossomed through hard work into fifteen such secondhand men's shops, making up Lee Averett's Saving System within five years. The flagship of their operation rented space in the newly opened Michigan Avenue Garden Apartments as soon as it opened in 1929.

Necessity dictated that labor consciousness grow. Of course, hundreds upon hundreds of porters and Pullman workers remained indifferent—or in some of the latter cases, frightened—by the might of the Pullman Company. When E. Franklin Frazier (1929) wrote sarcastically that Chicago "is the headquarters of the peripatetic Knights of the Whisk-broom—the generic George of the largest independent Negro labor union in the country," he revealed the prominence of labor consciousness as part of New Negro thinking and motivation. This new mentality willing to challenge Pullman's house union was championed locally by Milton P. Webster, whose propensity toward leadership and independence was exhibited early in childhood. Described as bombastic to Randolph's quiet demeanor,[130] Webster proved the right counterbalance for Randolph and a person with whom assertive Chicago porters and others like them could identify. The ultimate step in labor organization resulting from discontent with wages and working conditions culminated in the rise of the Brotherhood of Sleeping Car Porters in 1925.

Many African Americans considered work in the postal service as "honorable, respectable, and reasonably remunerative." Civic awareness, if not involvement, along with proper deportment became paramount in postal life. Postal workers gave support to the NAACP disproportionate to their numbers and actively participated in the struggle to attain full citizenship as well as workers' rights.[131] In addition, one's behavior outside the workplace counted for as much as adherence to a mandatory code inside postal facilities. Novelist Richard Wright's main character in *Lawd Today*, Jake Jacobs, lived an imbalanced social life filled with marital discord and other aspects of socially disrupted behavior. When his personal failings reached a boiling point, his wife threatened and followed through on reporting his conduct to his postal employers. As a last resort to save his job, he bribed a politically connected barber and a postal official to dismiss the charges of untoward conduct brought by Mrs. Jacobs.[132]

Considering post office employment to be desirable work with decent pay and high status, many workers gravitated to this employment source. By 1921, 1,400 black workers were employed as clerks and carriers. They represented 3.4 percent of the male black force over ten years of age in 1930. Gosnell claimed that double that number were employed, moving the figure to 3,000 workers on the job. The Chicago Urban League agreed somewhat, reporting that by the end of the decade 3,400 persons worked for the U.S. Postal Service.[133] According to Albert Brooks, a future Chicago NAACP branch president and four-decade member of the National Association of Postal Employees, too many of these workers in both

Gosnell's and the League's tally enjoyed only substitute status.[134] There were so many African Americans employed in the postal service that more racist-minded whites in the city alerted fellow travelers of their ilk sitting in the U.S. Congress of the danger to them of black men working. There, a South Carolina congressman attacked the blacks, leading to a debate on the floor with Rep. Martin B. Madden.[135]

The Large Base of the Multidimensional Working-Class Persons

An enormous base of working-class persons formed the bulk of black Chicago's citizenry. Different from the previously mentioned classes by virtue of its hard work yet limited wealth-producing efforts, its places of residence, its preferred forms of entertainment, and both the social and physical distance between it and the other classes, the working class was sometimes considered the lower class. For purposes of this historical exposition, it is described as the working class by essence of its reason for being and the virtue of its existence: work. The quality of life for the working-class living arrangements related directly to their ability to find adequate housing at affordable rental rates. The quest proved difficult, if not nearly impossible, for some people. Kitchenette living, where apartments were subdivided by both white and black landlords to facilitate more housing units—and, it must be said, to make money off the misery of others—dominated the housing market by this period. Single women, especially, felt adrift in the cold, impersonal urban vortex of the big city as they sought suitable living arrangements.[136] Richard Wright, the writer, arrived in Chicago in 1927 with expectations too lofty to be actually realized. The one aspect of life he anticipated as most easily attainable was decent living. But instead of a spacious, comfortable apartment he would share with his Aunt Cleo, Wright was introduced to her one-room housing unit, the kitchenette.[137]

According to Timuel D. Black Jr., "As I remember, even if you could afford a big apartment, you couldn't find one to rent. The landlords cut up all the larger apartments and converted them into smaller units so they could make a lot more money. We lived in one of those huge apartments at 5000 Grand Boulevard. . . . But we had to move [in conformance with the landlord's wishes and avarice]." James "Jack" Isbell agreed with Black's assessment of the housing situation of the times, adding, "We moved thirteen times from 1929 to 1932."[138] Bishop Arthur Brazier of the Apostolic faith recalled how he was born at home in the Hyde Park community in 1921. "As you recall, back in those days most of us were born at home since we were not allowed in hospitals. Hospitals were totally segregated. . . . So I was born at home on the third floor of an apartment in Hyde Park."[139]

The problem of accumulating enough money to pay the rent was solved by some by having a lodger, or roomer, join the household. This addition of an unrelated family member meant that there was another essential resource to pay the weekly or monthly rent on an apartment or home. Langston Hughes perceived yet a different dimension to this problem of meeting the rent. Rent parties in apartments meant freedom from white interference in cultural creation. "Then it was that house-rent parties began to flourish—and not always to raise the rent either. But, as often as not, to have a get-together of one's own, where you could do the black-bottom with no [white] stranger behind you trying to do it, too."[140]

Meanwhile, as a counterpoint, Gwendolyn Brooks lived with working-class parents who aspired for a world where talent led to attainment. Her parents, both Kansans, never accepted the racial status quo as so limiting that their daughter's dreams could not be achieved. The father constantly read and recited from the classics in the Brooks household. His deferred dreams of a medical career had failed to deter his commitment to providing a nurturing home for his family and for his own personal achievement of independence, despite his work as a corporate porter. The mother had once taught school in Kansas and prepared her daughter to become the first female Paul Laurence Dunbar. Arriving in the city in advance of the Great Migration, the Brooks family first lived in Hyde Park in the African American enclave along Lake Park Avenue and in the early 1920s purchased a home at 4332 South Champlain Avenue in the Grand Boulevard community to the north, which was opening to prospective African Americans homeowners.

The Brookses' two-level frame house featured a broad front porch from which Mrs. Brooks and the children entertained and interacted with their neighbors. There were limits, however, to the amount and type of social contact that Gwendolyn and her younger brother, Raymond, could maintain with the neighborhood children. The wrought iron gate formed a self-imposed barrier to any possible assault to proper decorum or a disruption to order.[141]

Health care to these classes was limited by income and racist exclusions to about six hospitals. It was estimated that only eight of every hundred beds in the city were open to African American patients.[142] Working-class individuals did without essential care until emergencies arose. Part of this explains the high incidence of death and disease in the black areas of the city. The poor health experienced generally by the African American nationally, and in Chicago locally, afforded an opportunity for those providers of institutional medical services to achieve two worthwhile ends. Altruistically, serving the community was one way to improve the quality of life. Maintaining financial stability meant the facility would remain open and continue to serve the needs of humanity. As a business, at least four black hospitals provided the residents of the Black Metropolis with care and simultaneously opened the door to a business opportunity. These facilities, along with the public-run Cook County Hospital on the West Side and private St.

Luke's Hospital located in the 1700 block of South Michigan, provided the basic lifelines to black health care.

Sociological observer Charles S. Johnson made reference to two, including the best known and nationally recognized Provident Hospital, which was still located at Dearborn and 36th Street. Then there was the (possibly white) Fort Dearborn Hospital, the Dailey Hospital, and the John T. Wilson Medical Foundation, all providing competition and services to the Black Belt community. The saga and success of Provident Hospital is a well-told tale beginning with its founding in 1891. In its twenty-first year, when Daniel Hale Williams's biographer, Helen Buckler, reported that the Williams–Hall feud reached its peak, resulting in Williams's resignation, former judge and NAACP official Robert McMurdy wrote to Julius Rosenwald's representative, William F. Graves, that fiscally the hospital was holding its own. "The hospital has property worth $100,000, and is entirely free from debt except a usual current deficiency which on December 1 was $2346.66, it being one of the light months of the year always." Notwithstanding the professional animosity brewing between Drs. Hall and Williams, evidence of the split apparently did not affect the ability of the institution to remain open and function with some degree of normality. As to efficiency, that is a matter where documentation is missing but needed. Moreover, the entire economic picture appeared rosier than would be expected from the impression of the Buckler account based on Williams's most avid supporters, who happened to be Hall's strongest detractors.[143]

To its credit, Provident Hospital had established itself as the anchor of black health services for three decades. Rising black use meant more of the impoverished and underpaid populations of the Black Belt were using it instead of remaining at home and suffering from a lack of health care. Rising black donations from the mass level in support—for example, from baseball—indicated that independence rather than dependence was seeping into the consciousness of the African American community. The linkage to the South and Tuskegee Institute demonstrated that Booker T. Washington's friendship with both Williams and Hall benefitted the hospital, and thereby the Black Metropolis as a whole, more than the elite. Perhaps importantly, the charge that Hall was promoting the hospital as a business was being validated. By 1927, it had served 100,000 patients with 220 young women having been trained as nurses and 146 graduate physicians being trained as residents (and thereby meeting Illinois medical registry requirements). In medically segregated Chicago, there was nowhere else to go for the latter professionals. In regard to indigent patients who could not afford to pay for medical care when surgery was needed and therefore had to forgo any specialized care at all, one donor offered to finance two beds solely for them.[144] Thus, Provident acted as a major community preserver of life.

As a business operation, it experienced severe financial difficulties throughout the duration of its years of service. Under the shrewd guidance of Dr. George Cleveland Hall and the generosity of Julius Rosenwald, it managed to keep its doors open. The big meatpackers also contributed heavily during this period, notably Swift, Armour, Wilson, and Libby, as well as Carson, Pirie, Scott, and Illinois Steel. When the lean years became apparent, plans to build a new hospital were deferred until a future date. Repair of the existing Provident structure was suggested instead, for a sum of $35,000. As a final business solution, Rosenwald's son-in-law, Alfred K. Stern, who handled some of his philanthropic activities, considered affiliating with the University of Chicago as other black institutions had done elsewhere in the nation to further strengthen a financially weaker institution. Stern argued with a businessman's logic:

> A modern building is needed to provide adequate facilities for the Negro population of this city, and the affiliation with the University will be a guarantee of proper standards of personnel and service. I can well realize that these aims cannot be accomplished without some delay, and meanwhile that the institution must carry on its work. The care of out-patients is less affected by the nature of the hospital building than most other hospital activities. At the same time it is in my judgment one of the most helpful types of work in which a hospital can engage, being largely preventative in purpose and touching large numbers of people. It seems to me that without waiting for the acquisition of a new plant, your hospital would do well to develop this service to its maximum efficiency. In order to indicate my sympathy with the policy which you have mapped out, I am pleased to contribute . . . the sum of two thousand dollars ($2,000) for the out-patient department.[145]

The Fort Dearborn Hospital was located at 3831 South Vernon Avenue with little known about its operations. As the neighborhood experienced demographic change from white to black, the owners sold to an African American, Dr. John T. Wilson, formerly a native of Atlanta, Georgia. The entity created was the brainchild of Wilson and appreciative trustees named the facility appropriately—the Wilson Foundation. As to Wilson's medical background, "He studied in Chicago, Philadelphia, Pa., and spent time as a clinical observer during fifteen years in the Mayo Brothers Hospital at Rochester, Minn."[146] Dr. Wilson organized his hospital with $50,000 and operated from two buildings, one being of modern design and construction and completed in 1924. With x-ray rooms, five operating rooms, laboratories, and nurses' quarters in place, the facility opened with 124 beds. It was located approximately three-quarters of a mile east of Provident Hospital.

On the other hand, Dr. U. G. Dailey had established himself as a physician of note by the 1920s, and in November 1926 he established his own hospital in two mansions at 3734 and 3736 South Michigan Avenue.[147] A graduate of Northwestern University, Dailey won recognition as a medical scholar and first-class surgeon. As a protégé of the brilliant surgeon and hospital builder Daniel Hale Williams, he sympathized with his mentor in the now four-decade personal and professional conflict between Williams (joined by his close confidant and friend Charles Edwin Bentley) and fellow surgeon George Cleveland Hall. Most likely, the establishment of Dailey Hospital had to do with the alienation of Williams and Bentley from Provident under the supposedly despotic and idiosyncratic reign of Hall. The subsequent resignations of Williams in 1912 and of Bentley in 1917 not only left a void with their departures but also broke a link with up-and-coming physicians such as Dailey and Carl G. Roberts. Dailey eventually faced the same stifling pressure from Hall and left Provident.[148] In any event, the professional fate along with the fiscal fate of Provident passed into the hands of Hall.[149] When Ida B. Wells-Barnett became ill in March 1931, she was taken to receive treatment at the Dailey Hospital, not Provident.[150] Late in this period when the Roman Catholic Church proposed building a large hospital that would accept black patients, it was met with mixed support and opposition from African Americans.[151]

Just as with the middle classes, military affiliation accorded a member of the working class an opportunity to elevate his status in the community as well as build his personal sense of self-esteem. The 8th Regiment enjoyed immense popularity in the Black Metropolis and upon its return from overseas duty in France in 1919, each and every member of the unit was accorded a hero's welcome to be followed with communal recognition of a job well done to advance their race's image in the struggle to achieve full citizenship rights.

Langston Hughes's contribution to the literature of the day offered insight into the workers' thinking with their attitude toward work, the enjoyment of life, and personal responsibilities. In both *Not without Laughter* (1930) and *The Big Sea: An Autobiography* (1940), Hughes shared his experiences and his knowledge on how the working class lived and persevered in Chicago. Hughes's trove of feelings and information was based on the time following the war that he spent residing with his mother, who worked in a hat shop in Chicago's downtown.[152] Yet other sources were the childhood experiences of future Pulitzer Prize winners Gwendolyn Brooks and Richard Wright. Brooks's writings on her formative years as a preadolescent provided valuable insight into working-class life of the "respectable" element, which contrasted with Richard Wright's young adult trials and travails as a newcomer to Chicago in 1927.

These wellsprings of contact with the working class served to inform any person inquisitive of the dynamics, nuances, diversity, and complexities of black life a clearer view of the emerging Black Metropolis. Hughes's bases of information, which he repeated in different settings later in time throughout his writings, followed the Great Migration. Chicago was the partial setting for his *Not without Laughter*, which depicted life in an urban setting during the Depression through the eyes of a young man named Sandy and his earlier arriving mother, Annjee Rogers. Both were natives of mythical Stanton in the South, where the pace of life and living conditions stood in sharp contrast to that experienced in Chicago. On the South Side their housing unit consisted of a single room on Wabash Avenue with two windows facing the elevated transit structure known as the "El." The daily presence of the foreboding steel railroad structure that hovered over all humanity within eyesight and the inescapable noise within earshot has made an indelible mark on South Side life that continues to this day. The El rested a little more than a hundred feet east of State Street in an alley and greatly influenced all manner of social aspects of life along State Street. It made a lasting impression on the novelist, compelling him to talk about its importance in depicting it as an overwhelming presence over the lives of those who lived near and were influenced by it. The El produced constant noise and shook structures while it offered a glimpse of the world to anyone who rode on it. "A trip on a local elevated from the Chicago Loop will not only make visible . . . different sections of the population . . . yet . . . [also] a certain unity expressed in a community consciousness that is missing in the cosmopolitan life of New York."[153] After Hughes's Kansas and Cleveland experiences, which lacked rapid transit, to him the El helped make State Street and its Stroll and its shops and people appear even more as "a fabulous street."[154]

When the fictional migrant Sandy arrived in Chicago after five years of separation from his mother, who was portrayed as working in a beauty shop, Hughes had an opportunity to share insight into a life of abundant love contrasted against economic scarcity. Sandy's mother once treated him to an inexpensive dinner at a local restaurant. The mother, Annjee, "picked carefully from the cheap menu so that their bill wouldn't be high." Beyond the joy she experienced in being reunited with her son, the economic reality for the working class dictated life. She cautioned, "But don't think this is regular. We can't afford it. . . . I bring things home and fix them on an oil stove in the room and spread papers on the trunk for a table."[155] In the noisy, crowded room they shared (for they had no apartment to speak of), they ate, slept, and joyfully embraced each other as a family unit as they maneuvered through the unpredictability and difficulties of urban life. In *The Big Sea* when Hughes wrote of the residents of Cleveland, he applied their existence to that of Chicago's labor scene. "I never tired of hearing them talk, listening to the thunderclaps of their laughter, to their troubles, to their discussions of the war and the men who had gone to Europe from the Jim Crow South, their complaints over the high rent and the long overtime hours that brought what seemed like big checks, until the weekly bills were paid. They seemed to me like the gayest and the bravest people possible—these Negroes from the Southern ghettos—facing tremendous odds, working and laughing and trying to get somewhere in the world."[156]

Hughes repeated the reference to Chicago's State Street from *Not without Laughter* in *Fine Clothes to the Jew*: "Since the whole book [*Fine Clothes to the Jew*] was largely about people like that, workers, roustabouts, and singers, and job hunters on Lenox Avenue in New York, or Seventh Street in Washington or State Street in Chicago—people up today and down tomorrow, working this week and fired the next, beaten and baffled, but determined not to be wholly beaten, buying furniture on the installment plan, filling the house with roomers to help pay the rent, hoping to get a new suit for Easter—and pawning that suit before the Fourth of July—that was why I called my book *Fine Clothes to the Jew*."[157]

Recreation for the working class came in many forms: spectators at the black-owned American Giants baseball games, active participants in baseball at Washington Park, dancers throughout the community at the many venues dedicated to jazz and blues, gambling, movie going, and house parties. Black Chicago's pride and joy in competitive sports remained the American Giants Baseball Club. With two decades of semiprofessional play in their resume, the Giants won championships in the Negro Baseball League constantly. For the less adventurous and boisterous, however, entertainment was available for the churchgoers at the Ada S. McKinley Settlement House on 32nd and Wabash Avenue.[158] For one family, the eastern portion of the 29th Street beach provided respite from heat, boredom, and inertia. As reported in *The Negro in Chicago*, "The whole family belongs to Salem Baptist Church and attends twice a week. The husband is a member of the Knights of Pythias. He goes to the parks, bathing-beaches, and baseball games for amusement."[159] The absence of day-to-day recreational outlets bothered Irene McCoy Gaines. She became concerned with the plight of 10,000 girls who needed constructive recreation.[160]

Music offered respite and enjoyment for others, for which academic cynicism could find fault. As to the blues, the civic-minded *Half-Century Magazine* complained of the descent of this musical form into vulgarity and coarseness.[161] There was even sufficient appreciation for classical music from members of the working class to question the snideness of the observation of E. Franklin Frazier, who wrote of domestics in 1929: "At the recital given by George Garner, who returned from triumphs abroad to entertain the home folks in Chicago, many an old woman struggled up the stairs of Orchestra Hall after the day's work to hear him sing. Some of them were uncouth and greasy and thought he was singing an English number on the program when he was singing Schubert's *Der Linderbaum*. But they were happy to hear one of their own."[162] Based on the experiences with high culture in black Chicago's history, quite possibly some of these women were accustomed to attending the Orchestra Hall and listening to opera both in concert with and in imitation of their upper-class "betters."

Gwendolyn Brooks remembered dances where the boundaries of ladylike decorum could be tested and her commitment to a future life of writing could possibly be diverted: "I went to few parties. I was uncomfortable at the parties. I danced the Charleston very well, but that was not what you did at parties!—besides the Charleston could not stay in style forever. The one-step was all right, and the two-step—and I knew something about these. But you needed more, at those teen parties. You needed to be FAST. You needed to sashay, with loud laughter, into the mysteries of the 'Kissing games.'"[163]

For adults, rather than appearing in public acting uncouth in deportment and greasy in appearance, the working-class man and woman in Chicago sought to act and look acceptable to both their social peers and betters. When enjoying leisure and recreational activities, it was important to always present yourself in a manner that was never embarrassing and always enhancing to your reputation.[164] According to Frazier, "A woman from the South in speaking of the care she was exercising concerning her behavior in Chicago emphasized the fact that she did not want her friends back home to read any unfavorable news concerning her in the *Chicago 'Dee-fender.'* . . . Negroes in Boston or other cities may have inhibitions about reading their own papers in public but in Chicago Negroes read Negro papers anywhere and whites read them as well."[165] With so many people literate and reading as a recreational activity as well as an educational device, the education of the young assumed an importance in the Black Metropolis that was notable.

When parents dreamt about their children's futures, education furnished the escape route but its availability in the North came with some difficulties. As the old Black Belt filled with more and more families with more and more children, overcrowding followed. Interracial fighting among schoolchildren also became common. One solution came from the *Chicago Defender* as it attempted to build young people's appreciation of education through its weekly Bud Billiken column. Advice was given on school problems and encouragement rendered on the values of learning and preparation for the future.[166] The Chicago branch of the NAACP contributed to better schools by encouraging parents to pick up grade cards and to visit their children's schools in order to show education to the children in a holistic light.[167]

The streets of big city Chicago as well as perilous streets elsewhere lured too many youth into socially destructive attitudes toward learning and school. Maintaining discipline posed a major problem in schools where blacks predominated and the necessity of strictness by teachers was often misunderstood. The recollections of persons who were students during this period indicate that discipline in predominately white schools was better, hence several blacks touted their experience in the latter.[168] But as the adage of the day—"The proof is in the pudding"—illustrated, the end result of an action often carries the greatest importance. Many of the Black Metropolis's distinguished citizens of the latter part of the twentieth century today proudly boast of their educational experiences at neighborhood elementary schools and at Wendell Phillips and Du Sable High Schools.

Policy could be viewed as a form of recreation to women and men, especially those of the sedentary types. Part of the Black Belt's gaming tradition that included betting-oriented card play, horse racing, prize fighting, and roulette wheels placed the participant into a lively world of church folk and street folk, working class and the lowest income group, all seeking to get rich on a single nickel or dime's play. As recreation, playing the numbers involved the lonely as well as the gregarious in daily social contact with family, relatives, and friends and neighbors to discuss the possibility of "hitting," or winning at policy. Discussing the meaning of a number could lead to gossip or even the exchange of valuable information with a family member or contact. Waiting for a "pick-up" man who was well dressed and well mannered opened up the socially isolated to the world around them, if only for several minutes, because the runner's schedule was tight. Walking personally down to a policy station meant fresh air, a chance for sightseeing, and an opportunity for conversation with the collectors at the policy bank. It also meant a chance to glance at piles of money, the likes of which most players would never win or see if they held a bank account. A decade later, with the ideological climate unchanged and the economic situation completely in chaos, this assessment was reiterated: "It must be remembered that in Chicago there are a large number of competing interests and an event has to be something that everyone WANTS or is in the nature of a 'natural.' Civil rights are not yet popular like policy or Joe Louis and cannot be considered as a natural drawing card."[169] The manner in which business, a most popular undertaking, contributed to the making of an economically viable Black Metropolis warrants our attention next.

Better housing. *Source*: Chicago Commission on Race Relations, *The Negro in Chicago* (1922).

Overton Building. *Source*: NIC, Vol. II.

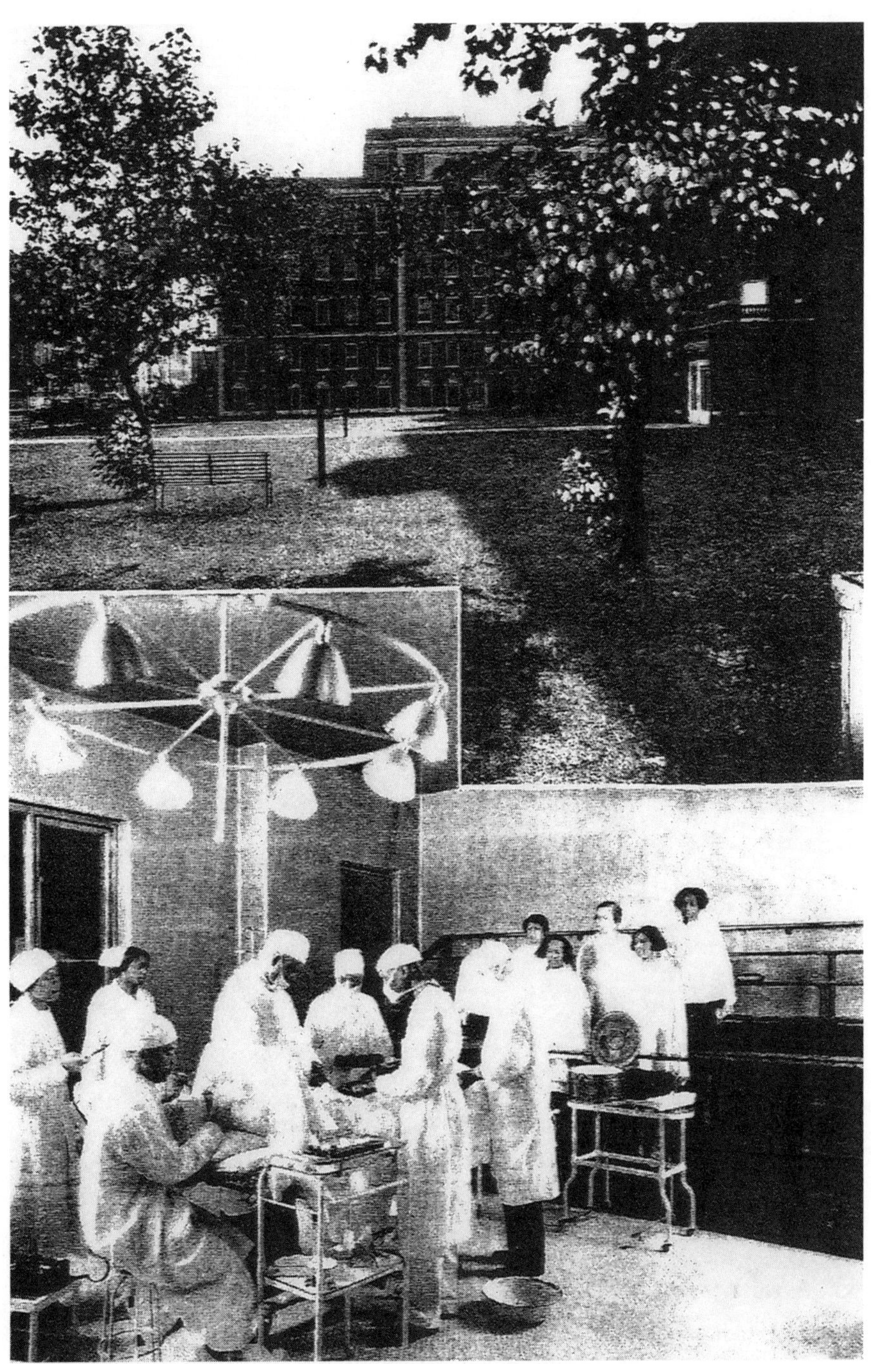

Wilson Hospital. *Source*: NIC, vol. II.

Supreme Cab Company. *Source*: NIC, vol. II.

Leo Holliday. *Source*: NIC, vol. II.

Monarch Tailors. *Source*: NIC, vol. II.

(*at left and above*) Workers. *Source*: NIC, vol. II and the Chicago Commission on Race Relations, *The Negro in Chicago* (1922).

Oscar Micheaux. *Source*: *Simms' Blue Book And Directory* (1923).

Pilgrim Baptist Church

CHAPTER 3

The Golden Decade of Black Business

> Measure the Negro. But not by the standard of the splendid civilization of the Caucasian. Bend down and measure him—measure him from the depths out of which he has risen.
>
> —Frederick Douglass, World's Columbian Exposition, 1893

> The condition of the Negro business man in Chicago today would be a warning to every Race-loving Negro in the United States TO GET TOGETHER . . . [now] every Negro must be found cemented together "ONE FOR ALL, AND ALL FOR ONE."
>
> —Liberty Life Insurance Company, 1920

> Chicago has become in the last decade one of the great business centers of the Negro race, surpassing New York's Negro community, which is larger in population. . . . The banks and the seven insurance companies having headquarters in this city have Negro stockholders, Negro officers and Negro personnel.
>
> —Carroll Binder, *Chicago Daily News*, 1927

The complementary wing to politics within the Chicago political economy—the business sector—claimed as its leadership the triumvirate of black Chicago commercial enterprise: Robert S. Abbott, Jesse Binga, and Anthony Overton. These men dominated the business activities of the Black Metropolis with their control over finance and information like no others in their community and very much like the business titans found throughout other major Chicago economic enclaves. Business was national king at this time and their collective presence provided a significant part of the foundation of making the Black Metropolis a reality. The economic influence of the 1920s built to such a crescendo that other interests and activities were virtually submerged to it as an epicenter. One internal memorandum of the NAACP analyzed the temper of the times and concluded the following: "There are so many diversified interests in Chicago that the N.A.A.C.P. really suffers greatly from indifference on the part of the people."[1] These were diversified interests related to economics and the emergence of a consumers' society—*working* for extra money from which to increase spending and buying; *spending* for recreation and leisure rather than just for necessity; *buying* property, automobiles, and the new technological devices such as the refrigerator, clothes washer, and record player; and *investing* in oil exploration, stocks, bonds, and real estate.[2]

Although the Chicago NAACP was the vanguard organization in the fight for advancement of civil rights, it was suffering because of other interests; no organized body or activity could fully attract the attention of the mass of the people during this decade with the exception of business, and in particular, business success. Indicative of this point was Charles S. Johnson writing in 1923 of there being 1,800 business establishments in operation.[3]

Robert S. Abbott's role as owner and publisher of the *Chicago Defender* newspaper has already been highlighted. Along with Anthony Overton and Jesse Binga, these men—whose stature reached that of titans—influenced and directed the business affairs of the Black Metropolis as no other force. Overton reigned absolutely as one outstanding figure over black Chicago during this period while operating his economic empire, from the Overton Building near the epicenter of the Black Metropolis at 3639 South State Street to his proposed Chicago Bee Building at 3647–3655 South State Street. His multifaceted business operations ranged from manufacturing to finance (in banking and insurance) to publishing. Peering through the fourth-floor windows of the Overton Building, Anthony Overton had truly become the proverbial "master of all he surveyed."[4]

The Overton Hygienic Building was originally proposed and architecturally conceived as a six-story, multifunctional structure, but construction costs led to temporary modifications in this structure, leaving the building as an impressive feat nonetheless.[5] Overly ambitious, Overton revised his plans and the exceedingly expensive Overton Building emerged as a four-storied, multipurpose structure. An elevator trip down from the fourth floor to the third floor (the journey being a rarity in a South Side structure) allowed him to see how well his core enterprise—the Overton Hygienic Company, which manufactured toilet and cosmetic products—was performing. While on the third floor, he saw the sales, accounting, and advertising operations of the company. Descending again and alighting on the second floor, he could see the workday routines of the Victory Insurance Company as well as other, disparate professional activities. Once on the first floor he encountered the nationally known financial giant he controlled—the Douglass National Bank—along with a rarity, an enterprise he did not own: a fully functional drugstore.[6] Publishing of the *Chicago Bee* newspaper, Overton's sedate Sunday alternative to the sensationalistic *Chicago Defender*, took place next door at 3649 South State by 1931.

In the mold of Chicago's founding father and economic inspiration—the immensely successful oldest New Negro, Jean Baptiste Pointe Du Sable—the personal dream of twentieth-century New Negro Anthony Overton in the commercial world was encapsulated as the dream of an entire people. If group self-sufficiency was to be proven feasible over time, the efforts of this phalanx of New Negroes would have to prove themselves viable by demonstrating the profitability of their business operations. It was incumbent upon them to set the standard of achievement for future generations to emulate. Evidence of the African American spirit toward economic advancement was noted far away across the Atlantic in 1928 when the editor of London's *Daily Express* published his accounts of a nationwide tour of U.S. cities. "He describe[d] Chicago as 'a wonder city of some millions, each and every one, including Negroes and gunmen, eager to become a millionaire over night.'"[7] Despite the notorious character of the company, the compliment to black agency could be appreciated nonetheless.

Overton demonstrated his competitive nature when he competed with Madame C. J. Walker and Mrs. Annie Turnbo-Malone in the cosmetics industry to produce the best products in the market, and Robert S. Abbott with W. E. B. Du Bois in publishing to articulate more clearly the views and dreams of the respectable element within African American society. The self-assured Overton was given to overexpansion because of a supreme confidence that he could effect change in his environment despite the circumstances and against all odds. This resiliency of spirit against adversity led him to enter the political arena as an advocate, but not a candidate, for reform government in 1928.

In Dickensian terms, Overton's empire peaked in the decade of the 1920s that represented "the best of all times." Temporally, the decade provided the ideal circumstances for the actualization of the economic component of the Dream of the Black Metropolis. Talent was abundant and competence high.[8] By 1929, Frazier took note of an expanded business spurt in the Black Belt, one that he attributed to the purchasing power of thousands of energized wage earners and consumers who arrived on the wave of the Great Migration.[9] Existing pro-business attitudes held by black entrepreneurs and businesspersons as well as fellow consumers greeted these new Chicagoans. The result was a melding of these forces that allowed business enterprising souls to take advantage of the prosperity of the decade. The foundation of the twentieth century's black business community rested on nearly a full century's experience in the sphere of market activities.

Moreover, several generations of professional persons, female and male, created a highly competent echelon of service providers. When the Binga State Bank needed a cashier of proven skills, C. N. Langston, a graduate of Oberlin College, was available. Douglass National tapped Arthur J. Wilson, a CPA educated at Northwestern University, the University of Illinois, and the University of Chicago. Supreme Life Insurance Company had the same experience when it sought an actuary with competent assistants. Mathematician and University of Illinois graduate Lloyd G. Wheeler III impressed the company and was immediately hired as an assistant to compile and analyze statistics in order to determine risks and premium amounts. In the distant future, Wheeler would eventually lead the company as president. These individuals and firms kept consumers' portfolios healthy, provided the legal expertise to incorporate and regulate procedures, extended credit for startups and operational maintenance as well as homes, maintained accounting ledgers, rationalized insurance rates, designed the structures holding business operations, presented visualization of products and services in an attractive manner, built an ideological base for sound practices and group pride, discovered new products and uses for them, and very importantly, created employment opportunities.

Jesse Binga was another person so resilient as not to be beaten down by mundane challenges as well as unanticipated adversities. The level of fortitude he exhibited amidst the terror bombings of his home and business offices was sufficient evidence of his courage and dauntless character. Nor was he overly impressed by competitors such as Overton, who was stealing his thunder as the biggest mover and shaker in the Black Metropolis. As Overton's empire grew, Binga not only kept pace with his state-chartered bank but, by January 1929, he had made plans to enter the field of national banking. The U.S. Treasury authorized his opening of the South Park National Bank of Chicago, which was to be situated in the new epicenter of the Black Metropolis at 47th and South Parkway.[10]

The Image and Reality of Black Business

In any discussion or analysis of historical African American economic advancement, especially in the field of business, the basic pitfall to be avoided is that of comparative analysis between the totality of white endeavors and that of limited black business self-help efforts, nationally or locally. The illogic to thinking that the creativity and production of a composite white effort—inclusive of every national, ethnic, and religious group claiming European roots and current connections—could be matched by a single minority group emerging from two hundred years of crippling bondage is self-evident. Frederick Douglass stated it aptly in Chicago at the World's Columbian Exposition in 1893: "Measure the Negro. But not by the standard of the splendid civilization of the Caucasian. Bend down and measure him—measure him from the depths out of which he has risen."[11] Accordingly, assertive African American molders of their race's image sought to demonstrate the group's progress and achievements at the sentimental guideposts of 1915, the fifty-year mark since emancipation, and in 1940, its seventy-fifth anniversary.[12] Nevertheless, the potential to demonstrate racial progress presented by participating in the upcoming World's Fair of 1933, dubbed officially "A Century of Progress," offered another more inviting signpost. Black business could step forward and show its success, and therefore, advancement. Black advancement in the business sector represented indubitably a major step forward in community and neighborhood progress. Further, the Black Metropolis rested solidly on its merits as an integral contributor to Chicago's overall economic progress, of which the major downtown and some outstanding community businesses led the way.

Although these visible achievements (of which contemporaries were aware) warranted historical attention generations later, they also attracted cynical evalu-

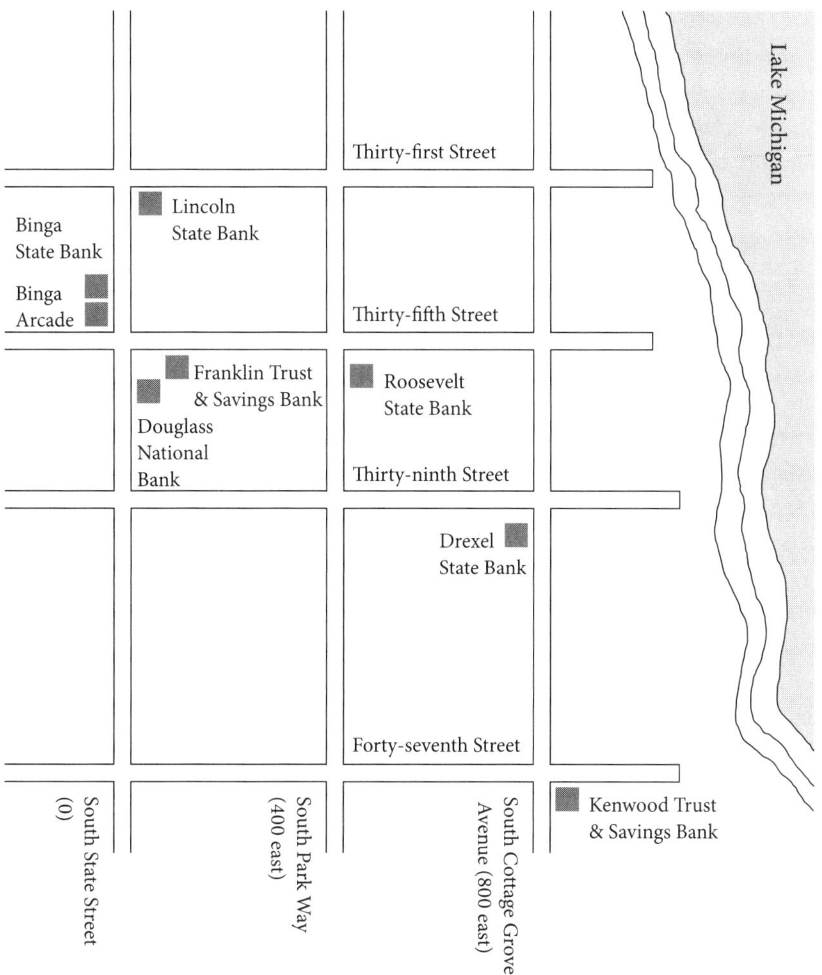

Location of Banks

ation from critics of black business activities. The 1919–1920 edition of *Black's Blue Book* subsequently reported in the face of this criticism on the existence of five banks among 1,200 black-owned businesses, along with 48 real estate offices, 106 physicians, 40 dentists, 70 lawyers, 3 insurance companies, 6 hotels, and 11 newspapers.[13] Likewise, *Simms' Blue Book and National Negro Business and Professional Directory* (1923) advertised the services of 116 physicians, 52 dentists, 81 lawyers, and 32 pharmacists.[14]

As the decade progressed, so did growth. Business development depended on the personal initiative of entrepreneurs and businesspersons; an influx of consumers with cash to spend, invest, and save; and improvements in the provision of quality goods and services, accompanied by the guidance of business and professional associations such as the Associated Business Clubs, the Chicago chapter of the National Negro Business League, the Cook County Bar Association, the Chicago Commercial Association, and others of this type. According to Carroll Binder's contemporary investigation on the extent to which the African American community had kept abreast with Chicago's dynamic economic growth, he was able to conclude that "Chicago has become in the last decade one of the great business centers of the Negro race, surpassing New York's Negro community, which is larger in population. . . . The banks and the seven insurance companies having headquarters in this city have Negro stockholders, Negro officers and Negro personnel."[15] Modern-day business-history scholar Juliet E. K. Walker explored both the past and current business traditions and carried the argument further, writing that "Chicago has been the major city where black businesses were established with national markets, particularly black hair care products, manufacturing enterprises and publishing enterprises. . . . [Not surprisingly, it was] the national center of multimillion-dollar black businesses [with] a distinctiveness [as it] emerged as the quintessential city for black entrepreneurship."[16]

A significant portion of that growth originated directly in the expanding African American market. As to its impetus, Drake and Cayton maintained that "the Great Migration created the 'Negro market'" as white and black merchants took notice of the purchasing power of several hundred thousands of consumers during the 1920s.[17] The success in creating and sustaining a new commercial epicenter relying on a black consumer base at 47th Street and South Parkway lent proof to the Negro market's viability, wherever its location. Even during the Great Depression, this commercial district thrived. Supporting their contention with detailed data, Drake and Cayton established the entry of the Black Belt's population into the American consumer age in which they began to use their ability of consumption as a measure of citizenship and social status. The success of a black business base related to demographic increase, increased income, the success of advertising, and a racial ideology that stressed group advancement and citizenship in the most materialistic of terms. Over one thousand businesses operated in black areas of the city and attempted to meet the consumptive needs of a population that expanded from 108,456 in 1920 to 233,903 by 1930.

The Dream of a Black Metropolis—a city within a city, with a flavor to life consistent with African American values, behavior, and tastes and under the control of leaders and spokesmen of their own choosing—dominated the near South Side and adjacent lakefront cityscape. Totally consistent with the patterns assumed by other new groups arriving in the city, it proved anything but an anomaly. The basic difference appeared in its nonconformance with white wishes and expectations of performance, or nonperformance, by blacks. The success of Jesse Binga and Anthony Overton in banking proved the blind spot in Julius Rosenwald's perception of the Black Belt's nonexistent potential in the financial field.[18] Moreover, progress in the insurance field demonstrated that the competency and abilities of

African Americans could compete in the financial industry for the black dollar. The impression they gained ran counter to the stereotype of a prostrate community completely overwhelmed by obstacles and embracing a collective sense of pessimism and resignation.

Nonetheless, in their tome *Black Metropolis,* Drake and Cayton wrote contradictorily about black business in 1945. With the benefit of hindsight and the advantage of viewing the economic ruin of the Great Depression firsthand, they chided would-be dreamers of building a separate community economy such as the Black Metropolis. "Objective reality, however, is at variance with the ideal [that African Americans held of success in the business sphere]. No Negro sits on a board of directors [on the] La Salle Street [financial district], none trades in the grain pit [at the Chicago Board of Trade] or has a seat on the [Chicago] Stock Exchange; none owns a skyscraper."[19] Similar criticism flowed from both centrists and from radical economic voices on the left within the ranks of the Communist Party and associated groups.[20]

Other ethnic groups in the city at this time dreamt the same dream of indigenous control and followed the same path. Perhaps the qualifying criteria should have been how far blacks had advanced beyond dreaming into planning and implementing their economic visions. First of all, consideration should be given to the obstacles they faced and what alternatives existed beyond attempts at separate development. Without any attempt at a semblance of independence, the argument would have centered on black indifference or inactivity. Next, the question of how certain elements within Chicago's white power structure evaluated these black businessmen in terms of their fitness for economic success should be broached. When the Chicago Urban League wished to impress the members of the Race Relations Committee of the prestigious Union League Club with the contradictory nature of life on the South Side, for the negative they showed them deteriorating housing on Dearborn Avenue in the area of the "shacks." For the positive aspects, they visited the Binga State Bank, Liberty Life Insurance, the offices of the *Chicago Defender*, the Overton Hygienic Company, and several homes owned by blacks at the southern end of the Black Metropolis. Significantly, there *was* a positive side to reveal.[21]

Consistent with the temper of the times, at the onset of the decade, African Americans planned and implemented new construction along State Street during this decade, and the two black bankers led the way. As previously mentioned, in 1922–1923, Anthony Overton had conceived of building a six-story business center. Modifying his plans, he finished construction of an impressive four-story edifice that immediately opened for business. As a testimony to his fortitude and vision, this monumental structure stands today. The next year, not to be outdone by his chief rival for financial supremacy, Jesse Binga transformed his private banking operation at 36th Place and State Street into a newer facility at 3455 South State near the northwest corner of 35th and State. Once settled into the colonnaded Binga State Bank, he followed this development with the Binga Arcade, constructed in 1929 and located directly on that northwest corner. Later in the decade, he laid plans for establishment of another national bank in his community, the South Park National Bank, to be located at the corner of 47th Street and South Parkway, already in process of becoming the new epicenter of commercial activities for the black South Side. Meantime, the Knights of Pythias, a leading national fraternal order, commissioned black architect Charles S. Duke to design an eight-story structure for commercial and fraternal activities at 37th Place and State Street that was completed in 1928.

To be sure, most of the storefronts (and the lots on which they sat) along State were white-owned, even when black-operated, but the totality of economic vitality within the Black Belt need not have been evaluated solely on ownership of the land. Beyond new construction, the accumulation of wealth should have guaranteed progress in American society; however, the strength of ingrained racist notions worked to place doubt in the minds of the most hopeful and successful African Americans.[22] One glaring example of freedom of choice coupled with doubt was evident by the mid-1920s, when 90 percent of African American bank deposits sat in the largest of seven nonblack banks scattered around the South Side, leaving only 10 percent in the vaults and investment portfolios of the Binga State and the Douglass National Banks.[23]

The possibility of African American success in concrete terms was met again when the promoters of the World's Fair of 1933, led by World's Fair president Rufus C. Dawes, invited publisher Robert S. Abbott and banker and real estate investor Jesse Binga to join the initial investors of this signal event with $1,000.00 investments.[24] In the first instance, these leading men, because they were the wealthiest black businessmen, won recognition for their basic business attribute—they proved they could operate, sustain, and most importantly, profit from their endeavors. Yet the two men decided cautiously, and perhaps judiciously, in declining to participate with Dawes and his associates in this venture because of a contracted business climate. In doing so, they exposed the frailties of black businessmen and of the Black Metropolis ideal overall. At the same time Dawes sought a substantial outlay from these potential investors, Binga supposedly was planning an endeavor for mass-level black investment for a comparatively low $5.00 subscription amount.[25]

Further scrutiny of the state of black business by the 1920s reveals that *Black Metropolis*, a highly respected tome by Drake and Cayton (1945), rendered subjectively a commonly held assertion about black business capabilities rather than employing complete objectivity. Drake and Cayton engaged in minimization of persons and their businesses who made the positive images of the Black Metropolis more real than illusory. The name immediately coming to mind is that of the omnifarious magnate Anthony Overton, who pursued varied business interests in cosmetics manufacturing, banking, insurance, and publishing. As to their personal fortunes, both Binga and Overton were "reputed to be millionaires."[26] Abbott's prominence and accomplishments in publishing earned him hundreds of thousands of dollars, along with his tens of thousands of readers nationally. Likewise, Binga in banking and in his extensive real estate holdings had done well and prospered. The Binga State Bank not only met Illinois standards for chartering, it also held membership in the citywide Chicago Clearinghouse Association, the equivalent of "'sterling' on silver" in banking circles. The often racially charged and caustic *Chicago Tribune* featured banker Jesse Binga in one of its Sunday editions, giving him page one, column one treatment. Lending credence to this newspaper article, one banker-essayist declared Binga and his bank to be "one of the leading banks owned and operated by Negroes anywhere."[27]

The end-of-the-year banking statements throughout the decade indicated growth. Figures for 1928 showed $1,474,680.96 in deposits, a testimony to Binga's financial astuteness in his field. The next year's total for deposits was tallied at $1,752,200.54.[28] However, rather than describing Binga as an economic visionary, Abram Harris described him as an incompetent businessman who overextended himself with his future plans for a newer and larger nationally chartered bank to be opened during the next decade.[29] The proposed bank, the South Park National Bank, was slated to be located two miles south of the Binga State Bank at the new 47th Street and South Parkway commercial epicenter of the Black Metropolis.[30]

Overton's Douglass National Bank already held a federal charter and was therefore a part of the Federal Reserve System. Once Overton expanded his empire to include an old-line, legal reserve insurance company, the Victory Life, he plunged into the world of national insurance services. Victory "passed the acid test for an insurance company by qualifying to write insurance in New York [state]." His overall business achievements in 1927 earned him both the philanthropic Harmon Award for African American achievement in business and the NAACP's Spingarn Award for having "most signally distinguished himself or herself in some honorable field of human endeavor." With the usually racially caustic *Chicago Tribune* taking notice, the usually time-conscious and frugal Overton no doubt had to accommodate receiving the Harmon Award by clearing his work schedule and paying for a trip to nearby Indianapolis for the ceremony.[31] The accomplishments and success of Overton, Binga, and Abbott demonstrated to an entire community that a group could advance incrementally and through successful phases in America despite racism.

Without access to certain portions of now accessible documentation, such as data from the papers of "A Century of Progress" from the period 1927–1933, the true status of black Chicago's financial progress during this decade remained obscured to researchers until the 1970s. However, the NAACP's *Crisis* commented on black Chicago's noticeable growth in business in 1915, as did the Urban League's *Opportunity* as it examined the community at its apex in 1929. The period in between was examined in the pages of the *Messenger*, the *Chicago Daily News*, the compilations of community life in Frederick H. H. Robb's *The Negro in Chicago*, and in newsprint and marketing media—the *Defender*, the *Whip*, the *Bee*, and the *Tribune*. At least two business directories were published: *Black's Blue Book* and *Simms' Blue Book and National Negro Business and Professional Directory* illustrated the Black Metropolis's strengths and accomplishments in 1923 and 1927, respectively. Charles S. Johnson, in his contribution to the argument, wrote of businesses that varied "in size and characteristics from nondescript fly-traps called restaurants to the dignified Overton Building."[32]

As Drake and Cayton (1945) sought further to identify the point in time at which African Americans developed a market consciousness, they located it in the Great Migration of 1916–1918. Historically, the source of the business consciousness in black Chicago had roots that extended backward in time to the Chicago frontier experience of the nineteenth century, and imaginatively, to the exploits of Chicago's founding father and first commercial leader, Jean Baptiste Pointe Du Sable in the late eighteenth century.[33] As to recognition of an internal African American market with purchasing potential, the ample array of businesses that had sprung up by the turn of the century along State Street preceded the Great Migration, aided by Binga and Overton's examples. With nationalistic appeals always a part of business advancement, market consciousness expanded as more and more blacks shopped at stores operated by members of their own group.[34] In actuality, the Great Migration seemed simultaneously to have created—as well as greatly enhanced—the business chances of providers of goods and services to prosper and the ability of African American consumers to enter the American mainstream of indulgence. The success of the Liberty Life Insurance Company, for example, was linked directly to the Migration and to the capital the southern migrants brought to this northern market.[35]

So, although the contemporary image of black business was positive and at times critical, the image of black business in the highly touted tome *Black Metropolis* was somewhat skewed by time and circumstance into a caricature. The Dream of a Black Metropolis appeared at a time when America was filled with dreams, many of which were coming true and found some businessmen able to match performance with reality. If African Americans did not accept the NAACP's full-blown optimism as evidenced in its legal approach to transform American society over the long run, they allowed themselves the luxury of succumbing to the infectious optimism of the northern portion of the nation that convinced many to think in positive terms while acknowledging that race was a hindrance that had to be considered at all times. To some spokesmen and -women of the Black Metropolis idea, the fulfillment of the dream became an end in itself. Their strength of conviction in foreseeing a positive future was impressive since they lacked a crystal ball into which they could readily gaze. The likelihood of attaining a reasonable level of individual and group freedom of opportunity was to be a reality of the latter third of the twentieth century. The civil rights transformation of the 1960s was no foregone conclusion, so attaining some semblance of control over their own living and working space through community consciousness and hard work, and especially building tangible examples of what could be accomplished, also appeared more practical than hoping for a fair shake in employment or an Equal Employment Opportunities Commission (EEOC) by the 1960s, decent housing commensurate with their incomes, educational opportunities with employment equal to their training, or even recreation and sports participation open at a level where major league baseball seemed unfettered by racism.

If scholars of another generation and especially two or more generations in the future could see how myopic their view was through hindsight, they might see in contradistinction that those persons living in the third decade of the century with a sense of civic community, coupled with group consciousness and pride, saw themselves as reasonable in their approach to achieving happiness. Investing in real estate and creating structures such as the Overton and Bee Buildings, the Binga Arcade, the Jordan Building, the Knights of Pythias Building, the Masonic Temple, and other examples replaced hope in an uncertain future with practical examples of accomplishment at the current stage of their group's development.

The State Street Corridor: Locus of Economic Power

The locus of black economic power in 1920 remained the thoroughfare along which African Americans first chose to anchor their commercial district: South State Street.[36] Along this streetscape, the heart line of the Black Metropolis's thrust toward independence served as its national model for an African American entrepreneurial enclave. Chicago's State Street corridor, running through the heart of the old Black Belt, should be accorded a preeminent position among national black business enclaves and receive the same amount of attention given the business activities along Fayetteville and Parish Streets in Durham, North Carolina and on Greenwood Street in Tulsa, Oklahoma. South State Street served as one of the city's longest running thoroughfares, with black businesses extending from 18th Street to 55th Street and beyond on occasion. Remarkably along this roadway, black Chicagoans demonstrated great skill in organizing financial and service institutions to anchor their community as they constructed edifices from street elevation to sky level, testimonies to African American accomplishment. Of such importance was this location that relocations up and down the thoroughfare, and usually in a southwardly direction, became a common occurrence. Both the Binga State Bank and the Douglass National Bank occupied different locations before moving into their final street locations in the 1920s. Binga's bank was to be found at 3637 South State before it moved to its final corner location at 3455 South State. Douglass National Bank claimed space at 3201 South State before it occupied its own edifice at 3633 South State.

The success of the businesses along this street rested on a consumer base that proved itself capable of being in step with the times. Consumerism dominated the day as the expanding working class indulged itself in both necessities and luxury items. The growth in size of the service industry—with beauty shops, hair and skin care products, seamstresses and dressmakers balancing the proliferation of barber shops and men's stores grooming the male population, who hoped to match their fashion-conscious women in personal attractiveness—illustrated the temper of the times. The moniker of the street was "the Stroll" for the throngs who attended movie theaters, cabarets, and other entertainment venues where they spent their earnings in wild abandon so common for the period.[37] Every bit as American as the millions of whites who were spending themselves into financial limbo, the residents and customers of the Black Metropolis enjoyed life as though the good times would never end, or possibly sensed that they could end (and within a decade, as they had).

The recollections of hundreds upon hundreds of African Americans heralded the golden days of the thoroughfare. Abram Richard Wilson, the light-complexioned, red-headed raconteur who assumed the moniker of "Red Dick" over the decades after opening a haberdashery in 1916, remembered business, entertainment, and overall "gayety." "The Negro's rise in business and the professions was symbolized in the area," as a generation later he located with his eyes and a sweep of his hand the location of the Binga State Bank and other commercial operations. "Honky tonks prospered, and money seemed to flow from everyone's pockets as easily as laughter from [everyone's] lips." As Roi Ottley summarized Wilson's tale, "the south side had entered an era of noisy vitality, and 35th and State was the center of this triumphant existence."[38]

Participation in the Financial Industry

The core of the Black Metropolis rested on its economic vitality. Its banking and insurance institutions, along with its extensive real estate operations, provided the energy for investments and profits for growth. With an importance somehow minimized and at times overlooked in *Black Metropolis*, the level of involvement of entrepreneurs and businesspersons reached an impressive plateau by this decade. While Durham, North Carolina, claimed its "Hayti," Tulsa, Oklahoma, touted its "Little Africa" along Greenwood Avenue, and New York City boasted constantly of Harlem as examples of commercial success, South State Street running through Chicago's Black Belt assumed a secondary position to no other ethnic economic enclave in any other locale.[39] Together, the Binga State Bank and the Douglass National Bank, which represented the largest black banks ever established, controlled one third of all black bank resources nationally.[40] According to Columbia University–trained economist Abram L. Harris, "by virtue of their relative size these two institutions were looked upon as the titans of Negro finance, and the Douglass National Bank was especially singled out as symbolical of the Negro's possibilities in commercial banking."[41] However, beyond the progress that African

Americans made in banking and other related financial areas, these positive influences naturally encouraged related economic activities and produced successes. When the Binga State Bank closed in June 1930, the sentiment in black America was described as one of foreboding, reversing the pride and enthusiasm that had accompanied its opening in 1921.[42]

As a role model in the world of banking, the success of the "House of Binga" had inspired one of the policy world's Jones brothers a decade later to consider entering that sphere as his career in legitimate business climbed. He was aware of the need to study banking and that mastery of "theory [was] necessary."[43] Neither Binga nor Overton had studied theory in regard to banking, and part of their failures was due in no small part to business decisions made without the benefit of training and familiarity with banking theory.[44] Perhaps this explained part of Julius Rosenwald's response to a question as to his assessment about the feasibility of black banking success in the crumbling Black Metropolis, as he became convinced these efforts would not succeed over time.[45]

However, beyond banking, which had succumbed to the same pressures that destroyed thousands of the nation's smaller financial institutions, both white and black owned, the possibility that the totality of all businesses would generate revenue (or income) matching their scale of economy (number of businesses) seemed reachable (at least theoretically or ideologically). Growth in banking was apparent as the years progressed. Exceeding it was exaggeration in estimating how much money blacks did have on deposit. In 1923, Charles S. Johnson wrote that "three banks alone have $3,150,000 of Negro money on deposit. One bank has 4,000 depositors. One can make money in Chicago. This is its most respectable attraction."[46] At one time, Jesse Binga estimated that African Americans possessed deposits of $40 *million* in all Chicago banks, one tenth of which was in two black banking institutions, and owned $4 *billion* in taxable property.[47] In 1927, Carroll Binder estimated that African Americans had amassed a lesser amount of $2,800,000 in bank deposits at their two black banks, but higher figures of $50,000,000 and $60,000,000 on deposit at were attributed to Oscar DePriest and Jesse Binga, respectively.[48]

Most black businesses operated in the service sector, in spheres in which whites had little interest and therefore provided neither impediments nor competition. This meant that restaurants, beauty parlors, barber shops, funeral homes, cabarets and show clubs, and other efforts could and did grow. These operations increased as a result of the Binga State Bank's and Douglass National Bank's presence, influence, and loans.[49] The major test came in stages, first during 1926 when unemployment became noticeable, and then by 1930, the first full year of economic depression.

Competition from neighborhood white banks within the Black Metropolis was especially keen. The seven other banking institutions—Bankers State Bank, Industrial Savings Bank, Franklin Trust and Savings Bank, Drexel State Bank, Kenwood National Bank, Lincoln State Bank, and Roosevelt State Bank—attracted the lion's share of black banking resources during this period. According to Claude A. Barnett in 1929, "The Bankers State Bank and the Industrial Bank, each reported that more than 90 per cent of their depositors in the savings department were Negroes and about 25 per cent in the commercial department. . . . The Franklin, Drexel State, and Kenwood National Banks each reported a large number of Negro depositors. . . . The Lincoln State Bank reported it had 15,000 Colored depositors and the Roosevelt State Bank admitted it had about one million dollars on deposit from Negroes."[50] Despite these deposits, the employment of African Americans was minuscule to nonexistent. Especially interesting was the fact that all of the banks except one were located within the boundaries of the Black Metropolis.

In accounting for the heavy volume of black investment in white banking institutions, several explanations appear reasonable. One would have been the positive experiences with institutions such as the Lincoln State Bank located at 3105 South State Street. When the planners and primary investors of Liberty Life Insurance Company in 1919 sought startup capital of $100,000 to purchase a charter from the State of Illinois, they found their enthusiasm was unmatched by stock purchases by 1921. Needing $45,000 to meet a deadline, Frank L. Gillespie, the leading figure in this venture, proposed that supporting investors pledge their homes as collateral to officials at the Lincoln State Bank. The leadership at Lincoln was receptive and the venture proceeded forward, although with an unsteady gait. News of this support for an institution that provided both future opportunities for life insurance and home mortgages to many African American families had to have played a role in the tendency of some African Americans to support this institution. As impressive as this risky gesture appeared as a boost for economic nationalism and confidence in the future of black financial progress, it required the legal skills Earl B. Dickerson had gained at the University of Chicago as well as a bit of 1920s legerdemain to complete the capitalization.[51]

No doubt, living in close proximity to a financial institution influenced patronage. Location of businesses played a major role in financial success, and white store owners resisted opening choice spots to competing African Americans. This decade opened with most Americans walking to purchase goods and services, or in this case, save. Public transportation was expanding also, but mainly it was the day of the newness and expense of the automobile until the mid and late decade with expanded credit. (This might have been the case with the author's great uncle, Eugene Slaughter, who invested in a Christmas savings program at the white-run Roosevelt State Bank, located just three blocks south of his residence at 3159 South Parkway.) Other reasons might have been an unfamiliarity with black banks or any large financial ventures.

Besides, there was the case to be made for the intragroup mistrust that many African Americans had of African American businesses and their operators. Liberty Life addressed this issue head on with a rousing, full-page advertisement under the heading, "The Awakening of the Negro" in the *Chicago Defender*. Appealing to New Negro sensitivities about race, power, and economics, this argument followed:

> The condition of the Negro business man in Chicago today would be a warning to every Race-loving Negro in the United States TO GET TOGETHER. Because during the past fifty years those who have lived in Chicago have made Millionaires among every nationality known to civilization that offered them the least bit of encouragement for their patronage and made a PAUPER of every Negro who dared enter into competition with these people for our trade. The results of our loyalty to the other fellow find us without any State Banks, Legal Reserve Insurance Companies, . . . necessary for the upbuilding of a Race. The one fault that has retarded our progress . . . has been caused by allowing the other fellow to plant the seed of DISTRUST among us and so well did he plant the seed that not until the recent war did the Negro realize that his best friend was his own people . . . [now] every Negro must be found cemented together "ONE FOR ALL, AND ALL FOR ONE."[52]

Fortunately, the decade featured corrective measures to these problems in a short span of four years as both a state- and a nationally chartered bank appeared, as did a legal reserve insurance company in Liberty Life. Yet the culmination of decades of antiblack brainwashing, poor service, insufficient capitalization, limited inventories, and other variables invariably doomed immediate expansion of the African American market to reach a level commensurate with ideological expectations.[53]

The Black Metropolis's companion banking institution to the Douglass National Bank, the Binga State Bank, had an auspicious beginning for the decade, emerging as a state-level entity after its chartering in 1921. Its rhetoric was inspiring and would initially be matched by performance. Illustrating the important link between ideology and finance, Binga declared:

> It would not be the policy of the Binga State Bank to hoard a large amount of money [to] point at. . . .
>
> What we want is a banking institution that will solve our problems—we know ourselves as no other people know us, and we alone must develop our ability to relieve the present conditions that are said to be making our people the undesirable citizens of Chicago.
>
> What we want is an organization that will educate the ignorant people who are flooding our city, by gaining develop a thrifty and desirous person. . . . [W]e want it distinctly understood that the Binga State Bank will not be a one man institution, but a state bank under state supervision, operated by our people and for our people.[54]

It was capitalized in 1920 with $100,000 and surplus of $20,000, which compared favorably to other smaller, neighborhood banks in white ethnic areas. Any question as to whether Binga had the confidence of his black neighbors as investors was answered immediately as 1,100 confident residents deposited $200,000 on the first day of operations.[55] According to Binga biographer Carl Osthaus, "The new institution, located on a corner rivaled only by New York's 135th and Lenox as a commercial center for black Americans, symbolized the commencement of a new era in Chicago business."[56]

Pride in the institution remained high and in its second year, by September 1921, deposits on hand totaled $298,957.54.[57] A pattern of increasing deposits continued, with deposits reaching $1,153,450.59 in 1924 with capitalization at $200,000 and a surplus listed at $35,000. Stock value went up to $165 from $120. The bank's promise of job creation was fulfilled with the personnel level reaching eighteen employees.[58] The end-of-the-year banking statement for 1928 showed $1,474, 680.96 in deposits and the next year's total was tallied at $1,752,200.54.[59]

The Binga State Bank's biggest resource was its Achilles' heel, as it held $800,000 in real estate loans, a factor that was good news for the community and its chances for real and potential development. Some mortgages on property included elegant homes on Michigan Avenue and South Parkway, making them theoretically marketable. It also won the Binga State Bank praise nationally.[60] Yet these investments weren't seen as sound in the eyes of downtown white bankers, who looked at all black investments stereotypically. Investing in the African American community in this manner did not constitute a sound banking practice.[61] Overall, housing stock in the Black Metropolis represented a double dose of potential trouble in the purest capitalistic strategy of moneymaking as proposed by black bankers: It promoted segregation of their own people and increased economic disadvantage at the same time by loading the banks with less-than-liquid assets.[62]

The migration of the war years and thereafter stimulated home ownership, and so long as the level of employment for blacks was good, home mortgages looked like good investments for the bank. Also, as long as people were employed, high dwelling costs could be met even if it meant overcrowding of families and the absorption of nonfamily lodgers into the household. These social aspects of banking held no interest for white banks, which followed rigid economic rules of the field of business. They focused primarily on the value of relationship and rediscounted loans to black banks, reinforcing the aura of soundness to the arrangement. In their emphases aimed at building their community, the typical black bank held no large accounts. At closing, the Binga State Bank held 6,000 accounts under $100.00; 2,000 between $100.00 and $1,000.00; 1,100 in the range of $1,000.00 to $5,000.00; and 11 depositors with holdings between $5,000 and $10,000.[63] Examining these figures after closing might just distort what transpired before closing. Did friends of the banker receive a tip to draw down their accounts prematurely, for example?

Yet, as the pride of the Black Metropolis, the citizens of the South Side were quite delighted to witness the bank reach the pinnacle of recognition from the white business establishment with its appearance on page one of the *Chicago*

Sunday Tribune issue of May 8, 1927. How Binga achieved this status of front-page coverage during this decade of demeaning and minimizing depictions of African American life as well as achievement is puzzling. It was, nonetheless, appreciated. Given the newspaper's ambivalent relationship with the city's African American residents, we can only conjecture as to its meaning.

Perhaps it related to Jesse Binga's life philosophy, in which he accepted the tenets of the American capitalist society in its entirety, excepting its personalized, racial aspects. As Binga sought growth, he bought an older edifice a half mile north along South State near the northwest corner of 35th Street, at 3442 South State. It opened auspiciously as the new Binga State Bank on October 20, 1924. Architecturally the structure was imposing, featuring white bricks and two massive Ionic pillars over its one-and-one-half stories. Its footprint was frontage of 24 feet across State Street, with a depth of 123 feet and a height of 27 feet. Its interior featured "lofty reaches of marble and bronze, and . . . massive steel vaults and . . . mellow walnut panelings and . . . subdued hangings." As a special touch to match its physical elegance, a somewhat formally attired Binga personally greeted customers each morning with an assurance that he was in charge and the institution reflected his confidence and strength in them as residents of a Black Metropolis. By its physicality, it exuded the sense of stability an investing public required and "the assurance on the part of the bank's Board of Directors that it intends this institution to remain in this community permanently."[64] Its portals proudly carried the inscription of Binga's acceptance into the city's banking fraternity: Affiliated Member—Chicago Clearing House Association.[65] To contemptuous whites, it was as structure inappropriate for this setting, for it was what "you would expect to find in the Loop, but not in the Black Belt."[66] For the blacks walking by, it testified to an early introduction of black economic power.

Shortly thereafter, a more determined Binga constructed the Binga Arcade squarely on the northwest corner of 35th and State Streets at 3452 South State in order to better exploit business, and to further stabilize this epicenter of the Black Metropolis. When Binga built his arcade building, he erected a virtual skyscraper in his community.[67] His monumental dream amazed even the downtown establishment. As reported in the *Tribune*, "the prodigal way in which expensive materials are used calls for attention. For instance the exterior walls . . . are entirely of marble. A twenty foot return is announced for the north wall. Every window in the building will be of plate glass. The interior woodwork throughout will be of American walnut. The corridors will be of marble. It'll have foundations capable of carrying three more floors if business warrants. At present it will be only five stories, though the top floor has the height of two stories, so it virtually will be a six story structure."[68] It was designed by Joseph Scheitler and Wenisch at a cost of $325,000 and when completed in 1929, it produced stares of astonishment while attracting cheers from the Black Metropolis's multitudes. On a financial scale, it had little chance of financial success as it anticipated too high a revenue return from rental income. Binga also built a structure in the wrong place at the wrong time, because competition farther south at 47th Street and South Parkway posed a major threat that should not have been ignored.[69]

With the bank's demise in the Depression decade of the 1930s, it was evident that Binga was the victim of the basic weakness that plagued black banking: having to rely on a very unreliable economic group for investments and one that would fail to meet its obligations at various turns in the economy, such as recession. At the same time, his business dealings revealed that on occasions he had used the bank for personal purposes.[70] The same was being whispered about Overton.[71]

Chicago's lucratively attractive banking field made the same siren's call to African Americans that it did to whites, so Jesse Binga found himself joined in March 1920 by another companion and competitor. Ohio transplant P. W. (Pearl William) Chavers made his decision to enter the field of banking by salvaging what was left of the Woodfolk Bank's assets. With the creditors of the bank pleading with him to take over the trusteeship, he finally relented. According to his biographer, his motivation was as idealistic as it was entrepreneurial. He would protect and serve his and his community's interest and prove to those black persons who believed that a black bank could not protect its depositors' money were misguided. In the reconstruction of a conversation with his brother-in-law from Ohio, Chavers replied to his inquiry as to risk. "More of us should get into community affairs to make a place for our people. It is not enough that I am doing well for myself. . . . [W]e have to fit into the scheme of things in the big city . . . [and] the only way is for us to venture for survival, using our brains in the business world. That is how others got established in this country. We have to gain respect from people in business and one of the better ways is through banking."[72]

As his brother-in-law warned him about the resistance he would experience from his fellow blacks who were established and sometimes resented and distrusted more recently arriving newcomers, Chavers refused to be dissuaded. Chavers instead sought the advice of attorney J. Gray Lucas, a native-born Texan and Boston University–trained lawyer, who counseled him positively on this matter. Thereupon he also approached Jesse Binga, whose advice was valued because of his experience in real estate and banking and because of his impressive financial connections in the white world.[73] Then, working with Isidore Goldman, the court-appointed receiver of the old Woodfolk Bank, Chavers finalized plans for the transference of the liquid funds into a new Merchants and Peoples Bank located on the old bank site at 3201 South State Street in a two-story, rectangular structure.

Chavers faced the dilemma that Binga had in 1908, and Hunter and Woodfolk did in following years. He could either take a plunge and start a banking operation based on his personal assessment that the time was right (in regard to one's own talents to learn the business on the run and amass the capital) or wait for a day that appeared to never come in a society geared toward delaying black progress and deferring full citizenship on a level playing field upon which to compete. If black banks and building associations did not lend money to prospective African American homeowners, what entities would, given the racist climate in lending? And, if black banks had to rely on investing in real estate primarily instead of manufacturing and commercial operations from which they were excluded, what other course could they pursue?

In 1921, in the middle of a national economic recession, while responding to a new state law regulating banking activities, Jesse Binga converted his personal operation to an institution operating under a state charter. At the same time, P. W. Chavers secured a federal charter for the Merchants and Peoples Bank, while maintaining his efforts as trustee to pay off the black claimants to the Woodfolk Bank's remaining assets. At a November meeting held at the Bethesda Baptist Church, he laid out his plans for the opening of the new bank. Seeking a name with the power to inspire an ultimate level of confidence, he chose to name it the Douglass National Bank. When his wife protested why he couldn't get credit by using his own name, he replied, "The bank is a movement against economic slavery. The thing is too big to name after a local man."[74]

Ostensibly, black Chicago had the first black national bank in the Douglass National Bank, at least in name and in this, the planning stage.[75] By the time the bank opened in 1923, it was black America's second federally chartered bank. Implementation of the economic game plan took capital, connections, and competitive fortitude. Nationalistic to the core, Chavers planned to raise capital solely within the black community so capital was "to be sold exclusively to Chicago Negroes."[76] Before the bank could reach its full capitalization of $200,000, with $50,000 in savings, cosmetic magnate and publisher Anthony Overton was invited into the planning to assume control over the bank. This maneuver was unexpected. According to a biographical account by his daughter, Madrue Chavers-Wright, Chavers's efforts had been undermined by Rev. John W. Robinson, a leading Methodist Episcopal (but not an AME) minister whose primary desire was to recoup his church's funds from the defaulted bank. In describing her father, the biographer emphasized his high character that emulated that of his business hero, Booker T. Washington. P. W. Chavers excelled "in transcending the resistance he encountered in developing his ideas. This was the test of the man: how he encountered, endured, and surmounted betrayal. . . . All of his life [he] was fighting several groups at one time: both the black and white self-seekers, the entrenched older generation of politicians, the shady elements, as well as the apathy of the victimized, and the betrayal of those in whom he had placed unwarranted trust."[77]

Despite Chavers obtaining the initial support of what his biographer referred to as some leading "Old Settlers," including a financially manipulating Rev. John W. Robinson, a more important set of endorsements was needed. From Washington, D.C., the office of the comptroller of currency raised legitimate questions about the capabilities of the board of directors Chavers had assembled. These were basically inexperienced men in the world of banking who desired to operate an institution authorized under federal auspices. Whether he was or not, Chavers should have been embarrassed when he was informed that such membership required competent bank experience. In addition, endorsements were required from the offices of Congressman Martin B. Madden and Illinois Senator Medill McCormick. Chavers had met disappointment with this endeavor, but in the meantime had won an important victory for ordinary persons with an agreement with the court that provided for Woodfolk Bank depositors to be repaid 100 percent of their savings over a ten-year period ending in 1931.

Efforts to raise capital for the national bank proceeded rather slowly, with some subscribers being unable to continue making their stock payments. Chavers preferred stock as an alternative source of funding rather than interest and involved a great many smaller investors in democratic fashion, in contrast to Rev. Robinson's penchant to involve fewer, but bigger, investors. Robinson worked behind the scenes with either S. A. T. Watkins or Alderman Robert Jackson to originally get Anthony Overton involved.[78] The minister had proven himself adept with fundraising and handling money by clearing the debt on his small denominational church in an eleven-year period. Whether he possessed any knowledge of high finance and banking theory is conjectural. Evidently, one major reservation from Overton, who, with his expanding economic empire of a manufacturing firm and proposed six-story Overton Building on the drawing boards, was reluctant to contribute to the opening of a bank with Chavers, a relative newcomer to the city and with fewer resources at his command. This made good business sense, especially given Overton's expected large purchase of stocks and ability to raise the $200,000 needed for capitalization.[79] Moreover, Chavers had only a four-year track record in the city and therefore had not had time to develop a network of the type needed to ensure confidence in any venture as large as this. Overton had only been in the city six years longer, so control over financial resources seemed to be the real issue in this instance, but he was amassing a fortune in his cosmetic business and gaining a national reputation for his successful, profitable operations. He further promoted his business activities through his own monthly publication, which was gaining readers in the South and the East. The one person most directly affected competitively, Jesse Binga, meanwhile was quoted in the *Defender* as welcoming the addition of another black bank, especially one that offered commercial loans, which a state bank such as his was unable to do by state law.[80]

The formal opening of the Chavers-directed Douglass National Bank was scheduled for January 2, 1922, but delays related to raising needed capital, the unacceptable composition of the board, and internecine maneuverings as to Chavers's neophyte and newcomer status postponed this event. Rev. Robinson supposedly informed Chavers that Washington officials wanted someone who was either Caucasian or an African American of Anthony Overton's financial stature to head the bank. This was indeed an accurate relay of information, so it appeared that the Douglass National Bank would never open with Chavers as its head. At the same time, the imperturbable Chavers headed to the nation's capital in his continued pursuit of the charter, but this time with the backing of key fellow Ohioans, including President Warren G. Harding. Persistence in this case being its own reward, Chavers returned successfully with the charter in June.

Once back in Chicago at the first meeting of the Douglass National Bank's board of directors, Chavers was confronted with his own ouster from the presidency before he had an opportunity to perform in that capacity.[81] Not unexpectedly, economic titan Anthony Overton assumed the presidency. Completing the leadership team were Rev. Robinson and political powerhouse and Third Ward alderman Major Robert R. Jackson, who served as vice presidents. Chavers, who had refused a vice presidency, now had no role whatsoever. As his biographer recalled his disappointment and reconstructed his utterances, he had considered the entire affair the equivalent of a mutiny. "They turned on me. Not one single man spoke up for me. To think I personally selected each one, except [Overton], in whom they now place their confidence. . . . The Board Members agreed to vote [Overton] in as President and Chairman of the Board while [I] was away. They agreed in advance on their strategy, and they staged the meeting today to get me to hand over the presidency. They were not interested in learning how I had secured the charter."[82] Years later, Rev. Robinson would admit his culpability in the "mutiny" but explained it away along practical lines. He claimed that in reality the mutineers didn't want Overton over Chavers, only his prestige and money, and they had hoped that Chavers would be satisfied with the vice presidency.[83]

As Chavers returned solely to dealing in real estate, the newer version of the Douglass National Bank began its operations under the control of Overton and his backers. As part of the Overton economic empire of manufacturing, insurance, newspaper, and banking, the future of the Douglass National Bank looked promising.

No matter who ran black banks, or wherever they were located, they characteristically were overcapitalized and carried assets that were heavily illiquid. According to Harris, the healthy proportion of capital investment to total deposits for state banks should have averaged 18 percent. Instead, it was 32.9 percent in black Chicago. In national banks, the percentage was also 18 percent. Further, this financial weakness was exacerbated by the tendency to expand loan discounts disproportionately to deposits. So the test of the place of the black Chicago bank in history had to be based on both its internal and external functions as community symbol and *bona fide* banking institution.[84]

Internally, this economic institution did indeed serve the needs of its community, but it required questionable business practices to achieve that end. That meant extending loans and mortgages where demands of efficiency within the capitalist system would have denied them. The reality for a community such as the Black Metropolis was that banks were meant to process and facilitate the flow of capital to stimulate businesses and to prosper for the benefit of stockholders and depositors, not benevolently extend credit to lenders who were poor risks.

The question posed externally was, how well did these institutions manage their money in the marketplace? If a certain amount on investment was dedicated to community improvement, through home mortgages, how did this compare to investments in industrial and commercial undertakings, either local or national?[85] The answer was, too little in the latter case. A black bank carried the additional burden of signifying African American entry into the nation's mainstream as competent citizens. As *Opportunity* expressed the sentiment and expectations of an entire community, "It is a symbol of the Negroes' aspirations to enter the commercial life of the nation and it is a mark of his faith in the ability and competence of his own."[86] While Binga and Overton had great confidence in black professionals and their financially skilled personnel, the essence of banking resided in the return on investments.

One particularly glaring weakness was found in the origins of the black participation in the Illinois and federal banking systems. In Chicago, the first banks started as private ventures, indicating the limits of their financial strength rested solely with an individual's personal resources rather than a group, institution, or system (such as the funding operations of a state or the national government). With the advance of time, the composition of banking leadership as seen through its board memberships indicated another weakness—a lack of impartiality and objectivity in decision making. By 1929, the Douglass National Bank included Overton's sons-in-law: Dr. Julian H. Lewis as vice president and attorney Richard Hill Jr. as a member. Another vice president was LeRoy Johnson, with attorney S. A. T. Watkins serving as chairman and Edward S. Miller as secretary. Members included Rev. J. H. Branham of Olivet Baptist Church, Alderman Robert R. Jackson, and George T. Kersey. Binga by the same period had grown so autocratic as to make decisions without his board, necessitating their mass resignations to protect themselves legally.[87]

Able to extol its membership in the federal reserve system, the Douglass National Bank vaunted its depository status of holding funds from the City of Chicago and Cook County Treasurers' offices, along with major fraternal orders such as the Knights of Pythias, Masons, and Elks. Liberty Life Insurance Company "opened accounts with us."[88] What helped also was the backing of Alderman Jackson, with not only his political connections but also his network of fraternal orders who used his Fraternal Press's services, and S. A. T. Watkins, supreme chairman of the Knights of Pythias and president of the Appomattox Club. The bank was capitalized at its beginning at $200,000 and carried a surplus of $60,000. Its deposit liability was chiefly in savings except in the first year when one half of it was demand deposits. Under strict management, the proper ratio of capital investment to total deposits was maintained, except in 1922 and 1923. In addition to the bank's inefficiency in conducting an insufficient loan and discount business, it appeared that Overton personally lent fellow Baptist Rev. L. K. Williams and Olivet Baptist Church $20,000 through the bank to help establish the Baptist Publishing House in Nashville.[89]

Insurance

Remarkably, at this early period in African American northern urbanization, black Chicagoans organized their insurance companies for the most part on the modern corporate model, bypassing the stage common in the southern experience of evolution from mutual aid and fraternal activities.[90] During this decade, seven major insurance companies joined the banks in the financial sphere: Liberty Life (later known as Supreme Liberty Life), Metropolitan Mutual, Victory Life (a spin-off of Overton's bank and manufacturing firm), Unity Mutual, Public Life, Underwriters' Mutual, and Pyramid Mutual. Most of the organizers of these companies had amassed experience with some of the larger and most successful white insurance companies. Consistent with the country's true entrepreneurial spirit, they struck out on their own to amass wealth and experience success in their own right. This was also due to higher education, an awareness of what the modern urban market demanded, and recognition of the purchasing power of this enlarged African American market.[91] By 1927, Carroll Binder of the *Chicago Daily News* reported that African American Negroes carried $14,000,000 in insurance.[92]

Liberty Life Insurance Company began the decade in precarious fashion, with a failure to have raised enough capital to satisfy state requirements. The company was the brainchild of Arkansas-born Frank L. Gillespie, who had arrived in Chicago around 1889; Gillespie conceived of the idea of a black-owned and -operated insurance firm and thought the time ripe to bring it to fruition in 1919. He engaged in further planning in 1920, and in 1921 the company was finally ready to begin formal operations in summer of that year. Three such companies operated successfully in the South; nevertheless Liberty Life gained the attention of the city and the nation because it was the only legal reserve insurance company owned by blacks north of the Mason-Dixon Line.[93]

Gillespie had worked and gained valuable experience in insurance by working for two northern companies earlier in the century. His skills had led him into management as a supervisor with the Royal Life Company. Gillespie's sense of proportion convinced him of the need to run the institution as a modern corporation and avoid one-man rule, something the titans of the Black Metropolis were prone to ignore. As a former student at Harvard University Law School where precision in thinking and performance formed the standard, Gillespie knew the importance of using highly competent personnel. Consequently, it led him to seek younger, college-trained men to provide its administrative and operational leadership with an eye to the future of the company rather than to rely on his peers, who had limited capital and even less knowledge of the insurance industry.[94] W. Ellis Stewart and attorney Earl B. Dickerson fit the bill and remained with the institution for decades. A recent University of Illinois graduate and mathematical wizard, Lloyd G. Wheeler III later joined the firm and assisted in providing its actuarial needs. Wheeler's return to Chicago from downstate Illinois had additional social significance in that it marked the reemergence of the old pioneer family's presence in the city once again.[95] The search for suitable space in which to conduct business followed and led Gillespie to a vacancy on the second floor of the white-owned Roosevelt Bank Building at 35th and South Parkway.

In mid-1921, the Liberty Life Insurance Company opened its doors and began to sell life insurance to those who heretofore had not been considered insurable by white companies. Insurance premiums were invested back into the community from which they came and each dollar in the Black Belt began to have "double duty." The press reported that "the entire capital of $100,000 will be invested in high grade mortgages and improved property purchased by Colored people. . . . [I]t will no longer be necessary for Colored men to give up good options in high grade property because of objections by white neighbors who control the channels of financial aid."[96]

Within five years of tenancy, Liberty Life had purchased the entire building. After two years' work, the institution had $3,500,000 worth of insurance in force.[97] In another five years Liberty Life had $10 million worth of policies in force and owned $227,000 in real estate and "ha[d] placed $123,000 in first mortgages."[98]

The first seven years were tumultuous and indicated just how difficult it was to operate when the market was filled with limited capital from a workforce with meager wages, job insecurity, and little experience with insurance. In addition, hiring full-time staff was made difficult by the scarcity of trained agents and the company's ability to pay them advances.[99] A semblance of stability was reached in 1929 when Liberty Life merged with Supreme Insurance of Columbus, Ohio, and Northeastern Insurance Company of Newark, New Jersey. The merger brought two new faces: Frank Pace from Northeastern, who assumed the presidency, and Truman K. Gibson of Supreme, who took on the duties as chairman of the board of directors. A major shift from selling ordinary life policies to industrial policies followed, consistent with both the financial situation that blacks faced in the workplace and general economic conditions in the nation.[100]

The growing manufacturing empire of Anthony Overton was poised to extend into the financial world as he established Victory Life Insurance Company in 1923. Within two years, this titan had expanded Victory outside Illinois into eight other states where branches were established. In another two years, Victory reported $5 million worth of policies in force and that it had "loaned $233,000 to Negro property owners."[101] By 1929, when Supreme was born out of the ashes of Liberty Life, Victory Insurance operated in ten states outside of Illinois, including the New York market. Unlike Supreme, Victory was immediately successful, due in part to a hefty surplus helped along by its attachment to a profitable industrial undertaking. Very much like the old Liberty (and Supreme), the company's original capital was invested in home mortgage loans.[102]

The attraction to this financial field led other African Americans with capital to invest and a thirst for wealth to follow Liberty Life and Victory Life into insurance. Unique as to its origins, capital raised from underworld activities fueled Metropolitan Mutual Assurance Company's organization in 1925. These surplus funds were amassed through gambling and policy operations under the control of Metropolitan's primary financier, gambling czar and politician Daniel "Dan" Jackson.[103] Aware of the needs of the basically southern migrant population with its familiarity with funerary provisions, Metropolitan concentrated on selling burial insurance to the least affluent black Chicagoans.[104]

Of the four smaller companies (Unity Mutual, Public Life, Underwriters' Mutual, and Pyramid Mutual), they all provided industrial insurance. They operated on what was described as the assessment plan, wherein customers pay weekly premiums and are guaranteed payment for the beneficiary upon death. Public Life was founded by attorney A. L. Williams, who also was one of the chief stockholders. The company was incorporated for $500,000. Its directorate was diverse, including thirteen white and two black officers, of which Williams was one.[105]

Another company broke the mold of offering ordinary and industrial policies and focused on fire insurance, offering coverage against conflagration. The Lincoln Union Fire Insurance Company raised capital of $100,000 after selling 4,000 shares at $50.00 apiece. Touting itself as a reliable vehicle through which to amass profits, the Lincoln Union compared itself to the Hartford. Its officers included Dr. Richard A. Williams, who held the Lincoln Union presidency along with that of the Royal Circle of Friends of the World, and Dr. Carl G. Roberts and Robert S. Abbott, who occupied the posts of first and second vice president, respectively. State Senator Adelbert H. Roberts joined attorney Earl B. Dickerson along with Drs. A. W. Mercer, Charles M. Thompson, and O. A. Taylor as directors.[106]

Real Estate

The acquisition and trade in land, accompanied by construction of various types of structures on settled plots of solid ground, has always represented an integral part of Chicago's economy. Following a pattern begun by Jean Baptiste Pointe Du Sable, it paved the way for nonindigenous claims to control over space. Carroll Binder wrote in 1927 that "Negroes proudly point out that one of their number . . . was the first property holder in Chicago."[107] With American occupation of the place "where the river meets the lake," change came soon thereafter with the first federal platting of land in the 1830s as the Illinois and Michigan Canal was proposed. African Americans slowly accumulated property again in the city beginning in the 1850s, when the Joseph Hudlin family built their own home on land they owned. John Jones's acquisition of land and construction of his two-story business followed shortly thereafter at the corner of Washington and Dearborn Streets.

In addition to ownership of property, capital accumulation was made possible through the buying and selling of the land and structures on it. African Americans continued their interest in acquisition of real estate both as individuals and as part of corporate entities into the twentieth century with some of the largest fortunes amassed by men who entered the real estate market—Jesse Binga, Anthony Overton, Oscar DePriest, and many others, such as T. W. Champion with his Pyramid Building and Loan Association, later his T. W. Champion Realty Agency and Loan Company.[108] Binga was exemplary in this field and took advantage of opportunities whenever they appeared, showing his true trait as an entrepreneur. Early in the previous decade, he took control over the entire western side of State Street in the 4700 block and built it into part of his real estate empire. "He owned 1,200 leaseholds on flats and residences; by 1926 he owned more frontage on State Street south of 12th Street than any other person."[109] Overton's real estate dealings flowed through his Great Northern Realty Company, which anchored the entirety of his financial empire, including his bank and insurance company.[110]

Moreover, as a matter of record, the major financial institutions of the decade—the Binga State Bank, the Woodfolk Bank, the Douglass National Bank, and the Liberty Life Insurance Company—entered the commercial and mortgage credit market and invested heavily in South Side property, both inside the old Black Belt and in what was becoming an expanded enclave territorially in the Black Metropolis. African American desire to be an integral part of the wave of new homeowners in Chicago led to extensive real estate purchasing. The *Half-Century Magazine* reported in its January–February issue of 1924 that "More than $10,000,000.00 of Chicago real estate has gone over to Colored people in the past year. They are purchasing bungalows, flat buildings and community plan apartment buildings at the rate of about $100,000.00 a week, according to the latest reports."[111] By mid-decade, banker Jesse Binga estimated that "the realty holdings of his people . . . approximate[d] $400,000,000 in value."[112] For his part, Binga's bank held $800,000 in real estate loans, a significant factor signaling growth. Although this was good for community and with some mortgages located on Michigan and South Parkway, making them theoretically marketable, downtown white bankers believed this did not constitute sound banking practice.[113] Then Binga constructed the Binga Arcade on the northwest corner of 35th and State Streets in order to better exploit business, to stabilize that area of the Black Belt, and to thwart white commercial expansion farther south at 47th Street. The arcade opened in 1929 at a cost of $400,000.[114] Overall, Drake and Cayton confirmed that within the growing African American market "between 1915 and 1929 . . . not the less lucrative [activity] . . . was speculation in real estate."[115]

Aiding the rush were the real estate professionals who Binder, quoting Bolton, said numbered fifty-six dealers by 1927. In *The Negro in Chicago*, Robb lists at least forty-eight companies and real estate dealers on the South Side alone.[116] Within their ranks was Harvard-trained Alexander L. Jackson, lauded in *The Negro in Chicago* as an embodiment of success for his entry into the field. Jackson also worked as general manager of the *Defender* during this period.[117] The Chicago Real Estate Board retained its prerogative to determine qualifications for admission into the ranks as realtors, not just brokers, and no African Americans won this honor until the 1960s.

Liberty Life Insurance owned its own structure and held $227,000 in real estate and "ha[d] placed $123,000 in first mortgages."[118] Such investments in real estate represented a desire to live decently and sometimes beyond one's means. Similar to the South where property ownership carried status, so "the Chicago Negro who has saved a few thousand dollars is therefore a receptive client for a six-flat building." The danger in this practice would have not been apparent while the country was in the midst of boom days, but in the long run, some families and investors would pay the price for their financial overextension. On the other hand, Binder noted, "there are thousands who will soon own, free of debt, the homes which they purchased since the war." When the issues of shortage versus glut in housing units, and appreciation and depreciation in property values, are raised, the answers are as mixed as the choices of property available for purchase.[119]

When Dr. George Cleveland Hall was queried as to the status of boulevard properties purchased by persons such as himself and in his class, his response was encouraging to both races: "Panic-stricken white property holders in a changing district often let alarmist realtors talk them into selling their property at a loss 'because the Negroes are coming in.' Dealers have made fortunes by fanning these fears and then reselling the property at an outrageous profit. The property owner who exercises good judgment and sits tight will soon find a Negro purchaser who will pay him far more than he could possibly have gotten had his street remained a deteriorated white district. . . . Keep cool when you see the Negroes coming and you'll get twice what you will if you mistake them for goblins." Hall cited South Parkway properties along his block that sold for $10,000 at one point and then sold for double that amount several years later, with less expensive properties selling for $3,400 bringing three times that amount only three years later.[120] Obviously, the very personable Hall meant to both allay white fears of moving altogether from their black neighbors while making a case for African American deportment as good neighbors.

Money making from real estate came at a high price with the insidious exploitation of blacks by blacks mentioned by the *Half-Century*. The *Defender* saw the problem of the Black Belt as a two-edged sword that promoted housing segregation and economic disadvantage to the less well-off while allowing the more financially secure to profit from their needs.[121] As a problem throughout the North, J. A. Rogers criticized W. E. B. Du Bois for finding some value in its profit-making potential.[122]

Both old and new structures offered the opportunity to make money accordingly, as whites left neighborhoods and left hotels of note behind as part of neighborhood transition, African American entrepreneurs moved quickly to fill the void. Magnificent structures such as the Vincennes Hotel, located at Vincennes Avenue and 36th Street, and the Brookmont, located at 3953 South Michigan on the northeast corner, soon became places of high entertainment and important conferences frequented by the black upper and middle classes. The Vincennes Hotel and Annex offered 140 rooms, 73 with private baths.[123] The Brookmont advertised 200 rooms and almost as many baths.[124]

Lucrative commercial and professional operations in the old South Side led to new construction, a not-too-unfamiliar sight in the "new" Black Metropolis. The Jordan Building, erected by bandleader Joe Jordan, stood at 36th Street and State Street. A repository for safe deposit boxes, it fit the need for those with valuables to store at a time when whimsically it was stated that "Nobody had a key in those days . . . [because the night life never ended]."[125] Construction by the city's numerous fraternal orders likewise produced monumental structures. In October 1924, 25,000 persons turned out to witness the laying of the cornerstone of the new Prince Hall Masonic Temple located at 56th and South State Streets. Bond purchases were numerous, led by Your Cab Company's Walter H. Lee's investment of $1,000 and Robert S. Abbott's purchase of a $100 bond.[126] Not to be outdone, the Knights of Pythias planned an impressive edifice to be located at 3737–3745 South State Street to join the Binga Arcade and the Overton Building as monuments to black business success along South State Street.

The Knights of Pythias Building was to be the gem of the fraternal order's plans for economic progress among its brotherhood, and upon completion its interior and exterior achieved its goal of structural magnificence. As octogenarian Rosalia Holt recalled, the building appeared to thrive with "commercial leases filling the offices with various professionals, while other floors contained some residential units. Interior recreational facilities also added to the building's attractiveness."[127] Designed by African American architect Walter T. Bailey, the National Pythian Temple when completed rose eight stories and covered a quarter of a city block. At its completion in 1928 it had cost $850,000.[128] Shortly thereafter, Anthony Overton undertook another project of immense financial scope in planning for the construction of the multistory *Chicago Bee* building at 3647–3655 South State. With work beginning on the cusp of the Great Depression in 1929, it was not finished until 1931. A dream structure architecturally, it featured an Art Deco design that was the product of the creative mind of architect Z. Eroi Smith. Its front elevation, composed of colored terra cotta, reflected the *Bee*'s and Overton's philosophy of modernity.[129] Construction took place over a three-year period, lasting from 1929 through 1931. Elevator service was featured, a rarity in this section of the city.[130] Dominating the east side of the 3600 block of South State Street, Overton's latest building was located down the street from 3617–3627 where the recently built Overton Building stood.

In 1928, philanthropist Julius Rosenwald saw both profits and a level playing field in residential rental housing available to African Americans as he financed the construction of the Michigan Avenue Garden Apartments. Upon completion, the immense residential complex covered the entire block of 4600 South Michigan Avenue with 400 apartments. Constructed at a cost of $2.5 million, Rosenwald stated that "it is not a charitable venture; tenants will pay rents that will earn six per cent on the investment, at the same time enjoying the benefit of freedom from excessive rents necessitated by profiteering real estate operators." Over the next quarter of a century, Rosenwald's faith in African American responsible living as well as his investment paid dividends.[131] As to smaller builders, Joe Johnson built homes for families on the West Side as did others on the South Side.[132] Apart from his many accomplishments in the years to come, Robert R. Taylor was incorrectly listed as building homes for blacks in the Black Metropolis during this period.[133]

Manufacturing

Overton Hygienic Company stood in 1927 as the Black Metropolis's shining example of business success in manufacturing.[134] The company could also claim a Bradstreet rating exceeding $1 million and was called "the leading producer of cosmetics for [African American] women."[135] Overton Company claims over 4 million boxes of High Brown Face Powder sold in 1921: "evidence that quality is still appreciated—and will be always. Qualities, 25c, 50c, 75c. Four shades, Natural, White, Flesh-pink and Brunette." Worrying about fraudulent use of the Overton brand or false products, a warning was issued: "See that our name is on every package."[136]

Overton started the decade at 5200 South Wabash Avenue in a two-story, four-unit building in a residential neighborhood. Later, he built two new structures to house his enterprises on State Street. Strategically, they were located immediately south of the old Binga Bank building on the eastern side of State Street.

From its beginning with baking powder in the early twentieth century, the company advanced to sale of cosmetics. Concentrating on toilet articles, High Brown Face Powder emerged. The company sought patent protection for its innovative line of cosmetics and its line of perfumes, all of which had their own fragrance base. All bore the name "High Brown." Sales in the United States soared as women of color delighted in their enhanced appearances. An international demand ensued, with orders flowing in from Egypt, Liberia, and even Japan.

Competition increased domestically in 1922 as Mrs. Annie Turnbo-Malone expanded her manufacturing operations of beauty aids for women to now include skin care products.[137]

African Americans entered food processing with the manufacture of sausage products. Pork had been a mainstay of the African American diet since before the emancipation, so these ambitious businesspersons entered a field that brought them instant success. Searching for a manufacturing site and a headquarters building, Parker House Sausage Company located its base at 4607 South State Street and remains there to the present time.[138] The Matticx Creole Sausage Company began operations at 35th and South Parkway, and a third company was the Uncle Jerry Sausage Company. Frozen confections found a ready market, inducing the workmen to take a risk in 1922 and produce ice cream as the Seven Links Ice Cream Company (known as Baldwin's Ice Cream Company since 1946).[139]

In transportation, African American enterprise led to the operations of nine taxicab companies, nineteen garages, fifty-one express and storage operations, and fifteen transfer companies.[140] Creative businessmen such as Walter H. Lee and Lee Evans, among several others, started taxi services. Building on a three-quarter-century-old tradition dating back to Atkinson's hack service during the 1850s,[141] Your Cab Company and its successor, Supreme Taxicab Company, assigned dozens of vehicles onto the streets daily. In a city of migrants and big-shouldered dreamers, Oberlin, Ohio–born Walter Howard Lee dreamt big dreams after seeing his father operate a livery stable with seventy-five horses for thirty-five years on his two-acre demesne. W. H. Lee was not a person to make anything other than dreams as big as his contemporary Daniel Burnham. "When his father decided to sell out and give each child his share, Walter Howard refused to be given anything. There were too many brothers and sisters and Walter had plans of his own. He had determined to conquer Chicago." Working an independent carrier of first coal, then ice, he eventually gravitated toward transportation. With white competitors blocking his path as his various enterprises grew too large for an African American, he worked his way into insurance with the newly formed Liberty Life Insurance Company, eventually assuming the position of company treasurer. Finally, Lee started his own cab company after watching Yellow Cab Company dominate the transportation scene while sometimes mistreating its black customers with poor service on the South Side. In July 1923, Lee formed a stock company and placed ten maroon-colored cabs labeled Your Cab Company on South Side streets. All vehicles were well-equipped taxis with their drivers in chauffeur's uniforms.

Walter H. Lee demonstrated that he was not only a dreamer and initiator but an efficient businessman as he paid off his debt quickly, his employees' salaries timely, and claims promptly. By 1927, Your Cab Company was capitalized at $200,000 with eighty cabs on the streets and 250 employees on the payroll. The Your Cab Company garage at 415–421 East Pershing Road (39th Street) operated with a weekly payroll of $3,500 and made plans to add a company luncheon room, along with a tailoring and cleaning operation for employee uniforms. Company insurance was envisioned to keep customers protected, with an investment company to assist other African Americans who followed in their footsteps.

The *Crisis* concluded, "And when [Lee] has finally completed this and given employment and assistance to thousands in Chicago, then it is possible that the Chicago Colored people will let him go and organize along the same lines for other cities; they do not mean to be selfish."[142] The fate of Walter H. Lee's venture within the decade seemed to forecast something all too real about the state of black businesses: Over the long haul, too little experience, coupled with limited capitalization in an unstable neighborhood economy, spelled doom. Your Cab Company failed late in the decade.

In happier times, Supreme Taxicab Company had followed Walter H. Lee's example within two years after Your Cab Company began its operations. Under President Lee Evans's direction, the business worked to provide the Black Metropolis with a level of service both commensurate with needs and profitable for the times, the boom days of the "roaring twenties." Evans could boast of having efficiency in service from his fleet of seventy-five cabs, meeting proper insurance levels under state law and bonding protocols, gaining membership from the citywide Taxi Association, and fielding "the only Negro organization of its kind in the United States."[143] Each of Supreme's vehicles was driven by a uniformed chauffeur operating from a black-owned garage at South State and 51st.

The automobile offered other possibilities for the entrepreneur and businessman. In January 1929, Kansas City transplants Herman Roberts and Kenneth Campbell opened a new car dealership at 5046 South Parkway. The two had spent ten years operating a Hupmobile dealership in Kansas City, Missouri, and assumed that the Chicago market would prove even more lucrative. Dr. Midian O. Bousfield, the president of Liberty Life, and associates purchased the first three automobiles the Roberts-Campbell Motors Company offered to the public.[144] Servicing vehicles such as these led to the establishment of garages, such as Powell's Garage, which offered a variety of automobile services at his facilities located nearby.[145]

The publishing field nationally offered opportunities beyond contributing to civic betterment in the fourth estate. Publication of Ferdinand L. Barnettt's *Conservator* in 1878 and Isaac C. Harris's *Colored Men's Professional and Businessmen's Directory* in 1885 had set precedents for the city as to what African Americans could contribute to disseminating information and for the print trade. Chicago excelled in the early twentieth century as a publishing and printing center in its midwestern location, so it was no wonder that ambitious African Americans quickly entered the field. It was being reported that by 1927 black Chicago supported a field of twenty printers, four magazines, and six newspapers.[146]

Of course, Chicago was home to the *Chicago Defender*, boastfully declaring itself to be "the World's Greatest Weekly." Proving himself an astute businessman,

Robert S. Abbott expanded during this period of prosperity by reinvesting what he earned into this lucrative product. "Money he made through *The Defender* went back into *The Defender* to make it independent as to equipment and home." Consistent with his aim to enter the publishing world with a first-class operation, by 1921 Abbott relocated the paper's offices to 3435 South Indiana Avenue, two blocks east of the State Street corridor.[147] Abbott remodeled these offices with a modern decor consistent with his dream. Charles S. Johnson wrote of Abbott's accomplishments: "Here [in Chicago] also is the home of the world's greatest weekly—with a circulation of more than a hundred thousand and a plant valued at as many dollars." As a matter of fact, the number of newsstands and agents in the *Defender* network totaled 2,359 coast to coast. The entire physical plant was valued at $1 million. Abbott printed two editions a week on new presses he owned that were worth $100,000 and old ones that were valued at $48,825.[148] *Simms' Blue Book*, along with *Black's Blue Book*, reported the newspaper's circulation was 225,000 copies sold per week with an estimated total of 1,200,000 readers for each edition, leading Simms to assess: "The *Chicago Defender* is the greatest achievement in the history of the Race in journalism."[149] As an employer, Abbott's staff reached 100, performing in employment areas "the kind [of employment] that had been forbidden to them." Being a racially integrated staff, it was unique. Having to conform to union rules relating to the actual printing of newspapers, Abbott hired white typesetters and other skilled workers in his plant.[150]

According to Carter G. Woodson, the *Defender*'s mainstay in the early years was its sensationalistic and deliberately lurid articles that appealed to the masses. As a business practice it opened up a new market while meeting the cultural need of increasing the flow of information of African American affairs to an interested black public. No longer was reading interest to be a limited middle- and upper-class preserve. Overall, Carter G. Woodson assessed that Abbott had succeeded in making good on his pledge to make the *Defender* the world's greatest weekly, at least for African Americans. "Abbott deserves credit especially for what he did for the Negro press," analyzed Woodson. He continued, "Prior to the success of *The Chicago Defender* Negro newspapers were ordinary sheets which had little influence upon the locality in which they printed. Not a single one had a circulation exceeding 25,000 and most of them considered themselves doing well if the circulation ran as high as 5,000. When Abbott demonstrated, however, the possibility of the newspaper that would cater to the wants of the Negro people in publishing news concerning them and in a way that they could understand and appreciate it, the publications changed their methods and imitated Abbott."[151]

Making money from mass circulation as opposed to advertising made the *Defender* unique, but such was its appeal and its power to expand the spectrum of its reading audience into the thousands that it paved new territory indeed.[152] Accordingly, Robb wrote that "porters and cooks and stockyard workers came to look for their *Defender* regularly because they realized that it sought to cater to their needs as no other organ had ever done. They came to look upon the *Defender* as their champion in real deed as well as in name."[153] Accordingly, Abbott's heirs would later mount a tombstone engraved with the bold pronouncement of "He did for his race in the field of journalism what other great characters accomplished in the field of education. He was an inspiration and builder in the turbulent era in which he lived."[154]

The *Defender* had its competitors, both major and minor, yet it still managed to dominate the publishing field. Its oldest competitor, the *Broad Ax*, suffered the fate of its aging publisher, Julius F. Taylor, and began its fade into obscurity during the decade. In years past, it had come alive mostly at election time when advertising revenue from Democratic contestants was heaviest and the black Republican machine only in its earliest years of ascendancy. The *Broad Ax* was the only newspaper published outside the Black Metropolis and that corresponded to its impact during this decade as both a caustic social voice and a channel for the Democratic Party. The Republican Party held sway over the politics of the Black Belt and the idea of supporting the Democratic Party in any manner remained anathema.

The *Whip* had yet to distinguish itself as the decade began. After its opposition to the formation of the Brotherhood of Sleeping Car Porters (BSCP) in mid-decade, it carved out a niche as a militant voice for job procurement within the Black Metropolis. The newspaper itself was the creation of two Yale University graduates, Joseph D. Bibb and A. C. MacNeal, who started the newspaper in 1919.[155] The paper enjoyed a circulation of 30,000 copies per week during the 1920s. Henry H. Proctor served as city editor, fellow Yale graduate A. Clement MacNeal held the post of business manager, and Harold C. Thompson handled circulation matters. Its offices were located at 3420 South State, a half block north of the epicenter of the Black Metropolis. Advertising itself as an alternative to the *Defender*, the *Whip* heralded its independence with a submast heading of being "An Independent Weekly." It further touted its reach: "We cover Chicago territory like no other medium among black people" and "Get in Touch with the Whole Negro Race through *The Chicago Whip*." Objecting to the sensationalistic mass approach of the *Defender* in which violence and notoriety qualified as matters of utmost importance, the *Whip* proclaimed it followed a different path. It advertised, "The one paper that correctly interprets the latest news of interest to black people and which represents the thought of intelligent and right-thinking black people of the country."[156]

The *Whip*, moreover, distinguished itself for its crusade to increase job opportunities on the South Side. Its buying power campaign attracted notoriety by 1928–1930 under the slogan of "Don't Spend Your Money Where You Can't Work," a spur-of-the-moment idea of Bibb's.[157] Unafraid to indulge in hyperbole, the paper claimed to have secured thousands of jobs within the Black Belt by use of organized purchasing power and that the jobs "movement spread throughout the city like wild-fire."[158] The idea was not new, of course, and had been promoted in a more subdued form by the *Chicago Defender* as early as 1914 and organizationally by the Chicago Urban League in 1927.

Significantly in its use of the racial label *black*, the *Whip* pioneered a higher sense of race identity. When it used *Race*, it elevated its consciousness even higher. Its negative stand on the organizing efforts by Pullman porters proved it could take the low road to opposition to a cause that it questioned, however. Coupled with its tendency to engage in *ad hominem* attacks on A. Philip Randolph and the BSCP, the *Whip*'s leadership stood accused of being in the pay of the Pullman Company.[159]

Another publication, Overton's *Half-Century Magazine*, was unsuccessful after a decade's effort focused toward predominantly business and woman's audiences, with a touch of literary appeal. The *Half-Century Magazine*, established in 1916 with a cultural, business, and racial uplift outlook, became an economic competitor to the *Defender* (constantly bashing it on its choice of ads and emphasis on sensationalism) and the *Crisis* (criticizing it on its high-brow approach to accepting and publishing literary strivings and its assimilationist approach to racial adjustment).[160] In its appeal to the female market with its interest in personal grooming and improved housekeeping, the *Half-Century Magazine* preceded its final step toward transformation by January 1921 with its demise and subsequent market reentry as the *Chicago Bee* newspaper in April 1925. Its first office was located in the apartment complex at 5202 South Wabash Avenue that Overton had converted into a combination of manufacturing and living spaces. A second office appeared later on South State Street.

As for the *Chicago Bee*, black Chicago now had a major weekly newspaper that presented a more middle-class, conservative tone and content aimed at a sedate Sunday's reading. Not unexpectedly, it was also billed as a family enterprise. "The fact that the son and daughters of Mr. Anthony Overton are the principal owners of the *Chicago Sunday Bee* has naturally given this paper the benefit of the wise counsel of his seasoned business genius. This connection at the same time has afforded an adequate financial background." The *Bee* envisioned itself as taking an evolutionary step beyond Abbott's sensationalism, acceptance of fraudulent advertising, and promotion of superstitious, exploitative gimmicks. In promoting what it stood for, the paper mentioned higher education, amicable racial relations, civic and racial improvement, and accordingly, the promotion of Negro business.[161]

Two small newspapers reconstituted and renamed themselves: the *Chicago World*, which was formerly the *Enterprise* until 1926, and the *Heebie Jeebies*, which was later renamed the *Light*. The *Heebie Jeebies* remained under the control of Claude A. Barnett and his Associated Negro Press (ANP) and concentrated on the news of the theater world with a sprinkling of light literary renderings. The Associated Negro Press served as a news-clipping bureau for other newspapers. Anthony Overton's *Half-Century Magazine* criticized the ANP severely for its sensationalistic riot coverage in 1919.[162] More formidable in a political town was the *Chicago World*, the brainchild of Jacob R. Tipper of Bainbridge, Georgia. Another Georgian who reveled in the saga of his family's elevation from bondage to freedom before the emancipation, Tipper and his wife arrived in Chicago in 1908 in advance of the Great Migration. He prospered, running a grocery store, while engaging in Republican Party politics as a protégé of Edward H. Wright in the Second Ward. His first newspaper in the publishing field was the *Chicago Enterprise*, which began its run in 1918 and continued after 1925 as the *Chicago World*. From 1926 on, circulation grew until it reached 40,000 people each week. From its location a block away from the *Defender* at 3611 South Indiana, Tipper employed a staff of ten and operated from his plant with equipment valued at $35,000.[163] From New York, Marcus Garvey's *Negro World* offered only token competition; from Pittsburgh, the *Pittsburgh Courier* won a small readership, but it paled in comparison to the Chicago's own *Defender*.

Beyond the fourth estate among firms functioning primarily in printing operations, Simms listed Alderman Robert R. Jackson as a major printer in Chicago. Jackson established his own printing operation, Fraternal Press, in 1909 after handling printed materials for twenty-one years in the postal service. Fraternal Press "is said to be the largest printing establishment in the United States that is owned and operated by any members of the Colored race."[164] As a member of at least twenty social and fraternal organizations, Jackson garnered business by specializing in printing laws and constitutions for these and other kindred organizations. Fraternal Press also performed engraving and bookbinding as well as book and job printing. Its location was one-and-one-half blocks east of the State Street corridor along bustling 35th Street at 107 East 35th Street.[165]

Yet, ironically, the largest printing company owned by a person of African descent belonged to a certain Mr. Lee, formerly of Lee and Laird. This firm was located at the edge of the Black Belt, hired only white employees, and Lee as owner passed for white, a secret he kept until his death.[166]

Documenting this expansion, along with the explosion of newspapers, were at least two business directories. *Simms' Blue Book* and *Black's Blue Book* contained page after page of many smaller businesses in operation. In and of themselves, these publications were manifestations of business progress. *Black's Blue Book* was a publication of the Douglass National Bank and was issued free of charge. The same was true of a graduate student club's publication. The Washington Intercollegiate Club's record of African American progress, compiled by Northwestern University law student Frederick H. H. Robb and exploring a history purportedly extending back 8,000 years, appeared in successive volumes in 1927 and 1929 as *The Negro in Chicago*.[167] As a promoter of the need to recognize progress, especially black commerce, the publication appealed to its readers to comply with the slogan "Patronize the Prepared and Worthy."[168]

Competition for the retail trade within the Black Metropolis was exacting, with neither blacks nor whites having a clear-cut advantage over the burgeoning African American market. Some African Americans preferred white businesses over black establishments, while the reverse was true in other instances. The resort by African Americans to the ideology of the "double-duty" dollar demonstrated that black businesses would not find it easy to control the purchasing patterns of their own racial members. With this appeal, African Americans were exhorted to support the establishments of members of their group primarily rather than shop with vendors from other ethnic and religious groups. The argument was old, but the results were never guaranteed among blacks as they were in the other racial and ethnic communities of the city. Throughout Chicago's other enclaves, selective in-group purchasing was a given and black businesses were never to be found. It was in the Black Belt that economic democracy had its greatest opportunity to function unfettered by same-group considerations. This placed the black businessman at a great disadvantage.

Despite these circumstances, social observer Charles S. Johnson reported contemporarily that African Americans had established "1,800 business establishments." With an aim at providing goods and services to a market approximating 200,000 persons of color, well-anticipated opportunities as well as challenging responsibilities loomed. What these businesses encountered, according to Drake and Cayton, were five elements needed to attain business success. They had to amass capital and credit, something difficult at times to accomplish given the position of black workers in the labor hierarchy and the disadvantage of being "the last hired and the first fired." Black businesses also had to compete with certain white retailers, especially those operating grocery and clothing stores, who had the capital reserves to extend credit over long periods. The next problem involved having a competent, reliable, workforce that came about only through sustained employee training, accompanied by a commitment to the business operation and the role one held in it. Another consideration was securing a good location, with white shopkeepers already controlling the best spatial arrangements and being able to collectively exclude blacks from choice locations, such as 47th Street where Jewish shopkeepers dominated trade. Then, promoting consistent and expanding patronage among African Americans depended not only on competitive prices, good service, and an extensive inventory but also on the psychological edge that white businessmen had over the psyche of some black southern migrants and many northerners as being better equipped to handle retail goods and services. Lastly, for the Black Metropolis to reach its full potential, the economic network of the South Side in its entirety—businesspersons, investors, workers, and consumers—needed circumstantially to either develop a spirit of cooperation or elevate that quality, which was already found among the recently arrived European immigrant groups.[169] By the latter part of the decade, with a greater incentive than ever to exploit this lucratively appealing African American market, whites elevated the level of their investments in land, structures, services, and goods.

Advanced preparation for and having a proper funeral and burial ranked high enough in the life cycle for African Americans that burial associations, cemeteries, insurance companies, and funeral homes profited immensely in these business areas. In undertaking, only one business concern was listed in 1885, but research emanating from the University of Chicago reported that there were twenty-eight establishments by 1927.[170] Between the years 1927 and 1937, a tremendous increase was recorded so that by 1937, seventy were listed.[171] Maximizing the opportunities before them, these guardians of the dead organized the Chicago Colored Undertakers Association with George T. Kersey as their president.[172] The final component to this business endeavor was the purchase of land and operation of a cemetery catering to the needs of African American families. Lincoln, Burr Oak, and other cemeteries provided the solution to a proper "Christian home going."

Personal upkeep presented ambitious souls with the opportunity to become successful and prosperous. Beauty shops and barber shops operated throughout the Black Metropolis, monopolizing the trade fearlessly, knowing that competition from whites was nonexistent. Since the turn of the century, South Side black barbers had begun to cater to black customers exclusively while their Loop counterparts continued their tradition of catering to a white clientele. This latter situation proved foolhardy because soon into the new century, a racist, Social Darwinian backlash against African American service providers nationally, and specifically in Chicago, occurred. After having lost the trade of white customers, the possibility of regaining it disappeared. A rise in black income directed toward personal grooming in the Black Belt and manifested in the appearance of black men along the Stroll led the way. By the 1920s, Simms's business directory listed thirty barber shops located on South State Street or within a block east and west of State, with a dozen or so to be found farther east within half a mile.[173] David D. Berry, who married into the Slaughter family in 1901, now practiced his trade in his own barber shop in the Black Metropolis and was soon joined by two brothers-in-law in the trade, Albert and Eugene Slaughter.

The New Negro personality among women sought realization in redefining self and gender, such as the examples of the late Madame C. J. Walker of New York and Indianapolis and Mrs. Annie M. Turnbo-Malone of St. Louis and her Poro College. After Mrs. Walker's death in 1919, her company entered the next decade without her charismatic business leadership and soon fell behind in competition with the Overton Hygienic and the Poro College.[174] Turnbo-Malone increased her activities, moving a portion of her Poro College operations to Chicago after the decade ended, in 1930, offering black women a way out of poverty and domestic work. Mrs. Turnbo-Malone's Poro College expanded exponentially and grew strong enough to purchase the southern end of the 4400 block of South Parkway.[175]

The fairer sex continued to benefit from Overton's many hair products such as High Brown Hair Grower, promising a "live, glossy appearance" and advertised as "a straightener as well as a grower." Another product, Aida Pomade, was described as "a perfect hair dresser, especially prepared for usage with irons [ironing combs]. Gives hair a natural soft and silken lustre and keeps it in the desired position in the warmest weather." As the core of the Overton empire, his cosmetics line still reigned in Chicago as beauty products *par excellence*.

Several small department stores, haberdasheries, and dress shops existed. Among the shoe repair shops was that operated by Leo T. Holliday, located at Michigan and 35th Street, two short blocks east of the epicenter. A former Texan, Holliday had a varied career in the theater, war, and commerce. His eventual travels led him into the shoe repair business. The efficient look to his business belies the general assessment of inferiority placed on this area of African American endeavor.[176] Another small business operation of interest was Monarch Tailors, which operated at 3334 South State Street and was owned by William Little. Claiming to be "the Largest Ladies' and Gents' Furnishing Establishment of its kind in Chicago, proprietor Little had thirty years of experience in the trade and fifteen years in ownership.[177]

Ed's Toggery, a men's haberdashery located at 129 East 35th Street, opened its doors with an all-black staff and under black ownership in 1923. At age twenty-three, Springfield, Illinois, native Edward T. Lee supposedly lacked the business experience usually needed to start and sustain a business. An examination of his temperament and background provided answers to this retail phenomenon. Lee had begun to work at age fourteen for a wholesale manufacturer of men's collars, shirts, and toggery, logging in ten years of immersion in the field. With a meager capitalization of $1,250, he gambled on location, quality, service, and efficiency to put him over the top. His effort proved successful. Now at age twenty-seven, he carried an inventory valued at $10,000 with a business that "is constantly growing, and [with] a fine line of customers; among whom are Wm. Cowan, Col. Otis B. Duncan, David McGowan, Alderman R.R. Jackson, Chandler Owen, George Arthur, [and] Dr. U.G. Dailey."[178]

In addition to the retail establishments that flooded the Black Metropolis, a small amount of light manufacturing took place. Paul E. Johnson produced a therapeutic electric lamp that advanced the cause of medicine after meeting the many obstacles placed in his way by institutionalized racist practices. Arriving in Chicago in 1906 at age fourteen as part of the pre–Great Migration wave, he worked as a porter in a medical uniform repair firm. Ambitious to the point of believing that there were no impediments that could stop his progress toward commercial independence, he persevered despite every sort of discouragement, short of violence. "After coming to Chicago, he secured a position as an office boy for the Charles H. Killough Company whose business it was to receive the medical outfits [machines] in physicians' offices in exchange for new ones. These worn-out outfits were brought to the office and repaired. Johnson swept the floors, cleaned them, carried in the old machines, stored them and took them apart. He watched while they were being repaired. Finally, he did some of the repairing. Then he began to learn so much about it that he helped all of it; but he was still a porter at a porter's wages. There was no chance for promotion [for an African American]. The firm was sorry. They appreciated his work, but,—'you know how it is,' they said. Johnson was dissatisfied."

Johnson's final response was to start his own company. After several setbacks, expected in a new startup business, he traveled to Germany to learn more about the production of medical lamps. Negotiations with a monopolizing General Electric Company finally led to a commitment to purchase his products. After the electric giant reneged on their agreement, Johnson struck out on his own and continued to pursue his own dream independently. His factory employed both white and black workers in a work site covering 10,000 square feet and containing $65,000 worth of equipment.[179]

Johnson was not the only person to work with electrical manufacturing and power supply. In 1922, Sam Taylor founded Taylor Electric, an electric service store that sustained itself into the twentieth-first century.[180]

P. W. Chavers of Columbus, Ohio, had arrived in Chicago in March 1917 with his business in hand. His profitable, fourteen-employee apron and ladies' garment factory hit the ground running as he set up shop at 534 East 43rd Street, several blocks east of Grand Boulevard. Inside, "twelve sewing machines lined the walls on either side of the cutter's table from which [Chavers] handled the bolts of material when cutting the garments." His double-windowed storefront proved more than adequate for his operations that served both wholesalers and retailers such as Marshall Field and Company when its summer basement sales approached.[181] Chavers and his wife, Minnie, who began to run the family's apron and clothing factory after he became involved with the bank, made a move racially that shocked their employees and transformed race relations: They hired two neighborhood spinsters with experience in clothing and door-to-door sales. What was unusual was their race: Caucasian. Now their employees would experience a new dimension to race relations, one quite familiar to the Chavers as Ohioans, where race relations were somewhat more egalitarian.[182]

The Griffin family shared the transformative entrepreneurial business spirit of the age by starting out with a small candy store adjacent to the State Theater at 35th and State Streets. A chance display of a piece of sheet music in their window led to their decision to enlarge their business operations to include a fuller range of musical production, including the new phonograph recordings. A reflective Ida Mae Cress recalled the process:

> [a local musician] . . . came into the store, and he asked . . . if he could put a piece of his sheet music in the window so that people walking by would notice it and come in and ask about it, and that's just what happened! He sold a bunch of copies, and pretty soon several other people came in and asked about displaying or putting their music in a position where people would see it and want to buy it, and that's when Dad decided, "Well, I guess I might as well open a music store!" So then he moved down to 3637 South State [into the old Binga Bank facility] and started what was called the Griffin House of Music. . . . [We] delivered records and player piano rolls, and sometimes the boys would be sent downtown to pick up music or records that were a special request . . . people would call up and say, "Can you send me four or five records? or "Would you send me certain piano rolls?[183]

Associations and Organizational Linkages

The spirit of cooperation that was manifested throughout the decade among African Americans in various aspects of endeavor rendered the myth of ingrained disunity as patently unfounded. Collaboration within the ranks of major business and professional organizations reigned in anticipation of a time when chambers of commerce and professional associations would flourish. That time for the former came in 1923 when Jesse Binga laid plans for the realization of a unified local black business movement. Not since his successful State Street carnival in 1912 had Binga felt such enthusiasm about the possibility of bringing his idea to fruition. Within black Chicago, overall enthusiasm for the business credo and the probabilities of success ran so high that a localized business organization was formed in January 1924 under the banner of the Associated Business Clubs (ABC). Led by the three business titans of the Black Metropolis—Abbott, Binga, and Overton—the ABC promoted entrepreneurship and improved business management techniques and cooperation among the various business interests, professions, and trades.

The ABC's structure resembled a federation in that clusters of businesspersons with similar pursuits were lumped together in divisions, or exchanges, each with its own chair. The real estate exchange, for example, organized almost immediately and began to promote unity and encourage heavier investments by blacks in the vast property holdings found in the Black Metropolis.[184] So, despite the egotistical and tyrannical descriptions heaped on the heads of the leadership of this first African American chamber of commerce, democracy existed. What existed in the way of a hierarchy found Abbott assuming the helm as president and Binga settling into the executive secretary's chair. Mrs. Ethel Minor Gavin served as assistant to Binga and as head of the Women's Auxiliary. With his tendency to defer attention away from himself, Overton appeared to have silent input but was still considered one of the major sponsors. His views on how the Negro Sanhedrin (which convened in Chicago parallel with the start of the ABC) mishandled the linkage between education and business illustrated his frustration with anything less than a total commitment to business preparation, execution, and unity.[185] The *Defender* raised question as well about the conference's omission about labor issues, commenting "most blacks are working people."[186] Equally impressive was how the titans who had competing interests still managed to coalesce for the sake of economic unity and their group's advancement. Abbott and Overton competed in publishing, with Overton's *Half-Century Magazine* converting to a weekly newspaper, the *Bee*, in 1925; meantime, Binga and Overton competed for banking dollars and supremacy over the Black Metropolis through their construction of new buildings, charitable giving, and reputable civic stature. Overton also added another dimension to his empire building in 1923 by publishing a business directory, *Black's Blue Book*, free of charge and delivered to black households throughout the South Side.[187]

The absence of contention from the existing Chicago branch of the National

Negro Business League (NNBL), which had been founded around 1912 with Dr. George Cleveland Hall as its president, bode well for the ABC. When the NNBL held its convention in Chicago in 1912, it drew an enthusiastic response from black Chicagoans. It sustained itself, however, without making a major imprint. By 1923, with energizing Frank L. Gillespie, the president and founder of Liberty Life Insurance Company, becoming president of the local NNBL, the future looked somewhat more hopeful.[188] Instead of words denoting an ensuing rivalry, the inauguration of the ABC's activities elicited ebullient praise from Gillespie, who stated that "for the 35 years I have been living in Chicago I have been waiting to see the 'big Negro' join hands and start a co-operative movement like this. With such an example as the Abbott-Binga-Overton combination functioning in unison before them, the smaller business men will take heart and back them up. It means a new day for better, bigger Negro businesses."[189] Gillespie had an additional reason to applaud the ABC since the ABC committed itself fully to making the silver celebration of the NNBL's birth a success in Chicago with a full range of activities and large audiences.

An absence of dissension appeared likewise to exist nationally, relegating the false issue of national business supremacy by one locale as well as the real need for interregional collaboration among black businesses to their proper levels of importance.[190] The results of trips to the South, the Washington, D.C., area, and the West encouraging cooperation among businesses and extending markets became a staple of the weekly ABC meetings. One meeting even took on an international flair when Prince Kojo Tovalou-Houenou from Dahomey (now the Republic of Benin), West Africa, visited the ABC to discuss racial conditions in his country, France, and elsewhere.[191] His visit no doubt brought back memories of the last visitors from Dahomey to visit the city during the World's Columbian Exposition of 1893.[192]

The range of activities and meetings of various exchanges that took place appeared impressive for any age. Attorney A. M. Burroughs spoke on the role of bonds, trust companies, and the financial stability of any community. "He stated that a trust company . . . would have 150,000 of our group to draw from. Our Race has on deposit at various banks on the South side approximately $4,000,000 and $7,000,000 in the downtown banks. The largest theaters, hotels, and big buildings have been built by trust companies." Thirty-fifth Street was languishing because it lacked the big investors who are "looking for big profits and [do] not care for stocks and mortgages." Real estate purchases and sales proved a topic the ABC could deal with because of its familiarity. Jesse Binga spoke on one occasion on the controlling black Chicago through increased land purchases both to build profits benefitting the African American investor and community, and eliminating outside group influences and domination. The banker and realtor declared, "Property purchased by Colored people in Chicago during the last 10 years has advanced $10,000,000 in value, but values are now at their peak, and it behooves those who invested to be careful. The money market is tightening, and those who purchased two or three years ago need to be certain of their ability to meet the mortgages now falling due. Many of the people who sold property on the rising market are sitting back and refusing to renew mortgagees, with the intention of getting the property back again through the inability of the purchaser to refinance."[193]

On a later occasion, Jesse Binga introduced one of the more attractive features of black business marketing techniques when he suggested using coupons redeemable at ABC member stores. For every one-dollar purchase, a three-cent redeemable certificate was issued that various participating ABC member stores would accept toward purchases.[194] With growth, this black chamber of commerce purchased its own meeting facility at 3632 South Michigan Avenue in 1925 as its pursuit of a membership of 1,000 businesses was reached. Members were pledged to high standards and good service, so the ABC placard in a store's window made known that "standard and quality of merchandise are guaranteed and that courteous treatment and fair play are part of the service."[195]

When the ABC welcomed the NNBL delegates to the city in August 1924, it was done in grand style with a parade led by the *Chicago Defender* band under the directorship of the nationally renowned musician Major N. Clark Smith. Scores of business flats circled the territorial boundaries of the Black Metropolis while passing by hundreds of small businesses. Daily and evening sessions drew throngs to hear various speakers. The American Giants played a baseball game at their home field to honor the visitors, while a huge reception was held at the magnificently appointed ballroom of the black-owned Vincennes Hotel. What had been dreamt of now had been transformed into an actuality.

The success at collaborative efforts among the various professional, service, trade, and commercial groups extended to physicians who affiliated with the National Medical Association. At one time, Dr. Carl G. Roberts was the local president. Lawyers belonged to the Cook County Bar Association. Not to be outdone for his profession, Charles S. Duke contemplated forming an organization of engineers and architects during the 1920s.

* * *

Nineteen twenty-four brought yet another major conference to black Chicago; this one was Professor Kelly Miller's All-Race or Negro Sanhedrin. Probably scheduled in Chicago by reason of its location as the nation's rail center and mid-continental home to perhaps the most assertive aggregation of African Americans in the country, Howard University's Miller conceived of the conference in light of heightened Ku Klux Klan activities nationally as well as the current, transformative northern migration. The Negro Sanhedrin was scheduled to begin in Chicago during the symbolic second week of February in 1924. Almost sacred to many blacks because it contained both the birthdays of Abraham Lincoln and Frederick Douglass, the spirit of both men was invoked in Miller's call for national unity among all organizations and agencies dedicated to promoting African American advancement. Paralleling, but not replicating, the international perspective of the UNIA and Du Bois's Pan African Congress, along with the local thrust of the Black Metropolis movement, Miller foresaw the need for a union to "speak with the consent and authority" of all organizations and in behalf of African Americans. He emphasized it was "not so much an organization as an influence." Just as important, Miller invoked New Negro reasoning in writing that the "time has come when the Negro must think for himself and speak for himself in terms of his own understanding of his own conditions."[196]

Chicagoans eagerly awaited the conference of leading spokesmen and scholars and chose Dr. George Cleveland Hall as the chair of their Committee of 100. Dr. Carl G. Roberts assumed the vice chair with the ubiquitous Morris Lewis (from the Chicago NAACP and Oscar DePriest's political organization) serving as secretary. Preparatory meetings were held every Sunday at the Appomattox Club with the Wabash YMCA scheduled to hold daily meetings of the delegates. The general public had its opportunity to share in the proceedings in a series of general meetings to be held nightly at Wendell Phillips High School.

Once the conference began, 500 delegates representing sixty organizations filled their seats and took to the podiums addressing a variety of issues. What the delegates did not discuss was the major topic around which African American life revolved: work. Labor somehow escaped notice. The *Defender* recognized the omission as egregious and editorialized against this affront in the "Aftermath of Sanhedrin." The newspaper lambasted Miller and the planners critically. "The question of labor was given no place in the agenda, but was practically outlawed. And this despite the fact that 98 per cent of our group is in the working class. It is patent to all that cultural advancement of any group is conditioned upon the economic status of its masses. Therefore to have excluded such a vital issue would be like attempting to build a house before laying its foundation."[197] At the end of the conference, a disappointed spokesmen for black communists, Lovett Fort-Whiteman, criticized Kelly Miller and begrudgingly and belatedly approved of the UNIA position to avoid the conclave.[198] Although declared to have been a success, in its wake the All-Race Sanhedrin accomplished little more than to arouse sentiment for the need for tangible action. While these nationally focused proceedings had emphasized the worthiness of the trickle-down theory that had hierarchical benefits for the masses and all of the classes beneath a cooperative organizational umbrella, the Associated Business Clubs had chosen to focus on building a localized base from which all elements would benefit as they rose collectively. The importance of the role of labor was not to be denied and is covered in the following chapter.

Prelude to the World's Fair

As a prelude to the World's Fair of 1933, African Americans acted proactively to ensure participation, representation of their image under their auspices, and of course in the middle of a depression, employment opportunities. With memories as well as living reminders of limited involvement in the planning and execution of the World's Columbian Exposition of 1893, they were well aware that they had to act early and often years in advance of the opening of the Chicago World's Fair of 1933. This time, both on their part and the fair's planners and financiers, African Americans had the opportunity to demonstrate the extent of their advancement in a variety of ways. When Chicago's financial leaders moved forward with plans to host the World's Fair of 1933, these downtown financial backers took notice of the economic success of the South State Street black businessmen. Jesse Binga's face and philosophy had graced the first page of the *Sunday Chicago Tribune* of March 8, 1927, for all of midwestern America to see. That same year Anthony Overton had received had the prestigious Harmon and Spingarn awards for excelling in his business pursuits. Robert S. Abbott was a proven commodity in publishing and in civic affairs. For those whose capital was manifested primarily in ideological terms, the World's Fair represented another opportunity to demonstrate black achievement.[199]

So, totally unlike the situation preceding the 1893 fair, African Americans had something to offer to advance their claim to inclusion based on more than a desire for fairness. In the era of business, blacks had arrived and on terms that whites could respect. The fair, the city's second in forty years, was titled "A Century of Progress" and aimed to underscore the advancements made in all aspects of human endeavor, especially the material and scientific, over the past one hundred years. Chicago's centennial as a chartered political entity would buoy the celebration. Black Metropolis titans Robert S. Abbott and Jesse Binga, unfortunately, had to refuse the offer to invest before the fair got underway. Both Abbott and Binga had recently taken risks in their business operations that included, for the latter, building a new edifice in contradiction to the trend that favored the 47th Street white developers. Moreover, the consumer base upon which they depended for patronage was experiencing economic difficulties of the sort that increased fears of possible economic collapse sometime in the future.

But if the black business community could not engage to the fullest extent in behalf of their race, other African American men and women were up to the challenge. With a desire to reverse what some visitors and participants in the 1893 fair saw as a racial slight, part of that effort to ensure race recognition revolved on Jean Baptiste Pointe Du Sable's founding of Chicago as a permanent, nonindigenous settlement with a European-inspired economy. As early as May 1928, Dr. Arthur G. Falls, speaking for the De Saible Men's Division of the Chicago Urban League, approached the fair's planners with an idea for an exhibit honoring Du Sable, and in effect, African Americans. By November, an initiative under the leadership of Mrs. Annie Oliver united to form the De Saible Memorial Society, which was ready to promote African American cultural interests at the fair.[200] Overall, all classes and over fifty organizations eventually coalesced into the Colored Citizens World's Fair Council, which sought equal enjoyment of their citizenship rights on the fairgrounds, proper representation of their racial image based on contributions to Chicago and the world, and the all-important element in human survival—employment. By the end of the decade what amounted to a crusade was underway in the Black Metropolis to gain full inclusion. The backdrop in economic terms was influential enough to dominate all aspects of endeavor in the succeeding decade.

* * *

The economic outlook in 1927–1929 fell during that portion of the decade that Drake and Cayton labeled as the lean years, when a remarkable and contrasting trend manifested itself about two miles from the heart of the Black Metropolis business district. It was also at a time when retail operations appeared to have stalled everywhere and rising unemployment among black workers, who occupied the bottom of the occupational ladder, appeared acute. White competitors, seeking to penetrate the lucrative African American market beyond the small retail stores they maintained in racially changing neighborhoods, thought big and built bigger. These entrepreneurs and established merchants engaged in aggressive business ventures aimed at capturing the still-extant prosperity of the period. While Jesse Binga and the leadership of the fraternal order known as the Knights of Pythias were completing plans for the construction of the Binga Arcade and the impressive Knights building at the epicenter of black business, their white competitors had outflanked them farther south and east at 47th Street and South Parkway.

Whites rarely exhibited interest in development in this area, and on the contrary, abandoned various neighborhoods where they had lived for decades. Surprisingly, in 1923, outside white developers proposed building a fifteen-story athletic club for the enjoyment of African Americans at the corner of 35th and Michigan Avenue. Nothing came of the plan, but within three years, in summer 1926, Jewish commercial developers announced plans for a combined theater, ballroom, and department store complex to be situated in the 4700 block of South Parkway. Their plans startled residents of the South Side, who rarely expected developments of this magnitude, and especially in areas where they predominated demographically.

This new, first-class entertainment center would be located in the heart of what was to become the new epicenter of the Black Metropolis. The theater, the elegant likes of which had not been seen in an African American community, cost $1,500,000, replicating the best venues being built in white neighborhoods much farther north and west in the city. Its debut was planned for February 1928, but several months earlier, in December 1927, the adjacent building opened as the Savoy Ballroom. This venue featured two orchestras and employed an additional fifty employees. What was unusual for the times was to be found in the composition of the workforce: “this lavishly furnished place, produced entirely with the funds of white investors, plainly depended upon Negroes for the operation. From manager to doorman, approximately fifty employees, were Colored. . . . Indeed, never before . . . had Colored people in Chicago waited upon members of their own race with such finesse and civility."[201]

As an attraction, the Regal Theater represented state-of-the-art construction in its acoustics, seating, and design. Sociologist Clovis Semmes has written that "for Chicago's Black Belt community the Regal was truly unique. It was without question the largest, the most technologically advanced, and the most architecturally ornate movie house in the Black Belt, and the only deluxe theater or movie picture palace ever built expressively for a Black American community."[202] It contained 2,798 seats and specifically hired African Americans in all positions, from top to bottom.

Aware of the spirit of independence pervasive in the making and maintenance of the Black Metropolis, ambitious whites strove to capture their share of the African American market by providing goods and services heretofore only scarcely found on the black South Side. The same year that the Regal opened, Walgreen's drugstore chain located a branch in the same structure as the Regal. This chain, started by a Swedish family, adopted the same policy in place at the Savoy and Regal and hired almost all black personnel. Only the manager was white. Then, the South Center Department Store was completed and hired blacks to whites at a ratio of 16 to 1 among its 220 nonmaintenance and service staff. African American Richard Jones filled the position of general superintendent, astonishing the entirety of the Black Metropolis. As the corner looked all the more attractive, Neisner Brothers located a five-and-dime store next to South Center with a staff, including sales personnel, that was 40 percent African American. In rapid succession, other white stores opened and hired black staff as clerks and supervisors. One-half mile west on 47th Street, as it intersected with Michigan Avenue, philanthropist Julius Rosenwald financed a five-story, modern residential complex that catered to the African American middle class. As Rosenwald stated, "I built it to make money." Yet, the concept seemed novel to all but those who remembered a similar venture he supported in 1918 further north. Here, as was the pattern farther east, the management staff was African American.[203]

As Oliver Cromwell Cox analyzed contemporarily, business expansion involved African American capitalists also. "The movement was not left exclusively to white business men. A few Negroes with the necessary command of capital made some of the most daring moves."[204] African American efforts remained concentrated around the 35th Street epicenter, however. Binga's dream of a bigger and better edifice for his financial operations resulted in the finished construction of the Binga Arcade in 1929. At the newly constructed National Pythian Temple at 3725–3745 South State Street, the Knights of Pythias spent $1,200,000 to build this office and theater complex.

Regarding competition from 47th Street, Binga's attitude was combative and he was ready for the challenge. He was heard to utter, "I'll bring [them] back . . . I know how to do it." Part of his plan called for shoring up the corner of 35th and State Streets by luring the major utility companies to establish branch offices. This aspect he accomplished when Commonwealth Edison, Illinois Bell Telephone Company, and Peoples Light and Gas signed ten-year leases in the Binga Arcade.[205] Another portion of Binga's plans included establishing a new banking institution at 47th Street to be named the South Park National Bank. He received approval of his application to the federal government and proceeded by removing money from the Binga State Bank to funnel into the development of the new national bank. The impracticality of this venture convinced Binga's board of directors for the Binga State Bank to oppose it. His response was to replace them and any others who questioned his quest. "His board of directors found empty chairs, only to be filled with new faces at the next meeting. Binga had disposed of them, for they, it seems, had challenged his right as an overlord. Here was a mad genius now, building, wrecking and ruining. . . . But was Binga the tyrant many said he was? He couldn't have been. Binga was weak. His haughty manner was only pretense. Steel gives little, but the best of steel will bend. Binga could be beat."[206] Meanwhile, in pursuit of work to sustain hearth and home, the black laboring force demonstrated that if it was ever to be beaten down, it wouldn't be without a struggle. The next chapter explores that saga.

CHAPTER 4

Labor

Both Fat and Lean Years

Unions cannot expect to close the working door in [the black man's] face in peaceful times and expect his co-operation in troublesome times. They must be consistent.
—*Chicago Defender*, December 1921

Even in regard to its laboring population Chicago exhibits the possibilities of the Negro as an industrial worker as no other city.
—E. Franklin Frazier, 1929

Postal workers, as a class, give greater support to the National Association [for the Advancement of Colored People] than any other class.
—Daisy E. Lampkin to Robert W. Bagnall, 1928

Whatever halcyon days were seen in the business sphere failed to materialize into a comparable experience for the bulk of the black laboring class during the 1920s.[1] Although the war years had brought something positive into the lives of old and new black Chicago residents, the end of war brought a series of negative experiences and ones all too familiar to the black worker in America. Demobilization of the armed forces and the servicemen's return into the labor force produced a glut of workers. With the Chicago Urban League reporting that unemployment had reached serious proportions, the decade of the 1920s began on rocky foundations, to say the least.[2] With this decade beginning with such gloomy prospects of continuous postwar recession and with unemployment rampant, its conclusion inauspiciously produced a similar scenario in place. The recognized features of economic depression in the 1930s then easily came as no surprise to the African American worker in and outside of industry.[3]

New Negro economic visionaries—and in the reality of the times, actual business titans such as Anthony Overton, Jesse Binga, and Robert S. Abbott—stood tall as trailblazers in the best American capitalistic tradition as they exhibited the entrepreneurial traits of risk taking, strategic and futuristic planning, and an ability to transform dreams into tangible realities with both wealth production and job creation. Consistent with New Negro thinking, the results were manifested in institution building as well as the actual construction of new buildings that completed the visual element in the process of creating the Black Metropolis.

As impressive as the presence and influence of business and politics were over black life, the advent of World War I, which produced the black industrial proletariat, left an even more massive workforce seeking change and workplace opportunities in its wake. Moving to a phase in their awareness of their value to the nation's labor structure, elements of the laboring classes—in particular, Pullman porters and packinghouse employees—considered organizing along the lines of trade unionism to attain goals previously considered unimaginable. As a result, labor consciousness and successful organizing among these groups of workers produced black labor's most activist decade to date. Their efforts produced progress not only in the labor environment; the groundswell for a determined civil rights thrust was in progress among the ranks and organizational structure of packinghouse workers, Pullman porters, steelworkers, and postal employees as well.

Not to be overlooked were numerous contradictions existing in the domain of work that saw great expectations being heralded in some quarters while a reasonable semblance of full employment or even near full employment never materialized. According to the numerous economists and historians who have examined the role of the Brotherhood of Sleeping Car Porters (BSCP), the American Negro Labor Congress, and the various attempts to organize packinghouse workers, the problem of underemployment seemed to be overlooked as well—except for the activities of the aforementioned groups.[4] Black labor in the trades experienced racial discrimination within their areas of skills and responded locally by organizing under their own leadership, such as that exemplified by Edward Doty's Chicago Colored Plumbers Association and later the American Consolidated Trades Council.[5] Worsening economic conditions tied to global dislocations, constant migration from the South of workers seeking sustenance and causing a local labor glut, and the early advent of a massive depression in the Black Belt loomed as disruptions for members of the laboring class. These factors exposed the weakness in the black dream of a self-sustaining economy as unemployment remained constant and a threat to attaining a higher quality of life collectively.

Consistent with its mission from the previous decade, the Chicago Urban League took a leading role in the 1920s in advancing the interests of black labor. The organization reported, "In Chicago, there is diversified employment, to be sure, but there is a significantly heavier concentration in the basic industries; more than that, there are gradations of work from unskilled to skilled. In certain plants skilled workers increased from 3.5 per cent of the Negro working population in 1910 to 13.5 per cent in 1920 in Chicago."[6] The league then updated its assessment of the situation, reporting widespread unemployment among African Americans, while at the same time announcing a scarcity of workers in the South along with receipt of pleas from whites in that region for black workers to return to their former homes.[7]

Behind the picture of business expansion, the specter of unemployment worsened. By March 1921, the number of unemployed reached 15,000. One jobseeker was told by a white businessman who operated in the Black Metropolis, "If you want a job, go to Garvey!"[8] The situation was so dismal that the *Chicago Defender* considered telling persons anticipating migration to Chicago to remain in the South.[9] Absorbing a labor force of this size would have been an insurmountable task, so even heightened racial pride in the existence of two new economic institutions, the Liberty Life Insurance Company and the Binga State Bank, could not affect the needs of such a mass.

Charles S. Johnson observed at the beginning of the decade, as did Carroll Binder, Alma Herbst, Claude A. Barnett, and E. Franklin Frazier at its end, that this period nevertheless offered a ray of light in regard to labor opportunities for this workforce that was now transforming and filling with industrial workers. Employment in this sphere meant higher wages and a chance for black individuals and especially families to improve the quality of their lives in Chicago. A more balanced account of the meaning of these developments to this halcyon view emanated from a historical perspective two generations removed from the contemporary scene. The narrative and analysis of historian Arvarh E. Strickland in 1967 explored a sphere where yesterday's labor hero was a latter day's problem as a competitor for work.

While the Chicago Urban League and the Illinois Free Employment Bureau properly claimed credit for this breakthrough in employment and wage earning, maintaining it depended on good relations with the giants of the industrial world in meatpacking, steel, and other firms in heavy industry. This complicated the issue of unionism—to support it or oppose it. Recently arrived migrant laborers were a godsend for employers in meatpacking and steel, who wished to neutralize the growth and power of organized labor as the migrant from the wartime influx served as a bulwark to unified, collective labor organizing. Feelings of hostilities between blacks who had experienced antiblack animus and unscrupulous maneuvers by union leadership as well as hostility and condescension from rank-and-file white unionists themselves remained strong. Moreover, antiunion black workers represented a source of strikebreakers in the event that labor staged walkouts. Progressive-era reform thinking found a solution that relegated freedom of choice and movement as paramount to the migrants' dilemma—remain north and be manipulated or return south and be exploited. The migrants should stay.[10]

Packinghouse and Other Industrial Workers

The arrival of thousands of African American workers into the slaughterhouses during the war introduced black labor with no background to a highly organized and industrialized work world in which they had to learn new skills and immediately adopt new attitudes toward work. At one point during the war, the percentage of black workers reached an extreme level of 70 to 80 percent of all workers in Chicago packinghouses.[11] Of greater significance, Johnson described a situation in the slaughtering houses in which there were actually more semiskilled black workers who found employment than unskilled ones.[12] In terms of actual numbers, Frederick H. H. Robb late in the decade reported on totals of 6,580 black industrial workers divided among the Armour (2,084), Swift (2,278), Wilson (818), Morris (1,400), and Libby, McNeil, and Libby workforces.[13] The Chicago Urban League meanwhile gave its assessment of 8,000 workers.[14] About the same time Binder reported, "At least 30 per cent of the labor force in Chicago packing plants is Colored. Negroes hold important posts in the employee representation plans or company unions at Armour's, Swift's and the other plants."[15]

The experience of blacks on the "killing floors" placed them in a pivotal place in the dissembling operation of meat processing. This was the choke point from which the flow of the processing line was controlled. Skill and precision with the cutting knife were essential in this labor-intensive work environment, and more and more blacks qualified as butchers through the years, growing to represent a formidable component of a unified labor force. Labor historians Halpern and Horowitz cited the case of Jesse Vaughn, who began his career as a hog driver within the stockyards when he arrived in Chicago in 1924. "At that time, racial tension and prejudice ran high, and an informal white job trust restricted black workers to low-paying, menial positions. 'Them Poles wouldn't let you use no knife, not no black,' he recalled. Within a few years, though, Vaughn held one of the top jobs on the kill[ing floor]—thanks to a sympathetic Irish foreman who taught him the necessary butchering skills during breaks. Skilled black butchers like Vaughn could earn as much or more money than many black professionals in the 1930s."[16]

Unfortunately, the status of the black packinghouse worker was as precarious after the war as it had been before the Great Migration that had transformed these workers into desirable members of the labor force. Layoffs accompanied the end of hostilities in Europe and white workers resumed their dominant prewar positions and numbers. When African Americans joined unions such as the dominant Amalgamated Meat Cutter and Butcher Workmen of North America (AMCBW), the move enhanced their position within the ranks of packinghouse workers. More than one black worker felt like the white woman worker who stated, "while her work made her feel like a slave, union membership 'gave her dignity.'"[17] The distrust of the unions from the previous decades seemed to be lessening, as even the *Chicago Defender* began to urge a conciliatory tone toward unionization and consider struggling alongside whites for a "common cause and common destiny" as a basically working-class community.[18]

For those African American workers who refused to embrace unionism, with or without independent black labor organizer Richard Parker's urgings, their antiunion attitude related to many complex factors involving racism and previous negative experiences in the workplace. Basic distrust of whites and the union concept assumed too important a role. When the more urban acclimated, northern black worker entered the stockyards at the bottom of the work hierarchy, in general, he stayed at the bottom—unlike the various white ethnic groups that had preceded him.[19] Then unfamiliarity with organized labor's ideals and individual self-interest played their parts. Just as various immigrant groups with agrarian backgrounds had to be acclimated to industrialized, urban life and the notion of collective action, so it was with blacks in this phase of their national experience in the modernizing North. Then there was the antiunion rhetoric, fueled both by racial chauvinism and the influence of white paternalism, emanating from the street corners, restaurants, churches, and social service agencies of the Black Metropolis.

Importantly, once again the role of the black worker as a strikebreaker assumed its previously important role in the meatpacking industry. The role of the strikebreaker had always played an important role in meatpacker upper-level strategy as a controlling device over its extant workforce. The Irish and Germans had weakened the position of the members of the original white, Anglo-Saxon, Protestant (WASP) workforce, so that at the turn of the century the Slavic and black workers were used to undermining the position of the predecessor groups. Now with some black and huge numbers of ethnic white workers filling the ranks of the packinghouse labor force, the southern black worker (as opposed to his assimilated northern brethren) became a tool for the manipulation of the labor force. The disadvantages of life in the racist South had prepared black labor to jump at any chance for advancement, regardless of the collateral costs to any other group. Survival in both the moment and posterity was at stake. Accustomed to appealing to a dominant white on the plantation—or in the village or town, for that matter—African Americans in the South were reduced to sustaining themselves at a slavelike level even after the war. Moreover, in never having worked for sustainable wages and having developed a labor consciousness like northern workers, while suffering from a deficient level of racial consciousness, the southern laborer made an ideal pawn for the packers.[20]

Meanwhile, the influence of the Big Four packers—Armour (which acquired ownership of Morris in 1923), Swift, Wilson, and Cudahy—remained high in a northern black community like Chicago as the packers continued their support of African American churches and charities. In a similar manner to the Pullman porters' efforts to build popular support in 1925 and years thereafter, the paternalistic hold that large white economic concerns had on the black community assumed a dominant and controlling aura.

As the meatpackers acted in early 1921 to maximize their profits at their workers' expense, they proposed a reduction in wages accompanied by a return to a ten-hour day. The AMCBW exerted as much influence as it could to retain the loyalty of black workers who had been unionized during and after the war. At a large unity meeting held either in October or November 1921 that was attended by 600 black laborers at the famed Unity Hall, 3140 South Indiana Avenue, the benefits of unionization were stressed and supported by Oscar DePriest, Irene Goins, independent church leader Rev. William D. Cook, and two representatives of the Pullman porters (representing their pre-BSCP membership days).[21] Pressed by the meat companies, no doubt buoyed now with both black and ethnic white support, an overconfident AMCBW then led the union to call for a strike on December 5, 1921. In an attempt to gauge and hopefully ensure the black workers' support, African American unionists visited fifteen different churches on the eve of the strike and found pro-packers sermons being preached at all but one.[22]

Continuing as a major influence was black labor organizer Richard Parker, whose American Unity Labor Union kept its promise of not abandoning the black worker during the postwar period. This union—along with his American Negro Protective League and his newspaper, the *Chicago Advocate*—continued to promote his position on and publish his perspective of the labor situation. When the AMCBW was developing its strategy on a December 1921 strike, Parker advised against it and contacted the packers, advising them that 6,000 black workers in the stockyards would not strike at the behest of a white-led union. In fact, there was neither that number of black workers in the yards nor any more than 100 men listening to Parker's plan. In and of itself, Parker's idea had points that were appealing. While accepting the wage reduction—Parker allowed 20 percent for skilled workers and 10 percent for the unskilled—he insisted on retention of an eight-hour workday, overtime pay, and only a one-year agreement in regard to the wage cut.[23] With the strike in full bloom, the lack of black support became evident, but worse, the packers issued an additional call for southern laborers. The appeal reached responsive ears eager for a chance to simultaneously leave the South, to improve conditions for themselves and their families, and to finally work for decent wages. Swift recruited heavily and successfully doubled the number of African American workers in its plants from 16 percent of its 1921 total to more than 33 percent; another company among the Big Five (the Big Four by 1923) increased its total from 25 to 33 percent.[24]

In the North, circumstances made Chicago inviting as the 1921 stockyard strike led to the call once again for southern labor. For former Atlantans Alex W. and Julia Gates Walker, former service-sector workers and survivors of the infamous riot of 1906, postriot life in Birmingham, Alabama, had seemed more promising as he entered the industrial workforce at Bessemer Steel. Walker, whose armed defense of his family and home during the Atlanta racial catastrophe had earned him a prison term after being convicted of killing a white member of a violent mob, fourteen years of residence and work in Birmingham still offered few chances for real economic advancement. Not only Alex, but his wife, Julia, answered the call to come north and work in the packinghouses. Together, they joined two adult children who had already arrived in the city and were working as Pullman porters. Now it was their turn to enter the Chicago workforce as strikebreakers and begin a lifetime of Chicago residency.[25] Meanwhile, another southern family responded positively to the call to migrate, one destined to contribute mightily to Chicago's culture through their renowned musical prodigy, Herbie Hancock. The Hancocks arrived as a family unit from Atlanta under the leadership of their father, who immediately sought work as a strikebreaker at the Cudahy packinghouse.[26]

In the aftermath of the strike, Herbst wrote that since 1921, the percentage of blacks working in the packinghouses fluctuated around 30 percent.[27] The strike lasted only two months and ended in the unionized workers' defeat. As a result, the unions were demoralized and according to Spero and Harris, they were "driven from the yards."[28]

In the Black Metropolis, the new workers were looked upon as persons who increased the consumer base, expanded the electorate, reunited family and friendship networks, filled the churches with ebullient Christians, and added manpower in the event of another racial confrontation. The *Chicago Defender* spoke for many on the issues of strikebreaking and group economic survival. It published this rationale:

> The prospect of a job in these times of near-starvation looks good to any idle worker, black or white. Self-preservation is the first law of nature; add to this knowledge that such opportunities only come to the black worker on occasions like this and it can be readily seen why he fills the union worker's place. It is an ill wind that blows no one good, and while there is much to be said in favor of unionism, the powers that be must be made to realize that no strike can be effective in this country unless the black worker is part and parcel of it. To make him a part of it[,] it is necessary that he be taken unreservedly into every trades union. Unions cannot expect to close the working door in his face in peaceful times and expect his co-operation in troublesome times. They must be consistent.[29]

African Americans who entered as strikebreakers remained on the job as important production workers whose racial numbers continued to rise until the decade's end. Overall, by 1930, 4,500 black packinghouse workers were on the job, with close to half classified as semiskilled.[30]

Elsewhere in industry, in the area of steel production, African Americans had arrived from the South with knowledge of working in this field, although traditionally in the most arduous and dangerous positions. Alex W. Walker of Birmingham had this experience; so did Timuel D. Black Jr.'s father. In Chicago, this tradition of limited opportunities and placement in unsafe conditions continued. "The number of iron molders increased from 31 in 1910 to 520 in 1920, and this latter number represents 10 percent of all the iron molders."[31] One of largest producers, the Illinois Steel Works, increased the size of its workforce from 7 in 1910 before the Great Migration, to 35 during the migration, to 1,209 in 1919 at its closing phase. The postwar recession saw those numbers fluctuate downward to 338 and upward again to 1,014.

The famous steel strike of 1920 found 85 percent of all black steel workers walking off the job with their white co-workers, but without the lifelines of union and community support that came with a desire for true fraternity in the workplace and proximity to home. In the latter case, with the steel production facilities located on the city's far southeastern-most section and nearer the lake (in the so-called East Side), most African Americans, who lived in segregated residential neighborhoods, had long distances to travel of up ten to twelve miles. Unlike their white counterparts, who usually found housing accommodations near their jobs, blacks lived in the South Side's transformed Black Belt, now the Black Metropolis.

During the 1920 strike, for those blacks who were experiencing unemployment farther north in the city in the Black Metropolis, the appeal from the companies for workers, even as strikebreakers, proved too attractive and at least 600 men were recruited immediately from along the State Street Stroll and within other points of the black community. With a solid relationship already in place between the steel producers and the major social service institutions of the Black Metropolis, a typical pattern of easy access to the South Side's abundant supply of labor was revealed. "Big steel" had made substantial donations to the Chicago Urban League and Provident Hospital over the years, similar to their donations in the various immigrant communities.[32] For his part, labor leader Samuel Gompers made the unsubstantiated claim that 30,000 African Americans were brought from outside the Chicago area, thereby inflaming tensions that had already reached a boiling point.[33] Since the supply of men willing to work under any circumstances exceeded demand, in the case of this strike in this industry, there was no wholesale attempt, nor a need, to import outside workers from the South.[34]

Unfortunately, the economic fate of these men followed a familiar path in American labor relations as the manipulation of Labor by Capital meant that all of the temporary workers lost their jobs with the return of the members of the permanent workforce. If there was a bright spot in the steel industry at the close of the decade of the 1920s, the foothold gained in the previous period held firm as the average annual number of black workers employed was now 600.[35] Another plus was to be found in the growth of Chicago's industrial proletariat, which advanced slowly beyond meatpacking and steel into the chemical industry.[36]

The Pullman Porters Organize

In other industries and service areas, workers persisted in their demands for better working conditions along with higher wages and benefits. Pullman porters moved to protect their rights as workers, paralleling the experience of the first, large mass of African Americans who entered the industrial sector as packinghouse workers. Although they were being overshadowed by sheer numbers in black Chicago's workforce by packinghouse workers, the image and aura of the elegantly attired, manly Pullman porters accorded them attention beyond their actual circle of influence in Chicago. With the rise of their union in 1925, the Brotherhood of Sleeping Car Porters and Maids (BSCP), representing the first, large-scale, independent attempt at black unionization in the nation, their imprint in the popular imagination soared again. Historian William H. Harris, in his examination of the leadership of the BSCP, found that they "commanded attention out of proportion to the relative importance of the 12,000 service employees at Pullman compared to the total black work force, especially when at one time the union had fewer than 700 members."[37] Yet the BSCP earned a historical importance, in context, through its struggle and its culminating victory for union recognition by the Pullman Company in 1937. This triumph for black labor signaled that a new era had begun for African American labor and group advancement.

In Chicago, if indeed the BSCP presented the brightest light in securing a future for the African American worker within the American labor movement with Chicago's vast army of railroad employees, it had to come *internally* through a demonstration of effective organization of railroad porters, waiters, and maids who were willing to support the BSCP and reject the Employee Representation Plan sponsored by the Pullman Company, and *externally* by successfully gaining access to and entry into the conventional economic channels of labor advancement. The porters did not want to destroy the Pullman Company; they sought better working conditions and recognition as integral parts of the company.[38] Specifically, this required acknowledgment from the American Federation of Labor (AFL) of the BSCP's claim to being a bona fide labor organization representing a majority of the workforce, an accommodation with the Big Four railroad brotherhoods, and support at the federal level from both the legislative and executive branches of government. Finally, the major factor in recognizing success in the long struggle for BSCP permanence and effectiveness involved recognition as the legitimate bargaining agent for this segment of railroad workers by the Pullman Company, a long-earned triumph realized in the succeeding decade in 1937.

Overall on the Chicago labor scene, it appeared as if labor advancement would be the result of the Chicago Urban League's efforts that had focused on the industrial sphere where packinghouse workers and others employed in manufacturing seemed to be making a solid, but slow, headway. Yet the seemingly endless struggle of the Pullman porters and other railroad employees to obtain decent hours and pay increases had gone on unabatedly, although without notable progress. A breakthrough came when Pullman porters organized the Brotherhood of Sleeping Car Porters (BSCP) in New York in August 1925.

The formation of the BSCP represented the culmination of decades of legitimate labor complaints as well as individual and collective actions against the Pullman Company and its oppressive work practices. Long hours, company spying, and low pay, necessitating a reliance on tipping and feigned obsequiousness, remained as established, generational indignities to be suffered by these workers.

The logical consequence of prolonged struggle and a search for an effective outlet beyond the timid organizations that preceded the BSCP was for a newer, more militant approach to match the times. As A. Philip Randolph, destined to be their leader, pointed out, "You no longer have the wooden car, no longer have you the typical porter. That porter has passed and a new porter has come into being. He is urbanized; he is industrialized, subject to this standardized civilization, and he is thinking through this new medium and it is organized labor."[39]

A group of five porters, including the legendary organizer of porters Ashley L. Tottten, won some popular support for the BSCP at its inception in the East. They even induced an articulate young socialist idealist in regard to labor, A. Philip Randolph, to assume the presidency. The new chief executive immediately surrounded himself with able men such as Totten and Chicago's Milton P. Webster, who proved an effective spokesmen in the labor arena.[40] But initial success in New York did not equate with a support base in the heart of Pullman operations, Chicago. With the epicenter of both Pullman Company operations and expansive Pullman porter residency being Chicago and Chicago's Black Metropolis, respectively, activities toward the workers' advancement shifted geographically to the South Side. Part of the struggle would be fought as well at the federal level legally, legislatively, and juridically at the nation's capital.

Amid the "diversified interests" in Chicago—jazz and blues, sports, unskilled and semiskilled labor organizing in the stockyards, self-indulgence and self-promotion, group salvation sought through nationalistic means, early planning for black participation in the upcoming World's Fair in 1933 (the "A Century of Progress" exposition), to name only several—any serious, militant-appearing labor organization could anticipate obstacles before capturing the time and attention of workers and the public in general. Furthermore, Chicago in 1925 was full of opposition to an independent workers' union of this type particularly because of the Pullman Company's history of close association and support for every worthwhile charitable and community effort on the South Side.

Acting out of self-interest, many individuals and institutions adopted what historian Beth Tompkins Bates has described as the "don't bite the hand that feeds you" syndrome.[41] Although the targets of the organizing efforts of the BSCP were the porters, maids, and dining car waiters, the community played a role in that any hesitation among the workers could be neutralized, if not eliminated, through third-party pressure to accept the BSCP and its program as *the* way for labor advancement. At the time, many porters themselves doubted the wisdom of challenging a labor system that seemed to benefit them, as they had adopted many bourgeois values that had them being considered as "the aristocrats of black labor."[42]

In addition, the churches, financial institutions, politicians, and political organizations—and even Provident Hospital and the Wabash YMCA—belonged to a network of groups and institutions dependent on the Pullman Company for a portion of their organizational survival, placing the BSCP at a distinct disadvantage.[43] For their part as guides to a brighter future, the titans over the Black Metropolis's political economy—Abbott, Binga, Overton, Wright, DePriest—failed as they withheld their sympathy and support. Although this dependency ran contrary to New Negro thinking, it remained a reality of life.

As early as 1920, T. Arnold Hill had enunciated the Chicago Urban League's position as being one of opposition to separate unions "because he feared that 'whites and blacks organized in separate unaffiliated bodies will, sooner or later, be on opposite sides of some important labor issue which ought to affect all alike.'"[44] The possible loss of what the race had won through so many sacrifices played a role in this thinking as well. Ideologically, this explained one position.

Another and rather unflatteringly link showed its head when the black churches were encountered. These religious bodies had traditionally always enjoyed an interdependent relationship with prominent, old-line Protestant whites and had always appeared eternally grateful for the linkage. Worst, to the churchgoers, was Randolph's reputation for being godless and antichurch. Randolph, in fact, was the son of an AME minister and often resorted to biblical references in his speeches.[45] There were other factors to consider as to the nature of church opposition. Anti-BSCP porters who had positions as pillars of their church could influence a congregation as much as some ministers. Then, Bishop Archibald A. Carey Sr., now a pastor in rotation at the Quinn Chapel AME Church, represented a case worth examining. Positively, Carey dispensed jobs whenever they were available at the Pullman Company works, along with summer porter positions on the trains. Negatively, Carey opposed the BSCP to the extent that he forbade AME congregations from allowing the BSCP message to be heard.[46]

The case of major African American newspapers, which formed another formidable wellspring of opposition bloc, lent itself to another explanation, one that was unfavorable to their image as unselfish race saviors.[47] The *Chicago Defender*, which for two decades had been on the side of black progress, now was situated as a major impediment as it performed as a propaganda tool for the company. Renamed by the BSCP as the "Surrender" and the "World's Greatest Weakly," two major developments determined the *Defender*'s stance, both related to its financial status.[48] Direct economic considerations played a major part in Abbott's collaboration with the Pullman Company, as he served on Jesse Binga's bank board and participated in a money shift of $10,000 from the Pullman Porters' Benefit Association of America into the bank's vault during the 1920s. A. Philip Randolph remembered a friendly Abbott late in the twenties opening the *Defender*'s books to him and seeing the amount of Pullman-directed funds benefitting the newspaper. Previous to this gesture, an internal administrative change within the *Defender*'s hierarchy by the time the BSCP was organized had seen Abbott relinquish control of the paper to his brother-in-law and general counsel, Nathan S. McGill. It was McGill who chose to side openly with Pullman and against the BSCP after years of *Defender* support for the porters' cause. His motivation was financial and supposedly carried out in the interests of the paper to reverse the extravagant spending of Abbott as he maintained his upper-class standing.[49] Two events occurred of immense importance to the course the *Defender* would take in the future. Randolph confronted the paper's temporary leader McGill both in Chicago and New York about the paper's antilabor stance with the threat of a porters' boycott. Then, upon Abbott's return to the helm of the paper's operations and McGill's dismissal over finances and administration, the *Defender* ended its policy of opposition to the BSCP through silence by late 1927, thereby furthering the labor organization's cause.

The *Chicago Whip* had built an early reputation for independence also, but it also proved susceptible to its financial links to the Pullman Company. Brazeal wrote of a financial deal witnessed by Oscar DePriest in which 55 percent of the newspaper's stock was assigned to a Pullman Company representative.[50] On a personal level, Randolph proved an easy target for the opposition. The intellectual Randolph embraced socialism, which opened him up to smears of being a "red," "socialist," "Bolshevik," or "communist." Since the paper's leadership embraced the economic status quo, it came as no surprise that it reproached Randolph with the conservative-sounding comment "[T]he black people at large should align themselves as far as possible with the wealthier classes in America."[51] In entering into direct conflict with the BSCP's aims, the *Whip* received an equal amount of resistance from Randolph directly through the pages of the *Messenger*.[52]

The *Chicago Bee*, under Anthony Overton's control, proved equally susceptible to financial pressures. "For a while, the *Chicago Bee* . . . criticized the *Defender* for capitulating to the Pullman Company. But it, too, eventually succumbed and joined the opposition to Randolph."[53] A lesser news sheet, *Heebie Jeebies*, produced by Claude A. Barnett, who headed the Associated Negro Press, also joined the propaganda war while supposedly remaining an apolitical, theatrical review. In sum, under obvious pressure from the Pullman Company, the black titans with the stalwart New Negro mentality reverted to traits that historian Beth Tompkins Bates has referred to as "Old Negro," "Old Guard," or "Old Crowd."[54]

Not to be overlooked was the emergence of new source of opposition in the fledgling Communist Party (CPUSA). Beginning in 1925 with its support for a breakthrough in labor by way of the American Negro Labor Congress, within three years the CPUSA acted on its latest directive from Moscow to attack Randolph and the BSCP as irrelevant and dangerous to the real interests of working people. As demonstrable evidence, the CPUSA cited the BSCP's failure to follow through on a threatened strike scheduled for June 1928. This criticism of the BSCP could have been expected given the fact that the BSCP was seen as reformist and therefore basically supportive of the America capitalist system, whereas the CPUSA instead demanded a revolutionary approach.[55]

On a rhetorical level, Randolph could fight back—as well he did against all critics—through the pages of the *Messenger*. This intellectually charged monthly journal featured not only Randolph but also a spate of writers who provided an effective counterthrust to critics until it ended publication in late 1928 because of financial reasons. In contrast to their black counterparts, the white newspapers and labor organizations in Chicago generally looked upon the BSCP with favor. The local radio outlet of labor, WCFL, "the Voice of Labor," generously opened its facilities to the BSCP.[56]

Local success in organizing required a familiarity with potential recruits, along with a flair for attracting people to the message and cause. As articulate and charismatic as the energetic, thirty-six-year-old Randolph was, he was an outsider to the largest community of porters within the rail network. This factor provided another in a series of reasons as to why Randolph and the BSCP met opposition and resistance in a setting that annually welcomed conferences and conventions filled with temporary sojourners as well as migrants seeking permanent residence. Part of the character of black Chicago contained strains of parochialism, a trait noted by E. Franklin Frazier, which stood in vivid contrast to the city's other shared image of cosmopolitanism. Clustering around family and friends from the same plantation, town, city, and county in a city of various self-contained neighborhoods, a Chicago porter described his first impression of Randolph as "fast-talking New Yorker."[57]

So, the key to Chicago's organization was the proper use of a local voice such as Milton P. Webster. The latter proved to be an indispensable component of an indigenous leadership necessary to supplement Randolph's effective national charisma. Importantly, he was constant as Randolph's friend and this was a relationship that never wavered.[58] "Despite their reverence for Randolph, most porters, especially those in Chicago, looked on Webster as one of their own."[59] Neither the oppressive labor demands placed on porters nor leadership requirements posed any new challenge to Webster. From his previous service as a porter to his identifiable youth leadership as colonel in a neighborhood component of an 8th Regiment auxiliary group—the Marshall Chapter, named for the regimental commander in Mexico and France—Webster proved a good choice.[60] His involvement loomed as huge because he could personalize the porters' struggle with his porter's background and connect viscerally with the workers and their families, along with the greater black community. In 1918, he served as an officer in the Railway Men's Association and won a wage increase for all porters.[61]

His persona and local ties in being a true Chicagoan—assertiveness, competitiveness, previous Pullman ties, current Republican Party connections, and literally with big shoulders on his huge, imposing physical frame—meant that if all politics was local, including protest politics, Webster began this transformation of community attitudes and opinions with a great advantage.[62] At age thirty-eight years, he was Randolph's age mate and a man equal to Randolph in his commitment to the cause, yet different in temperament and demeanor. One biographer, Jervis Anderson, described him thus: "He was blunt-speaking, gruff, had a formidable-looking head, and with a cigar frequently in his mouth, seemed like a man who was most at home in the backrooms of political clubhouses. His stern face inspired fear, and declared its owner to be a man who fed on power and who was guided by the philosophy that 'you get nowhere unless you push people out of the way.' 'He was not a college man . . . but he was smart.'"[63]

Almost typical of so many black Chicagoans during this period, his thirst for independence even led him to consider pushing within the BSCP for greater autonomy from New York.[64] In his politics he was a Republican, but he did not belong to the South Side wards that were under the control of the Wright organization in the Black Metropolis. Rather, his affiliation was farther south in the white-dominated Sixth Ward organization, from which he secured a patronage position as a Cook County sheriff's bailiff. As for his growing into his administrative responsibilities, he was destined to emerge as first vice president of the BSCP.

The presence of Webster allowed the BSCP to engage in its most effective strategic maneuver and the one that dealt the biggest blow to the opposition. It came when the BSCP adopted a community-based strategy that reflected the influence and power of racial consciousness among the various special-interest spheres within the Black Metropolis. This approach validated the local definition of a New Negro (as enunciated by Frederick H. H. Robb) as one who avoided the philanthropy of a Pullman or a Rosenwald in pursuit of an independent course of action. Robb was impressed enough with the BSCP to write that the BSCP "has made more strides than most groups in Chicago. . . . [T]he time has come when Negro organizations should aid in advancing their cause instead of hindering it."[65] Furthermore, this approach ran consistent with the truly historical assertion of NAACP official Robert W. Bagnall in 1925 that this new way thinking and personality in black Chicago represented a complete transformation in race relations. Without a doubt, "there has been a revolutionary change in the psychology of the Negro. He now will work with whites or permit them to work with him; but he resents it when they work for him—he being their ward. He wants to control to a large degree, his own affairs." Coincidentally, his assessment defined the BSCP philosophy perfectly. At the same time, Bagnall's power of perception might have been shaped by the sympathetic views the NAACP held of the BSCP.[66]

According to historian Beth Tompkins Bates, the paradigm for advancing this approach from assertion and concept to actualization lay in the emphasis Randolph and his lieutenants placed on the concept of manhood and citizenship rights that would be attainable through the success of a thrust such as that which the BSCP proposed.[67] It was, of course, as much a case of tapping into the extant sentiment of the community and moving past the long-simmering memory of slavery not just as a historical tragedy but as a contemporary threat in the workplace. The specter of present-day slavery through debt peonage in the South and industrial and service-sector exploitation in the North pervaded thought with a perpetual resonance. On more than one occasion, A. Philip Randolph hit this responsive chord to black ears when he lambasted slavery, as he did in the *Messenger* in 1926 as cited by Bates.[68] And still, he referred to this labor horror as he mentioned that while Abraham Lincoln had emancipated the slaves from chattel slavery, his son, Robert Todd Lincoln, as president of the Pullman Company, "has bent his influence and name to the notorious exploitation of Negroes as *Pullman slaves*."[69] Again, in an essay he wrote for a transformed and supportive *Chicago Defender* in 1929, Randolph sounded much like Ida B. Wells-Barnett in 1893 in the famed, Columbian-era, protest pamphlet. Randolph wrote that "The dominant aspect of the Negroes' entrance into the Americas was that of a worker. . . . Upon their labor . . . was built the slave power of the South. . . . The development of the textile industries of the world is largely traceable to the exploitation of Negro slave labor. . . . Negro slaves . . . yearned for freedom. . . . History repeats itself today. Pullman porters are risking their jobs for industrial freedom by joining the brotherhood. Slavery was abolished. The porters, too, will win."[70] The BSCP had in effect adopted the agenda of fighting for uplift of their race, for their freedom, and for their manhood while they pursued the end of eliminating economic exploitation and the start of workers' independence.

Ironically, one of the most important paths to building mass support for this basically male organization was through the support of the women of the race. Almost immediately, women within the BSCP organized within their own ranks under the banner of the Chicago Colored Women's Economic Council. The ranks of the council were composed of the wives and relatives of porters who were expected to raise money for union activities and for assistance to the victims of Pullman Company reprisals. Likewise, they kept the membership and community informed about union events. The wives of porters could talk freely when their husbands could not, especially at public meetings.[71] While a near-contemporary observer, economist Brailsford R. Brazeal, emphasized the roles of wives, relatives, and friends of the porters, most recently historian Bates has emphasized the role of *organized* black women who belonged to the federated women's organizations and clubs.[72] The presence of an aging, but still vital, Ida B. Wells-Barnett at sixty-five years proved essential to the success of securing the Chicago base of the BSCP, according to twentieth-century historians Beth Tompkins Bates and Paula Giddings.[73] Wells-Barnett's avid admirer, social worker and pro-labor activist Irene McCoy Gaines, proved an especially important addition to the ranks of supporters of the BSCP. Gaines was also the wife of Republican politician Harris B. Gaines, a beneficiary of the very patronage politics the organized women purportedly opposed. In any event, Irene McCoy Gaines's credentials in behalf of labor, along with her membership in the Chicago Women's Trade Union League, proved invaluable.[74]

The first attempt to garner community support ended in failure in October 1925 when only the host minister at the Metropolitan Community Church, Rev. William D. Cook, appeared and participated among five ministers invited. Webster evaluated the situation for what it was. Secondary to convincing porters of the value of the BSCP to their lives and their families, popular support (meant to indirectly influence them) was missing and had to be won from the public in an environment where neither a black labor titan nor influential organization prevailed.[75] A year later, by October 1926, the idea of building a grassroots base of support for the BSCP bore fruit as hundreds of people jammed newly arrived Chicagoan Rev. Junius C. Austin's independent, racially conscious, Pilgrim Baptist Church pews. Among the city's black Baptist churches, Pilgrim retained its independence as a member of its denomination as well as its community. It was on the way to emerging as a competitor for Christian souls with Olivet Baptist, the megachurch of its day with a claim to 10,000 congregants.[76] Meanwhile, before Rev. J. C. Austin arrived in 1926, Pilgrim had already claimed Ferdinand L. Barnett as a member (although his wife had switched affiliation again from Grace Presbyterian Church and transferred her membership to the newly established Metropolitan Community Church). Mrs. Wells-Barnett had chosen to worship with the iconoclastic Dr. William D. Cook, late of the AME faith. This became an important factor in the next year's mass meeting, as now two of the most iconoclastic churches in the Black Metropolis declared themselves to be pro-BSCP supporters, who could now always secure a large meeting place when other doors were closed.

With a full year of pressure politics at the mass, activist level, a shift in public opinion and support was readily apparent. At the conclusion of the 1926 meeting, both Randolph and Webster were convinced that a corner had been turned and that now a level of enthusiasm reigned among porters and the public that meant smoother sailing.[77] This emerging victory allowed the BSCP to examine its accomplishments free of early anxiety and in relative tranquility. "Believing that money was all powerful, our detractors boasted glibly that we would soon be in the vest pocket of Pullman. But they reckoned without cognizance of the force of the idealism of the New Negro. They knew not of the rise of a newer spirit within the race which placed principles, ideals and convictions above dollars."[78] This new atmosphere of building support represented only a phase in the BSCP's upward climb to labor recognition of the union's relevance in achieving a just result for porters and others. Yet remnants of the old opposition remained. Just a month after the successful community meeting at Pilgrim, the BSCP's rival, the Pullman Porters' Benefit Association of America (PPBAA) held its annual conference in Chicago and praised the Pullman Company. As the *Defender* reported, the conferees "voiced their loyalty to the company." Purportedly, at the same time, banker Jesse Binga questioned the BSCP's challenge to labor's already beneficial arrangement with Pullman. Binga had another incentive to offer in the form of promises of loans and mortgages to porters who belonged to the company-friendly union, the PPBAA.[79]

This shift in labor sentiment in the Black Metropolis possibly reflected a transformation in political power arrangements, coinciding with Edward H. Wright's fall from power after a clash with former Mayor "Big Bill" Thompson. Since the black Republican political organization of the South Side acted as a "patron of minority groups and a broker for business," it could be assumed that Wright had exhibited no public sympathy for the BSCP.[80] And then there was the lobby of the Appomattox Club, which featured a portrait of George M. Pullman, so some link between the company and an anti-BSCP stance seemed obvious. At this juncture of South Side politics, Dan Jackson replaced Wright as leader of the Second Ward and symbol of Wright's loss of control over politics in the Black Metropolis. Meanwhile, Oscar DePriest resurfaced in the public spotlight as the political powerhouse over patronage over the Third Ward and heir apparent to the Black Metropolis's political machine. Whatever direct effect Wright's removal from the political scene had or did not have in opening a breach in the wall of opposition is unknown. However, since the popular and opportunistic DePriest, who was friendly with Webster, seemed to be in the thick of every street-level struggle for black progress, he might well have played a positive part in the change in the community's attitude.

In any event, another mass meeting was held at Metropolitan Community Church in October 1927. The results were even more favorable and in the aftermath, a total shift was noticeable as the Chicago Citizens' Committee formed with the influential civic and community leader Dr. George Cleveland Hall now firmly supporting the organization.[81] Coincidentally, it was at this point as well that the *Chicago Defender* formally changed its stance and not only started to report on the activities of the BSCP but also carried Randolph's column on union activities. Growth in the BSCP's membership was apparent, as it reported that its membership rolls had reached 5,700, with Chicago boasting 1,100 members. Unfortunately, many were delinquent in their dues.

Cementing the bond between community and labor organization, in 1929 Chicago played host to the annual convention of the BSCP. It was at this meeting that Webster emerged as near co-equal to Randolph as the BSCP constitution and organizational structure were changed and power divided. New York was the loser as Webster was elevated from a divisional leader and elected first vice president and chair of the executive board.[82] Other attempts at achieving advances came, although incrementally. Nonetheless, they provided the necessary conditions for BSCP success. These involved federal-level investigations, and legislation and executive bodies that produced results that the BSCP hoped optimistically, and sometimes naively, would be favorable to the BSCP's cause. Significantly, by May 8, 1929, Randolph and the BSCP won recognition and a charter from the American Federation of Labor (AFL).[83] At this juncture, the effects of the national economic downturn plagued the BSCP to the extent that total dues-paying membership dipped to 1,342 nationally and to 430 in its top division, Chicago.[84] Subsequent to this decline, membership within the BSCP succumbed to the worst days of economic depression when the membership rolls declined to less than one tenth this size during these acknowledged "dark days." While the BSCP continued to face internal dissension and external pressures, what the future wrought was anything but gloomy.[85] In its ultimate triumph, in 1936 at an overcrowded ceremony at the newly opened Du Sable High School (named after the Black Metropolis's ultimate hero who exemplified independence of spirit and success in accomplishments), AFL president William Green bestowed on the BSCP an international charter, and the BSCP achieved a monumental feat in becoming the legitimate bargaining agent for all railroad porters, dining car waiters, and maids. The BSCP now stood as co-equal with 105 other federal unions within the AFL. The lesson taught to black labor in the United States served as a stimulant to other workers' groups to trust the value of sustained, independent action while allowing for positive collaboration across racial and organizational lines whenever possible.

Postal Workers

United States postal workers represented another group within the ranks of labor that enjoyed a level of relative wage and job stability among African Americans, resulting in both pride and envy. Considered a haven in a world of intense job discrimination, "the post office was a microcosm of society as a whole. For the most part, blacks associated with blacks, both on and off the workroom floor and whites did likewise. There did not seem to be any open hostility between the races. They just seemed to go their separate ways."[86] The blacks who held their positions had earned them through merit for the most part and they worked under favorable working conditions compared to other spheres of employment. The U.S. Postal Service employed over 25,000 black workers nationally by 1928—representing 9 percent of its total force—with the Chicago postal service having 31 percent of its workforce being African American (compared to New York's and Detroit's 16 percent).[87] Similar to the case with the Pullman force, Chicago indeed proved to be a workingman and -woman's town.

With a racist job ceiling in place, the ranks of the postal workers included some of the finest minds in the Black Metropolis. The highly educated and artistically talented, such as Cornelius Pierce (soon to be a distinguished artist and twin brother to America's first graduate in chemical engineering), along with physicians, lawyers, and members of other professions filled the work stations of the post office daily. Some were destined for unparalleled later success. Future Chicago postmaster Henry W. McGee was unaware of how challenging, successful, and fulfilling a career awaited him when he entered the postal service in 1929. The ambitious young nineteen-year-old Texan was soon working and attending Crane Junior College on the city's West Side with the likes of Cab Calloway and future legal giant Robert Ming. Given a chance to work inside the main post office building in downtown Chicago, he tackled the perplexing and demanding "scheme." As described by McGee, "a scheme was a system which when mastered enabled a clerk to distribute mail by railroads to all 102 counties in Illinois. Each town in each county was listed on a small card and [an employee] had to pass an exam correctly distributing these cards. There were easier schemes like North and South Dakota and Utah, but Illinois, Pennsylvania, Ohio and other heavily populated states were more difficult. Whenever possible, blacks were given the more difficult schemes and whites were given the easier schemes. By this method, they could have some sections mostly black and others mostly white. I marveled at the ingenuity of those who practiced racism. They really had to work at it."[88] For another nineteen-year-old, future writer Richard Wright, the postal scheme represented an obstacle from hell, designed to push the worker to his limits of mental endurance.[89]

Blacks combated racism in a variety of ways, preferring the effective means of collective action. Organizing extended back into the early part of the century with separate racial groups such as the Phalanx Forum, but now included extensive memberships in larger multiracial postal unions. Economists Spero and Harris assesses their intent thus: "These groups do not pretend to take the place of the regular postal unions but merely aim to supplement their work [as well as] to consolidate the political power of the Negro worker and to guard his interests before the local postal officials."[90]

Municipal Workers

The city's municipal workers included many categories of workers, from the highly skilled and educated to those persons who were unskilled and subsequently fell prey to seasonal employment. Four hundred African Americans held civil service positions at the decade's end, out of a total city workforce of 30,000 workers. Another 300 held positions that weren't covered under civil service. Over 1,000 seasonal workers secured employment during the summer or during heavy winter snowfalls.[91] As to the distribution of which African Americans found *appointive* work, residents of the Second and Third Wards with strong political connections were favored.[92]

Members of the Chicago Fire Department—in particular, those serving with the historic Engine Company 21—who had been counted among the city's employee workforce since 1872, fared the worst in job advancement. Twenty-two blacks proudly donned the dark blue uniforms of the department, which consisted of one captain, one lieutenant, eighteen firemen, and two engineers.[93] An unwritten racial protocol relegated competent African Americans to assignment to the one firehouse in the city in the old Black Belt, giving silent testimony to the fact that the ideal of the Black Metropolis—power within producing respect and positive results without—had not been completely realized. Decades-long anguish at this injustice, coupled with an unrelenting campaign aimed at resolution, boiled over in the 1920s with political pressure being applied from the black aldermen onto the newly re-elected Mayor Thompson's shoulders in 1927.[94]

In his examination of the plight of firemen, Robinson found this arrangement prevailed in violation of the highest aims of civil service meritocracy:

> For over forty years, there has been a Negro fire company in Chicago, and the practice has been to appoint only Colored applicants to the Colored fire company. The practice is obviously discriminatory and perhaps illegal within the meaning of the Civil Service Act. But a devious method of circumventing the law was found whereby all Colored were appointed to the same company. Any person whose name is on the eligible register may "waive certification in cases where it (the Commission) considers the reasons given for such waiver as good and sufficient, and where it is desirable to keep a name of the eligible on the register from which the certification is made."
>
> A waiver may with permission be withdrawn in thirty days. The practice is thus: Whenever a vacancy occurs in the [Colored] company and the name of a Colored applicant is below those of white applicants, the Colored person secures waivers from all of the whites higher on the list, who relinquish their higher positions on the list until the certification is made, and then by withdrawing their waivers secure their former standing upon the register. Should a vacancy occur in one of the other [white] companies and a Negro's name be highest on the list, the Negro waives his appointment in order that the highest white may be appointed. . . . [S]hould one [Colored] insist upon certification to another company the certification would be made and that the Negro might accept the appointment. But . . . more than likely, he would not survive his probationary period of six months [because of retaliatory written reprimands and objections].[95]

With the mechanics of discrimination explained, it was left to renowned political scientist Harold F. Gosnell to describe in personal terms how this egregious practice functioned.

> One of the former Negro fire captains stated that after he had been in the department for a few years he took a lieutenant's examination. He was eleventh on the list. When it came time to appoint him, the fire marshal asked him to waive his right to appointment as there was no place for him in the Colored company. Twelve years passed and he was still waiting for his appointment. Finally under a Republican administration, one of the Colored assistant corporation counsels who was a friend of his wife's sister-in-law 'went to the front' for him and he was appointed as a lieutenant. When he took the examination for the captaincy one of the Colored alderman, a friend of the fire marshal supported his candidacy and there was no trouble.[96]

In contrast, the Chicago Police Department included 113 sworn officers, in whose ranks were to counted three lieutenants and seven sergeants.[97] The number of black policemen increased due partially to the ability of the Chicago Police Department to assign its African American officers into an expanding black territorial base. During this period, only one woman served as a police officer.

Women in the Work Force

The solitary figure of a woman in the police department represented accurately the limitations placed on women in the workforce. Indicative of the power of the "glass ceiling," in direct contrast, the number of women still relegated to work in the domestic sector was as high as ever, at 75 percent.[98] The major difference in this postwar decade was the number of women who had gained a foothold in industry and who now could work in areas beyond low-paying domestic service. The number of women working in laundries increased so that they became a dominant force.

Surveys conducted under the auspices of the Chicago Urban League, which evaluated its efforts at job placement outside the domestic sphere, revealed that by 1929 the number of women employed in fifteen large establishments totaled 3,700 workers, of which 790 were African American. In six factories processing date, fig, and nut products, African Americans had a near monopoly on jobs, filling 635 out of 683 positions. In women's dresses and men's clothing, 900 blacks were on the job. In overall and apron factories, 1,000 women had found work. The popularity of lamp shades for electric lights provided 4,000 women with work.[99] A review of hiring at Sears, Roebuck, and Company revealed the employment of 1,423 women in its mail order house.[100]

Conditions at date factories were such that some women took up organizing their fellow workers to improve the circumstances of their employment.[101] In terms of geographical and residential placement in the Black Metropolis, the farther southward one moved along the South State Street axis, the higher the number of women in the professions, the lower the number of women in domestic service, and the increasing percentage who did not work at all, obviously because they did not have to.[102]

Cosmetics manufacturer Anthony Overton also promised women the same future successes that Madame C. J. Walker and Mrs. Annie Turnbo-Malone had in the way of another outlet to use their God-given talent at sales and attain a semblance of independence. His homegrown economic ventures opened doors in light manufacturing as well as in finance and journalism. Overton's business directory, *Black's Blue Book*, carried its message of racial self-sufficiency to a level previously unseen in black Chicago. "The length of service of the Overton Hygiene Mfg. Company to the public, its growth and the quality of its products, are reasons why every *Loyal* Colored man and woman should demand and use High-Brown Toilet Preparations. Still another reason is that every person in our institution from the President to the janitor is Colored. Give us your support by purchasing our products and we will show you some surprising results by the increasing number of positions of all kinds we can offer to *Our* men and women" [emphases in original].[103]

The Underground Economy

Among the diversified interests in the Black Metropolis, one segment of the population sought a solution to its economic needs and desires through activities beyond the pale of legality. Criminals and noncriminal types generated capital for investments and purchasing from sources outside mainstream channels in what was considered the underground economy. Most notable to outsiders were subletting apartments, gambling, and bootlegging. Lesser known were the intricacies of the policy racket, a lottery-type activity run solely by African Americans and engaged in daily by thousands of black workers in all economic sectors. The significance of policy rested on its acknowledged power to produce hundreds of jobs, along with thousands of dollars for self-indulgence as well as donations to charitable, community, and civic institutions and activities. Binder estimated in 1927 that at least 2,000 men and women made their living in various gambling operations. Correspondingly, the slump noticeable in business produced a decline in gambling revenues as cash flow through the hands of persons who loved gaming enterprises decreased.[104] White politicians in the Loop, along with those purportedly serving the best interests of the South Side, collected hundreds of thousands of dollars in payoffs every month.[105]

Bootlegging flourished to the extent that it challenged the role of gambling as a generator of illegal revenue. Al Capone's Italian syndicate seemingly acquiesced in South Side operations and allowed blacks to engage in the trade that the former dominated by outright violence in other areas of the city. The name of illegal places of distribution and consumption of alcohol was the "blind pig," the near equivalent of the speakeasy in white areas. Efforts at reform proved ineffective as decent citizens were forced to tolerate this lawlessness.[106]

The linkage between politics and the underground economy was direct, open, thoroughly corrupting, and profitable to many aspects of life, excepting morality. Why good citizens engaged in these activities was often the result of a choice between accepting unemployment as a way of life or securing employment under a cloud. As to the immorality involved, E. Franklin Frazier summarized the dilemma and solution chosen:

> The political consciousness of the Negro community on the whole is the same as the white community. Chicago has long been known as the political paradise of the Negro. His political leaders have been part of the machine that has controlled the city. The Negro's political power has given him jobs which have helped in his economic emancipation. At the same time his political strength has been used to benefit those who receive contributions from the underworld. White people have constantly decried the political morality of the Black Belt. When there was considerable agitation about cleaning up the vice on the South Side the greatest emphasis was placed upon the mingling of whites, especially white women,

with Negroes in places of amusement. But since Negroes have quite naturally preferred living in hell as equals than living in a Jim Crow heaven supervised by white folks, the so-called reformers have not found much comfort among Negroes. The so-called debased elements among the political powers offered the Negroes something concrete in the way of jobs and protection. The mass of Negroes have not been inspired by nobler aims of political action but they are nearer reality than the white people who expect Negroes to be bloodless saints casting their votes altruistically for a purified city that left them to feed upon their idealism.[107]

Advent of Economic Depression

Foreboding signs of economic dislocation appeared as early as 1926, notwithstanding the somewhat idyllic picture of industrial and overall economic stability presented by Frazier and Barnett on the eve of the Great Depression.[108] Contrary observations on the status of the labor scene complicate any assessment. At the end of the decade and on the eve of the Great Depression, E. Franklin Frazier reported on a bright picture on the status of black labor.

> The number of men employed in manufacturing and mechanical pursuits according to the United States census was one-third more than the number in domestic and personal services which generally ranks first. Among the women the same situation does not exist but nearly one-fourth of the women employed were in manufacturing and mechanical occupations. Nearly two-thirds of the women were classified under domestic and personal services. A large number of Negroes in manufacturing and mechanical pursuit is in the Stockyards. In the case of some industries they are shut out completely; and in other cases the laboring force is Colored. One box factory employs only "light" Colored girls. In some industrial plants whites and Negroes work side by side in all occupations. In other industries there is segregation as to work and recreation. In still others separation exists either as to recreation or as to work. The unions in their relations to the Negro worker offer every possible form of advancement with rationalizations to suit each situation. Nevertheless, the place which the Negro has secured in the industrial life of Chicago is indicative of the Negro's future in industry.[109]

The truthfulness of the old economic adage depicting the precarious position of the black worker in the American labor force of being "the last hired, the first fired" began to take its toll within the Black Belt and throughout the surrounding black enclaves. Depositors at the Binga State Bank began to live off their savings after having "saved for a rainy day. That day had arrived and the response of the black community was both timely and appropriate, personal and organizational. Withdrawals of deposits forecast even bigger problems ahead and accounted for the individual's reaction."[110] The formation of the Joint Committee for Employment aimed at amelioration of the crisis illustrated the larger response.[111]

At the same time, the Chicago Urban League likewise geared its resources to fight this pending disaster. With a new executive secretary who joined the organization in 1925, the league was more than adequately prepared to meet this challenge. During 1925, the employment picture looked bleak but in 1926 job orders and placement held their own.[112] By 1927 and 1928, conditions were being described as resembling those that existed in the recession year of 1921.[113] In a reversal of labor progress, the activities conducted under Foster's direction resulted in the league being able to place some workers in traditional black-dominated service jobs such as in laundries and private households. Yet the league's main targets were those that had been traditionally opposed to fair employment practices. The league then mounted its campaign against the utility companies, especially Illinois Bell Telephone Company, and the A&P food chain. The results of the campaign, although aggressively pursued, were not very impressive.[114]

The next year the league aimed to move a step beyond its emphasis on seeking traditional "Negro jobs" in the Black Metropolis to place blacks in a greater variety of jobs within their community.[115] Significant but not fully recognized in this period was the idea that a community that supported businesses located within its boundaries could demand jobs from them whenever it needed to do so. This idea of using "buying power" as a tool to relieve the perennial employment problems blacks faced would form the basis of more militant action beginning in 1929 under the auspices of the *Chicago Whip*. These efforts, in turn, reached their peak in the next decade under the banner of the well-known "Don't Spend Your Money Where You Can't Work" campaign. At this time, though, the league's Department of Industrial Relations merely acted to fulfill its responsibility "to advocate new opportunities for Negroes" by using research techniques and the data gathered to explore the efficacy of making demands within the Black Metropolis on white businesses. The department issued a news communiqué that explained the rationale for its action: "[Since] 75% of the money spent by Race residents on the south side goes to south side merchants who are in most cases of the white race . . . the League is planning to campaign to secure more employment for Race men and women and boys and girls in the mercantile places on the south side or wherever in the city our people spend a large part of their money."[116] Aware that a united front of numerous organizations might be able to accomplish what a single agency could not, the league solicited and successfully gained support from the member organizations of an umbrella group formed in 1927 under its auspices of the federated Joint Committee on Emergency Relief and Unemployment on the South Side. The Joint Committee included in its ranks the Chicago NAACP, the Wabash YMCA, the Appomattox Club, the Cook County Bar Association, and many of the community's churches. In addition, all of the black newspapers pledged their support to its work, as did the two black aldermen, Anderson and Jackson.[117]

The response from the white store owners was neither enthusiastic nor cooperative even in instances where the "business was almost 100% among the

[Negro] Race."[118] One contributing factor was the knowledge that the store owners had of the basic, conservative nature of blacks in eschewing the aggressiveness needed in situations involving direct action.[119] Therefore, this more assertive approach that had relevance and an allure to blacks held no such significance to, and produced no fear in, many of the whites against whom it was directed.

During 1927, slight gains were noticed in the effort to reduce unemployment because of the use by the league of its still basic, conciliatory tactics. The Silver Dollar Stores opened a branch on 47th Street that included twelve clerks in its workforce. The A&P stores added two additional black clerks, and a black man was made head clerk of the Charles Foote Shoe Store on 47th Street. However, the most important and significant success in employment had come at the South Center Department Store, located at the corner of 47th Street and South Parkway, at what was destined to be the new epicenter of commerce and culture of the Black Metropolis in the 1930s. The grand opening of this store on March 17, 1928, with a fully integrated staff that was 33 percent black (and soon would become 50 percent within a short period of time), was to become a symbol of what could be done in securing employment opportunities for blacks. The league was instrumental in bringing about this change, and it was reported that "the Urban League and the other agencies communicated the temper of the people to the financial backers of the new store who wanted to do something [equitable treatment in hiring], but were afraid, of inexperienced [black] help, of the possibility that black clerks and white clerks would not be able to work together. On the one hand, there were 250,000 African Americans saying: 'We will not buy if you don't hire.'"[120]

Offsetting these gains were the losses occurring with greater frequency as white workers began to feel the crunch of the approaching depression. Thirty-five blacks lost their jobs in the Black Metropolis when the Stop and Shop Store moved to the Loop, where few blacks were welcomed as workers.[121] More detrimental was the mass dismissal of black workers and their subsequent replacement by white workers. In separate incidents, "a large department store in the Loop district dismissed most of their Colored help employed in the laundry. The reason advanced was that they wished to experiment with white help in the department. [And,] a company which manufacture[d] clothing for men dismissed seven of [its] eleven porters all of whom had been employed from 8 to 12 years. The general manager, when interviewed, admitted that honest and efficient service had been rendered. This change was also made for experimental purposes."[122]

By 1929, the *Chicago Whip* newspaper, which had always evinced an interest in improving the economic status of blacks as a means of racial advancement, joined the job protest effort and assumed the responsibility for promoting it through greater activism.[123] It inaugurated a job campaign against the white-owned, nationally operated Metropolitan Life Insurance Company that was, first, consistent with the needs of the workforce in the Black Metropolis, and, second, more militant in tone and methods than any other ever undertaken before on the South

Side. This was the introduction into black Chicago of the modernized version of the buying power idea conceived earlier by the *Chicago Defender*. With Joseph D. Bibb and A. C. MacNeal at the *Whip*'s helm, the middle class had allied itself with the interests of the working classes. As radical as that alliance appeared, the tactics used seemed just as unusual for the times. The gradualist approach of Booker T. Washington gave way to Chicago-style, confrontational methods that moved beyond persuasion and cooperation. A massive propaganda effort was conducted through its pages and from the pulpits, along with a boycott against the company. Metropolitan Life, with its power, refused to bend and never considered hiring blacks as insurance agents.[124]

The *Whip*'s course of action was made possible because of its independence, not being subject to any major constraints upon its activities from sources within or outside the Black Metropolis.[125] It proceeded in its activities subject to pressures dictated only by conscience, ideology, or whatever its leadership deemed economically expedient.[126] The imprint on organizational protest by the *Whip* and its *ad hoc* subsidiary, the Commercial Service Employees Bureau, was significant in 1929 but it would be even greater during the period of the Great Depression.

In comparison to the *Whip*'s campaign against the Metropolitan Life Insurance Company, the league's activities in the job sector had been relatively innocuous. However, to the conservative, business-minded league supporters, they no doubt appeared to pose a threat to the economic status quo. Any linkage rests entirely in conjecture.

The Communist Party made some inroads among black workers, especially through activist members of the African Blood Brotherhood (ABB), who were revolutionary in their thinking and call for effective action. Along with having a firsthand experience beyond the service sector, their being "black building tradesmen in plumbing, electricians, bricklayers, and stockyard workers. Ed Doty, a plumber, led Chicago's ABB and had already organized the American Consolidated Trades Council."[127] They shared a hostility to Garvey's pro-capitalist UNIA, of which some had been former members, along with the reformist Chicago NAACP and Chicago Urban League. In 1925, the party convened a meeting in the city to make plans to further the interests of blacks in the ranks of organized labor. The American Negro Labor Congress (ANLC) emerged from this assemblage, which was organized in the name of racial and labor equality under the auspices of a black man, Lovett Fort-Whiteman. The latter individual was impressive and articulate as a journalist, but just as important, he was a non-Chicagoan who lacked a base and familiarity of the nuances of life in the Black Metropolis. Fortunately, he could rely on Doty's members to lend their knowledge of and links within the South Side community for direction. Seeking a place to inaugurate their labor movement, pro-labor Rev. William D. Cook of the Metropolitan Community Church obliged, and that same year he also opened his doors to the newly organized Brotherhood of Sleeping Car Porters (BSCP). The two labor organizations were destined to collide as each sought to be the voice of black labor. Their tactics proved antithetical in regard to indigenous participation and direction: The BSCP relied on an existential relationship with the people as it guided their advancement, while the ANLC took its orders from Moscow and black communists, who proved ineffective in the long run in fostering an understanding of the nuances of African American life. On one occasion, the ANLC presented a Russian play in the Black Metropolis with Russian actors who, naturally, performed in their native tongue, much to the bewilderment of their audience.[128]

The presence of Fort-Whiteman in Chicago, elevated in Communist Party circles to the highest level an African American had achieved, was significant primarily because of his racial background and the importance that the communists realized African Americans attached to the powerful race factor in the Black Metropolis. However, Marxist-Leninist doctrine assumed primacy, so underscoring Fort-Whiteman's commitment to the aims of the party was the description he earned of being the "reddest Red of them all."[129] Several glaring problems doomed this labor organization to an early lack of success. The initial meeting itself was dominated by white communists and attended by only a small number of blacks.[130] More importantly, too few blacks were members of the Communist Party in Chicago, perhaps fifty, and too few African Americans overall worked within the industrial workforce where a labor consciousness was more prone to be built. Along with their racial consciousness, the average black worker still struggled to sustain himself or herself and often a family, many times on a daily basis. When African Americans were found in other productive areas, they were clustered in small numbers and lacked a "labor consciousness," a key component in organizing labor.

Furthermore, the weakness that exacerbated the situation to a point of failure was the communists' ideological insistence that the American Negro Labor Congress was formed to address itself to what they considered the most pressing need of the black populace: strength through labor unity rather than racial solidarity. However, in pushing the concept of all-black, independent labor organizations, it violated the Communist Party's doctrinal commitment to building a color-blind working class.[131] The fate of the ANLC was almost predictable, as it existed solely on paper for the next three years and failed to leave a distinguishable mark on the labor scene.[132] The lesson it learned would be better applied in the next decade in the name of true worker solidarity.

Considered as tolerable by the African American editors of the *Opportunity* and *Crisis* magazines because of deep-rooted American racism that eroded the life chances of black workers, the ANLC in contrast incurred the suspicions of the American Federation of Labor (AFL).[133] For his part, Du Bois saw this conference "as one of the most significant gatherings in recent black history. As far as he was concerned, progress of black people was more important than the vehicle through which progress was achieved."[134]

The activities of the Communist Party persisted during the 1920s as the left attempted to increase its influence among American workers. African Americans were the focus of the left since their numbers and exclusion from the ranks of organized labor left them vulnerable to any alternatives presented to their chronic condition of unemployment. With American racism as the culprit, Communist Party leader and labor organizer Lovett Fort-Whiteman appeared a savior as he led the organization of the American Negro Labor Congress in 1925. The congress assembled in Chicago in October, and Raya Dunayevskaya, a devoted communist with organizing skills to match her zeal, helped Fort-Whiteman with his news organ, the *Negro Champion Magazine*.[135]

Its failure in this endeavor notwithstanding, the interest of the Communist Party in the plight of unorganized black labor placed it far ahead of the Chicago Urban League, which in following a policy enunciated from New York engaged in opportunism in contacts with white labor organizations. The league avoided open support of the unions because of their discriminatory records against blacks but, at the same time, refused to condemn them despite its reliance on contributions from businesses to support the operations of the league.[136] When the most severe part of the wave of unemployment hit the Black Metropolis in the late twenties, the Communist Party was as unprepared as the rest of the city and the Black Metropolis to address the problem decisively—so it did nothing of consequence. The Communist Party branch in the Black Metropolis held meetings but did not produce any outstanding activity or results in any area.[137] It was handicapped by the same problems the league and the early NAACP faced, since its leadership was predominantly white in a milieu where racism was highly significant. In addition, its revolutionary message that advocated overturning the capitalist system and, with it, racism was too extreme for the population of the Black Metropolis, which had not quite accepted completely the far more moderate buying power idea. Its limited influence among African Americans was indicated by a black party membership in the CPUSA that was no doubt minuscule, since national black membership was fewer than 200.[138]

The next decade would bring a level of economic deprivation that shattered the dreams and even hopes for a better future. The challenge to the creators and supporters of the Black Metropolis was to maintain its stability with a vision for growth in the distant future. The question of the day became, would the buoyancy of the Black Metropolis give way to the dismality in job opportunities of the early Black Belt period?

CHAPTER 5

The Struggle for Control over Black Politics and Protest

> Probably no racial group in the country (unless it be the Irish) is more manifestly "political" in its everyday life than the American Negro. . . . [T]he Chicago group is one of the most progressive of the country, economically, politically, and culturally.
>
> —Ralph J. Bunche, 1928

> What a change ten years has wrought in the affairs of our people! . . . The changes wrought seem almost revolutionary and not a gradual and continual change in the regular or evolutionary course of affairs.
>
> —Joseph D. Bibb, 1929

> [To the query as to who controls the Black Metropolis's voting bloc] "I am the group."
>
> —Edward H. Wright to the Special Committee Investigating Expenditures in Senatorial and General Elections, 1926

Maintaining the stability of the Black Metropolis within the dynamics of the city's political economy meant more than promoting growth and development in the business arena and expanding employment and housing opportunities. Politics was to be utilized to meet communal needs in employment and housing, offering the most direct means of improving the collective quality of life in black Chicago. These necessities, rather than signs of racial equality, remained as the primary measurements of progress at a time when civil rights attainment still appeared theoretical and its movement forward seemed stymied. The national office of the NAACP noticed this sentiment and assessed the situation thus: "There are so many diversified interests in Chicago that the N.A.A.C.P. [with its mission of promoting racial egalitarianism] really suffers greatly from indifference on the part of the people."[1]

With energy, courage, and entrepreneurial daring, Chicago's New Negro thinkers had modified a gradual ascent in racial progress into an accelerated thrust forward in the political and economic spheres. Two diametrically opposed, non-economic channels were poised as well to contribute to the realization by black Chicagoans of their various material needs, dreams, and aspirations.[2] Politics and protest, the latter represented primarily by the program and activities of the

Chicago Urban League and secondarily through the limited efforts of the Chicago NAACP, demonstrated that even a moderately confrontational approach could contribute to a modicum of improvements in the lives of the city's black citizenry. In any instance where the limitations of achieving positive social action through government operations and political institutions discouraged citizens, the alternative means to solving economic crises through civic advocacy or protest provided another type of choice. These efforts were exemplified in the housing struggle against terrorist bombings through measures conducted by the *ad hoc* Protective Circle. At the end of this decade and in the earliest phases of Great Depression in which unemployment increased throughout the Black Metropolis, the ameliorative efforts of the Chicago Urban League, accompanied by the "Don't Spend Your Money Where You Can't Work" campaign initiated by the *Chicago Whip*, appeared on the scene to confront the problem of job discrimination head-on. Not to be overlooked was the indirect support given to job expansion by the Chicago NAACP (preceding its open and direct support furnished in the years after 1932) as well as various *ad hoc* organizations and their actions.

From the American left, the early recruitment and organizing activities of the Communist Party funneled through the American Negro Labor Congress, and a nudge toward raising labor consciousness among the black laboring class seemed appropriate for the times if economic gains were to be made at all. In effect, protest activism extended beyond the quest for equal citizenship rights to include seeking economic parity in an implementation of a "dual agenda."[3]

* * *

Chicago's New Negroes who dared to lead the way politically were anything but young chronologically. Conspicuously, they were mature members of a generation that had either braved slavery personally, such as John R. Lynch, or had witnessed their parents' ascent from the influences of that degraded state of existence. With community powerhouses Edward H. Wright and Oscar DePriest leading the way, year in and year out political involvement grew in popularity and prideful admiration among both the African American masses and the other classes during the 1920s. This acceptance of and near obsession with politics resulted from the successful efforts of the black Republican politicians to convince the electorate that many of their basic needs such as securing jobs and protecting business operations (even the illegal variety) were being met by a responsive, party-driven, governmental apparatus. Contemporary records abound with both descriptions and analyses of this phenomenon, while a wave of recent scholarship disputed the extent to which tangible, long-term benefits accrued from this relationship.[4] Hundreds of patronage jobs, provision of political favors, and police protection for activities within the underground economy represented economic advancement and accounted for the high level of interest and support for politicians and electoral politics.

Joseph D. Bibb, the erudite editor of the *Whip*, reviewed in 1929 what the decade of the 1920s had wrought: "A decade ago we had no congressman, no state senator, no members of the Industrial Commission, no municipal court judge, only two men in the legislature. We had no men of color on the Illinois Commerce Commission, no civil service commissioners. We had only one man in the corporation counsel's office, one attached to the state's attorney. We had no alderman or committeeman in the Third Ward nor were the hundreds of our people holding state and municipal positions."[5] Indeed, in Bibbs's estimation, political advancement had been of the highest necessity to the people of the Black Metropolis, and the results tangible and successful. In a metropolis committed to spending $1 billion in public and private funds in the near future for infrastructure, improvements, and innovations in making money and life more pleasurable for its three million residents, the daring of the New Negro seemed quite appropriate.[6]

The Whirl of Life in the Political and Governmental Spheres

The black political leadership of Republicans Edward H. Wright and Oscar DePriest during this decade energetically set old Black Belt politics on a new programmatic course, that of maintaining and expanding African American political control over the Black Metropolis. The political watershed reached in 1915 as blacks gained their first aldermanic post with DePriest's election to office proved only a stepping stone to greater realizations. In 1918, African Americans secured a second seat in the Chicago City Council, so at this time blacks now had representation through Louis B. Anderson in the Second Ward and Major Robert "Fighting Bob" Jackson in the Third. Further, blacks secured the most important and powerful position at the local ward level, that of committeeman in 1920 as Wright took office and became the Second Ward's first black patron over municipal jobs.[7] From their political bases in the Second, Third, and Fourth Wards, all situated within the elastic boundaries of the Black Metropolis, blacks elected the only black magistrate in the nation as well as Illinois's first black state senator in 1924. Their state-level complement of legislators grew to number five representatives. And, significantly, they would elect the first black representative in the U.S. Congress in the twentieth century when Oscar DePriest won his seat in November 1928.

Answering the professionals' plea for job placement, they negotiated successfully for the appointment of black lawyers as assistant states attorneys and assistant corporation counsels. Topping off their achievements, in 1927, a black man became a member of the Civil Service Commission. AME church leader Bishop Archibald J. Carey satisfied his personal appetite for power as African Americans chose to recognize him as their own group's watchman and monitor over this bank of municipal jobs. As these positions were being secured, the Black Metropolis's political organization under Edward H. Wright's leadership continued to work on the major items that made up their agenda: broadening job patronage; increasing influence over decision making in municipal legislation (with Second Ward Alderman Louis B. Anderson as the mayor's floor leader in the Chicago City Council); and negotiating with white politicians with greater authority on all issues that affected the members of their race.

However, satisfying the needs of the professionals solved only a minor part of what constituted patronage management. According to Harold F. Gosnell, black politicians worked somewhat successfully to secure jobs for their constituents within the municipal workforce with "2,785 Negroes [placed, representing] 6.4% of the total." Claude A. Barnett put the number at 3,400 and located an additional 124 workers in the police department and 21 in the fire department. The federal government hired even more workers, mainly in the post office. Robinson's figures were lower, even when he accounted for 1,000 seasonal workers without civil service status.[8]

Conventional Politics

The conventional vehicle chosen by overwhelming numbers of African Americans who lived in the Black Metropolis for individual and group advancement was the black political submachine of the Republican Party. This formidable political body reached the zenith of its existence during the twenties, winning the support of an ever-increasing number of migrants as soon as they arrived in the city.[9] Besides a high degree of African American assertiveness, black successes had been related to the timely convergence of certain personalities and developments on the political scene shortly after the turn of the century. To begin, strong-willed individuals with an ardent interest in politics—such as William "Big Bill" Thompson (who would become a three-term mayor with his victory in 1927), Edward H. Wright, and Oscar DePriest—were all dominant influences in the Black Metropolis. They and the black electorate were overwhelmingly Republican in their allegiance in a milieu that was dominated by Republicanism, from the precinct level to the White House. For their part, Chicago's Democrats occupied a near-invisible place in the Black Metropolis, which appeared in sharp contrast to their status citywide. Attorney Earl B. Dickerson was one among only a few who dared carry the banner of the Democrat Party on the black South Side, and he was called a traitor for his affiliation. Next, housing discrimination helped consolidate the bulk of the black population into the compact area of the Black Metropolis and produced initially a potentially powerful voting bloc that eventually evolved into an actual one. In addition, a high level of racial consciousness combined with politics developed, nurtured by positive cultural identifications under the well-directed leadership of Wright and DePriest. Last, there was a willingness among white politicians such as Bill Thompson and the Black Metropolis's spokesman in Washington, U.S. Representative Martin B. Madden, no doubt based on expedience, to relinquish their former white-populated territories to black political aspirants without engaging in internecine warfare with their fellow Republicans.[10]

As a matter of political reality, no matter how impressive their victories and acquisitions were, black politicians remained members of a subordinate racial group with limited access to the mechanisms of control over society and, most importantly, the quality of life in the Black Metropolis. African American involvement in the political system followed a pattern that was quite similar to that adopted by the city's white ethnic groups, who engaged in the attainment of benefits accruing from special-interest politics. The Republican machine under Thompson and his predecessors recognized diversity without attempting to stymie, destroy, or stigmatize it. As contemporary scholar Harold F. Gosnell described the Republican machine in the thirties, it was a "patron of minority groups and a broker for business."[11] However, even as the patron of non-WASP minority groups, the Thompson machine still had as its primary goals the maintenance and enhancement of its own citywide organization. These self-centered concerns always took precedence over all other involvements such as the need for good government, open housing, opportunities for employment, and a progressive school policy. And, as a racial adjunct in political matters, whites in authority and their constituents, whether Republicans or Democrats, would tolerate advancement by blacks only as long as it did not alter the structure they governed or the racial system from which they benefitted.[12]

Black political leadership was then, at times, more beholden to its source of power, the seemingly omnipotent Republican machine, than it was to the Black Metropolis constituency that elected it. As a counterbalance to this situation, blacks worked to develop greater political leverage within the party based on their impressive strength at the polls where they usually led the city with their registration and actual voting percentages. Since all of the Republican factions were aware of this strength that could provide the balance of power needed for crucial victories in primary elections, they offered concessions to blacks as they attempted to attract this bloc of voters.[13]

The head of the most powerful and prominent faction in the Republican machine was Mayor William Thompson, who derived part of his strength from his affiliation with the black electorate and its leadership. His presence in city hall when the decade began meant that blacks had a municipal leader who was ostensibly friendly to their causes. The most impressive manifestation of this was his record of appointing blacks to office (after negotiations with black leaders) in scores of lower-level jobs, and in a selective number of highly placed professional positions. Because of these actions by Thompson, by the late twenties his white detractors had derogatorily labeled Chicago City Hall as "Uncle Tom's Cabin."

Conversely, among blacks, Thompson's actions led to the creation of a myth that found him being referred to as a "Second Lincoln." This appearance was based to some degree on reality, but more importantly, it was a result of careful cultivation of good relations among black people by Thompson personally, by black politicians allied to his faction, and by certain black community leaders, especially the ministers. However, the myth was nothing more than the sum of several distorted perceptions. Several facts illustrate this point. First, Thompson refused to recognize the black claim to the seat in the First Congressional District (which blacks dominated both in terms of voting and population) until 1928 when the death of white incumbent Madden immediately before the general election and subsequent pressure from DePriest forced him to act. Second, he never appointed a black person to the Chicago Board of Education despite the constant pressures placed upon him by blacks, the number of qualified persons available, and the validity of the black demand.[14] Third, his administration never took a firm stand against the bombings of black homes and other housing restrictions that impeded black residential expansion.

Yet, since most whites were so disdainful of having anything to do with African Americans, any white person who showed the slightest degree of civility or humanity toward blacks, or performed any gesture that appeared in any manner to be genuine, received an outpouring of enthusiasm from African Americans. Thompson showed that interest and he benefitted accordingly. Placed in its proper perspective, it is apparent that the popularity that Thompson enjoyed was not the result of any unique character trait or even charismatic personal qualities. As Harold F. Gosnell has pointed out, any white politician coming into prominence under the same circumstances would have enjoyed similar popularity among blacks.[15] Thompson's high level of popularity among the black electorate also should not be interpreted to mean that he had full control over the behavior of the black voters at the polls. Black voters were loyal to the principles of the Republican Party as they perceived them in the Lincolnesque tradition and to those white leaders who appeared genuine in their utterances and actions.[16] This attribute of loyalty can also be traced directly to the success of a program of awareness conducted among the black masses by black Republicans and the sophistication of the black leaders such as Wright and DePriest in the political sphere. In addition, those white politicians who received support on election day were the ones who furnished jobs, pledged protection from both police misbehavior against law-abiding citizens and police vigilance against black criminal elements, and tailored their appeals in such a manner that indicated a sensitivity to the wishes of the diverse elements within the black electorate by class or length of residency in Chicago. On those occasions when a politician like Thompson misjudged his influence with blacks—as he would in the U.S. senatorial election of 1930 and the mayoral election of 1931—he was quickly made aware of his miscalculation on election day by either threatened or actual loss of votes.

Paralleling the collective attention of political scientist Harold F. Gosnell and his team of participant observers at the University of Chicago, the *Chicago Defender*'s political analyst A. N. Fields credited any political advancement within the Black Belt to a coterie of politicians groomed under the auspices of the Second Ward's populace, leadership, and vision. "The political progress made by our people during the past 50 years when summed up revolves around such personalities as Edward H. Wright, Oscar DePriest, Louis B. Anderson, and Major R. R. Jackson . . . men [who] were largely responsible for whatever political policies were shaped and formulated having to do so with our interest," Fields reported.[17]

Of significance to this circle of men were the factors common to successful professional politicians. Their world revolved around a sense of racial vision transcending any externally proscribed social status, a desire to move beyond perfunctory officeholding to policymaking, the status of being financially independent, and the inclination to increase their competitive position within the dominant Republican political apparatus, yielding to other groups only when absolutely necessary. These were also men who had come of age during this decade and constituted a generation of persons who shared the common goal of breaking free from external influences to the extent that they could regulate their lives and those of their constituents in the most expansive sphere of influence possible. Likewise, a level of personal and political maturity marked their claim to leadership. In 1920, Wright was fifty-four years old, DePriest was forty-nine, Anderson was forty-nine, and Jackson was fifty. Although loyal to the only party that paid their constituents any attention, they all possessed turn-of-the-century frustration with political voicelessness under white control. So, although they publicly supported national Republican claims at being the party of "Freedom and Equal Opportunity," the words seemed hollow to them given the maldistribution of power within the city.

Without a doubt, the two leading black politicians on the South Side were Edward H. Wright and Oscar DePriest. These two men were recognized by both whites and blacks for their political sagacity within the party and leadership abilities among their racial constituents. For his part, Ed Wright started the decade right by winning party support in 1920 for his run as Second Ward committeeman, which he won handily at the polls. "As ward committeeman Wright was aggressive in race matters, strict in discipline, indifferent to personal publicity," and last, according to Gosnell, "loyal to his word at all costs."[18] He was above all a "Race man" and therefore a racial champion regardless of the odds and circumstances.[19]

His awareness of the importance of developing a civic network that could enhance black racial and political prospects for success was manifested in the founding of the Appomattox Club in 1900. This club served as a meeting place for black political leaders as well as influential community leaders from all endeavors and for the Cook County Bar Association (the all-black counterpart to the white, racially exclusive Chicago Bar Association) in 1916.

Because of his tenacity and astuteness in political dealings, Wright had earned the sobriquet of the "Iron Master." Under his leadership, the black component of the Chicago Republican machine took on legendary qualities of iron-willed discipline and invincibility at the polls during its lifetime.[20] It also produced tangible results in securing work for the city's African American citizens. The

Black Metropolis Republican faction reflected somewhat the personality of its leader, who was known for his intelligence (as demonstrated by his education at the College of the City of New York), honesty in dealing with the people of the Black Metropolis, and strength when dealing with whites (whether friendly or hostile to what he perceived to be his race's interests).

New Negro assertiveness became the hallmark of this decade's political behavior. Likewise, confrontation with whites in positions of power became a trademark practice of Wright's. First Congressional District Congressman Martin B. Madden incurred the "Iron Master's" wrath when a promise to promote highly qualified blacks to postal positions commensurate with their education and job skills went unfulfilled. A delegation from the Phalanx Club, a union-like postal workers organization, "complained to Ed Wright that it had among its members individuals working at the post office with college degrees with the title of postal clerk but actually working as laborers on the docks, throwing mail bags into the trucks." Wright's response was immediate and pronounced in its fury and resolution:

> Congressman Madden was summoned from the House floor to take Wright's call . . . [the telephone call followed in this one-directional manner:] Congressman Madden, I have a committee from the Chicago Post Office sitting at my desk. I have talked to you about the condition in that place. I also told you that there were black men down there that were college-trained and with years of service but being relegated to the lot of common laborers. I am damned tired of you making me an embarrassment to my people. We are delivering something like a 25,000 [vote] majority to the damn Republican Party in my ward. I want a black supervisor in the Chicago Postal System before the damn sun goes down this day. Do you hear me?

The congressman, at this time chairing the House's committee on post offices, complied. A black man assumed supervisory responsibilities at the Armour Station later that day.[21]

Wright imaginatively recruited women in a role equal to men as precinct captains, breaking in the process an archaic gender distinction. Utilized by the Republican machine in all wards, the Third Ward in particular led in their widespread employment of women, reaching 25 percent with noticeable effectiveness.[22] A woman serving in the capacity of precinct captain could also approach women in a manner that a male could not without offending their husbands. When necessary, some captains resorted to baby-sitting while a female voter went to the polls or finishing the woman's washing chores during her absence.

Under Ed Wright's tutelage and direction, municipal authority took a light brown tone as Second Ward alderman Louis B. Anderson became floor leader for Thompson and the first African American to sit on the Finance Committee of the Chicago City Council. Anderson, sitting as alderman from 1917 through 1933, possessed and used the skills in parliamentary procedures for which he would gain legendary status.[23] Appropriately, the decade began with a triumph for Anderson as he engineered a pay raise for all municipal employees.[24] Every bit the political survivor, Anderson's political patron's power swayed his actions. Ed Wright and Anderson often did not agree on political matters; still, the "Iron Master's" will regularly won the day.[25]

In a national analysis of historical and contemporary black political involvement made in 1971, political scientist Martin Kilson found that the blacks of Chicago had represented a unique strain in politics in that they avoided that brand of politics of finding favor with certain white groups in a superordinate–subordinate arrangement.[26] Kilson's model was based on a note of reality about Chicago politics that this book (*The Rise of Chicago's Black Metropolis, 1920–1929*) uncovered. Black politicians were neither totally subservient to the Thompson machine nor were they completely independent to do what they wanted in political, racial, and economic matters. They operated most often in a middle ground where they usually voted along with the party for its programs but were not normally called upon to vote against their group's racial interests. In a northern city like Chicago, there was never a serious attempt to impose discriminatory statutes on the law books to proscribe the rights of the city's black citizens.

The most common situation that a black politician would face involved discrimination against them or other blacks by omission, or through the lax enforcement of safeguards that afforded protection against civil rights violations. In 1925, Alderman Anderson had a policeman removed from the police force because of an act of brutality committed against a black man (who in this case happened to be his son-in-law). And, in 1926, Wright and an entourage of black political leaders, which included Anderson, faced a discriminatory situation in the Loop as they were denied the use of an elevator at the Palmer House. Wright protested and Anderson responded by shouting, "We're going to use that elevator and we're going to use it damn quick, or there'll be a houseful of trouble."[27] In response to these protestations, they were quickly boarded on a front elevator by the hotel's management. It was in these latter situations that black politicians had their opportunity to prove their mettle as race champions to their constituents or, using the descriptive term applied during the period, as "Race men." Yet they rarely, if ever, engaged in direct activities that clearly challenged the discriminatory public policy that existed in the city. One notable failure that involved Anderson occurred in 1922, when the Chicago NAACP branch secretary, upon finding the screening of *The Invisible Empire* in Chicago objectionable, contacted the alderman to formally protest, which unfortunately he did not.[28]

Of equal importance was the fact that in the Black Metropolis, the actions of black politicians were carefully scrutinized on the issue of race, and any deviation from the racial norm (which treated selective reactions as acceptable and courageous) was quickly noticed by the black electorate and by the black press. As for the black politician and his freedom of action on racial matters, Gosnell observed that "he might sell out his group on many matters but on certain fundamental race issues he could not go contrary to the deep seated convictions of his constituents and hope to be reelected."[29] This was due to the high level of racial consciousness that was a part of the ethos that pervaded the Black Metropolis's political milieu. Gosnell also held that "race pride [was] an ever occurring theme at political rallies" and "the qualities that seemed to be appreciated by voters were fearlessness in race matters, activities in coping with situations of importance to Negroes, and a friendliness toward the masses."[30] Every black politician was a symbol of racial progress, and blacks were cognizant of the fact that "the power of [the black party] member depended primarily on black votes and not upon the favor or success of a given [white] party faction [alone]. He was, in a measure, independent of the white bosses and their financial resources."[31] Furthermore, an important ingredient aiding in this far from total dependence on whites was the existence of a black funding base for black political activities that was derived from illegal gambling operations in the Black Metropolis.

Political year 1923 produced several other breakthroughs. Mayor Thompson's reputation was so tainted with charges of political corruption and malfeasance (which included his connivance with mobster Al Capone) he was dissuaded through a combination of public and party pressures from running for a third consecutive term in office. The 1923 election saw blacks transfer their support temporarily from the Republican slate because Thompson was removed from the ticket to avoid embarrassment at the polls. African Americans voted for local Democrat William Dever in a well-calculated and -coordinated pirouette that denied any future Republican challenger to Thompson an opportunity for possible victory. With Thompson poised to return within four years, black Republicans adhered to a *modus vivendi* with the Democratic mayor. This was the first completely successful move toward independence by African Americans in Illinois politics.[32]

With Democrats in control of city hall, Wright wrestled key appointments for his supporters. Of the highest significance, "His chief lieutenants were located in such positions as assistant states [*sic*] attorneys, attorneys for the sanitary district, deputy sheriffs, deputy coroners, deputy bailiffs, and many other responsible positions. As he later put it, 'Every conspicuous political appointment of a Colored man or woman in Chicago and Illinois from industrial commissioner and Illinois commerce commissioner down, has been brought about by the Second Ward Republican organization under my leadership.'"[33] Meantime, he had Governor Len Small, who owed him a favor from 1920, appoint him a member of the Illinois Commerce Commission.

However, the fact that a Democrat took control at city hall in 1923 meant that white and black Democrats advanced their interests also. The door was opened for Democrat and University of Chicago law school graduate Earl B. Dickerson to become assistant corporation counsel in 1923.[34] Thirty-two-year-old Dickerson's rise to political prominence began from this point in his career, at a time upon which he reflected that he was one of very few black Democrats in the city. Conceding the field to the Republicans except for a bit of national attention in 1924, it would not be until the next decade that Democrats sought full, local African American participation within their party.[35]

Meantime, Ed Wright moved forward to position himself for the day when he would be the first and deciding voice in certain party matters concerning African Americans outside the confines of the Black Metropolis. Accordingly, Wright and other black political leaders decided that 1923 was a propitious time for them to once again nominate an African American for a municipal judgeship. In 1924, the nation's first African American popularly elected municipal magistrate took office, as did the first black member appointed to the Chicago Library Board. He (Albert B. George) and she (Fannie Barrier Williams), respectively, were joined by the nation's first popularly elected state senator (Adelbert Roberts) the same year. Key state appointments followed on commissions. Not since the political debacle with Ferdinand L. Barnett's defeat along racial lines in 1904 had a black man been able to advance onto the citywide ticket. Barnett had been well qualified but fell victim to the caste-like system that prevented black advancement into the ranks of the judiciary.

A year earlier, in 1923, Wright had advanced the name of Albert B. George for the party's consideration for placement on the 1924 ballot. George was a well-qualified candidate whose racial heritage was obscured by his near-white complexion. Wright "practically forced his [name] on a reluctant Republican party."[36] Running citywide posed the risk of a white backlash if George's lineage became public knowledge, so it was suppressed. Wright's strategy continued: He promised the white Republican committeemen unqualified black support for the party's entire ticket if George was supported.[37] The result was that Albert B. George won a seat during the 1924 municipal election with a plurality of 78,000 at a time when the black vote totaled 60,000 registered voters. At the same time, Adelbert Roberts was pushed for election to the state senate, the first African American to win that seat. Roberts, a graduate of the University of Michigan, had arrived in the city in 1888.

Concerned with equal access to learning and education, Wright pressured the mayor's office to have civic leader Fannie Barrier Williams appointed as the first black person to sit on the Chicago Library Board. The significance of this latter appointment meant that the interests of blacks in literacy, an encouragement of a higher appreciation of the world, and the acquisition of a broader knowledge base were enhanced with a presence on this prestigious but weak board. With municipal resources having been siphoned off in favor of Mayor Thompson's projects, along with widespread corruption, library services throughout the city had suffered. Williams, now a widow, served inconspicuously from June 1924 to September 1926, when she returned to Brockport, New York, to care for her sister who was in poor health. She was succeeded by Dr. George Cleveland Hall, whose length of service lasted from October 1926 to June 1930 with his death.[38] It was under Hall's tenure that he again proved himself a credit to the civic mantle he wore as he pursued funding through municipal and private sources to construct a library to serve the black community. At that time, there was virtually none available and scarce amounts for libraries in general.[39] Hall managed nevertheless to procure $100,000 of public funds and additional funding from the Julius Rosenwald Foundation to complete funding for the branch library. Full evidence of his success came in 1932 when a library bearing his name opened in the Black Metropolis.[40]

Hall had to walk a proverbial racial tightrope as he assuaged white concerns that a racially exclusive facility was being proposed in a city that ostensibly laid claim to its fairness and openness of public facilities. African American sentiment in the meantime proved to be quite adamant that the Chicago Public Library meet the needs of the perpetually underserved and normally overlooked black community. The reality of the matter was that a facility located where it was planned at 48th Street and Michigan Boulevard would, in fact, be considered a black library in an exclusively African American area recently abandoned by whites. While managing this problem, Hall sought to broaden employment for aspiring librarians and writers among the African American population.[41] One name that appeared eminently qualified was the rising black star Vivian G. Harsh.

As to African Americans securing a position on the board of education, membership still remained elusive.[42] African Americans consistently exerted pressure on political leaders from both parties, but the response from white political leadership reflected the wishes of a united white constituency that looked upon black advancement onto this body as a threat to municipal stability and their children's future. This was a sentiment that existed into the mayoralty of Harold Washington (1983–1987).

Honoring the military tradition of black Chicago reached a fever pitch as well by mid-decade. In response to opposition to a monument to the Black Metropolis' military cohort, the famed "Black Devils" of World War I, Wright acted decisively, harshly, and successfully. The fight over erecting the 8th Regiment statue at 35th Street and Grand Boulevard (later, South Parkway) was ferocious. Threatening the defeat of a needed bond issue for the governing body, the South Park District, the board acquiesced to African American demands. The well-recognized Victory Monument was thus constructed in 1929 and has since been revered through the years.[43]

Wright remained the publicly recognized leader of the black electorate until 1927 when he fell from prominence as a result of a major dispute with the Thompson faction over power and political independence. This exercise in black empowerment climaxed in the wake of the corruptive 1926 senatorial election that led the U.S. Senate to investigate irregularities in campaign funding. At this point Ed Wright, in response to the question as to what individual or group told him and his Black Metropolis cohort what to do and when to do it, boldly told the Senate Select Subcommittee, "I *am* the group."[44] Interestingly, in the eyes of many white Republicans, millionaire politician George F. Harding was still the "boss" of the Negro wards.[45] Political reality, however, dictated otherwise. In the core of, and extending out to the boundaries of, the Black Metropolis, Ed Wright reigned supreme as the political leader.[46]

During this heyday of black power, the voting strength of the Second and Third Wards gave Wright proportional power within the ranks of the Republican Central Committee to select the candidate for sheriff, one George Arnold, a white state official with the Illinois Department of Labor. Further, with Wright's power and influence within Republican circles at its zenith in 1926, "Big Bill" announced his intention to run for a third term as mayor of Chicago. In a pivotal move in the politics of the Black Metropolis and one unparalleled until the winter of 1982–1983 with the independent, broad-based mayoral race of Harold Washington, Wright opposed Thompson and sided with a physician named Dr. John Dill Robertson, the white candidate of Republican Party boss Fred "Poor Swede" Lundin. Then a rift in party ranks caused Wright to shift his support to another white candidate, Edward R. Litsinger. Wright also induced Democrat Earl B. Dickerson to run as an independent against the incumbent alderman, Louis B. Anderson, now a DePriest ally. Weakened with this late move, Litsinger was soundly defeated by a resurgent Thompson in the three wards of the Black Metropolis while Dickerson was defeated as well.[47] The usually friendly *Chicago Defender*, now under the control of Robert Abbott's brother-in-law, Nathan S. McGill, reported that the people of the Black Metropolis rejected the "Iron Master's" machinations and had "begun to think for themselves."[48] They recalled Thompson as being good for their varied interests—legal and otherwise, pro-wet and committed to black patronage—and had voted accordingly.

This tactic of having backed a loser inevitably cemented Wright's fall from power, both because of Litsinger's impossible chance to win and the cost of bucking the Thompson avalanche. The Black Metropolis had been accustomed to supporting Thompson to a great extent because of Wright's efforts. Now they seemed incapable of switching sides again, even when it benefitted their long-term interests. As Fields recounted, Wright "called his captains into council, telling them that what had happened and finally said, 'I have chosen my own course. I am not asking any of you to quit your jobs, but I am able to take care of myself. You go over to Dan Jackson—he is your new leader.'" Wright was very much aware of the value of retaining short-term gains for a people acclimated to disappointments and the crumbs from any table's leftovers. One such person realizing the need to protect his gains was Alderman Louis B. Anderson, who remained with the organization under Daniel "Dan" Jackson's leadership.[49]

Wright realized too late the folly of building up another politician to become bigger than his race's cause—in this case, long-range black political empowerment. Wright blamed himself later for having created the Thompson aura in the black mind and voting habit.[50] This had been the case with Thompson, dubbed "the Second Lincoln." A cynical Earl B. Dickerson considered this to be an appropriate appellation since Lincoln had never extended patronage to African Americans during his short term in office, and Thompson's support for black employment in government had been limited in actuality rather than being as extensive as it was in perception.[51]

Wright warned in 1926 and 1927 that past friends of his race were preparing to break the black power grip they held over their own dominions. Thompson saw things the same way—an independent South Side organization under Wright's control was intolerable. According to Fields, "When [Wright] told them that there was a conspiracy to lessen the political influence and activities of the Race by white men presumed to be their friends, they looked upon it as the last appeal of one who sought to retain himself in power."[52]

Dan Jackson, an ally of Oscar DePriest, already sat as Third Ward committeeman and he now moved into a position of greater prominence within the Thompson camp. A physically ailing Wright then yielded his seat on the Illinois Commerce Commission to Jackson in September 1928, with a public explanation citing Wright's health complaints. Armed with fifty patronage positions, taken at the expense of Wright, Jackson now surrounded himself with men of his persuasion, which meant the momentum toward political independence through black empowerment that Wright had fought so long to build was lost. Anderson, although no longer a Wright supporter, was excluded from Dan Jackson's inner circle. He did manage to retain his aldermanic post until 1933 when William L. Dawson replaced him.[53]

Meanwhile, the 1926 race for the seat of the First Congressional District was conceded by black party regulars to the white incumbent, the Hon. Martin Madden, whose tenure extended back to 1900 and whose service in behalf of constituents had proven invaluable. Rising nationalistic tendencies within the Black Metropolis at this time created a climate in which Madden appeared vulnerable to rumblings in neighborhood meetings, while still solidly entrenched among Republican Party stalwarts. Would-be banker P. W. Chavers, who had arranged the chartering of the Douglass National Bank only to be undermined and ousted, now sought Madden's seat and ran on a racially charged program. Chavers articulated his position in this manner:

> I now call your attention to the issues created in this Congressional campaign. . . . Between Madden, a white man, and myself, a Colored man. I say to you that we must respect our God-given skin color, the skins with which we were born. We cannot, we must not, accept the doctrine that white is the only official color in America and that a white man can represent us better than one of us can. No white can feel the sting of uncivilized lynchings and the constant assaults of discrimination and segregation that we suffer simply because of our God-given color. If we accept the doctrine of white representation, then we are forever condemned, for we are not asserting ourselves as we should. . . .

> We are competing in the economic arena and we must rise to this challenge and earn our place in this society, side by side, with the white man. This is our right and our responsibility. We must protect what we achieve . . . and never let them take away what is rightfully ours.[54]

Out of nearly 12,000 votes cast in a district that was predominantly black, Congressman Madden received 9,682 votes to challenger Chavers's 2,015 tallies.[55]

When compared to Wright, DePriest's role in Black Metropolis politics had a lesser but not an altogether insignificant place until 1927. He challenged Wright's leadership vigorously on several occasions as he did in the aldermanic races of 1923 and came out the loser as the candidates whom he sponsored were defeated. As a local leader, he also projected an image and had a reputation that stemmed from his being the first black member of the Chicago City Council. His election in 1915 had made him a symbol of racial success that brought admirers to his side whenever he appeared on the streets of his ward.[56] However, during the twenties, his involvement in politics took on a surreptitious tinge after he was forced from open participation in politics following his indictment and subsequent acquittal on bribery charges in 1917. DePriest officially resurfaced fully in 1927 as Wright slid from power.

Governance, the administration of the city's affairs, and electoral politics still dominated the Black Metropolis's landscape even with increased civic advocacy by groups outside the political sphere aiming to improve the quality of life in their portion of the vice-ridden city. For example, the year 1927 brought heightened political tension as the mayoral election marked the return of Bill Thompson into the public's arena. What was unusual was Thompson being slated without Wright's blessing. Racism was strong with growing white resentment to black political gains, and the theme of "Bye, Bye, Blackbirds" gained in popularity as a Democratic campaign song. If the political demise of Edward H. Wright and resurfacing of DePriest as a conspicuous public figure did not bring enough discomfort to certain segments of the African American electorate, the daylight assassination of black aldermanic candidate Octavius C. Granady in April 1928 did. Running for office in the West Side's corrupt Twentieth Ward, attorney Granady was killed by machine fire in front of a polling station in broad daylight. The reaction within the Black Metropolis extended beyond its usual range of apathy among so many of the masses to indignation within the ranks of the civic-minded.

By the end of the year, concerned, reform-minded citizens of the South Side led by banker Anthony Overton, Rev. L. K. Williams, and attorney S. A. T. Watkins had begun to organize to defeat the Thompson machine, which they held accountable for Granady's death and the widespread criminalization of life in the Black Metropolis. In addition to Mayor Thompson and his white cronies, Oscar DePriest was targeted for defeat at the polls. "Policy men and street walkers have become so bold down here that they invade our best homes and neighborhoods. The gambling evil shows up every day in the banking business. Hard working wage earners draw out their savings accounts, drop their life insurance, and neglect their families so they can throw their money away on policy tickets. Protected prostitution is worse than it ever has been," observed Overton.[57]

Overton's involvement in electoral politics was indeed unusual for the black business community, which traditionally committed itself solely to providing financial contributions to politicians. His involvement in 1928 was overlooked by Harold F. Gosnell's researchers, as the banker took the next step beyond indignation and joined a predominantly white businessmen's organization that had undertaken as its goal the restoration of good government. The candidate of choice of this group was Hon. John A. Swanson, who ran for state attorney, Cook County's chief prosecutor.[58]

Meantime, the 1928 congressional election saw Rep. Martin B. Madden run for his fourteenth consecutive term in office. He won handily in the spring primary with black party loyalists supporting him again because of his standing in the Congress. It was a position from which many blacks continually benefitted directly. At the time, ambitious African American attorney and Republican Party loyalist William L. Dawson (whose star would rise during the 1930s) actively entered electoral politics at age forty-two, seeking the congressional seat. He was defeated through the efforts of numerous individuals within the party organization, including Oscar DePriest.[59] Once again the contest was fought by independents along racial lines. Dawson challenged Madden along familiar lines. He argued that "By birth, training and experience I am better fitted to represent the district than any other candidates now in the field. Mr. Madden . . . does not even live in the district. He is a white man. Therefore, for those two reasons, if no others, he can hardly voice the hopes, ideals and sentiment of the majority of the district."[60] Despite Dawson's racial appeal in a district that was now heavily African American, the electorate followed Mayor Thompson's preference in retaining Madden and the dictum of party first, race second. This position was, ironically, a notion that Dawson himself would espouse later in his political career. Dawson received only 29 percent of the votes; Madden won the primary with over 60 percent. Dawson's ambitions and skills at conciliation proved resilient as, instead of punishment, his career took an upturn in summer 1929 when he was appointed by the governor (with DePriest's backing) to succeed the late Dan Jackson as a member on the Illinois Commerce Commission.[61]

It was at this critical juncture, just weeks before the general election, that man, ambition, and circumstance meshed. Madden died, and Oscar DePriest reemerged from political oblivion and vacation at Idlewild, Michigan, to seize the moment. With the backing of Second Ward committeeman Dan Jackson, "Big Bill" Thompson, and three Italian ward committeemen, including one of Al Capone's lieutenants, DePriest garnered sufficient party support to have his name placed on the ballot.[62] In a classic case of opportunistic politics, DePriest maneuvered himself into a position to win as an individual, which he did. In the general election DePriest defeated Harry Baker, a white Democrat, with a tally of 23,141 votes to 20,261.[63] An independent black candidate named William H. Harrison ran as an alternative to the tarnished DePriest and won only 4,008 votes, while the other alternative, the Communist Party candidate Edward "Ed" Doty, won 101.

Significantly, by 1929, now U.S. Rep. Oscar DePriest had become "a national figure, admired by Negroes and feared by many whites." In the eyes of his supporters, who ranged across the social spectrum from the members of the intelligentsia to the masses who turned out and voted faithfully in every election, "he fought segregation, discrimination and oppression. His influence spread into every phase of civic life. He used his political power and prestige to open new doors of opportunity and to press for advancement." Also, he was known as a man who would "kick down a door to help a member of his race" and as one "who always could be counted on to do something for his race."[64]

However, DePriest was more complex than presented in his popular image. In contrast to his being lionized both inside and outside of the Black Metropolis, he was criticized for his financial and political opportunism. He was known to be a real estate speculator and rent gouger, and "compared with some of the other leaders of his time DePriest was less bound [than they were] by tradition and party loyalty. [To many,] he was a supreme opportunist [who] calculated each step coolly and shrewdly."[65]

As the Republican Party of Chicago and the Black Metropolis approached the end of the decade, their prospects looked promising in spite of ominous signs of an unraveling of the economic fabric both locally and nationally. Politically, the Black Metropolis had accomplished the impossible in incredible fashion: Chicago had sent the first African American in nearly three decades to sit in the chambers of the U.S. Congress.

The Linkage between Traditional (and Nontraditional) Politics and Disparate Protest

In the best of all worlds—one in which good, representative government worked in the people's behalf—no alternative was needed to improve society. In 1920s Chicago, with politicians of all stripes serving their parties' needs first, along with the quest for their own individual pursuits of seeking and holding office before considering what citizens wanted and needed, the public good was often treated sacrificially. The election day assassination of reform-minded aldermanic hopeful Octavius C. Granady in 1928 showed the extent to which personal courage was needed to serve the citizens of the Black Metropolis. These tensions created a complex, multidimensional relationship between traditional political leadership and their black constituents in regard to activists' expectations of racial progress in the areas of representation, employment, housing, education, and citizenship rights. Correspondingly, this made the response of black politicians to advocacy groups that either worked within the limits laid down by the dominant white culture or challenged the status quo exceedingly problematic.

The black politicians' perception of which organization had the best program to aid in the struggle for an improvement in their race's status, like that of the constituents they served, was often a matter of individual preference. As loyal members of a political machine, they had to be responsive to the realities of political life in the city and therefore could be indifferent on occasions to their race's best interests. Importantly, depending on the issue involved, they could be very responsive regardless of the political climate or other ordinarily influential factors such as personal aggrandizement and group advancement. Yet the most common situation that a black politician encountered paled in comparison to what his constituents had to endure.

These parallel responsibilities forced politicians into a dual strategy in which they worked to survive personally while pursuing the racial goals their constituents sought. Despite the racial protocol alive in Chicago that accommodated black advancement within political channels based on the necessity of the day, there were occasions when the growing strength of the Black Metropolis electorate made Wright and his political cohorts appear too aggressive to Republican Party leaders and allies. Public display of this hegemony led the "powers that be . . . [to decide] that Wright's ambition was becoming too elastic and that something should be done to curb him. He was becoming a menace to the power and influence of such men as George F. Harding and his lieutenant, Charles Krutchkroff. Wright was not a Harding man because he thought he knew better what his race wanted than Harding did."[66] In a clash in 1920 over whether Wright would become the nominee and victor as Second Ward committeeman, Wright and his forces won, making him the first of his race to enter the councils of the Republican Party's Cook County Central Committee. Now, as committeeman, he possessed the power to dispense jobs to his constituents as he saw fit.

Meeting the needs and aspirations of African Americans through governmental partisan politics brought some successes, but mainly for individuals and politicized cliques. These pathways offered only limited advancement for the masses of African Americans when pitted against entrenched white racial interests, procedures, protocols, and institutions. African Americans were forced to mount a vigorous multifaceted crusade in pursuit of achieving a broadened agenda. This programmatic wish list ranged in intensity from the attainment of civil rights to economic parity and espoused such measures as conciliation to militancy to revolution.

Alternative channels through which change was to be effected, for example, involved reorganization and redirection of the Chicago branch of the NAACP's programmatic thrust to gain relevancy in the lives of black Chicagoans. Other efforts aimed at improving the lot of workers occasioned the emergence of the first national union among Pullman porters, along with a radical labor organization committed to revolutionary trade unionism in the American Negro Labor Council. These appeared, in turn, as competitors to highly nationalistic activities involving thousands of the city's blacks, who coalesced along racial and cultural lines. In the totality of the scope of all of these activities, the interests and needs of black labor, business, the professions, schoolchildren, and broad social groups were encompassed.

The program of the Chicago Urban League, which was primarily jobs oriented and therefore consistent with the most immediate needs of the people of the Black Metropolis, appeared to have been supported by all of the politicians. It was given, after all, the open support in writing of political leader DePriest[67] and was consistent with their program of expanding the black labor base that formed the backbone of the black Republican organization until the advent of the Great Depression. DePriest distinguished himself in defense of black workers during the race riot of 1919, and at the dawn of the Depression decade in 1930 he would once again emerge at the forefront of the fight for jobs as long as it did interfere with national Republican policies.

Without exception on absolutely organizational terms, Alderman Robert Jackson of the Third Ward was the most enthusiastic supporter of the Chicago Urban League. He worked perennially as a financial campaigner for the organization and even headed the annual drive for funds and members as a working leader on a number of occasions. His colleague in the council, Alderman Louis B. Anderson of the Second Ward, got the city council's approval in 1926 for the establishment of a municipal shelter for the homeless men of his ward during the Christmas season of that year. He then shared the credit for his action with the league, which subsequently agreed to maintain the shelter on an ongoing basis.[68]

The program of the Chicago branch of the NAACP placed the organization at variance with both the black politicians and the Chicago Urban League because it followed an ideology that endorsed—and a program that employed—confrontational tactics. This change in approach took place after 1925, when a black-led leadership replaced a patriarchal, biracial clique that had operated since the branch's founding. The Chicago NAACP aimed to change the status quo through the use of publicly embarrassing civil suits directed against discriminatory practices and their perpetrators.[69]

Nonetheless, there were those occasions when black politicians supported the branch with unrestrained enthusiasm. In 1925, when the branch president, Dr. Herbert Turner, issued a call for a meeting and support for Dr. Ossian Sweet of Detroit (who had repulsed a white mob attacking his home), it was Ed Wright's Second Ward organization that helped kick off the fund-raising with a $100.00 contribution, an especially large gift for that time.[70] In 1926, preceding Oscar DePriest's visible public return to politics, he served as the chairman of the Citizens Committee that helped sponsor the NAACP's national conference held in Chicago, and later in the year, sponsored the organization of the first women's auxiliary, dubbed the "Flying Squadron."[71] In a display of allegiance to the cause of securing first-class citizenship, DePriest took out a $1,000.00 life membership in the NAACP.[72] Once in Congress as black America's first twentieth-century national legislator, DePriest appointed the branch's former secretary, Morris Lewis, as his congressional secretary. Lewis's reputation as an avowed egalitarian rested on his having vigorously pursued civil rights cases for the branch before 1925, when the biracial leadership tandem of Judge Brown and Dr. Bentley advised caution.[73] Lewis had occasionally personally extended himself beyond the scope of his official responsibilities and pursued cases involving civil rights violations, much to the displeasure of Dr. Bentley and Judge Brown.[74]

Other than these cases, however, the record involving collaboration between black Republicans and the Chicago and national NAACP was limited. Black politicians also had to live with the persistent problem of economic dislocation during the postwar period. However, their response was virtually unnoticeable. Black politicians did nothing—or, as members of the machine, could do nothing—legislatively of significance in the midst of deteriorating economic conditions among Chicago blacks. During this period preceding the Great Depression, the black politicians, like their white counterparts, were basically ignorant of the need to take sweeping, systemic action when faced with widespread and growing unemployment.

When the politicians were confronted during this decade by the Chicago chapter of the Communist Party, an economic-oriented, revolutionary organization (that had not yet established itself in the twenties as an organization to be reckoned with by the governmental establishment as a direct threat to American economic institutions), they ignored the chapter. The politicians, as well as their constituents, remained supportive of the political and economic systems that in the twenties had not yet been branded disreputable and culpable for the nation's economic shortcomings. Although the activities of the black politicians might have appeared limited in regard to the scope of what was needed to be done to change the racial and economic status quo, they were quite ambitious in relation to how the politicians and many of their constituents perceived their responsibilities. They fought to secure, maintain, and enhance their race's political position in the city through which progress was to be made. In this, they were meeting some success. In addition, at this time, neither a well-coordinated protest movement nor an individual organization existed that could provide a better solution to the race's ills.

One internal change within the structure of the Chicago NAACP surely impressed the politicians. The branch reached a critical phase of its development by 1925 with the emergence of the black presidency, which would sustain itself for decades to come and lead the branch to organizational and then institutional status. Characterized by generational as much as racial nature because of the New Negro influence, the most salient feature of the differences between the generations was age: The generation of the founders, the neo-abolitionist egalitarians, produced very little in the way of programmatic or ideological successes.

Politicians were now included on the NAACP's executive committee, which now peaked in size to a membership of twenty-six. Its ranks were diverse occupationally, though predominantly black and male, and included politicians such as Oscar DePriest, state senator Adelbert H. Roberts, and state representatives William E. King and George W. Blackwell; lawyers, such as Democrat Earl B. Dickerson, the West Side's Graham T. Perry, and recent Mississippi migrant Theophilus M. Mann; the manager of the *Chicago Whip*, A. C. MacNeal; ministers; and social workers. The meetings of the executive committee were held in the most densely populated area of Bronzeville, which meant that they were in the midst of the populace the branch purported to serve. However, the executive committee reached programmatic decisions that aimed primarily at alleviating the plight of the professional and middle strata of blacks rather than that of their working-class black brethren. The former groups encountered problems that were more legalistic in nature and therefore the opposite of the employment and housing problems faced by the majority of the black people in the Black Metropolis.

The disparity between what the branch's program offered and one that addressed the needs of the mass of the Black Metropolis's citizenry stemmed from the closed hierarchical character of the executive committee. First, with the small pool of persons chosen for service, the branch faced a problem in regard to attendance at its leadership meetings where it was difficult to get more than a quorum at most sessions. One group, the politicians, never attended meetings because they were probably too busy or considered the meetings unimportant. Second, those members who did attend represented only a small portion of the population of the Black Belt because of their higher status, occupation, and income levels. Third, the membership of the branch was neither informed of nor invited to branch meetings and therefore had no input into decisions regarding policy and program.

When the people of the Black Metropolis looked at the Chicago NAACP, they saw an organization that conducted its business as an exclusive club without apparent regard for the divergent interests of the Black Belt's inhabitants. A change in conditions over time would bring a series of transformations. The year 1925, for example, brought the branch to a critical phase in its development—the emergence of a new patriarchic leadership that excluded whites while acquiescing partially to African American nationalistic sentiment. This hegemonic change was as much generational and ideological as it was racial, with differences in age and the experiences of black Chicagoans maturing during the New Negro era assuming great saliency. Dr. Carl G. Roberts assumed the presidency over the predominantly African American branch. Having shared the same experiences with racial prejudice and discrimination that other black Chicagoans had, his appointment appealed to his fellow African Americans. Yet, within eight months, Roberts abruptly left the presidency and Dr. Herbert Turner, another surgeon and a devoted racial egalitarian, succeeded him. Permanency of black leadership had been established.

Linkage among Civic Organizations and the Antiestablishment Communist Party

The histories of the Chicago Urban League, the Chicago branch of the NAACP, and the Chicago chapter of the Communist Party were somewhat similar in the earliest years of their founding in that they all shared certain characteristics: They all emerged from primarily all-white ideological and leadership bases and were reliant on funding from primarily outside the black community for their initial maintenance. In the case of the league and the NAACP, they shared the same white personnel in leadership roles in what was a civic version of an interlocking directorate. However, in the unique case of the Chicago Urban League, it was able to develop a relatively substantial black contributory base of long duration. The majority of the people of the Black Metropolis were supportive of organizations and institutions that were organized and led by persons from within their own racial ranks and were suspicious of, if not hostile to, outside persons and groups. The most notable examples of the organizations and institutions that they supported were the churches, lodges, social clubs, and fraternal orders that abounded in the black community on the South Side. Therefore, the three organizations met at least four significant problems that hindered their operations during the 1910s and 1920s: the adverse image of the racial outsider in a tight-knit racially inclusive community, a precariously unreliable funding base to sustain activities, a small membership where volunteerism was necessary to fulfill programmatic and operational responsibilities, and a strained relationship among the interracial board and staff personnel that reflected the national tension that existed between the races.

Of the three new nonpolitical organizations, the Chicago Urban League was able to move farthest beyond its problems to advance, first in the direction of racial advancement by providing assistance in the economic sphere and the building of better race relations, and second in the direction of protest activism in the job sphere in the late twenties. The kind of improved race relations most prevalent in the Urban League's earliest years was the type that benefitted whites as well as blacks, but for different reasons. At the point that the league's leadership, white and black, attempted to work in earnest for racial equality as well as opportunity, a more racially conservative element, such as represented by the business interests, threatened to, and then did, withdraw their support in 1929 over this and other similar issues. Yet there were strengths possessed by the league, and they were found in its having an economic program that was accepted by the people it purported to serve, in operating with a permanent, paid, professional staff, and in receiving continuous financial and volunteer support from blacks.[75]

Unfortunately for the league, the decade of the twenties did not bring a continuation of its early efforts and successes between 1917 and 1919. According to

Arvarh Strickland, a historian and authority on the organization's development from its founding, conditions changed as the decades did. Strickland noted that "the League had reached the climax of its effectiveness and public appeal during the riot of 1919 and the two years following this disturbance."[76] This was due to the nature of the decade that first produced economic stagnation and in its wake growing unemployment among blacks, and then a curtailment, both early and late in the decade, of essential financial contributions from major, white funding sources. The city's job market, always restrictive for blacks, was affected by the recession of 1920-1921 and rapidly constricted after the war. The league was then forced to face a problem with which it lacked familiarity as the number of black unemployed workers either remained constant or increased. Further compounding of the league's woes was a diminution in its financial support from white contributors who, after 1921, no longer saw conditions as being as dire as they had been earlier and subsequently discontinued their aid. They fell into two categories: those who had contributed originally because the deterioration of race relations that culminated in the riot of 1919 seemed a problem of paramount importance; and those who assisted the league in its employment mission when the halcyon days of the pre- to postwar boom existed.[77]

The consequence of the dwindling financial base was the curtailment of basic services and an attendant concern about the organization's chances for survival during the mid-twenties. Then, in 1929, a second financial shock came as the Chicago-based Rosenwald Fund, which at times in the organization's history had contributed as much as one third of its operating budget, decided to withdraw all of its funding as a result of personal and philosophical differences with the league's leadership over the direction of its programs. Uncertainty about the future of the organization under these dismal economic conditions in the mid-twenties began to have an influence on its professional staff. T. Arnold Hill, the black executive secretary, felt so uneasy about working conditions in 1923 that he considered an alternate career in "the more promising field" of politics.[78] Hill decided in the affirmative and broke with national and affiliate league policy on political noninvolvement as he chose to enter the city's political arena as a reformist candidate for alderman in the vice-ridden Second Ward. Noninvolvement had always been sound policy because the league depended heavily on contributions from a diverse contributory base, and Hill's decision to sully heretofore clean waters placed the league in a position of alienating some of its large financial supporters. No financial losses were immediately discernible after 1923, but the league's image had been altered and there was a loss of prestige.[79]

Although the standing policy of political noninvolvement had been strictly adhered to by both board and staff members when it came to overt displays of political involvement, covert and private activities by board and staff members as individuals had been prevalent through the organization's history. For example, Rosenwald had always taken an interest in the city's political life and future. He had consistently opposed corrupt and radical political elements and was especially appalled by the machinations of machine politicians since the beginning of the century through the days of the Thompson regime.[80] Other board members also had opposed the corruption that ran rampant in the city. The attitude of Harry Oppenheimer, a prominent meat distributor and friend of Salmon Levinson, the internationally known peacemaker, was reflected in a message about Hill in 1923. He communicated that "Hill . . . is running for alderman from the second ward, that disgraceful part of Chicago which urgently requires cleaning up. . . . Primaries take place in [a] few days and money [is] urgently required."[81]

From a political standpoint and one that eluded advocates of good government, Hill's candidacy was misconstrued by some black people to be a demonstration of the league's open opposition to Second Ward Alderman Louis Anderson. This challenge did not endear itself to either Wright's Second Ward organization or to Mayor Thompson. However, a contest with reform elements was never considered a viable threat to the formidable Second Ward organization. In the campaign, Hill objected to the deplorable vice conditions in the ward while Anderson countered by raising the specter of Hill's candidacy being a white-directed impediment to race advancement. Although on the surface Anderson's charge appeared to be without merit and merely a device used to sway voters by manipulating the sensitive issue of race, the dissolution of the Second Ward black political faction (which had police support in allowing vice conditions to exist) would have meant a loss of thousands of jobs in the Black Metropolis. In the cold, hard economic terms that made life in the Black Metropolis as bleak as it was, corrupt government that tolerated vice conditions also worked to produce an environment where blacks could find constant employment.[82] The black electorate's response to Hill was to soundly repudiate him at the polls on election day, with Anderson tallying 6,360 votes to Hill's 2,572.[83]

Having been subjected to the rawness of Chicago machine politics at its most insidious levels, Hill left the Chicago Urban League in early 1925 to take a more secure position in New York with the National Urban League as director of industrial relations. His successor as executive secretary in 1925 was A. L. Foster, who arrived in Chicago to become the staff leader of an enfeebled league. Foster was perfect for the occasion since he brought energy and an aggressiveness that was rather at variance with the league's and Hill's overly gentlemanly and accommodationist approach to the problems of economic and racial advancement. The racially conservative Rosenwald, who was also a supporter of Booker T. Washington and the Tuskegeean's gradualist approach in race relations, had once described Hill as a good man in the job, being "a very conservative, vigorous, educated Negro."[84] Foster shared Hill's latter two traits but he would prove to be anything other than conservative.

Foster also brought with him a set of ideological views that, while not totally contravening, were subject to generate conflict, as they did late in the thirties during a period of economic discontent. He balanced them carefully into this personal philosophy; on one path he traveled, he endorsed racial conciliation consistent with the league's avowed purpose; on another, he was an advocate of racial solidarity among blacks, a belief more acceptable to the black masses and politicians than to the white members of the city clubs and boardrooms. Building on this second ideological characteristic, Foster adopted more aggressive tactics as part of a strategy to combat joblessness. Focusing the league's efforts in the geographic area of the Black Metropolis in an area that was most likely to respond to the pressure exerted by blacks, he mounted an intensive campaign of education and persuasion to increase employment opportunities in an area where black consumer power was high.

The new executive secretary was faced immediately with two ills that were directly related to the deteriorating economic conditions that continued throughout the decade: high unemployment among black workers and the sagging financial status of the league.

The league's strategy on behalf of labor (chapter 4) had evolved into one geared to winning battles in a constricting job market filled with both pervasive unemployment and underemployment. With this change, it had been transformed organizationally into a prime agent of a movement for job protest. However, the limits of its ideology (in particular, that portion dealing with racial conciliation) and program restricted its ability to respond on an activist level with any means other than those of persuasion, education, and cooperation. The result of this heightened activism disturbed the representative of one of the organization's biggest financial backers, Alfred Stern, who was Julius Rosenwald's son-in-law. Organizational turmoil lay ahead.

The league did not change its approach and Stern announced that a suspension of financial assistance would take place immediately if certain changes weren't forthcoming. The tactic used by Stern was to condemn league activities in the area of social welfare as being inefficient and to accuse the staff and board of incompetence in dealing with the economic problems affecting blacks. Stern in particular accused Foster of being an incompetent for not pursuing a program that was viewed as irresponsible in the eyes of Rosenwald, although what exactly was desired was never fully enunciated.[85] Also, Alonzo Thayer's presence as the director of Industrial Relations disturbed Stern. Thayer, who was newly returned to the league, was a key staff member of Foster's and a former employee of the *Whip*, which had a known anti- Rosenwald bias.[86] Thayer was described by Stern as being "very opinionated and antagonistic in his attitude to executives in plants where he was trying to locate Negroes or to improve their positions. In public addresses about the Negro's problem he made tactless statements which also created antagonism . . . [and as for the board, it] is made up largely of social workers and ministers and is dominated by a few women."[87]

Stern's solution was not aimed at the Chicago Urban League alone because he saw what he perceived as weaknesses in the organization's approach and program holistically in national terms. When he recommended a merger on the national level between the NAACP and the National Urban League, he was also dealing with an acknowledged enfeebled Chicago affiliate. Strategically, a dual agenda would have been adopted. As attempts to mollify Stern on all points proved futile, subsequent funding from the Rosenwald family ceased and was never resumed.[88]

Sometimes out of trials and travails come a strengthening and a pathway to future solutions. The intertwining of three developments in the late twenties placed the league on a course that was preparing it well for the challenge of the Depression decade. At this time the league was adopting a wider view of economic processes because it now had experience with the problem of unemployment as it reached disastrous proportions, not only for the inhabitants of the Black Metropolis but for all Chicagoans. Moreover, the response of the league to the job crisis had advanced along a course that led it to develop an appreciation of the rudiments of the buying power idea, which seeped ever so slightly into its program. Then, the reaction of its more conservative philanthropic contributors portended the difficulties the league would encounter as long as it attempted to approach the job crisis with a more militant stance and a program in which the contributors saw no value. In challenging those groups that benefitted from the political and economic status quo, the league acquired a greater vulnerability than ever before in its history. In the thirties it would survive or fail based on its ability to reach a compromise with political and economic forces that it obviously could not overwhelm, and in fact, upon which it was dependent.

Unlike the Chicago Urban League, the Chicago branch of the NAACP was one organization in the civic realm that was distinctly founded to challenge the status quo. While the branch adopted a program that called upon it to work "for the advancement of Colored people [and at] efforts to lessen race discrimination and to secure full civic, political and legal rights to Colored citizens and others," the adoption of this program never led to the necessary organizational goal of full implementation. The branch's primary concern was always one of organizational survival. It moved listlessly through its earliest years until the Depression decade, when it finally showed some vitality as it overcame its problems of poor leadership, small memberships, and inadequate funding. Even a dramatic change in the racial composition of its leadership on the governing executive committee in and after 1925 proved inadequate to propel it into full organizational efficiency.

The branch's leadership ranks were always divided between the ideological poles of caution and assertiveness, the latter bordering on militancy. Of course, status and wealth played their part. On one end of the spectrum in the early days, one could find a person like Julius Rosenwald who, like his deceased friend at Tuskegee Institute, did not wholly accept the idea of a militant, activist organization that aimed primarily at achieving racial equality at the expense of creating racial opportunity.[89] On the other, there stood a militant like Ida B. Wells-Barnett, who did not wholly accept the idea that a black-oriented program, and the organization that promoted it, needed white leadership. Interestingly, neither of the two remained with the branch for any length of time during its earliest years or returned any time thereafter. Their absence and the spheres they represented merely served to highlight the two problems that would beset the branch for years to come: inadequate funding and a lack of a militant, recognized black leadership needed to attract the masses within the black populace. In regard to one of the basic, divisive, and lingering differences between the races, that of status, whites held upper-class or upper-middle-class status while the blacks were lower-middle-class professionals who enjoyed an elevation of status only among blacks. Because of this inequality in status, wealth, and power, a relationship developed that bordered on paternalism. With the arrival of black leadership in 1925, divisive class concerns and the division of support into building the Black Metropolis produced only a black patriarchy and no meaningful program aimed at ameliorating the problems of the laboring class.

One positive point was recognizable as this decade began: a rise in activities of its corps of attorneys, both white and black, who were willing to defend black citizens accused of participating in the riot disturbances of 1919. Significantly, it did so only after the national office dictated that this course of action be taken. In the eyes of the branch's leadership, the fear that some of the defendants might be criminals and might therefore tarnish the organization's image unfortunately had subverted the branch's interest in protecting legal rights. The cautious leadership of Judge Brown and Dr. Charles E. Bentley feared what they perceived as the branch's mission being contaminated with imagined mass-level tendencies toward criminality. Among the defendants, though, was A. C. MacNeal, a militant branch officer (and future branch president) accused of assault with intent to kill as he opposed a mob that assembled outside a house in which he was trapped.[90]

After this brief period of success in an area in which the organization was best able to act, the legal, it reverted to its old status. During the twenties, its pattern of inactivity was so pronounced that its existence except on paper as a chartered body was even doubted.[91] Its handicaps of having an elitist, white-dominated image and an inadequate funding base plagued it, and this problem of funding consigned the branch to a position where it was never able to pay its expenses or meet its obligations to the national office.[92]

By 1924, the year after the Chicago Urban League's executive secretary, T. Arnold Hill, considered leaving that organization because of its financial and organizational problems, the Chicago NAACP branch's executive secretary, Morris Lewis, pondered the same course of action. His decision was to leave to take a position as circulation manager with the *Chicago Defender* newspaper, which was the city and nation's most widely read black publication as well as, ironically, a hostile voice to the Chicago NAACP. While in office, Lewis had provided the counterweight to the slow and cautious organizational approach of the branch's white president (from 1922-1924), Harold L. Ickes, and of Dr. Charles E. Bentley, the vice president.[93]

At the time of Lewis' departure in late 1924, Ickes also had been considering resigning his post due to his frustrations with the organization over funding and the dearth of Black Metropolis and citywide white financial support. His view had moved in this direction, which he shared with Robert W. Bagnall: "The feeling has been growing in me that probably one difficulty with our local branch was that we were too 'high brow.' In addition to that I felt that if the Branch was really to succeed and do anything worth while it would be because the Colored people themselves realized its worth and were sufficiently interested in the organization to get back of it. I stated that in my opinion a Colored man ought to be selected as president. . . . I think the Board itself should be composed of Colored men and women leaving whites to serve, if desired, in an advisory capacity."[94] Ickes's sentiments were shared by Morris Lewis, who took Ickes's suggestions one step further to include the president as one of the impediments holding the branch back. He described Ickes as being "ultra-conservative. He has not got the Negro viewpoint. This is true of most white men. It is impossible for them to put themselves in our places."[95]

Since James Weldon Johnson, the national secretary, shared his views on the need for a change in racial leadership, Ickes's suggestions as well as his resignation were accepted in late 1924. The next year, the Chicago branch elected its first African American president. The choice of the branch was Dr. Carl G. Roberts, a physician with a record of staunch commitment to the NAACP's cause and one who had worked assiduously in its behalf. It was hoped that the change in racial leadership in 1925 would be viewed in the black community as a sign that not only had blacks secured the power to shape what they would view as being their own organization's direction but also its composition of only 200 members.[96]

The future of the branch was indeed to be shaped partially by roles relegated to the whites and to the rank-and-file blacks. The role of whites during the remainder of the decade was severely diminished, with whites serving in three areas: as advisors, activists, and financial contributors. However, the inclusion of working-class blacks as branch members was an essential ingredient that remained missing. It would have to be this group, through the payment of membership dues, that would have had to sustain the branch financially.

This was especially true because the Chicago NAACP, unlike the Urban League, depended on membership dues rather than on white philanthropy to finance its operations. Fewer and fewer whites also meant diminishing financial contributions. Those whites who did remain became important links between the races. Recognizing this, James Weldon Johnson commended the Chicago NAACP for retaining the influence of Mary McDowell on the advisory board. McDowell was so well respected in the black community that this move proved especially wise.[97] Johnson aptly stated, "She will give you a close means of contact with various white groups in Chicago."[98] She would do for the NAACP what Rosenwald did early on for the Chicago Urban League. It was envisioned that other whites would serve the branch as activists investigating civil rights violations in situations where blacks couldn't obtain information. Once aware that school segregation was becoming a serious problem, James Weldon Johnson suggested to the Chicago branch that, in order to facilitate the investigation of the charge, "you might get a clever young white woman, say, one connected with the University of Chicago . . . to do the job."[99]

Morris Lewis felt that to attract the mass of the population of the black Chicago and make the branch truly democratic in its governance and consistent with its governance, a complete change in approach and attitude was needed. He wrote, "What we need here . . . is to begin anew; not as a high-brow organization or as an anti-high-brow organization but of the people, by the people, for the people."[100] In a similar vein, from the association's New York headquarters, Robert W. Bagnall confided to Dr. Carl G. Roberts, after being asked what had been wrong with the branch in Chicago, stated not only the obvious but remarks that have to be considered prophetic. Bagnall wrote perceptively with an awareness of the influence of New Negro thinking: "The Association in Chicago has so long been regarded as an organization dominated by whites and a few Colored individuals that it will take some time to educate public opinion to the realization that it is an organization of the people."[101]

The racial shift in leadership did not mean that a change in class orientation had occurred. What evolved in Chicago was anything but a black-led, egalitarian organization. Internal bickering, which centered on personalities and social standing, prevented a change in direction toward democracy. Within several months of leading the branch in this milieu, Carl G. Roberts left his office in disgust over internal squabbling, presumably over procedures. Roberts was then immediately succeeded by another rising black physician, Dr. Herbert A. Turner. The new president enjoyed high status in the Black Metropolis and began late in 1925 what was to become a seven-year tenure in office. He was described as an activist leader by Morris Lewis and as being "not too proud to do anything anyone else is willing to do. He has good ideas but is not deaf to good plans from others."[102] Very importantly, he also had an established medical practice and substantial income, which he generously shared with the organization.[103] A more complete description of Turner would have also included information that would have shown him to be much more akin to the thinking of Dr. Bentley on social matters and not in the least the assertive egalitarian leader that the branch needed. Turner's attitude was to change in that direction though, early in the next decade.

As a direct result of the branch's continued elitist image, which was supported by the attitudes of its leadership, a broad base of popular support did not develop. Another factor was significant to explain this failure to gain the community's support. The branch failed to develop a comprehensive program that reflected the needs of the people of the Black Metropolis. The people needed jobs and the branch offered them an incomplete and perhaps not immediately attainable civil rights program. What program activities it did muster centered on lukewarm support for a school segregation case at a school located several miles south of the Black Metropolis, in the Morgan Park enclave. This was at a time when the primary issue in education inside the Black Metropolis was overcrowding. Occasionally, the branch protested civil rights violations in places of public accommodations such as restaurants in the Loop and others located on the fringes of the Black Metropolis, but the *Chicago Defender* and other aggrieved blacks did much more than the branch's legal redress committee and actually brought civil suits to court, which they won.[104] The branch also took an interest in cases involving discrimination in interstate bus transportation, but a large number of persons in the Black Metropolis did not utilize this service since they were recent migrants from the South and had little interest in traveling back to that region. And the branch failed to conduct regular public meetings, except for those held for issues of national importance, such as the Sweet Defense effort in 1925 and the Dyer Anti-Lynching Bill rallies in the mid-twenties.

The notoriety of the Sweet family case assumed national importance. The trial was being heard by a jury in Detroit in June 1926 as the branch hosted the NAACP's seventeenth annual meeting. The Sweet case was as notable for its cast of characters as it was for its impact nationally on standing racial protocol. The previous year, Dr. Ossian Sweet, a dentist and professional man of standing, had defended his family in their newly purchased home in Detroit at the end of a gun. When a white mob attacked his home, he fired on it and killed one of its number. His defense attorney was the noted Clarence Darrow, and his support mechanism included the weight of the national office of the NAACP. In defending the sanctuary of his home, he attached himself to a time-honored right in Anglo-Saxon jurisprudence and something white men had honored as sacred for generations. Black Chicagoans in 1925 firmly supported the Sweets. When newly installed branch president Dr. Herbert Turner appealed for a fund-raiser, Ed Wright's Second Ward organization helped. As mentioned previously, Oscar DePriest's assistance to the branch was essential to its well-being as well.

Much like the fourth annual conclave in 1912, the seventeenth annual conference held in 1926 afforded Chicagoans an opportunity to demonstrate just how well the NAACP movement was progressing in the city. W. E. B. Du Bois made the following observation: [The choice of Chicago was] "peculiarly appropriate . . . inasmuch as one of the most serious race riots ever known in America arose [here and] . . . as a direct result of attempts at the restriction of the homes of Negroes to segregated areas."[105] The conference featured intense discussions on housing segregation, which assumed national proportions, as well as on Southern disfranchisement. The creative surge associated with the New Negro movement was not ignored, as younger, assertive blacks participated throughout the program. Importantly, the conference headquarters in 1926 was the Pilgrim Baptist Church, located in the heart of the Black Metropolis. An increase of interest among blacks in racial equality counterbalanced a decline among whites, who, when they thought of the Black Metropolis, imagined its many recreational delights. The more substantive aspects of life, especially if they projected a bleak picture of America's unkept promises, seemed all too mundane. Chicago's jazz clubs along State Street were not unlike Harlem's night clubs that had become magnets attracting erstwhile racial liberals.

Totally unlike the conference held in Chicago fourteen years previously, whites were scarcely seen. The few familiar faces included Julius Rosenwald, Clarence Darrow, and Theodore Roosevelt Jr., along with Mary White Ovington and other national officers. Nevertheless, enthusiasm prevailed in the aftermath of the conclave, prompting the director of branches, Robert W. Bagnall, to write to Assistant Finance Secretary Weaver that "I hope the effect on the Chicago branch will be most telling, and that as a result there will be a large increase in memberships and interest."[106] Beyond the enthusiasm, the recurring problems of big city life remained. Along with racial discrimination, the distraction caused by "diversified interests" ranging from the economic to the political to the nationalistic to the hedonistic presented the branch with a major set of challenges.

The branch encountered many obstacles in maintaining its operational status during this period of financial exigency, but none was overwhelming. Not having to pay a salaried staff or for office space removed major challenges and were two major advantages. Despite this slim silver lining, there were limitations imposed by the branch's ability, or inability, to raise funds. Money was always desperately needed to pay for essential goods such as office supplies, along with services such as printing, telegrams, and telephone usage. The effort to secure these funds was also a reliable indicator of the community's support, an annual reminder of the branch's necessity to promote a program that met the needs of its membership and the times.

With Dr. Turner's tenure in the presidency, the branch received the administrative leadership needed to place it on a sound footing. Turner brought with him a sense of commitment that was ably manifested in his personal fund-raising activities, leadership, and most importantly, in the length of his volunteer service. Despite the local popularity and national office exposure to the work of the branch secretaries, the locus of power within the organization now lay firmly in the presidency. Turner directed the branch to an organizational level where committees functioned with both enthusiasm and efficacy.

In its programmatic thrust and corresponding methodology, the Chicago NAACP set itself apart from every other active and activist group seeking mainstream acceptance while operating on the South Side, excluding the Communist Party that emerged from obscurity after 1925. In tandem, the Chicago NAACP, its national office, and the Urban League all agreed as to the danger the Communist

Party posed to the nation's values, institutions, and interests, so a permanent line of confrontation existed. The Chicago NAACP's choice of confrontational tactics, especially after mid-decade with the advent of the black patriarchy, aimed to change the status quo through the use of publicly embarrassing civil suits directed against discriminatory practices and their perpetrators.

Indicative of what was transpiring during the period of black hegemony over the branch was a meeting held in December 1927 that featured the national secretary, James Weldon Johnson. Twelve hundred persons were in attendance at the meeting, where they were told that "Chicago, probably more than any other city in the United States, shows only a lukewarm interest, yet Chicago needs a live, wide awake branch more than any other city in the country."[107] The response of the audience to this appeal was reflected in the action of the fewer than one hundred persons who joined the branch that night. Notwithstanding the problems that resulted from the branch's lacking a program from which to attract a base of support for its financial needs and membership, Dr. Turner felt enthusiastic enough on the eve of the Depression decade, in October 1929, to state that "it is believed now that many of the black people of Chicago are ready to enroll and come out in the open for full citizenship rights under the law."[108]

Yet in the background, Chicago machine politics always stood lurking as a detrimental influence affecting the branch's vitality. This strong influence was usually felt indirectly.[109] Even-numbered years brought congressional elections, and the climate in the Black Metropolis was such in 1922 that Morris Lewis wrote, "The November elections will soon be on and our fund raising campaign must be shaped with that in view."[110] Politics also drew the attention and presence of both the leadership and the membership away from meetings and the branch's business. This was the case in 1923 during the hotly contested mayoral race when it was impossible to get a quorum for a meeting.[111] When faced with choosing a president for the branch, the preference was usually a person who was free of affiliations with the political machines. In 1922, this was one of the major reasons that Harold L. Ickes was the choice of the branch's kingmaker, Dr. Bentley, who wrote the national office, "I did not want the office of president mixed with the local politics for reasons that are obvious."[112] The obvious implication of having black political involvement in the office of presidency was seen in both the venal image and influence that Chicago politics projected nationally. In 1924, as Ickes prepared to leave office in favor of a black man, Mary McDowell, speaking for the whites and cautious blacks on the board, opposed the naming of Bishop Archibald Carey to the office because of his close ties to the Wright and Thompson organizations.[113] Virtually no activities were reported for the branch during 1928 and this was probably the result of its lacking a volunteer staff to serve during a volatile political year.

Despite the branch's desire to remain both nonpartisan and free of the influence of politics, occasions did arise on which it was asked to enter that sphere because it represented a positive civic force in the Black Metropolis and the city. Octavius C. Granady's assassination convinced the branch to join the citywide, interracial effort to raise funds and pressure government for an investigation of the murder. From all indications, it appeared the branch did not do much better than the city government in this matter in that it failed to produce any positive results.[114]

Surprisingly, the existence of a limited political presence on the executive committee throughout the twenties seemed to neither help nor hinder the branch as the black politicians evidently respected it as a neutral body. In fact, two politicians, Oscar DePriest and his loyal lieutenant, Morris Lewis, were active and provided immense assistance to the branch. This showed that politicians could serve two masters if one did not pose a threat to the other's interests. Of course, since the Chicago NAACP never entered the political arena directly, as the league had done with Hill's aldermanic candidacy, there would not have been reason for the politicians to be disturbed by it. The branch closed the decade without having registered any notable accomplishments in either the racial or the economic spheres. The next decade would hold more severe tests for the branch, with which, based on past performances, it would have difficulty in dealing unless its leadership modified its attitude toward activism.

To their credit, the national leadership of the NAACP in New York accurately assessed part of the branch's problems as they noted the "diversified interests," the high-brow image of the branch, and the Black Metropolis's need for a "wide awake" protest effort. Another factor appearing in Chicago was the rise of a middling group composed of highly talented, hardworking, underemployed workers particularly found in Pullman service and the U.S. Post Office. Their desire for an unmet improvement in both their citizenship and economic statuses convinced them to form their own organizations with dual agendas to promote their interests. Many postal clerks and carriers belonged to the Phalanx Forum Club (1911) and the National Association of Postal Employees (NAPE, 1920), while Pullman porters, maids, and dining car waiters joined the Brotherhood of Sleeping Car Porters and Maids (BSCP) in 1925. These labor organizations reflected the decision of its members to determine their own destinies. Both groups supported the Urban League and NAACP through the years after establishing platforms directly relevant to their own primary interests.[115]

From the emerging American left, the Chicago chapter of the Communist Party, U.S.A. (CPUSA) directed its energies primarily toward a program of vilification against what it assessed as a stultifying economic system in monopoly capitalism. Beyond its verbal criticism of the capitalist system, the CPUSA used the constraints of the racial status quo as a lever to attract African Americans to their aims. Rather than a complementary thrust to the league and the Chicago NAACP, the Communist Party was seen as posing a threat to these bodies because of its anticapitalist and antigovernmental stances. Importantly, unlike the other two organizations, the Communist Party had ideological roots that were unfamiliar to the Black Metropolis's populace. This decade saw the rise of American capitalism at its apex in the Black Metropolis, with its hundreds of businesses and an ever-expanding consumer base of support. Coincidentally, the national organization of the CPUSA was founded in Chicago in 1919 following the Russian Revolution and a local chapter was formed shortly thereafter. Between 1923 and 1927, the national headquarters of the party relocated to Chicago, giving a stimulus to activities conducted here. Nevertheless, the local chapter stumbled through the decade of the twenties due to poor organization and, perhaps most importantly, its failure to build a constituency among the white workers of the city, who rejected it while enjoying the boom years of the twenties. It began the next decade with limited resources as well.[116] As recognition of the plight of the blacks, who were facing a contrasting economic experience to whites, and acting in ideological conformance with the tenets of Marxism-Leninism, which called for the inclusion of all workers regardless of racial or ethnic background into the ranks of the workers' party, the chapter opened a branch on the South Side in 1924.[117]

The program of the communists in the Black Metropolis was the same as that employed citywide except that the race issue was given heightened attention. On the South Side, the Communist Party directed its efforts toward enlisting the black population's support around the issues of inadequate, substandard, and expensive housing (which the Chicago Urban League also considered its area of expertise); violations against the civil rights of blacks (which the Chicago NAACP, the black politicians, and the *Chicago Defender* also saw as their spheres of interest); overcrowded and unsafe schools; and the need for greater interracial cooperation among the members of the working class. In its fight against housing ills, it was able to antagonize the second-most powerful black politician in the city, Oscar DePriest, who was criticized for exploiting his black tenants as were the other black and white landlords of the Black Metropolis. The tactics used in support of this program were petitioning, mass meetings, and printed criticism presented through the pages of the *Daily Worker*, yet the communists called for mass meetings that did not attract black crowds and relied on a news organ that blacks ignored favoring the *Chicago Defender* as well as the other two major black newspapers, the *Chicago Whip* and the *Chicago Bee*. Since the overall tone of the communists' activities was pervasively geared toward persuasion rather than coercion, the level of police and political harassment was lowered so much that the communists lacked press exposure. Its record in electoral politics was consistent with its other failures and it was an insignificant force in the Black Metropolis before 1930.[118]

Overall, the twenties was not a conducive time for the communists to make any advances in the Black Metropolis despite the growing level of unemployment. The Communist Party would have to wait for more propitious times and circumstances to promote its interests, and the Depression decade would provide it with those. The relationship of the black Republican political organization of Wright and DePriest and these three organizations was one that followed several patterns. The black politicians were able to work somewhat compatibly with the two civic organizations, the Chicago Urban League and the Chicago NAACP, whenever they shared common interests that were primarily racial in nature that had not reached a level where either the politicians or the civic organizations had to exert themselves against the status quo. These organizations also shared a basic sense of unawareness of either the possibility or the need for a massive systemic assault against economic injustice and inequality. Further, they often shared the same personnel in organizational activities, especially civic fund-raising. Only the very weak Communist Party had a well-defined approach to solving the nation's racial and economic woes and that involved a remedy equally unacceptable to black and white Americans alike. Its hostility to all of the black organizations in the Black Metropolis with capitalist affiliations also did little to give it acceptability or credibility in the Black Metropolis. The absence of conditions that could exacerbate already existing racial and economic problems allowed stagnant organizational evolution to suffice in the place of dynamic, innovative development and action. The Great Depression would alter this condition by setting into motion new forces that would challenge the nature of this relationship.

Black Nationalism as an Alternative Political Course

The axiom that man could not live by bread alone but needed nurturing from other sources led some residents of the Black Metropolis to seek answers beyond traditional economic or political solutions. In this light, unconventional politics took on a more favorable aura when contrasted to the unproductive alternatives that existed on the South Side. One interesting case commanded the public's attention during the fall months of 1919 when tensions of the past summer's rioting still lingered. Into this scenario, black nationalist Grover Cleveland Redding brought forth a new movement: the Star Order of Ethiopia and Ethiopian Missionary to Abyssinia. As an unauthorized offspring of the Universal Negro Improvement Association (UNIA), it was destined to hold a prominent position in the history of Chicago.[119] The movement emerged from the current predicament and the discontent of adjusting to urban life, and it afforded hope for a better existence through identification with a foreign state and culture. One of the contributing factors to its birth was the interest of some black residents of the city in various nationalistic projects and a growing interest in emigration. The UNIA led by Hon. Marcus M. Garvey was currently recruiting new members as well. Yet another factor was President Woodrow Wilson's welcoming of a group of Ethiopians to the United States, whose purpose was to work for the reenactment of an expired treaty between the United States and Ethiopia. This treaty concerned trade concessions and guaranteed the right of Ethiopians to unrestricted travel throughout the United States with the usual protection by the federal government for visiting foreign nationals.

Redding readily realized what this could mean to black people who wished to travel unmolested throughout the country if they too, like native Ethiopians, could be assured of federal protection. This particular period in the history of the United States was one of nationwide intimidation and murder of black citizens. The number of lynchings was nearing its zenith. And with the resurgence of the Ku Klux Klan, the nadir of public safety and responsibility was being reached. It was reasoned that if black people became Ethiopians, or Abyssinians, they too could demand special protection of the U.S. government. Redding now saw a bulwark against the unjust network of Jim Crow laws that were present in the nation.

As a self-announced political leader, Redding began proselytizing on the city's South Side with the false claim of being a native Abyssinian as well as governmental official with a commission from his government.[120] Not only did the Abyssinians hold organizational insignificance, they represented a fringe group among others of their ilk.[121] Propaganda disseminated by the group alluded to millions of supporters, which was useful in the recruitment of new members. Most of their meetings were highly emotional, filled with the fervor of propaganda, and described as riotous.[122] With a following composed of persons of limited education and economic means, and with an indulgence into emotional religious rites, the Abyssinians were able to exploit their nationalist appeals to an alarming degree of effectiveness. On June 19, 1920, at a secret meeting held at a blacksmith's shop, a plan was announced by Redding to a small cadre to create an incident to provoke an atmosphere for insurrection in the city.[123]

For some unexplained reason, some Abyssinians had visited the offices of the Japanese consulate in the downtown area several days before the incident was scheduled to take place. When they were asked to state their business, they left without explanation.[124] It is possible that they were there in an attempt to enlist the assistance of the Japanese government. What their purpose was in going is not known, but Japanese colonization projects in Mexico and South America, coupled with California's fear of the Japanese, could have led these Abyssinians to believe that it would be to their advantage to align themselves with an emerging "Colored" nation.[125]

On the afternoon of June 20, 1920, a planned parade headed southward toward 35th Street with Redding mounted upon a horse and clothed in full Abyssinian regalia. At the corner of 35th Street and Indiana Avenue, a flag was burned; and when two white policemen challenged the group, they were chased away by Abyssinians who had taken guns from an accompanying limousine. A third policeman, a black man, happened on the scene; when he remonstrated, he was shot. A second flag was burned and an Abyssinian shouted, "As we have destroyed these flags, we are going to destroy your government. Our government is backing us."[126] A white sailor who stopped was shot; sporadic shooting took place and at least twenty-five shots were fired.[127] Having accomplished the first part of their task, the Abyssinians fled to prearranged destinations.

The threat of a riot was enough provocation to warrant the calling of every South Side police district to send twenty men and a commanding officer to the scene. Allegedly, seven hundred policemen responded in twenty minutes.[128] However, there was no further violence, the South Side community remained calm, and within a week all of the participants were captured. Nonetheless, this concluded only one phase of nationalist agitation for political solutions beyond traditional political channels.

The Hon. Marcus M. Garvey's Universal Negro Improvement Association represented another major alternative to conventional politics in achieving black advancement. The UNIA continued its activities with a vigor unimaginable in the previous decade. As an influential organization with nontraditional political aspirations and an acknowledged agenda that extended beyond a restrictive national perspective, the UNIA was recognized at this historical juncture by friend and foe as the first mass movement ever assembled among persons of African descent. Significantly, the influence of the UNIA reached levels of support that found UNIA divisions in all but eleven of the forty-eight states (mainly in the far northwest), the United Kingdom, portions of Africa and South America, and throughout the Caribbean.[129] E. Franklin Frazier called the UNIA "a crowd movement essentially different from any other social phenomenon among Negroes." And how well did the UNIA measure up comparatively to the ubiquitous fraternal order and church, which offered "self-magnification?" He found that "these [latter] organizations ha[d] failed to give that support to the Negro's ego-consciousness which the white masses find in membership in a political community," while the UNIA accomplished this feat handily.[130]

According to Garvey's biographer, Tony Martin,

> Garvey's unparalleled success had the effect of arraying against him a most powerful conglomeration of hostile forces. The United States government opposed him because its leaders considered all black radicals, whether racial egalitarians or nationalists, subversive; European governments confronted him because he was a threat to the stability of their labor rich and wealth producing African colonies; the Communists initially opposed him because he successfully kept black workers out of their ideological grasp; the National Association for the Advancement of Colored People and other integrationist organizations challenged him when he argued that white segregationists were the true spokesmen for white America and because he advocated black separatism. His organization also had to contend with unscrupulous opportunists who were not above sabotaging its workings for personal gain.[131]

Garvey rightly blamed his arrest in 1919 in Chicago on Robert S. Abbott, who he felt had used his influence to bring about his arrest in order to discredit the UNIA. This incident was to mark the beginning of a period of personal antagonism between Garvey and Abbott that would remain unabated until 1927. Until then, Robert S. Abbott remained as Garvey's most ardent opponent in Chicago.[132]

Although Garvey visited Chicago only on special occasions, his activities in the Harlem section of New York City were carefully scrutinized by the *Defender* reporter in that city.

The *Chicago Whip* both praised and attacked Garvey and the UNIA. On the one hand, it welcomed an aroused black citizenry that challenged its subordinate status. Then, because it could not envision racial progress evolving from a program of racial separatism, it accused the nationalist leader of illusory when posturing on the issue of African redemption. The outspoken Joseph D. Bibb equated Garvey's Black Star Line (a fleet of shipping vessels) as just another foolish scheme that would eventually fail and disillusion further the already disenchanted black masses. The *Whip* wrote that "parades, loud bands, and colored regalia, black horses and pompous street marshals . . . [proved] emotions [were being] played upon. . . . [The editors exclaimed that] if this zeal and enthusiasm [were] put into labor organizations and behind Negro businesses, oh how different things would be!"[133]

The UNIA's appeal as a program for black people can be summed up as one of personal redemption through an understanding of the black man's history and present worth, of group solidarity to show the world that the black man in either hemisphere was not inferior to any other racial group, of mutual economic and political aid between Africans and persons of African descent in the Old and New Worlds, and of reorganization of the black community into an area of economic and social solidarity. This appeal was refreshing to many within the Chicago black community and had a salutary effect on the socially estranged by providing an avenue for both protest and identification.

While the Garvey movement had a positive platform in helping black people "to destroy their inferiority complex, and to make them conscious of their power," certain positions taken on public issues bordered on the ridiculous. For example, Garvey openly supported President Harding's plea for national racial tranquility that was to be achieved by ending the protests for social equality.[134] The *Whip* reacted to this statement by commenting, "Garvey would do well to cut out the Uncle Tom tactics and maintain his original policy of uniting the black people of the world."[135] Flirtation with the leadership of the Ku Klux Klan further eroded some of Garvey's appeal.[136]

The ranks of the UNIA's membership swelled to 7,500 by 1920.[137] Branches were established on both the city's South and West Sides, with South Side headquarters, called Liberty Hall, located at 49th and State Streets. Although Garvey used Harlem as his base, his Chicago lieutenants ably carried on the movement's program as evidenced by an increase in membership to over 9,000 by 1923, and many more sympathizers supported the movement with their nickels and dimes.[138] Several divisions (or chapters) of the UNIA were organized and massive parades and relatively profitable business operations followed—in variance to the impression given by Drake and Cayton, who evaluated the leader, his organization, and its ideological influence two decades later. Drake and Cayton wrote that "Garveyism was never very popular in Chicago, but the UNIA did recruit several thousand fanatical members from the lower class and lower middle class, who spread its influence far beyond the small circle of its membership."[139] The evaluation was perhaps too critical as to the popularity of the UNIA, for Garvey's supporters—who were far from fanatical—included Ferdinand and Ida B. Wells-Barnett, Rev. J. C Austin, politician and World War I officer Col. William Warfield, and members of the Chavers banking family.[140] While the Barnetts gave support to some of the Garvey programs and once entertained him for dinner in Chicago, in the end, Wells-Barnett lost confidence in Garvey became she felt he had become too egotistic with plans too grandiose to maintain the momentum he built initially.[141] Showing that the popularity and respectability had not completely been extinguished after Garvey's departure from America, the nationalistic group had as its speaker at one meeting none other than Judge Albert B. George, the first black man to be elected to a municipal judgeship in Chicago. Overall, UNIA active members included segments of the middle class and middling class, as well as the working class, and churchgoers as well as delinquent Christians.

From Liberty Hall every August, the UNIA's annual convention parade would march forth into the contiguous black neighborhoods of the South Side, winding up and down the more densely populated streets in an attempt to attract as much attention as possible to the presence and strength of the organization. Royally attired black men would lead the parade, marching in military precision, for they were members of the Legion of Honor. The Black Cross nurses would follow, affirming the positive role women played, along with other auxiliary and juvenile groups. Everyone in the parade held a rank from corporal upward in the military hierarchy, there being no privates to remind a race used to subordination of their past statuses.[142]

Although the movement eschewed even considering, let alone formulating, a mass program for emigration to Africa, popular sentiment held that Garvey promoted a mistaken scheme to take black people "Back to Africa." With assimilationist thought predominating within the thinking of the bulk of African Americans, as clearly manifested in their loyalty to America despite ancestral ties they had with Africa, the UNIA had undertaken an uphill battle. Nonetheless, Garvey's prime concern lay in areas that African Americans easily recognized as meaningful to their lives—seeking success in the economic sphere, particularly in northern cities, and in the establishment of a profitable steamship line trading throughout the Caribbean.[143]

Garvey was indicted by a federal grand jury in 1923 because of the mismanagement of funds in the administration of the Black Star Line, but with the passage of time, past wounds seemed to heal. In 1927, the *Defender* published an editorial stating that Garvey had been imprisoned long enough and that whites who perpetrated worse deeds served shorter sentences. The *Defender* now stated that his organizing abilities were valuable to the efforts to achieve racial solidarity. As soon as Garvey was released from prison, Abbott stepped forward to claim partial credit for the federal government's action. As a Jamaican citizen, Garvey was subject to punitive action by the government, which ordered his deportation. He never set foot on American soil again, although he spoke from across the Canadian border in the next decade. In his absence, the movement continued to function in Chicago with some viability; however, Garvey's charismatic persona proved in the long run to be the cement that had held the UNIA together.

Opposition to the UNIA extended across the ideological spectrum beyond the sentiments of the sensationalistic, American-oriented *Defender*. The communists initially considered the UNIA as a worthy ally because of its mass-level constituency and focus on workers' concerns.[144] Hostility developed shortly thereafter as the communists realized that racial consciousness of the UNIA left no room for workers' consciousness and unified multiracial action.

The decade that had been described as vigorously alive with diversified interests proved to be accurately depicted. Continuous activities involving conventional politics seemed on the surface to dominate life. Yet, from the Abyssinians to the UNIA, the nationalist voice gained strength. In the year following Professor Kelly Miller's centrist Sanhedrin in 1924 and in the same year that the American Negro Labor Council from the left was organized, 1925, the nationalist Moorish American Science Temple was organized by prophet Noble Drew Ali. The next chapter examines the religious energy that abounded in the Black Metropolis.

CHAPTER 6

Transformed Religion and a Proliferation of Churches

> A Negro people coming from the country to cities find more diversions and more things bidding for their time and patronage. . . . City churches must offer the people and carry through a religious program that will be passionately human, but no less divine. It must be a program dealing with the life and everyday problems of the people.
>
> —Rev. Lacey Kirk Williams, 1929

Granted that political and economic forces and influences greatly affected the whirl of life in the Black Metropolis, they did not preclude the dynamic power of religion from exerting its sway. African American religious belief and practices were indeed unfettered in their scope. The case was so much so that E. Franklin Frazier in his analysis of religious practices could have added that they manifested themselves among Christians in the increase in independent, Spiritualist religious bodies housed in storefronts along major thoroughfares, along with the breakaway community churches that were founded in 1920 as part of the nationwide Community Church Movement. Further evidence of religious zeal appeared within the Abrahamic tradition, expanding from the Ahmadiyya Movement in Islam to adherents of the Moorish American Science Temple that was founded in Chicago in 1925 by Prophet Drew Ali. From Judaism, the black Hebrew, or Jewish, movement arose.

This liberating fervor in religion that at times seemed to hold reign over all other matters also crossed the gender divide. A synergy in religious belief strengthened during the decade, related also to new economic opportunities, to the transformation in the status of women who now possessed the ballot and were separated from traditional domestic roles, and to the wave of restlessness that enveloped the nation.

The migrants from the war years and those still arriving daily in Chicago brought more than muscle for labor and capital for commercial investment; they introduced into a black society in flux their particular spiritual needs and accordingly sought out groups and institutions to meet them. The black institutions that nurtured them attempted as best they could to serve dually the spiritual and social service needs of this variegated Chicago African American community, which had reached over 200,000 persons by 1930. In the midst of all these forces fomenting change, the determining influence of this period emerged from the folk religious beliefs readily discernible since the beginning of the century, and now blossoming because of the demand of the tens of thousands for spiritual relief of one kind or another. Any other than a spiritually based solution paled in comparison. These included the political sway of the black South Side organization under the control of Wright and DePriest that proved effective only in the sense that it helped arouse popular awareness of material possibilities. Interestingly enough, the reverse situation existed as a counterbalance, with neither a leadership nor domination from religious ranks in the political sphere.[1] The economic world likewise affected this world to a lesser extent, with folk belief allowing believers to transcend economic deficiencies and seek relief in alternative experiences in this world or the next.

The older churches among the Baptists and African Methodists (AMEs) struggled to retain their prominence as "first churches" as the full effect of the new migration was being felt. While a Baptist church such as Olivet counted over 10,000 members, the AME bodies overall experienced decline as the newcomers sought newer religious outlets.[2] A portion of the emerging segmentation by class and culture was evident likewise in this turnover. "The mass of the working class Negroes are to be found in the orthodox churches, principally Baptist and Methodist," reported the usually authoritative Frazier, "where they enjoy a service which is free for the most part from the primitive forms of worship."[3] But how accurate was he? Contemporary documentation indicated that this decade witnessed a chasm in religious practice and preference that further presented a challenge to the melding process that brought all African Americans into a cohesive racial cohort but with vastly different religious preferences. As to the mythical Old Settler–migrant divide, the variegated migrant experience pushed that inaccurate depiction of intragroup tension further backward into a disposable past. Yet divisiveness about and over religion was corrosive to the social fabric and required more of a solution than found in adequate seating in church. Persons desirous of spiritual nurturing demanded a familiarity in greeting and intimate fellowship, energetic and interactive preaching, fervency in music, and a sublimation of ritual to informality and warmth in worship. Rev. Lacey Kirk Williams thought he recognized the problems inherent in accommodating this group and explained it in, of all places, the frequently hostile *Chicago Tribune*. As a recognized civic leader, his opinion was sought and given an outlet for expression. He wrote:

> The same things that caused white people to move to the cities have likewise influenced Negroes. But Negroes have some special reasons for their city ward drift. Among these are: A desire for new, better environments and living con-

ditions; a desire for justice and better police protection; a desire for the best educational advantages, wider industrial opportunities and better wages and improved religious opportunities. . . . They soon discover strenuous economic and complex social conditions . . . just so the newcomers find marked differences in matters of church and religion. They were constant and faithful church supporters because there were fewer diversions. . . . In most cases they were well known in the communities from which they came. Their contacts were close and they enjoyed the honors and bore the burdens of church leadership. . . . [But in the North, there has been a defection from the church.] Why this defection? The new migrants are accustomed to a rural religion. . . . A Negro people coming from the country to cities find more diversions and more things bidding for their time and patronage. . . . City churches must offer the people and carry through a religious program that will be passionately human, but no less divine. It must be a program dealing with the life and everyday problems of the people.[4]

The reasons behind these changes among AME churches were easily discernible as problems arose in several areas. When the AME church suffered externally from a decline in membership, it was related directly to its strict adherence to its centralized structure with uniformity in obedience to hierarchical dictates, a liturgy full of rituals that many southerners found unfamiliar and unimpressive, along with musical selections and styles to which only southern AME members could find favor, but not black Southerners with Primitive Baptist or Spiritualist backgrounds. Influential, national AME Bishop Daniel A. Payne held "shouting, jumping, swaying, and dancing—in utter disdain" and his will predominated. AME Bishop Archibald J. Carey Sr. responded independently and creatively in welcoming migrants at special Monday meetings, while helping secure jobs for both men and women in the packinghouses as well as for women in the homes of wealthy whites.[5] Overall, the AME church's unwillingness to change to meet the desires of migrants in their preferred style and content of worship resulted in the AME church's increase of only 5,000 members between 1915 and 1920, a number exceeded by one church, Olivet Baptist Church, on its own.[6]

When the AME churches suffered internally, it was from problems involving church politics within the AME bodies. With Rev. Archibald J. Carey Sr. furthering the politicalization of church life while presiding as the forty-fifth bishop of the AME Church and serving as overseer for 250 churches in Chicago, Illinois, the Midwest, and Canada, he habitually imposed his will over churches in his jurisdiction. Bishop Carey explained his position in this manner: "I have many duties that press [upon] me. I have no leisure, and I seem not to have time for the enterprises in which I am engaged, but they are all important and I do the best I can."[7] As a *Chicago Defender* editorial praised him upon the occasion of his death, it pinpointed the nature of the man as well: "He won distinction in ecclesiastics but his was a political mind."[8]

These factors of overextension and unbridled ambition, along with Carey's dominating personality and bureaucratic posture, guaranteed contention in administrative matters under his bishopric. They played important roles in prominent breakups within the denomination, with friction first appearing among the South Side Methodists, and then on the West Side. Rev. William D. Cook of Bethel AME Church suffered under the bishop's iron-handed rule and was reassigned to another church despite his successes in his assignment at Bethel. Recognized as a "consecrated and able pulpiteer" and "a devout Christian leader, a fountain of living inspiration—a living sunbeam, welcomed by all,"[9] Cook's popularity was such that Carey's actions precipitated a split within the congregation at Bethel. Rev. Cook then sought freedom from denominational hegemony by establishing an independent church in 1920 called the Peoples Community Church in Christ, the result of these divisive church politics and ecclesiastical tyranny. Rev. Cook hence became a symbol among African American Christians of revolt against the rigidities of denominationalism and the formalities of established churches. Through his efforts at church democracy, he formed a highly successful, nondenominational community body to be known as the Metropolitan Community Church.[10] His seemed to be the model of the spirit of the times.

On the first Sunday after leaving his old church, Rev. Cook received 1,500 congregants into the new church body where he could independently and democratically lead his flock of recent migrants and others. With neither a temporary nor a permanent structure, this body of believers rented space at Wendell Phillips High School on Sundays until their financial position improved enough to allow them to purchase a church home. Longtime Bethel AME member Ida B. Wells returned from a self-imposed exile at Grace Presbyterian Church to become one of his loyal congregants in this pioneering nondenominational endeavor. She assumed roles as a teacher in the adult Sunday School and president of the Sunday Forum that had been established decades earlier during the pastorate of the famous Rev. Reverdy Ransom. For Metropolitan Community Church, an eight-decade history of religious freedom and humanistic triumph thus began.

Meanwhile, those congregants at Bethel who remained faithful to their denominational moorings continued to worship as AME Church members. Their new pastor was the son of renowned AME Church figure Rev. Benjamin T. Tanner and brother of equally religious artist Henry Ossawa Tanner. Described as scholarly and energetic, Rev. Tanner led the church forward and to financial stability as well. But during his tenure, the perpetual threat to church buildings struck as fire destroyed this church and forced the congregation into debt and wandering. Bethel ended up holding its services at the Wendell Phillips High School, following in the footsteps of Rev. Cook's Metropolitan Community Church. Bethel continued to persevere as a spiritual force and does so even today.[11]

On the West Side, Bishop Carey had reason to discipline Rev. M. C. Wright of St. Stephen AME, now in its sixty-eighth year of serving the community of

African Methodists. In 1929, the dream of the congregation to finally occupy a first-class edifice was realized as Rev. Wright led the church into its new quarters in the old St. Paul Presbyterian Church at Damen Avenue and Washington Boulevard. The location and structure heralded a new day for St. Stephen with enthusiasm running high until an internal dispute erupted, one possibly related to the move and the costs incurred, which amounted to $42,000. With opposition to Wright's plan for building and his desire to end the controversy, Bishop Carey responded by reassigning Wright to Coppin AME where additional squabbling with the congregation ensued. Wright then requested an assignment in Ohio but was unable to secure one. As a last resort, he rejected what he considered a Carey reassignment amounting to an exile in southern Illinois and left the AME Church altogether. Blaming his independence on church politics and the un-Christian-like behavior of his fellow African Methodists, Wright formed another church on the South Side that was independent of the AME bureaucracy.[12]

AME leader Bishop Carey, then at Quinn Chapel, with demonstrated skills at fund-raising as well as recognized heavy-handedness, interposed himself in another situation in which he might or might not have interfered. He claimed credit for assisting Bethel AME Church to rebound from a disastrous fire with a new church home in the recently vacated Temple Sinai synagogue on South Parkway.[13] That was at the time when historian Beth Tompkins Bates wrote that the Brotherhood of Sleeping Car Porters began its push in 1925 toward establishing a social movement aimed at increasing the citizenship rights of black Chicagoans. The militant labor organization stumbled in Chicago, however, as Carey ordered opposition to the union from all AME pulpits.[14] Then, as Bishop Carey was preparing to host the General Conference of the AME Church in 1928, he designed it to be as much a demonstration of his influence on the South Side as it was to be an ecclesiastical conclave. Carey was successful in this regard, and this only served to increase the spiritual dismay felt by his old nemesis in Chicago, the more spiritually minded Rev. Reverdy Ransom. However, the weight of too excessive an involvement in Republican Party affairs as a member of the city's Civil Service Commission in Mayor William Thompson's regime undermined Carey's reputation to the extent that his honesty and integrity was publicly questioned. Once on "the civil service commission . . . he wished to stand between his Race and discrimination. Others, who enjoyed his confidence saw silver and gold where he saw only service and brought him sorrow and an early grave. He trusted the flattery of acquaintance and thought that friendship spoke. Innocent of wrong of state or man," the *Chicago Defender* opined, "he wore a thousand griefs."[15]

The Baptists adjusted better than the Methodists to the challenge in providing for the spiritual needs of the newcomers. Because of the basic organization of the Baptist denominations—a decentralized structure in which each minister and congregation had the independence to do as he or it pleased—and with its traditional familiarity with folk religion, church after church built memberships.

Under the leadership of Rev. Lacey Kirk Williams, Olivet appealed easily to those seeking a less-structured religious environment. Olivet Baptist Church, in particular, earned a reputation as being an institution with a social gospel grounding as solid as its spiritual foundation. This pattern continued at Berean, Bethesda, Ebenezer, and other institutional offshoots of Olivet from earlier days. Rev. Williams still maintained the allure of being a dedicated theologian, which is what convinced aspiring divinity student Benjamin E. Mays to follow in the footsteps of Rev. Richard R. Wright Jr. at the University of Chicago and affiliate with Chicago's corps of dynamic pulpit ministers.

With its large membership, Olivet had expanded its services from the previous decade to include an employment bureau "for worthy persons." It had a staff manning the bureau that numbered thirty-one persons, further increasing employment in the community. It advertised "a free labor and rooming directory . . . [as well as] the largest church kindergarten in Chicago . . . a free child's clinic [and] a working girls home."[16] Church members belonged to all socioeconomic classes, with banker and fellow Baptist Anthony Overton apparently helping his denomination establish the Baptist Publishing House in Nashville in 1923 with a $20,000 bank loan.[17] Earlier, Rev. Williams had opened a savings department in Overton's Douglass National Bank to assist church members get in the habit of saving and to facilitate the process of securing home mortgages.[18]

With growing popularity, the Pilgrim Baptist Church—located a short one-half mile walk north of Olivet—soon became a competitor with Olivet for Christian souls once the Rev. Junius C. Austin reached the city from Pittsburgh in 1926. Austin's arrival followed some internal turmoil involving an assistant pastor, Rev. Edward Seals, and the senior pastor, Rev. E. J. Watson. Watson had acquired the reputation of being dictatorial, a "czar," a common accusation against black Baptist ministers whether accurate or not. In Watson's case, this was the second such confrontation with a junior pastor in several years. When Seals charged overwork, a reduction in salary, and punishment for not voting properly in the 1923 mayoral election for a Democrat in accordance with the manipulative wishes of the Republican Second Ward organization, a final clash occurred. As of January 1, 1925, Seals's services and affiliation with Pilgrim were terminated.[19]

With Austin's ascension to the pulpit succeeding Texas-born Rev. E. J. Watson, a far-reaching transformation took place that was both physical and metaphysical. The church first experienced a physical transformation in the decade's familiar dance of the churches as Pilgrim purchased a new church home, a Reform Jewish synagogue from a congregation of long duration in the city. In 1922 Rev. Watson arranged the purchase of synagogue, Kehilath Anshe Ma'ariv, located at 33rd Street and Indiana Avenue. This architecturally significant edifice was home to descendants of old Israel, and now African Americans had been taken into its bosom, worshiping as new children of Israel in this sacred edifice as well as finding a home for eternity. The physical specialness of the building originated with its design by the renowned architectural team of Louis Sullivan and Dankmar Adler. Church members described this physical treasure thus: "This structure, seating 1500 plus, embodies the masterful and planning skills that characterize Louis Sullivan's contribution to modern architecture and the acoustical principles that Dankmar Adler perfected. . . . Our church is a three story rectangular block surmounted by a set-back clerestory with a deeply pitched roof as a traditional element between the base and the clerestory. . . . The Romanesque entry arch and striking lines give it an expression of magnificence . . . [it is truly] a masterpiece in the fine arts."[20]

Most importantly, spiritual transformation arrived due in no small part to its neophyte minister, a Virginia-born youth minister at age eleven with seminary training and a gift for connecting with a people he loved and whose welfare he treasured. Rev. Junius C. Austin took over a recent migrant church body only several years old (1917) and only recently housed in this magnificent structure. Austin prepared to build a new tradition upon the expression of an older one. He immediately attracted a following and challenged the ministerial and spiritual magnetism of the formidable Rev. Lacey Kirk Williams of the Olivet Baptist Church as the church populace became aware of his independent and expressive style of preaching, which featured pulpit gyrations and gesticulations as well as dancelike movements.

Pilgrim's transformation would continue in future years as it was destined to be the home of a music revolution in the Christian church as well. At a Baptist convention in 1921, pianist and composer Thomas A. Dorsey became a born-again Christian. This transformation in his life affected his music, which now turned toward the religious and away from the secular. So began the creation of a new musical genre, gospel, by 1933. This congregation, like so many other Baptist bodies, was composed of a mixture of persons from all walks of life. And with the liberal attitude present at Pilgrim, acceptance of this new form of music was forthcoming, making the church an even more attractive institution to join for migrants who longed for the emotionalistic renderings in music.

Pilgrim's membership included future business, housing, and law notable, attorney Oscar C. Brown Sr. The lawyer's presence was highly significant as he provided free legal counsel for the church in its affairs for decades and demonstrated how flexible class lines were in the Black Metropolis. Upon reflection years later, Brown recalled how it was his pleasure to sit regularly beside the church's founder, J. A. Finnie, a man who neither mastered writing nor reading but who completely was absorbed in the spirit of the Lord.[21]

Like Pilgrim, the Bethesda Baptist Church planned to join Chicago's institutional migration as members searched for better housing and accommodations in which to worship. Led by Rev. Eli T. Martin, on January 14, 1925, Bethesda found and purchased a new home in the former Temple Isaiah Israel for $217,000 with a down payment of $52,000. The church's legal corps provided the expertise for the transfer of title and related matters and Deacon Anthony Overton offered his assistance with "business expertise, knowhow and connections" to the financial world. Trouble followed, however, as the congregation attempted to relocate into this commodious edifice seating 1,400 persons on South Michigan Avenue at 53rd Street. The previously all-white neighborhood was undergoing racial succession and blacks were unwelcome. Terrorists bombed the building, causing extensive damage totaling $25,000. With resolve, the damages were repaired and Bethesda continued on its religious path toward collective and individual salvation.[22]

In a rare situation in the history of black Chicago churches, the congregation of Berean Baptist Church remained in place at 52nd and Dearborn Avenue with no thoughts of movement. In fact, they celebrated a mortgage-burning ceremony on January 23, 1920. With their pastor, Rev. William S. Braddan, and dozens of war veterans returning from France and into the congregation, the future looked bright. Then fire struck their church in February 1921, destroying the upper portion of the structure and forcing the congregation to worship in a basement section. This faithful congregation was undeterred with adversity and rebuilt within the year.[23]

Among the Congregationalists, the spirit of the times convinced a group of the faithful from the Lincoln Congregational Church in February 1922 to found a new religious body, the Church of the Good Shepherd. A religious wave sweeping across the nation demanded greater democratic participation in worship, broader involvement in church decisions, and a heightened awareness of the problems of the world around and engaging them. Such changes ensued in the Community Church Movement and provided a workable model. Three congregants from Lincoln—Dr. Lawrence Blanchet, Mr. William McSee, and Dr. John L. Campbell—"met for the purpose of organizing a strong Christian church[,] a church with a broad field of Christian service where men from all walks of life could come and worship together as fellow Christians." Then they sought a proper location that would not intrude on the sphere of influence of Lincoln Congregational in the Woodlawn community at 6500 South Rhodes Avenue. "It was decided that the ideal location would be north of 63rd Street, south of 47th Street and east of State Street." Lacking financial resources for any elaborate edifice, they sought a living room to rent on Sundays or a vacant storefront. Choosing the former at an initial cost of $2.50 weekly, they began worship with thirteen Christian souls led in worship by the assistant pastor at Olivet Baptist Church, Rev. Odell B. Thompson.

Remaining in good ecclesiastical standing required consistency with the guidelines of the Congregational Union, the ecclesiastical advisory body of the denomination. Consequently, Rev. Thompson had to be replaced with an approved Congregational minister. Helping to smooth the transition was the Chicago Theological Seminary, which supplied ministers with regularity throughout the city. Needing a name, the small church body first chose the "Langley Avenue Congregational Church because of its location." Then, almost as from above, a series of seeming miracles took place. As whites abandoned the Washington Park Congregational Church at 5347 South Michigan Avenue, the Congregational Union allowed the Langley congregation to occupy this structure (valued at $50,000) for $800. Another gift fell from heaven as the services of the director of Congregational work among blacks in the North, Rev. Harold M. Kingsley, were made available on a full-time basis.

Rev. Harold M. Kingsley had distinguished himself by this period as a leading religious and social theorist after leaving the AME Church to become a Congregationalist minister. In August 1927, Kingsley headed to Chicago where he led the new church for seventeen years as, first, the renamed Michigan Avenue Congregational Church, and then a year later as the Church of the Good Shepherd as it miraculously occupied a vacated white Presbyterian church facility at 57th and Prairie Avenue. In spite of Rev. Kingsley's level of training, as if heaven-sent and -directed, he never insisted on standards of worship that would have proven inconsistent with the social status and needs of his congregation: "Our type of service is orthodox Congregational, in which we observe our racial religious contributions," explained Rev. Kingsley. "We make a frank emotional appeal on an intelligent basis. Of course, you would expect to have the music strongly emphasized. With the church came an unusual organ with Mr. L. Sterling Todd at the keyboard, and in front of it is gathered a large choir under the leadership of Mr. William L. Dawson [not to be confused with the political leader of the same name]."[24] Good Shepherd grew and grew through the years to become a leading religious body on the South Side.

Across the Christian divide, African American Catholics belonged to an international body that denied them the recognition they deserved as fellow Christians but they remained faithful nonetheless. Relegated to a single parish on the South Side, St. Monica's, the church was unlike most ethnic Catholic bodies in that they worshiped without a spiritual leader of their own group once the erudite Father Augustin Tolton died in 1897. The white priest who ministered to their spiritual needs beginning in 1921, Father Eckert, was highly regarded and drew praise in this vein. Rev. Harold M. Kingsley offered his assessment: "If the Roman Catholic Church had a hundred such men as Father Eckert, it would sweep the Negro race [with converts]."[25]

With their numbers growing, their situation had not improved in a quarter of a century until 1924 when St. Monica's at 37th Street and Wabash Avenue merged with the more spacious St. Elizabeth Roman Catholic Church at 41st Street and Wabash Avenue. It appeared that the short journey of one-half mile had taken the congregation from one century into another. This meant that there would not only be adequate seating for the adults on Sundays but also adequate space for the children who attended the school. Double seating at a single desk ended, for example. The educational setting had always been pleasant with the teaching nuns who belonged to the Sisters of the Blessed Sacrament treating the children with discipline and, importantly, "with respect, like human beings."[26]

In a familiar scenario among all Christian groups in the city, blacks and whites neither lived together peaceably nor did they worship in unison as co-religionists. As whites moved away from a parish, blacks moved into the neighborhood and assumed spiritual domain over the vacated church.[27] The extent to which there was a noticeable number of black Catholics among the recent migrants is unknown, but one former church member recalled that as a youngster she never knew the extent to which discrimination existed in the nation until she left St. Monica's School and Chicago and returned to racist Kentucky in 1925, just in time for the lynching of two black men.[28] Whatever its social composition, the newly revived St. Elizabeth's congregation did include three of the leading Catholics on the South Side in banker Jesse Binga, realtor James Madden, and physician Dr. Arthur G. Falls.

With the complex problems the newcomers encountered, many new faces and new institutions appeared on the religious landscape of the Black Metropolis. Just as Rev. L. K. Williams had described, these pressures were exhibited in the extreme forms of materialism on constant display and so abundantly in the celebration of anonymity and snobbishness instead of friendship within the community, found even in the churches, and in the sublimation of a spiritual-based religion in the name of modern self-absorption. The migrants' desire for a meaningful, more worldly connected, and usable mode of worship that contemporary scholars labeled as primitive demanded a personal bonding with God while they remained linked to the everyday occurrences that fascinated them so much in the big city. With an emphasis on worshiping an imminent God, they demonstrated a freedom that considered excessive ritual and elaborate ceremonies as interfering with their desired form of worship that stressed personal contact with their creator.

As could be expected, the ubiquitous E. Franklin Frazier spoke on this matter from personal observation. "In a trip through the Black Belt one can find Negroes enjoying their religion in the primitive form in which they enjoyed it in the South. This type of religious experience appeals to those who have not broken away from the Southern way of life. In the numerous store-front churches which are found along State Street, an effort is made to keep up the primary relationships that existed in the South. One recent migrant complains that she left the big church because the pastor did not know her."[29] This woman's personal needs occupied as much importance in her life as the core of the Christian faith—belief in God and subordination of one's personal whims. As much as African Americans enjoyed the decade as consumers of material culture, they remained a deeply spiritual people whose essential needs could only be met through religious beliefs and practices they accepted on their own terms. The waves of migrants who preferred a personal, emotional, and spiritualist church environment indeed posed a challenge to the old-line Protestant church establishment, one that new forms of churches and worship provided. Of the latter characteristic, one modern-day account depicts the situation with great accuracy: "Typically, as [one particular minister] neared the end of his sermon, he would punctuate every chanted sentence with a rapid inhale of breath and a thunderous clap of his palm on the pulpit Bible."[30]

In the lives of the African American faithful, the force of spiritualism could not be denied. It found dramatic physical expression in prayer, incantations, dance, and speaking to the dead. In mid-decade, a courtroom episode caught the attention of a major white daily newspaper in what was presented on page one as African American theater for its white readers. The plaintiff, Mrs. Julia Johnson, who headed the Church of Divine Inspiration, sued her neighbor, a Mr. Ezekiel Morris, who headed the Morris Spiritualist Church and Power Center, for slander. With each religious leader claiming to be in contact with the spirit of a Mr. Jones, Morris reported throughout the neighborhood that Jones had shared damning information on Mrs. Johnson's secret, sinful-like activities to various individuals who knew of both spiritualists. Challenged by the judge to explain their joint powers to communicate with the spirit world, Mrs. Johnson was granted an opportunity to demonstrate her abilities and contact Jones as a witness. In a darkened courtroom, made so for the purpose of the séance, several attempts at contact were made in an atmosphere reported to be "mystic and eerie." "The spirit of voodoo seemed to hover over the proceedings," so the reporter observed. The judge intervened only to ask if his deceased relatives could be contacted. After incanting by Mrs. Johnson on the witness stand and a restless jury and spectators, resolution came with a dismissal.[31] The core of the matter was that, to any black subscribers, this represented a serious experience in the lives of the litigants and was no more ludicrous than other religious rituals with sightings of the decreased to be found in any other belief system. Other courtrooms would accommodate black Protestants, Muslims, and other groups throughout the decade in disputes brought before the government for adjudication. In most instances, the dominance of the state and the law proved ineffective in settling matters of the spirit, heart, and mind.

Meanwhile, very quietly, one of the most dominant figures of this and the next several decades was extending his influence among black Chicagoans, including newcomers. Rev. Louis M. Boddie, who began his Greater Harvest Missionary Baptist Church in 1912, was to rise to prominence within the next decade with his preaching, community service, and ability to connect with persons seeking to fill a void in their lives through a belief in a power greater than themselves. Rev. Boddie was installed as religious leader of Greater Harvest in an unusual manner, in that he received his ordination not from a Baptist network such as the Illinois, southern tier, Wood River Baptist Association or northern tier Bethlehem Baptist Association; rather it was from a member of the Holiness Church. The influence of the Holiness Church, which required a bonding with God every day of the week of a Christian's life, was reflected in Greater Harvest's pulpit as well as the congregation's enthusiastic response in worship services. Exuberance in the name of the Lord replaced placidity in Sunday services. The tambourine accompanied musical selections to raise the level of intensity to its optimum peak. Heavily criticized by other Baptists, it nonetheless met the needs of these congregants as they worshiped.

Near the end of the decade, in 1928, a religiously inspired newcomer to Chicago, twenty-year-old Clarence H. Cobbs, received his calling to preach the gospel. The next year, Rev. Cobbs organized his own church in a storefront on South State Street under the banner of the First Church of Deliverance.[32] Taking the next step, in August 1929, the church sought and received recognition and denominational affiliation with the Metropolitan Spiritual Church of Christ based in Kansas City, Missouri.[33] Its religious motto encapsulated its theologically motivating path of action: "Jesus is the light of the world." With this divine direction, and having chosen to become Pentecostal in flavor, Rev. Cobbs relied on an innovative approach that was highly emotionalistic and introduced "divine healing, psychic phenomena, and séances." Wallace D. Best wrote that "in other ways indistinguishable from a Pentecostal church, First Church of Deliverance heavily emphasized religious iconography (candles, incense, robes, sacred objects) and put communication with the spirit world at the core of its ministry."[34] In the years that followed, the church edifice, which had been designed in the Art Moderne style, also "reflect[ed] the innovative character of the congregation that built it."[35]

Furthermore, historian Best has tied the emergence of women in the pulpit to the contradictions at work as a result of the Great Migration. With the migrants exhibiting a high level of religiosity and too few houses of worship of a variety to match their enthusiasm, coupled with the reluctance of the AME and even some Baptist churches to modify their established forms of worship to meet the conditions of the times, new habits in worship had to be expected. A number of new churches—independent, southern based, folk laden, preponderantly female, and heavily emotionalistic—filled the void. According to Best, "in every way, black women migrants found in Chicago a whole new world."[36] Women of faith in this transformative urban setting were more than willing to break tradition and overcome deep-rooted gender animosity by African American male clergy against the participation of women as religious leaders. Two women initially broke tradition and subsequently pastored major church bodies for decades. Successfully advancing within religious circles as heads of their own churches were Rev. Mary G. Evans, who pastored to her flock at the Cosmopolitan Community Church at 52nd and Wabash Avenue, and Elder Lucy Smith, who led the popular All Nations Pentecostal Church on East Oakwood Boulevard. In another rarity for that century, Rev. Clarence H. Cobbs even appointed a female, Rev. Mattie Thornton, as assistant pastor, which existed as a replicated, denominational model. However, Cobbs's church, the First Church of Deliverance, still maintained the male dominance associated with the denomination in its governing body, the board of trustees.[37]

The niches that Revs. Evans and Smith carved out for themselves were also places of gender and personal advancement for black working-class women. "The African American Protestant churches of migration-era Chicago provided arenas where black women became principal agents of change in conceptions of religious authority, worship, and social outreach."[38] They built church edifices from the ground and initiated programs geared specifically toward female needs. Both Evans and Smith left established denominational bases—Methodist for Evans, Baptist for Smith—that had encumbered their deepest instincts of fulfilling a divine mandate to lead their people. In particular, that meant the segment most overlooked in power arrangements, women, would be welcomed into their heavily female congregations.

Elder Lucy Smith was as much a titan in her field of endeavor as Binga, Overton, Wright, Abbott, and DePriest. She had arrived in Chicago in advance of the Great Migration but was every bit a migrant culturally until her death. Accordingly, her God-given physiognomy allowed her to literally tower over her congregation, standing over six feet and weighing over 300 pounds. Her church raiments of simple white dresses and her mastery over simple language were geared to invoke transparency of purpose in the manner of her Lord. Her greatest achievements came in the following decade when she took to the airwaves with her sermons and fed the multitudes on an economically depressed South Side.

Rev. Mary Evans was smaller in physical dimensions yet also as commanding in spiritual stature as Smith. As a child prodigy of the AME Church, she had been impressed with the need for discipline in worship, so later she demanded that feature of her congregants in their worship. Attracting both professionals from the middle class as well as working-class persons, she tapped her membership for competent leadership as she simultaneously managed her church's financial obligations through a successful reliance on tithing from members. She, very much like Smith, assumed the role of biblical mother over her congregation and led with strictness and conviction. It was in the next decade in a time of ultimate stress that she also made her mark as a dynamic religious leader.

The iron grip of Christianity on black Chicagoans that had been disturbed during this period allowed an interest in Islam to take hold. While the Garvey movement had stressed penetrating the political economy through its activities, the Ahmadiyya Muslims, Moors, and others interested in an alternative to American Christianity found the basis of their salvation through the religion of Islam. Garvey had used the Christian religion as a vehicle for protest, while the Ahmadiyya movement in Islam sought salvation through an emphasis on the peaceful character of the religion and the stress it put on global brotherhood.

A much more popular strain of Islam emerged under the leadership of Prophet Noble Drew Ali. The group-identifying name of Negro was replaced with that of

Moor. One important variation for African Americans was the prophet's invoking the most attractive parts of Islam, those dealing with brotherhood and peace, so all meetings began and ended with an emphasis on brotherly love, and members were urged to adhere to a principle that embodied peace, truth, and love. Prophet Noble Drew Ali, although reported to be semiliterate, had an eloquent flair that would both excite and incite his followers. Just like Elder Lucy Smith, a deficiency in education did not translate into a lack of charisma and the ability to bond with followers. Ali's teachings were found in the Holy Koran, which for Ali was a mixture of Moslem writings, biblical verses, Garvey utterances, and anecdotes from the life of Jesus.[39] This mixture of secular and religious statements was to inspire the Moors into activities that deviated greatly from their past experiences as members of an oppressed group. Each member carried an identification card, and to the Moor this gave him additional strength in the area of social and interracial relations. "The hundreds of Chicago Negroes who carried these cards believed that the mere sight of the card would be sufficient to restrain a white man who was bent on destroying or harming its owner."[40] It was recalled that the cards, when "displayed to Europeans (whites), would convince them that the bearer was enlightened and a member of an organization to be feared and respected." Members were to drop the surnames that they had used since emancipation and adopt Asiatic (Moorish) names, such as El and Bey. "My husband and I once met an old schoolmate of his on the street. My husband greeted his old acquaintance and stated, what have you been doing, Davis? The fellow gave my husband a very mean look and stated, my name is Bey, not Davis. This man stated again that his name was Bey and had always been Bey. He then walked away. My husband stated to me that the man's Christian name was what he had called and that his identity was clear. At that time we did not know too much about the Moors."[41]

This newfound strength became not only a social equalizer but also a source of trouble that led some Moors to believe themselves possessors of a superior nature. The sight of persons wearing red fezzes and beards began to present trouble for the city's white citizens as some members began to openly harass white people on the streets. The situation became so acute that Ali was forced to restrain his followers. However, no riots occurred. This is best explained by the constitution of the movement, which emphasized adherence to the laws of the community in which a member might reside. It clearly stated that "all members must obey the laws of the government, because by being a Moorish American, you are part and parcel of the government, and must live the life accordingly."[42]

The expansion of the movement led to the first Moorish convention being held in Chicago in October 1928. It won the praise of the *Chicago Defender* and was spoken of in the most complimentary manner.[43] The financial status of the movement had improved along with membership increases, and the signs of prosperity were apparent after the conclusion of the convention. The financial report for 1928 reported that at least $35,000 had been collected for the prophet, although contradictorily, Ali's secretary stated that he personally did not use the movement's money.[44] He was reported to have slept on a bare mattress and lived a life of abstinence from material pleasures. Prosperity can also bring strife, and this was what happened the following year.

The enlarged movement encountered problems the likes of which Ali could not administer alone. And, unfortunately, he had surrounded himself with persons whom he could not trust. Soon, in 1929, Ali was challenged by Claude Green, a former aide. One of Greene's first acts was to seize the movement's meeting place at 3140 Indiana Avenue, in Unity Hall. Fearing the results of prolonged strife and its effects on the movement, it is alleged that Ali concocted a plan to have Greene eliminated from a position of competition through his death. On or around March 10, 1929, Ali supposedly arranged for a secret meeting to be held and Greene's executioner was selected. Greene was killed on March 15, 1929, in the temple headquarters. The murder prompted the federal government to investigate the movement, and Ali was later arrested by local law enforcement officials for Greene's murder. He was released on bond but died under mysterious circumstances a short time later.[45] With Ali's death, the movement has continued but in an exhausted state until this day. Beyond the world of the spiritual, the material sphere of recreation and culture beckoned, and it found Chicago to be a nurturing host.

CHAPTER 7

Cultural and Aesthetic Expressions

> I feel I owe a great debt to black people because it was through the music of Louis Armstrong and King Oliver that I got my best inspiration and direction. I didn't learn anything from just ordinary black musicians. It was the geniuses of jazz music who really gave me my lessons . . . King Oliver, Louis Armstrong, Earl Hines and Bessie Smith.
>
> —Bud Freeman, tenor saxophonist

The whirl of life in black Chicago appeared dramatically in many cultural and aesthetic expressions. In its ability to overwhelm most other aspects of life, along with the heightened sentiment during the decade toward materialism and consumption, this composite spirit of creativity, rebelliousness, and celebration submerged reform and civil rights advocacy and challenged religion. Once again, the NAACP memorandum that analyzed the temper of the times and cited the "many diversified interests" that attracted the attention of the mass of the people bears interrogation as to the confluence of time, place, and character.

As a venue, Chicago historically was a proven incubator from which cultural creativity arose from various sources, institutionally, organizationally, and individually. The city also had established itself as magnet, locus, wellspring, and actualization of cultural expression, appearing as an especially nurturing hostess.[1] With the advent of the Jazz Age and its musical force in the 1920s, black Chicago's literary production unfortunately drifted into a penumbra. Contemporaneously, an upsurge of creativity manifested itself in the performing arts, and to a lesser extent, in the visual arts. When economic depression and reform dominated life during the succeeding decade, literary revitalization matched growing musical versatility and visual production, producing a "Black Chicago Renaissance."[2] Changes in the socioeconomic class structure found elite, middle-class, middling, and proletarian interests often coinciding around several aspects of the arts in an almost democratic fashion, but still often colliding as well as dividing.

While Johnson and Frazier depicted black Chicago of the 1920s as devoid of an intelligentsia and a creative, supportive, cultural milieu, for reasons lost to posterity, the conclusive bases for their combined lack of awareness of what historical evidence has revealed about the previous decades—creativity, innovation, independence, and cross-class fertilization—are unknown. *A priori* assumptions, personal inclinations, and perhaps a preoccupation with the celebrity of Harlem during the 1920s provide possible answers.[3] By 1927, a more complimentary Carroll Binder assessed the community and its standards thus: "Chicago's Negro community includes a number of men and women of high professional and intellectual distinction. It shelters writers and artists whose work is favorably known among both whites and Negroes, but from both a literary and artistic standpoint there is no group in Chicago comparable to the Harlem Negro literati."[4]

The demographic onslaught that brought 51,000 newcomers carried along an expanded talent pool as well as eager consumers of popular, African-based culture. Beyond what polite society enjoyed in choral production, ragtime provided the arrival of a new type of music into the public's heart and feet. Ferdinand "Jelly Roll" Morton, the self-proclaimed inventor of jazz, thrilled audiences throughout the city during this transitional period. When the end of the war ended employment opportunities, it fortunately did not end migration, as numerous musically talented individuals from New Orleans, the Mississippi Delta, St. Louis, and Kansas City headed to Chicago. Not to be overlooked within this wartime migration were the professionals and educated persons who supported the arts in their totality, producing even more aesthetically interested black consumers, customers, and enthusiasts. As to their tastes, they leaned more toward their own cultural productions, for example, the first phase of blues from the Mississippi Delta to join with vaudeville and song. For film, they looked to producer and director Oscar Micheaux, in the estimation of John Hope Franklin "the most important and prolific producer of black film during the 1920s."[5] Micheaux filmed on the streets of the South Side and chose his characters from passersby, from millionaire Robert S. Abbott to the average pedestrian.

Important for the arts, African American businesses such as Binga's, Overton's, and Abbott's lent essential support for the arts by building venues for the performance and enjoyment of the arts, maintaining a workforce with money to spend on entertainments, directing donations to artistic enterprises, and providing a class of persons who felt they elevated themselves through their rising sense of appreciation of the arts, primarily of the indigenous or popular varieties.

Nonetheless, the artistic production from such painters as William Edouard Scott and Archibald Motley Jr. found only a limited market among African Americans as individual collectors. Scott resorted to selling his services wherever his paintings were accepted—in public buildings, churches, and schools. Although he originally focused on French genre scenes following his training with Henry O. Tanner, back home in his adopted Chicago, he pioneered "a school of racial art" a decade before Alain Locke's call for such an endeavor.[6] Further, he exhibited in Paris, London, Chicago, and many other locations. His talent was recognized contemporarily as he earned the Jesse Binga Prize, the Fredic Magnus Brand award, and the Harmon Foundation special gold medal.[7]

These developments and events contributed immediately to the making of the Jazz Age of the 1920s. Various new forms of aesthetic expression bloomed, and significantly, a distinct "Chicago style" of this mesmerizing music appeared. Jazz, which had entered the musical sphere in the form of ragtime, was now transformed into the most influential musical form of the times. It was so dominant a cultural phenomenon that it lent its name to the decade. Individualistic, syncopated, invigorating—it was prone to leave the listener moving and dancing. Originally centered on the piano, string bass, and drums, now the cornet (or trumpet) and saxophone evolved as lead solo instruments. Structurally, the attention given the individual performer now rivaled that previously accorded the ensemble.

Fueling the spirit of independence in creativity was the mind-set of the period described by African American intellectual Alain Locke.[8] Locally, Robert S. Abbott's *Chicago Defender* analysis in 1920 as to the aesthetic preferences of the New Negro—whether he or she was working class, middle class, or "dicty" (snobbish)—was one of individuals determined to enjoy the black aesthetic to the fullest, and whenever he or she desired, in the *beaux arts* too. Well-defined territorial boundaries defined the Black Metropolis that existed as a physical affirmation of the African American tendency toward gregariousness as well as a confirmation of white hostility.[9] Within the South Side black community, a new sentiment affecting artistic appreciation and enjoyment among the masses, the *petit bourgeoisie*, and elite prevailed. In jazz clubs throughout the South Side, indigenous music reigned free from the cultural compromises dictated in Harlem. Racially, whites and blacks mingled as well in "black and tan clubs." In the latter venues, "sophisticates, street mongrels, businessmen, and chimney sweeps alike were in love with [jazz]. It transcended race and class like few other art forms."[10]

Positioned along major half-mile thoroughfares such as 31st Street were pugilist Jack Johnson's stamping ground, the Club du Champion's Cabaret, and the Lincoln Gardens Café. On 35th Street, the Grand Terrace, the Sunset, and the Plantation held sway; on State Street with its famous Stroll that millionaire publisher Robert S. Abbott deigned to walk,[11] the Vendome, the Dreamland Café, the Elite Café, and the Deluxe Café stood supreme. With droves of multicultural, mixed race, and cross-class patrons always at the doors, the major drawback found in Harlem had been overcome for the most part in Chicago as black patrons had as much direct access to black entertainers as whites from outside the South Side community.[12]

Significantly, Harlem historian David Levering Lewis found that artists in Chicago performed their music in a manner suitable to their tastes rather than those of their white patrons, as was the case in New York.[13] Aesthetic compromise was avoidable. In music, whites, in fact, became imitators of blacks. Tenor saxophonist Bud Freeman remembered: "I feel I owe a great debt to black people because it was through the music of Louis Armstrong and King Oliver that I got my best inspiration and direction. I didn't learn anything from just ordinary black musicians. It was the geniuses of jazz music who really gave me my lessons . . . King Oliver, Louis Armstrong, Earl Hines and Bessie Smith. When you heard Bessie Smith sing, you heard a whole symphony of jazz in one song."[14]

While true independence in performance might have reigned in Chicago, production was another story. As the number of homes owning phonographs grew, so did recordings of African American performers. King Oliver earned the credit for making the first black recording on April 6, 1923, which was in reality the *second* jazz recording produced. The actual manufacture of records was in the hands of outsiders at studios such at Okeh, Paramount, and Vocalion.[15] Nonetheless, the tastes of the masses were being satisfied along with that of other groups.

Musical giants such as Joseph "King" Oliver leading his Creole Jazz Band, Jimmie Raglund, famed clarinetist Jimmie Noone, and Louis "Pops" Armstrong and his talented wife, Lillian "Lil" Hardin, among others, perfected and then recreated over and over again America's only indigenous musical genre. On block after block, male and female musicians contributed to the musical vitality of the Jazz Age, while sharing the Black Belt's landscape with the New Negro. King Oliver's Creole Jazz Band performed at the Royal Gardens Café (later renamed the Lincoln Gardens Café), which accommodated 800 music listeners, and then the Dreamland Café between 1917 and 1922, to be followed by pianist Earl "Fatha" Hines at the Grand Terrace.

In 1917, Lil Hardin preceded her later husband Louis Armstrong to Chicago. An accomplished pianist and composer, she played with Freddie Keppard's Original Creole Orchestra and then King Oliver's Creole Jazz Band. Later in life, she led an all-female orchestra. When Armstrong arrived in Chicago she encouraged and molded him socially while encouraging him professionally to reach his full potential free of his mentor's (Oliver) influence. He naturally grew restless and headed to New York to seek his fuller recognition, playing with the renowned Fletcher Henderson. Instead he found disappointment because of the comparatively stagnant (in relation to Chicago) music scene. Lil Hardin convinced him to return and when he did, he took the city by storm, becoming the city's and globe's preeminent jazz cornetist. Wherever he played, the crowds flocked to hear this premier soloist's brash, loose, and propulsive rhythms. Together again, they recorded as part of Louis Armstrong's Hot Five and Hot Seven.

Farther south, in what had been a white residential domain for decades, the Savoy Ballroom (1927) and the Regal Theater (1928) emerged on elegant South Parkway near 47th Street as magnets for black consumers of culture. The scope of the Regal's musical fare was exemplified by the opening year's regular lineup. New York's master showman "Fess" Williams led the jazz orchestra on stage at the commodious theater while Eddie Peyton led the pit orchestra, which played European symphonic music. Peyton was also a jazz innovator of renown who played with the great Wilbur Sweatman, who contributed immensely to Chicago's becoming a jazz hub. Meanwhile, diagonally across the street at the Metropolitan Theater, Erskine Tate's orchestra handled pit duties to enthusiastic crowds.

The clamor for jazz had to share its enthusiasm with the blues, which rose to musical prominence during this period also. Migrants from the South were often reluctant to totally discard their musical heritage, so they more often than not promoted a musical tradition beloved to them. At times, older settlers with a class bent toward high culture disparaged the newcomers' love of "plantation melodies," Southern revival music, work songs, and boogie-woogie—the ingredients that made the blues that Ma Rainey and Bessie Smith sang so popular. Of this cultural-class clash, the *Chicago Whip* observed that "It's no difficult task to get people out of the South, but you have a job on your hands when you attempt to get the South out of them."[16]

Before the days of commercial radio broadcasts, remote production from hotels and nightclubs was common. Significantly, African Americans enjoyed great exposure. As early as 1922 Clarence Jones and his Wonder Orchestra appeared on Westinghouse station KYW. It was radio station WBBM that led the way in broadcasting of African American bands, but it was to white audiences.[17] Then, Earl "Fatha" Hines could be heard live from the Grand Terrace Hotel in the mid-1920s.

With a burgeoning Jazz Age population of 109,458 persons, which grew throughout the decade to reach to 233,000, variety in aesthetic preferences could be anticipated. More and more working-class persons expressed their predilections for African-based music and dance while a smaller number saw fit to visit the activities at Orchestra Hall as Frazier has described. When Frazier criticized a washerwoman who attended the Orchestra Hall recital of a black man, he failed to appreciate the meaning of her attendance. The scholar interpreted the act as one of racial vindication—that one of their own had achieved great musical heights recognizable by high-status whites—and she wished to give him their support. Then he assumed that she (and others of this occupational grouping) lacked a background of musical appreciation individually or collectively to appreciate the performance because of aesthetic deficiencies related to class and a background of Southern or urban cultural and educational impoverishment. This might very well not have been accurate, given the exposure of laboring class persons to high culture even throughout the previous century.[18] Whether motivated by group recognition of a member's achievement in the highest rungs of white society or full appreciation of mastery over high culture's musical forms, the case is intriguing. Probably unknown to Johnson and Frazier, black Chicagoans organized the Imperial Opera Company in 1930 and presented "Bohemian Girl" in the Loop's Kimball Hall. As to accomplished classical singers and musicians seeking recognition in the Loop at Orchestra Hall and the Auditorium, this seemed simply a case of seeking acknowledgment from the highest authority within the artistic sphere, so these artists went to where true recognition flowed.

Financially undergirding the various forms of the arts in Chicago was a small group of African American patrons of the arts who provided a level of financial support that stimulated independence and eliminated the need to compromise black creativity. Incomparable to Harlem's more extensive and wealthier white patronage network, nonetheless Chicagoans—through the likes of Robert S. Abbott, Jesse Binga, Anthony Overton, Dr. Charles E. Bentley, and others—financially supported the arts. Several merited recognition as part of Chicago's *Who's Who*. From their ranks and from various strata—entrepreneurs, businesspersons, and professionals—a discernible elite grew with money to satisfy the aesthetic tastes that matched their growing wealth. Carroll Binder reported on this aesthetically supportive arrangement when in 1927 he wrote of "Well-to-do Negroes [who] patronize the arts and letters and have country estates and country clubs like those of white people of the same economic and cultural status."[19]

Cosmetics magnate-banker-publisher Anthony Overton had already proven himself supportive of black Chicago's literary strivings by publishing the *Half-Century Magazine* and the Sunday weekly *Chicago Bee* newspaper. For the Bentleys, Charles and Florence, their interest in and support for the *beaux arts* remained strong even as the doctor's health began to fail.[20] Others, such as Drs. A. Wilberforce Williams and Ulysses G. Dailey, identified closely with and supported the *beaux arts*.

As exhilarating as the Jazz Age was in stimulating creative production in the performing arts, development of a literary foundation continued its slow growth. Locally, black Chicagoans promoted their own young literary aspirants, who specialized in poetry and short stories.[21] Poet Fenton Johnson began and ended the decade in 1920, writing *For the Highest Good* and *Tales of Darkest America*. Outlets existed aplenty. It was reported that by 1927 black Chicago supported a field of twenty printers, four magazines, and six newspapers.[22] Kathryn M. Johnson, who had worked as an editor for Overton's *Half-Century Magazine*, left the publication for a stint with the Red Cross in France during the war. When she returned, she and her colleague, Addie W. Hutton, immediately put their experiences down on paper in *Two Colored Women with the American Expeditionary Forces*. Following what was shaping up as a literary tradition, Rev. William Braddan of Berean Baptist Church and chaplain in the 370th Infantry Regiment (the "Old Eighth" Illinois Infantry of the Illinois National Guard), wrote *Under Fire with the 370th Infantry*. Braddan experienced combat at the front and replicated the experiences in print of black Chicagoans McCoslin during the Civil War and W. T. Goode during the Spanish American War.[23]

As to building a literary tradition through encouragement and publication, nationally the major African American outlets for literature, *Crisis* and *Opportunity*, edited by Du Bois and Charles S. Johnson, respectively, contained almost no Chicago contributions. At the same time, Robb's *The Negro in Chicago* in 1927 claimed eight budding poets in addition to the established Fenton Johnson as "Greater Poets in Chicago." Then, throughout the text, the work of poets of lesser note appeared.[24] Seeking, ironically, to credit black Chicago with a critical, scholarly breakthrough, some twenty-first-century scholars have included the writings of Charles S. Johnson and E. Franklin Frazier, who were visiting scholars at the University of Chicago during the decade, as examples of local African American literary productivity.[25] Johnson, as the chief planner and writer of the Chicago Commission on Race Relation's *The Negro in Chicago* (1922), and Frazier, with his influential study *The Negro Family in Chicago*, have been appropriated into the ranks of Chicagoans. What was authentically Chicago remained the efforts of publisher and "Race" champion Robert S. Abbott. Meanwhile, Richard Wright, who arrived in 1927 used this period to polish his skills and seek out like-minded creative individuals.[26]

Patronage from whites, such as that generated in Harlem, transformed an indigenous-oriented arts movement into a sham imitation of what its origins had promised. According to Langston Hughes, who wrote from within this creative locus of the black world, "Harlem nights became show nights for the Nordics. Some critics say that is what happened to certain Negro writers, too—that they ceased to write to amuse themselves and began to write to amuse and entertain white people, and in doing so distorted and over-colored their material, and left out a great many things they thought would offend their white brothers of a lighter complexion."[27]

Back in Chicago, with such attention being given the other spheres, the visual arts were not ignored. In fact, Frazier acknowledged that "Art has become the proper subject of conversation among a certain class who condemn the idle women who spend their time over bridge. . . . Chicago's artists are making significant contributions; among them are Scott, Farrow, Dawson, Barthe, and Motley who brought the latest Harmon Award to Chicago. The recognition that was given to Negro art during the Negro in Art Week has created a new appreciation of racial contributions in this field and is gradually being reflected in the homes of the Negro community."[28]

Muralist William Edouard Scott's star continued to rise, for he was now considered the dean of African American painters. His reputation soared and his repertoire broadened during the 1920s. Of his talent, it is written, "Although Scott had a special interest in genre scenes portraying the black experience, portraiture and mural painting were his principal livelihood."[29] He virtually painted the town, as his works were seen from the far North Side to the South and West Sides in public buildings, art galleries, and churches. In recognition of his high level of artistic production, Scott was awarded the Binga Prize in 1931.[30]

Within the Black Metropolis, use of public space presented another sphere in which the creativity of the individual and group reflected a community's consciousness and appreciation of public art. As a channel of expression of both its martial ardor and appreciation of the sacrifice of the fallen dead during the First World War, an appropriation for a military monument was proposed in 1924 by State Representative George T. Kersey.[31] In what assumed the vitality of a movement, a concerted effort involving the *Chicago Defender* and the entire

Black Metropolis's political apparatus gained steam to construct a monument to honor the men of 8th Infantry Regiment. Later, a statue was added that featured a black doughboy with bayonet raised in a combat stance. Both were eventually built at 35th and South Parkway. At the other end of the generational spectrum, African American youth were honored through an annual public extravaganza, the Bud Billiken Parade and Picnic sponsored by the *Chicago Defender*. As the brainchild of Robert S. Abbott and various members of his staff, they wanted to recognize the loyalty and hard work of *Defender* newsboys nationwide, organize them into a force for good citizenship, and build a continuous camaraderie among young people as buddies, not antagonists. The celebration utilized public space to bond together a community and earned designation on the second Saturday of every August as Bud Billiken Day. With this confluence of time, space, and racial consciousness, another element in the construction and cohesion of the Black Metropolis was added. Religion and the spirituality that further nurtured the resiliency of this community are discussed next.

Conclusion and Legacy

Perhaps there is a certain amount of irony in the fact that the declarative pronouncement on the meanings and achievements of this single decade of historical significance emanated from the perceptive mind of Joseph D. Bibb. The Alabama native, who attended and graduated from Yale University before beginning his sterling career climb in Chicago politics, had experiences across the ideological spectrum that ranged from conservative to liberal to militant to establishmentarian. He, along with A.C. MacNeal, had excoriated the Pullman porters as they organized independently against the railroad establishment under A. Philip Randolph's Brotherhood of Sleeping Car Porters, denounced derisively Marcus M. Garvey's Universal Negro Improvement Association, and initiated fervently and supported the "Don't Spend Your Money Where You Can't Work" campaign aimed at job creation at the behemoth Woolworth's Company. Bibb had lived through the whirl of life that Chicago offered and ended his career as the highest-ranking African American in state office.

Now satisfying the fundamentals of historical inquiry and substantiation as to the actual presence of an African American metropolis in real time and existence, Bibb acted as a participant-observer and reported on it in Frederic H. H. Robb's encyclopedic *The Negro in Chicago, 1929*. The potential of the fledgling "Black Belt" community, 1890–1920, built upon its pre–Great Migration, along with wartime migratory experience, to revitalize itself into the Black Metropolis of the 1920s. The Dream of the Black Metropolis, in historical perspective for all of the city of Chicago's various ethnic communities, persisted partially because it fit into the city's dynamic fabric as well proved consistent with the spirited character of the ever-migrating southern black population. Compositely, they snared what control over their lives that they could by establishing a political base led by their leadership, started small businesses in the shadow of the giant downtown colossi in banking and retail, and worshiped under indigenous leaderships. Yet, they were to live through a trial in the next that affected them all in a manner that was even more transformative.

The 1930s brought the Great Depression. Black Chicago had accommodated itself to economic deprivation years earlier with its labor force always being the last hired and the first fired, so the mounting unemployment rates of the late twenties acted as the first measures of trouble not only for them, but for the entire city and nation.

In advance of the Great Depression, black Chicago had accommodated itself to economic deprivation years earlier. Always the last hired and the first fired, the mounting unemployment rates of the late twenties acted as the first measures of trouble not only for the residents of black Chicago but also for the entire city and nation. The dream of the Black Metropolis foundered, unfortunately, on the rocks of the Great Depression in which its black banking giants failed, as did one of the three community insurance giants and its real estate empire, along with so many smaller businesses. The era of the Great Depression, moreover, produced both economic and technological disruptions that counterbalanced artistic promise. Despite the devastating effects of the Depression on politics, business, labor, and class, black Chicago demonstrated resilience in the face of adversity and responded with a level of assertiveness that left an indelible imprint on the city's landscape into the twenty-first century.

The pillars of the Black Metropolis—the Binga State Bank and the Douglass National Bank—along with the leading white banks of the South Side, faltered during the pre–New Deal period. By 1935, however, industrious entrepreneurs and businesspeople resurrected financial dreams with the organization of the Illinois Federal Savings and Loan. They were joined by a reorganized Victory Life Insurance Company under new management. Supreme Life and Metropolitan Assurance Company weathered the storm. Most small businesses unfortunately did not. Within years after the end of World War II, African American initiative and skill led to an economic rebound with the appearance of black-owned and -operated Independence Bank and Seaway National Bank in the Chatham neighborhood several miles south of the old and depopulating Black Metropolis. In that new locale, the best of the housing dreams of the old district were realized as Chatham became a sustaining middle-class model of residential stability.

Politically, the old Republican machine of Bill Thompson collapsed and the once-powerful black submachine of Ed Wright was rendered too effete to even make promises that would not be kept. Under Oscar DePriest's leadership, African Americans continued to vote Republican even when the party lacked hope, let alone patronage.[1] The former Black Metropolis's realignment to the Democratic Party was exceedingly slow in coming and did not occur until late in the 1930s and into the 1940s because of the strong pull of previous party affiliation. Nonconventional political action offered an alternative to attack the economic problems of the day in unemployment and housing.

The formidable and pervasive influences of the Great Depression extended beyond the effects they had on black politics on the South Side with the major race advancement and protest organizations being affected to a sizeable extent as well. Significant changes occurred within the Chicago Urban League, the Chicago NAACP, and the Chicago chapter of the Communist Party. The league suffered financially, faced the threat of its possible demise, and consequently changed the direction of its program. It did, however, manage to survive organizationally over the long haul. The Chicago NAACP transformed itself into an organization that could perform effectively in the economic arena under diverse leadership. The Communist Party seemingly thrived as it rallied behind a banner of protest and because of the apparent collapse of the American economic system that it vehemently opposed. It was, nonetheless, relatively ineffective in its attempts to control, first, a stagnant Republican-dominated milieu and then a progressive Democratic one.[2] The people of the South Side, on which each organization depended for memberships and financial support, gave assistance to these organizations but it was limited. During this period, when blacks were dissatisfied with the actions or inactions of the political or civic organizations, they engaged in continuous activities that were initiated by *ad hoc* and special interest groups within their midst and led by unconventional leaderships. In pursuit of jobs, the "streetcar riots" ensued. To meet the housing crisis, the populace took to the streets in pursuit of justice and instigated the "eviction riots." Delayed governmental assistance resulted in the "welfare station riots."

With American involvement and ultimate military victories in World War II, the stage was set for a vigorous black population benefitting from positive racial change stimulated by that conflict to disperse itself far beyond the territorial confines of the old Black Metropolis throughout the Chicago land area. Becoming more upwardly mobile and assertive, it reestablished itself as a formidable force in Chicago's lifeblood by the 1980s with the election of Harold Washington as mayor in 1983 and with even more dynamic advances to be made.

NOTES

Introduction

1. Joseph Bibb, "Achievements of Ten Years," cited in Frederick H. H. Robb, *The Negro in Chicago* (hereinafter referred to as *NIC*) (Chicago: Washington Intercollegiate Club, 1929), 2:96.

2. "Booker T. Washington Takes Chicago by Storm," *Chicago Defender* (hereinafter referred to as *CD*), December 10, 1910, 1.

3. *Crisis*, September 1915: 236.

4. St. Clair Drake, *Churches and Voluntary Associations in the Chicago Negro Community* (hereinafter referred to as CVA), (Chicago: Work Projects Administration, 1940), 136–37.

5. St. Clair Drake and Horace R. Cayton, *Black Metropolis: A Study of Negro Life in a Northern City* (hereinafter referred to as *BM*), (New York: Harcourt, Brace and World, 1945), 75.

6. Drake and Cayton, *BM*, 81–82.

7. Harold M. Kingsley, "The Negro Goes to Church," *Opportunity* 7 (March 1929): 90; E. Franklin Frazier, "Chicago: A Cross-Section of Negro Life," *Opportunity* 7 (March 1929): 71; "Unique Assemblage Meets at Home of Misses Shaw," *CD*, December 29, 1928, A4. Rather than living in social isolation from cultural and intellectual personages with whom one would have expected them to bond, the Fraziers-Marie and E. Franklin-interacted with the residents of the Black Metropolis. On one occasion they attended an interracial gathering on the fringes of the enclave that was devoted partially to a discussion of the Baha'i movement and poetry readings, with Mrs. Frazier rendering an original piece of her creation. Interestingly, Charles S. Johnson pointed to religious expression as an indicator of different levels of cultural progression. He observed "200 churches ranging from the air-tight store fronts of illiterate cults, dissenters and transplanted southern churches to the imposing structure of the Olivet Baptist Church with a membership of ten thousand. The different stages of culture of the Negro population are accentuated in the religious life of the Negro community in Chicago."("These 'Colored United States,' VIII: Illinois: Mecca of the Migrant Mob," *Messenger* 5 (December 1923): 928.)

8. Dennis C. Dickerson, "African American Preachers and Politics," *The Careys of Chicago* (Jackson: University Press of Mississippi, 2010).

9. Richard Courage, *The Muse of Bronzeville: African American Creative Expression in Chicago, 1942–1950* (New Brunswick, NJ: Rutgers University Press, 2011).

Chapter 1. Demography and Ethos

1. Arvath E. Strickland, *History of the Chicago Urban League* (Urbana: University of Illinois Press, 1967), 72.

2. Lizabeth Cohen, *Making a New Deal: Industrial Workers in Chicago, 1919–1939* (Cambridge: Cambridge University Press, 1990), 34. Overall nationally, 749,000 persons migrated from the South between 1920 and 1930 at an average annual rate of 74,900, U.S. National Advisory Commission on Civil Disorders, Report (New York: Bantam Books, 1967), 240.

3. Harold M. Kingsley, "The Negro Goes to Church," *Opportunity* (March 1929): 90.

4. For the Davises' experience, see Sarah Davis Elias, *Recalling Longview: An Account of the Longview Riot* (Baltimore: C. H. Fairfax, 2004) and interview with Mrs. Libby Davis Topps on July 13, 2007, in Chicago. For the Arthurs' experience, see Dahleen Glanton, "Running North: A Family History," *Chicago Tribune*, February 12, 1998, Sect. 5 [Tempo], 1, 4. For the Walkers' experience, interview with Patricia Walker Bearden on November 2 and 9, 2007, in Chicago, and an unpublished manuscript on the life of Alex W. and Julia Walker. For Alex W. Walker's involvement in the 1906 event, see Mark Bauerlein, *Negrophobia: A Race Riot in Atlanta, 1906* (San Francisco: Encounter Books, 2001), 246–49, and Leon F. Litwack, *Trouble in Mind: Black Southerners in the Age of Jim Crow* (New York: Alfred A. Knopf, 1998), 315–19, which covers the episode in its broader context. See also interview at http://atlanta.creativeloafing.com/gyrobase/PrintFriendly?oid=oid%#A125219. For the Brown family, see Oscar C. Brown Sr., *By a Thread* (New York: Vantage Press, 1983), 49.

5. See Richard R. Wright Jr., *87 Years behind the Black Curtain: An Autobiography* (Philadelphia: Rare Book Co., 1965).

6. Anthony M. Platt, *E. Franklin Frazier Reconsidered* (New Brunswick, NJ: Rutgers University Press, 1991), 85–94.

7. E. Franklin Frazier, *The Negro Family in Chicago* (Chicago: University of Chicago Press, 1932).

8. Frazier, *The Negro Family in Chicago*, 117. Today's mislabeled "ghetto" with its many deficiencies and imperfections has dominated purported scholarship in later years in complete blindness to whatever existed as the features of a community with diverse lifestyles.

9. Herbert G. Gutman, *The Black Family in Slavery and Freedom, 1750–1925* (New York: Pantheon Books, 1976), xviii, xix, 433–34.

10. Frazier, T*he Negro Family in Chicago,* 126; E. Franklin Frazier, *The Negro Family in the United States* (Chicago: University of Chicago Press, 1939; rev. ed., New York, 1948), 333.

11. Irene Graham, "The Negro Family in a Northern City," *Opportunity* 8, (February 1933): 48.

12. Interview with Judge Earl Strayhorn in Timuel D. Black Jr., comp., *Bridges of Memory: Chicago's First Wave of Black Migration-An Oral History* (Evanston, IL: Northwestern University Press, 2003), 468.

13. Interview with George Johnson in Black, *Bridges of Memory,* 344–45.

14. Frazier, T*he Negro Family in Chicago,* 118–25.

15. Frazier, *The Negro Family in the United States,* 240.

16. E. Franklin Frazier, "Chicago: A Cross-Section of Negro Life," *Opportunity* 7 (March 1929): 71. This is an interesting position because in 1929 he would have been comparing a black group with the capacity to increase its numbers, both through natural increase and continued migration, with a group that had its number curtailed by war between 1914 and 1918 and by national legislation in 1924 with the implementation of the National Origins Act.

17. Frazier, *The Negro Family in Chicago*, 136.

18. Frazier, *The Negro Family in Chicago*, 117.

19. Frazier, *The Negro Family in Chicago*, 101.

20. Frederick H. H. Robb, *The Negro in Chicago* (hereinafter referred to as *NIC*), 2 vols. (Chicago: Washington Intercollegiate Club, 1927), 2:193.

21. Philip T. K. Daniel, "A History of Discrimination against Black Students in Chicago Secondary Schools," *History of Education Quarterly* 20 (Summer 1980): 147–62.

22. Philo A. Otis, *The First Presbyterian Church of Chicago, 1833–1913*, 2nd rev. ed. (Chicago: Fleming H. Revell, 1913; updated 1925), 214.

23. James R. Grossman, Ann Durkin Keating, and Janice L. Reiff, eds., *The Encyclopedia of Chicago* (Chicago: University of Chicago Press, 2004), 156.

24. Grossman, Keating, and Reiff, *The Encyclopedia of Chicago*; Frazier, *The Negro Family in the United States*, 278.

26. Frazier, *The Negro Family in Chicago*, 137.

26. Frazier, *The Negro Family in the United States*, 252–55.

27. Frazier, *The Negro In Chicago*, 81–82, 72.

28. Chicago Commission on Race Relations (Charles S. Johnson), *The Negro in Chicago* (Chicago: University of Chicago Press, 1922), 487–88 (hereinafter referred to as CCRR).

29. Roi Ottley, *The Lonely Warrior: The Life and Times of Robert S. Abbott* (Chicago: Henry Regnery, 1955), 109–10; also, *Chicago Defender* (hereinafter referred to as *CD*), May 2, 1920, 16. The nineteenth-century effort of Ferdinand L. Barnett, editor of the *Chicago Conservator*, the city's first black newspaper (1878), to have the letter "n" in Negro capitalized in 1878 demonstrated the level of concern with racial pride and nomenclature in that time. Today, it would thus be linked with eliminating the "N" word in today's street language.

30. "By What Name Shall the Race Be Known," *Half-Century Magazine* (November 1919): 1, 15; "Are We Ashamed of Our Lineage?" *Half-Century Magazine* (January 1920): 1.

31. Marcus M. Garvey, "Who and What Is a Negro?" in *The Philosophy and Opinions of Marcus Garvey*, 2 vols., ed. Amy Jacques Garvey (New York: 1923; repr., New York: Atheneum, 1970), 1:8. See also Tony Martin, *Race First: The Ideological and Organizational Struggles of Marcus Garvey and the Universal Negro Improvement Association* (Dover, MA: Majority Press, 1976). See chapter 2, "Race First and Self-Reliance," for an elaboration of Garvey's views on racial identity and racial independence.

32. CCRR, 488.

33. Alain Locke, "The New Negro," in *The New Negro*, ed. Alain Locke (New York: Albert and Charles Boni, 1925), 4.

34. *CD*, January 3, 1920, 15.

35. Robb, ed., *NIC*, 1:16.

36. Frazier, "Chicago: A Cross-Section of Negro Life," 73. See "Unique Assemblage Meets at Home of Misses Shaw," *CD*, December 29, 1928, A4, and "Minutes," Department of Fine Arts and Literature, Chicago and Northern District Federation of Colored Women's Clubs, December 5, 1927, Box 1, Folder 8, Gaines Papers. Rather than social isolation from cultural and intellectual influences, the Fraziers enjoyed what appears to be a somewhat fuller life of the mind. See also "Mrs. Frazier Honored," *CD*, May 18, 1919, 5, on the occasion of her birthday; present were Dr. and Mrs. William Thompson, Mr. and Mrs. Charles Dawson, and two Howard University personnel. In regard to working-class black women, based on the experiences of their class with high culture in black Chicago's history, quite possibly some of these women were accustomed to both attending the Orchestra Hall

and listening to opera. See the type of entertainment planned for the silver anniversary celebration for the National Negro Business League in "Galaxy of Musicians to Entertain Business League, *CD*, July 26, 1924, 8, and Maude Roberts George's weekly column, "News of the Music World," *CD*, January 26, 1924, 8. Moreover, see chapter 2 of this book (*The Rise of Chicago's Black Metropolis, 1920–1929*) and Christopher Robert Reed, All the World Is Here! *The Black Presence at White City* (Bloomington: Indiana University Press, 2000),107–10 and *Black Chicago's First Century*, vol. 1, *1833–1900* (Columbia: University of Missouri Press, 2005), 396–400.

37. Frazier, "Chicago: A Cross-Section of Negro Life," 73.

38. Kingsley, "The Negro Goes to Church," 90–91.

39. Frazier, "Chicago: A Cross-Section of Negro Life," 70.

40. Robert W. Bagnall to Carl G. Roberts, March 31, 1925, NAACP.

41. "The New Negro Woman," *Messenger* 5 (July 1923): 757.

42. Frazier, "Chicago: A Cross-Section of Negro Life," 73.

43. "Other Papers Say [the New York Times]-New Negro Leadership," *CD*, September 1, 1928, A2.

44. See chapter 4 of this book.

45. Richard Wright, *American Hunger* (New York: Harper and Row, 1977), 1–2, 5–7, 10, 20, 31–32.

46. George F. Robinson Jr., "The Negro in Politics in Chicago," *Journal of Negro History* 17 (April 1932): 182.

47. St. Clair Drake and Horace R. Cayton, *Black Metropolis: A Study of Negro Life in a Northern City* (hereinafter referred to as *BM*), (New York: Harcourt, Brace, and World, 1945), 77, 29.

48. August Meier, *Negro Thought in America, 1880–1915: Racial Ideologies in the Age of Booker T. Washington* (Ann Arbor: University of Michigan Press, 1963), chap. 14, "The Social and Intellectual Origins of the New Negro."

49. Allan H. Spear, preface, *Black Chicago: The Making of a Negro Ghetto, 1890–1920* (New York: Atheneum, 1969), v.

50. Interview with Dr. Arthur G. and Mrs. Lillian Proctor Falls on November 4, 1983 in Chicago; Charles S. Johnson, "These 'Colored United States,' VIII-Illinois: Mecca of the Migrant Mob," *Messenger* 5 (December 1923): 928; Frazier, "Chicago: A Cross-Section of Negro Life," 70 ; J. L. Nichols and William H. Crogman, comps., in their dedication to *New Progress of a Race* (Naperville, IL: J. L. Nichols, 1925) pose this question to their national audience: "How many people know . . . that Chicago's first settler was a Negro?"

51. Frazier, "Chicago: A Cross-Section of Negro Life," 70. As for the riot defense, E. Franklin Frazier saw the riot of 1919 as a watershed in thought in black Chicago, accompanied by the rise of a new professional and business leadership that had New Negro sentiments. (Frazier, "Chicago: A Cross-Section of Negro Life," 73).

52. Johnson, "These 'Colored United States,'" 928.

53. Robert W. Bagnall to Carl G. Roberts, 31 March 1925, Branch Files, NAACP.

54. Drake and Cayton, *BM*, 81–82.

55. Drake and Cayton, *BM*, 495.

56. Herbert G. Gutman, *The Black Family in Slavery and Freedom, 1775–1925* (New York: Pantheon Books, 1975), 261, 262.

57. Robert W. Bagnall to Carl G. Roberts, March 31, 1925, Branch Files, NAACP.

58. Johnson, "These 'Colored United States,'" 933.

59. Frazier, "Chicago: A Cross-Section of Negro Life," 70.

60. Frazier, *The Negro Family in the United States*, 233.

61. City of Chicago, *Chicago Historic Resources Survey* (Chicago: Chicago Department of Planning and Development, 1996), appendix 16. See Roger Horowitz, *"Negro and White, Unite and Fight": A Social History of Industrial Unionism in Meatpacking, 1930–1990* (Urbana: University of Illinois Press, 1997), 61.

62. Wright, *American Hunger*, 1.

63. Frazier, *The Negro Family in Chicago*, 116; Frazier, *The Negro in the United States* (repr., 1957; New York: MacMillan, 1949), 258–61. "[Importantly,] for short periods the restrictive covenants . . . have succeeded in confining the Negro population to certain areas. But in the long run the restrictive covenants have not proved effective" (261).

64. Frazier, "Chicago: Cross-Section of Negro life," 70–71. When Allan H. Spear talks of Harlem/Black Manhattan in his preface to *Black Chicago*, he says that "its institutions and services were inferior to those of the white community" (p. xiv).

65. Carroll Binder, *Chicago and the New Negro* (Chicago: Chicago Daily News, 1927), 3.

66. Michel Fabre, *The Unfinished Quest of Richard Wright* (New York: William Morrow, 1973), 80.

67. "Giles-Calumet District," Preliminary Summary of Information, Commission on Chicago Landmarks, July 2008, 11, 13.

68. Johnson, "These 'Colored United States,'" 928.

69. This included the twentieth- and twentieth-first-centuries designated community areas of Douglas, Grand Boulevard, and Washington Park.

70. Herman H. Long and Charles S. Johnson, *People vs. Property* (Nashville: Fisk University Press, 1947), 12.

71. Spear, *Black Chicago*, 22.

72. For Binga, see John Landesco, *Illinois Crime Survey: Organized Crime in Chicago* (Chicago: University of Chicago Press, 1929), 128–29; for Woodfolk, see Madrue Chavers-Wright, *The Guarantee: P. W. Chavers-Banker, Entrepreneur, Philanthropist in Chicago's Black Belt of the Twenties* (New York: Wright-Amstead, 1985), 6.

73. Binder, *Chicago and the New Negro*, 3, 8. Also, *CD*, February 14, 1920, 16, citing the Real Estate News on the new economic reality of blacks having money to invest in property wherever they wish. For the historian, this bore similarities to the pattern of the Puritan "Great Migration of 1630–1640" in which whole communities moved across the Atlantic to Massachusetts Bay Colony.

74. Landesco, *Illinois Crime Survey*, 131.

75. CCRR, 131.

76. Walter White to George N. White, January 11, 1929, NAACP Adm. file, Subject file, 1910–1940, Segregation-Chicago, NAACP.

77. *CD*, January 17, 1920, 13; February 7, 1920, 1, 19; February 14, 1920, 16.

78. The author contacted Taylor's daughter, Mrs. Barbara Bowman of the Ericson Institute, who challenged the veracity of this belief. See "Many Negroes Owe Happy Homes to R. R. Taylor," *Chicago Tribune*, May 21, 1955, 5.

79. "Garden Flats for Colored Earn 6 Percent," *Chicago Tribune*, September 25, 1930, 26.

Chapter 2. "The Whirl of Life"

1. St. Clair Drake and Horace R. Cayton's *Black Metropolis: A Study of Negro Life in a Northern City* (New York: Harcourt, Brace and World, 1945) has not only endured throughout the twentieth century but has actually expanded in importance as a guide to under-

standing northern black urban life in its totality. This volume, *The Rise of Chicago's Black Metropolis, 1920–1929*, with its reliance on *Black Metropolis*'s (hereinafter referred to as *BM*) basic premises and outlines, stands as only an additional testimony to the latter as a major academic influence. Drake and Cayton's interpretations were, of course, influenced by the thinking emanating from the University of Chicago's "Chicago School" of sociology, among whose works included those of Charles S. Johnson (Chicago Commission on Race Relations [hereinafter referred to as CCRR], *The Negro in Chicago*, [Chicago: University of Chicago Press, 1922]) and E. Franklin Frazier (*The Negro Family in Chicago* [Chicago: University of Chicago Press, 1932]). So, in fact, a circular mode of thinking was involved.

2. Charles S. Johnson, "These 'Colored' United States," VIII-Illinois: Mecca of the Migrant Mob, *Messenger* 5 (December 1923): 933.

3. See the muddled world of the "aristocracy" presented in embellished narrative in the final remarks about the popular master of ceremonies at many social events; Julius Avendorph, "All Chicago Mourns the Death of Julius Avendorph," *Chicago Defender* (hereinafter referred to as *CD*), May 12, 1923, 5. This article influenced the interpretation of the period, in Wallace D. Best, *Passionately Human, No Less Divine: Religion and Culture in Black Chicago, 1915–1952* (Princeton: Princeton University Press, 2005), 40.

4. Interview with Dr. Spencer C. Dickerson on "Social Stratification," January 20, 1938, 8, 9, Box 23, Folder 4, Illinois Writers Project (hereinafter referred to as IWP).

5. Carter G. Woodson, *The Negro Professional Man and the Community, with Special Emphasis on the Physician and the Lawyer* (Washington, DC: Association for the Study of Negro Life, 1934; repr., New York: Negro Universities Press, 1969), 109.

6. See Arthur I. Waskow, *From Race Riot to Sit-In, 1919 and the 1960s: A Study in the Connections between Conflict and Violence* (Garden City, NY: Doubleday, 1966; Anchor ed., 1967), 63, 68.

7. PJB[yrne] to Foster, February 17, 1932, Fie 1–3310, "A Century of Progress" (ACOP).

8. See Christopher Robert Reed, "Black Chicago Civic Organization before 1935," *Journal of Ethnic Studies* 14 (Winter 1987): 65–77; James Q. Wilson, introduction, *Negro Politicians: The Rise of Negro Politics in Chicago* by Harold F. Gosnell (Chicago: University of Chicago Press, 1935; repr., Phoenix Books, 1967).

9. See Christopher Robert Reed, *The Chicago NAACP and the Rise of Black Professional Leadership* (Bloomington: Indiana University Press, 1997).

10. E. Franklin Frazier, "Chicago: A Cross-Section of Negro Life," *Opportunity* 7 (March 1929): 73; Drake and Cayton, *BM*, vii, 539–40.

11. Drake and Cayton, *BM*, 543.

12. Frazier, *The Negro Family in Chicago*, 111.

13. The middling (or intermediate) class is situated between the lower rung of the middle class and the upper echelon of the working class.

14. "All Chicago Mourns the Death of Julius Avendorph," *CD*, May 12, 1923, 5; interview with Earl B. Dickerson on July 11, 1968, in Chicago.

15. Jeff Lyons, "Generations: A Quiet Quest to Honor a Family's Legacy," *Chicago Tribune* (hereinafter referred to as *CT*), February 23, 1992, 14, 20.

16. Roi Ottley, *The Lonely Warrior: The Life and Times of Robert S. Abbott* (Chicago: Henry Regnery, 1955), 219.

17. Ottley, *The Lonely Warrior*, 224.

18. Ottley, *The Lonely Warrior*, 235.

19. "N. R. Smith Is Winner in Hawaii," *CD*, November 22, 1930, 13.

20. "Editor Greets Queen and Old Friends," *CD*, July 29, 1933, 6.

21. Ottley, *The Lonely Warrior*, 329–30.

22. At the end of an interview during the 1980s, one woman confided in confidence that Abbott was referred to as that "old sooty Abbott" by at least two fair-skinned women he attempted to date.

23. Drake and Cayton, *BM*, 535. This coincides with the remembrances of civic leader Lovelynn Evans (1893–1989) whom the author interviewed on December 6, 1984, and whose interview appears in Dempsy J. Travis, *An Autobiography of Black Chicago* (Chicago: Urban Research, 1981), 219. According to Mrs. Evans, character was a determining factor. On the other hand, W. Lloyd Warner's later study from the University of Chicago as well (W. Lloyd Warner et. al., *Color and Human Nature: Negro Personality Development in a Northern City* (Washington, DC: American Council on Education, 1941) indicated that skin complexion and overall appearance played an inordinately important role in determining status in black Chicago.

24. E Franklin Frazier, "Occupational Classes of Negroes in Cities," *American Journal of Sociology* 35 (March 1930): 733.

25. Gerri Major and Doris Saunders, *Black Society* (Chicago: Johnson, 1976), 272, 292, 300–301.

26. Telephone interview with Ms. Major's coauthor, Doris Saunders of Jackson, Mississippi, on May 28, 2008.

27. Interview with Dr. Spencer C. Dickerson on "Social Stratification," January 20, 1938, 8, Box 23, Folder 4, IWP.

28. Joseph I. Boris, ed., *Who's Who in Colored America* (New York: Who's Who in Colored America, 1929), 1.

29. Ottley, *The Lonely Warrior*, 356–58.

30. Interviews with Josephine Reed Rhodes on July 21, 1968, in Chicago and Lloyd G. Wheeler III.

31. Ottley, *The Lonely Warrior*, 328.

32. "Individual Pledges for Three Years to Provident Hospital," c.1925, Box 31, Folder 7, Julius Rosenwald Papers, Regenstein Library, University of Chicago (hereinafter referred to as JR Papers).

33. John A. Carroll, "The Great American Bank Bubble and Why It Burst," *Real America* (April 1935): 20.

34. W. E. B. Du Bois, "Postscripts," *Crisis* (December 1930): 425.

35. Dewey R. Jones, "Chicago Claims Supremacy-Jesse Binga," *Opportunity* 6 (March 1929): 92.

36. Jesse Binga to Anthony Binga; January 30, 1930, Binga Family File (in the author's possession).

37. Lucius C. Harper, "Binga Represented a Business Era That Was Crude," *CD*, June 24, 1950, 7 (ProQuest version).

38. Major and Saunders, *Black Society*, 305. Photographs of Mrs. Binga show a large woman of some elegance rather on that one who could be ridiculed for her physical appearance.

39. "Old and Young Enjoy Binga Christmas Party," *CD*, December 30, 1922, 7. An interview with Mrs. Jeanne Boger Jones of the pioneer Hall family confirmed the importance of the Binga affair as well as stories of others who visited their home on South Parkway across from Washington Park. Binga is given short shrift by Gerri Major in *Black Society*,

possibly because of her unsuccessful marriage to his nephew, the popular bon vivant, Dr. Binga Dismond.

40. Major and Saunders, *Black Society*, 273.

41. Interview with Mrs. Jean Boger Jones by telephone to Grand Rapids, Michigan, on October 25, 2007.

42. Boris, *Who's Who in Colored America*, 32.

43. "Mrs. Binga Goes to Reward after Long Career of Service," *CD*, April 1, 1933, 1 (ProQuest version); and Inez V. Cantey, "Jesse Binga," *Crisis* 34 (December 1927): 352.

44. "Salvation Army Puts Doughnuts on Sale Today," *CT*, October 24, 1927, 23.

45. Theresa Dickason Cederholm, comp., *Afro-American Artists: A Bio-bibliographical Directory* (Boston: Boston Public Library, 1973), 249–50.

46. "Mrs. Binga Goes to Reward."

47. See these examples in *CT*: "Binga to Erect Tall Building at State, 35th," March 28, 1926, B2; "Plans, Work, Binga's Secret for Success," May 8, 1926, 1, 20; "Union League Goes Calling in Black Belt," July 23, 1926, 23; "Jesse Binga, Banker, Is Honor Guest at Banquet," September 22, 1927, 36; "Trio of Imposing Buildings for Neighborhood Centers," May 20, 1928, B1; "Shops Building Announced for Sheridan Road, New Bank for South Side," July 19, 1929, 18.

48. James H. Wesley, "Carter G. Woodson-as a Scholar," *Journal of Negro History* 36 (January 1951): 10; notes of James E. Stamps, c.1964, on the 1915 founding of the Association for the Study of Negro Life and History.

49. Gosnell, *Negro Politicians*, 110–11.

50. Major and Saunders, *Black Society*, 271–72.

51. Interview with Mrs. Lovelynn Evans in Chicago on December 6, 1984.

52. "To Visit Panama," *CD*, February 9, 1929, 1;2.

53. For who's who listings, see Boris, *Who's Who in Colored America*, 203, 410.

54. "Frank L. Gillespie, Insurance Head, Dies: Thousand Pay Last Tribute to Leader in Business World," *CD*, May 9, 1925, 12.

55. Rev. L. K. Williams, "The Urbanization of Negroes: Effect on Their Religious Life," *CT*, January 13, 1929, 12.

56. Harold M. Kingsley, "The Negro Goes to Church," *Opportunity* (March 1929): 90.

57. "Colorful Career of Church and Civic Leader Ended," *CD*, March 28, 1931, 1, 4; "Archibald J. Carey," *CD*, March 28, 1931, 14.

58. Kingsley, "The Negro Goes to Church," 90.

59. Philo A. Otis, *The First Presbyterian Church of Chicago, 1833–1913*, 2nd, rev. ed. (Chicago: Fleming H. Revill, 1913), 214; John H. Johnson, *Succeeding against the Odds: The Inspiring Autobiography of One of America's Wealthiest Entrepreneurs* (New York: Warner Books, 1989), 60–61.

60. Susan Perry, Commission on Chicago Landmarks, "Preliminary Summary of Information on the Metropolitan Apostolic Community Church" (typewritten copy, December 2006), 5.

61. Corneal A. Davis, "Corneal A. Davis Memoir," vol. 1, Illinois General Assembly Oral History Program, Legislative Studies Center (Springfield: Sangamon State University 1984), 57.

62. Sarah Davis Elias, *Recalling Longview: An Account of the Longview Riot* (Baltimore: C. H. Fairfax, 2004); interview with Mrs. Libby Davis Topps on July 13, 2007, in Chicago.

63. Interviews with Lloyd G. Wheeler III on February 26, 1997, September 3, 1998, and March 18, 2001, in Chicago.

64. See letters of November 10, 1913, and May 30, 1914, both in the JR Papers; also, see "Alpha Phi Alpha Hold Annual Meet," *CD*, January 3, 1920, 13. Their new address was 3633 South Parkway.

65. Interview with Mrs. Lovelynn Evans in Travis, *An Autobiography of Black Chicago*, 218.

66. Willard B. Gatewood Jr., *Aristocrats of Color: The Black Elite, 1880–1920* (Bloomington: Indiana University Press, 1990), 235.

67. "Funeral Rites of Capt. Robert Shaw," *CD*, January 14, 1928, 2.

68. Frazier, *The Negro Family in Chicago*, 115.

69. Interview with Dr. Spencer C. Dickerson.

70. Drake and Cayton, *BM*, 535.

71. Robert J. Blakely, *Earl B. Dickerson: A Voice for Freedom and Equality* (Evanston, IL: Northwestern University Press, 2006), 165.

72. "The Original Forty Club of Chicago: 50th Anniversary Record," program booklet, 1966, 5.

73. E. Franklin Frazier, *The Negro Family in the United States* (Chicago: University of Chicago Press, 1939).

74. Frazier, "A Cross-Section of Negro Life," 73.

75. Sanhedrin Conference, *CD*, January 26, 1924, 12.

76. Frederick H. H. Robb, *The Negro in Chicago* (hereinafter referred to as *NIC*), 2 vols. (Chicago: Washington Intercollegiate Club, 1927, 1929), 1:126.

77. Frazier, "Chicago: A Cross-Section of Negro Life," 73.

78. Drake and Cayton, *BM*, 661, 662.

79. Interview with Earl B. Dickerson on March 21, 1984; Reed, *The Chicago NAACP*, 21; Blakely, *Earl B. Dickerson*.

80. Interview with attorney Earl B. Dickerson on July 11, 1968, in Chicago.

81. Blakely, *Earl B. Dickerson*, 46.

82. Interview with Earl B. Dickerson on March 21, 1984. All of the five social leaders would pass to eternity between 1925 and 1931, thereby relinquishing the social scene to youngsters like Dickerson and others.

83. Blakely, *Earl B. Dickerson*, 53–54.

84. Interview with Earl B. Dickerson on July 11, 1968.

85. See Dickerson's rise and successes in the business world: Blakely, *Earl B. Dickerson*, 176, 179–80, as well as the photograph of the article on "Earl B. Dickerson: How He Chalked Up His First Million" included in the illustration and photographs section of the book.

86. Memorial Services for the Late Rep. William L. Dawson (Illinois), 91st Cong., 2nd sess. (Washington, DC: U.S. Government Printing Office, 1971), 1–74.

87. "Wm. L. Dawson Would Succeed Dan Jackson," *CD*, July 6, 1929; Robert Gruenberg, "Dawson of Illinois: What Price Moderation?" *Nation* 183 (September 18, 1956): 196; Memorial Services for the Late William L. Dawson; interview with Earl B. Dickerson on July 11, 1968; Christopher R. Reed, "William L. Dawson," in *Encyclopedia of African-American Culture and History*, ed. Jack Sulzman et al. (New York: Macmillan, 1996); "A Progressive Negro Candidate: Dawson for Congress," in *Midwest [Chicago] Daily Record*, June 18, 1938, n.p. in Arthur W. Mitchell Papers, Chicago History Museum.

88. Ford S. Black, comp., *Black's Blue Book: Business and Professional Direct Compilation*

of Names, Addresses and Telephones of Chicago's Colored Business and Professional People (Chicago: F. S. Black, 1927), 174–75; Carroll Binder, *Chicago and the New Negro* (Chicago: Chicago Daily News, 1927), 11, who cites 176 as the total.

89. Michael L. Flug, "Vivian Gordon Harsh," in *Women Building Chicago, 1790–1990: A Biographical Dictionary*, ed. Ruma Lunin Schultz and Adele Hast (Bloomington: Indiana University Press, 2001), 359.

90. Interview with Dr. Arthur G. Falls on March 10, 1978, in Chicago.

91. Frazier, "Chicago: A Cross-Section of Negro Life," 73.

92. Reed, "Black Chicago Civic Organization before 1935," 65–77.

93. Woodson, *The Negro Professional Man*, 204–7.

94. Binder, *Chicago and the New Negro*, 11.

95. See *Opportunity* (March 1929): 94, 96.

96. Gosnell, *Negro Politicians*, 108–9.

97. CCRR, 353.

98. "A Successful Engineer," Robb, *NIC*, 1:95.

99. "Architecture's Forgotten Pioneer," [*culture*] (Chicago, Illinois), Summer 2003, 22. For further comments on Walter T. Bailey, see Lee Bey, "Black Influence in Architecture," *Chicago Sun-Times*, May 2, 1998, 18.

100. See sample letter of February 12, 1930, W.T. Bailey File, ACOP.

101. Drake and Cayton, *BM*, 660.

102. "IIT Ready to Honor Trailblazing Alumnus," *CT*, October 5, 2007, 2:1, 7.

103. http://www.csupomona.edu/~nova/scientists/articles/ha//.html.

104. James M. Brodie, *Created Equal: The Lives and Ideas of Black American Innovators* (New York: W. Morrow, 1993), 123–127; see also http://www.csupomona.edu/~nova/scientists/articles/ha//.html.

105. Lloyd A[ugustus] Hall, "Opportunities in [the] Chemical Industry," *Opportunity* 7 (July 1929): 221–22, 229.

106. Binder, *Chicago and the New Negro*, 12.

107. Binder, *Chicago and the New Negro*, 12; Robb, *NIC*, 2:283; *Half-Century Magazine* (March–April 1924): 8.

108. Madrue Chavers-Wright, *The Guarantee: P. W. Chavers-Banker, Entrepreneur, Philanthropist in Chicago's Black Belt of the Twenties* (New York: Wright-Amstead, 1985), 88–89.

109. Interview with Ida M. Cress in Timuel D. Black Jr., comp, *Bridges of Memory: Chicago's First Wave of Migration-An Oral History* (Evanston, IL: Northwestern University Press, 2003), 81.

110. Interview with Alonzo Parham, in Black, *Bridges of Memory*, 120–23.

111. Obituary, "Harold Hurd, 90, Pioneering Black Aviator," *Chicago Sun-Times*, September 10, 2002, 64.

112. Robb, *NIC*, 1:11.

113. See the column "Black Society" for May 18, 1921, as an example.

114. Langston Hughes, *The Big Sea: An Autobiography* (1940; repr., New York: Hill and Wang, 1963), 206–8.

115. *Half-Century Magazine* (March 1920): 7. Also, Major and Saunders, *Black Society*, 180–81.

116. Drake and Cayton, *BM*, 710.

117. See Larry Tye, *Rising from the Rails: Pullman Porters and the Making of the Black Middle Class* (New York: Henry Holt, 2004).

118. Sterling D. Spero and Abram L. Harris, *The Black Worker: The Negro and the Labor Movement* (repr., 1931; New York: Atheneum, 1969), 430, 454. See Beth Tomkins Bates, *Pullman Porters and the Rise of Protest Politics in Black America, 1925–1945* (Chapel Hill: University of North Carolina Press, 2001), 25, for a view counter to the one presented in this study.

119. Frazier, "Occupational Classes of Negroes in Cities," 731; Frazier, *The Negro Family in the United States*, 253–54; Frazier, *The Negro in the United States* (New York: MacMillan, 1949), 257.

120. "The Life of the Pullman Porter," http://www.scsra.org/library/porter.html, p. 6 of 10 (accessed August 23, 2010).

121. Drake and Cayton, *BM*, 235; Frazier, "Occupational Classes of Negroes in Cities," 733.

122. Binder, *Chicago and the New Negro*, 10. Also, see Robb, *NIC*, 1:99.

123. District Manager, United States National Life and Casualty Company, Chicago to Pullman Company, May 8, 1925, Box 8, Folder 140, Pullman Collection, Newberry Library.

124. Drake and Cayton, *BM*, 549.

125. Memo on actions of Pullman porter G. Belcher, assistant general manager, January 12, 1926, Box 8, Folder 110, Pullman Collection.

126. Memo by W. H. Boggs, investigator on the application of William McKinley Griffin, January 19, 1929, Box 8, Folder 134, Pullman Collection.

127. Robb, *NIC*, 1:99.

128. For the Benevolent Industrial Association, see Robb, NIC, 1:169, 2: 196; for the Protective Union, see Brailsford R. Brazeal, *The Brotherhood of Sleeping Car Porters: Its Origin and Development* (New York: Harper and Bros., 1946), 10–14.

129. Robb, *NIC*, 2:209.

130. Interview with attorney Jewel LaFontant in Travis, *An Autobiography of Black Chicago*, 231.

131. Reed, *The Chicago NAACP*, 69–70.

132. Richard Wright, *Lawd Today* (New York: Walker, 1963), 17, 20–21, 109–11.

133. Claude A. Barnett, "We Win a Place in Industry," *Opportunity* 6 (March 1929): 83.

134. Albert Brooks, "Orphans of the Storm [Substitute Postal Employees]," typewritten copy of autobiographical sketch, c. 1985, 2.

135. Gosnell, *Negro Politicians*, 302, 318.

136. Best, *Passionately Human, No Less Divine*, 148.

137. Richard Wright, *American Hunger* (New York: Harper and Row, 1944).

138. Timuel D. Black Jr. in conversation with Ida M. Cress, and with Gwendolyn Davis and James "Jack" Isbell, in Black, *Bridges of Memory*, 80, 132, and 281.

139. Interview with Bishop Arthur Brazier in Black, *Bridges of Memory*, 548.

140. Hughes, *The Big Sea*, 228–29.

141. Gwendolyn Brooks, *Report from Part One* (Detroit: Broadside Press, 1972), 47.

142. Kingsley, "The Negro Goes to Church," 91.

143. Robert McMurdy to William C. Graves, December 30, 1912, Box 31, Folder 7, JR Papers.

144. Albert B. George to W[illiam] C. Graves, April 21, 1927; and, J. B. D. Lee to A. L. Jackson, October 5, 1927, Box 31, Folder 7, JR Papers.

145. List of corporate pledges, n.d. (presumed c.1925); A. L. Jackson to Julius Rosenwald, May 1, 1927; and A[lfred] K. S[tern] to Dad, December 27, 1927; A. K. Stern to A. L. Jackson, July 2, 1928, all in Box 31, Folder 7, JR Papers.

146. "The Personality behind a Great Institution," in Robb, *NIC*, 2:223–27; "John T. Wilson Hospital," Box 36, Folder 6, JR Papers.

147. The Daily Hospital was featured on the photographic page of the *Chicago Defender*, November 22, 1930, 22.

148. Helen Buckler, *Daniel Hale Williams: Negro Surgeon* (New York: Pittman, 1968), 261.

149. The basic source of information of this conflict is the highly detailed, interesting, but ahistorical account in Buckler, *Daniel Hale Williams*. Spear called the book "gossipy," yet somewhat perceptive; Allan H. Spear, *Black Chicago: The Making of a Negro Ghetto, 1890–1920* (New York: Atheneum, 1969), 236.

150. Robb, *NIC*, 1:106, 2:238. Also, Alfreda F. Duster, *Crusade for Justice: The Autobiography of Ida B. Wells* (Chicago: University of Chicago Press, 1967), xxx, xxxi.

151. Kingsley, "The Negro Goes to Church," 91.

152. Langston Hughes, *Not without Laughter* (New York: Alfred A. Knopf, 1930; repr., 1968), 303–4.

153. Frazier, "Chicago: A Cross-Section of Negro Life," 70.

154. Hughes, *The Big Sea*, 33.

155. Hughes, *Not without Laughter*, 303.

156. Hughes, *The Big Sea*, 54–55.

157. Hughes, *The Big Sea*, 54–55.

158. Corneal A. Davis, "Corneal A. Davis Memoir," 1:58–59.

159. CCRR, 170–72. Also available in "group of family histories-An iron worker (first story)," in http://historymatters.gmu.edu/d/4977/ (accessed August 23, 2010) [derived from CCRR].

160. Irene M. Gaines to Dear Friends, January 27, 1922, Box 1, Folder 6, Gaines Papers.

161. "Widening the Breach," *Half-Century Magazine* (January–February 1925): 3.

162. Frazier, "Chicago: A Cross-Section of Negro Life," 73.

163. Brooks, *Report from Part One*, 373.

164. The previous century's code of behavior influenced that of the succeeding century. See Christopher Robert Reed, *Black Chicago's First Century 1833–1900* (Columbia: University of Missouri Press, 2005), 396–400.

165. Frazier, "Chicago: A Cross-Section of Negro Life," 71.

166. See "Bud [Billiken] Says," *CD*, September 23, 1922, 14.

167. Reed, *The Chicago NAACP*, 62.

168. Interview with Judge Earl Strayhorn in Black, *Bridges of Memory*, 468.

169. A. C. MacNeal to Walter White, June 1, 1937, Branch Files, NAACP Papers.

Chapter 3. The Golden Decade of Black Business

1. Memorandum, To the Conference, June 22, 1927, Branch Files, NAACP Papers.

2. Recent historian treatment of the Black Metropolis has paid special attention to the phenomenon of consumerism. See Lizabeth Cohen, *Making a New Deal: Industrial Workers in Chicago* (Cambridge: Cambridge University Press, 1990), 147–50; Davarian

L. Baldwin, *Chicago's New Negroes: Modernity, the Great Migration and Black Urban Life* (Chapel Hill: University of North Carolina Press, 2007).

3. Charles S. Johnson, "These 'Colored United States,' VIII-Illinois: Mecca of the Migrant Mob," *Messenger* 5 (December 1923): 928.

4. "Plan $750,000 Negro Hotel on Indiana Avenue [and Overton Building], *Chicago Tribune* (hereinafter referred to as *CT*), November 12, 1922, A14.

5. "A Monument to Negro Thrift and Industry: The Overton Building," *Half-Century Magazine* (January–February 1923): 12.

6. http://www.cr.nps.gov/NR/twhp/wwwlps/lessons/53black/53visual4.htm (accessed August 25, 2010).

7. "London Editor Lauds Chicago, Even Its Gunmen," *CT*, December 10, 1928, 16.

8. Oscar C. Brown, *By a Thread* (New York: Vantage, 1982), 51–52.

9. See Carroll Binder, *Chicago and the New Negro* (Chicago: Chicago Daily News, 1927), 11, who cites a University of Chicago postgraduate student, W. H. Bolton, on the growth of business brought on by migrants from the wartime years; see also E. Franklin Frazier, "Chicago: A Cross-Section of Negro Life," *Opportunity* 7 (March 1929): 72; Frederick H. H. Robb, *The Negro in Chicago* (hereinafter referred to as *NIC*), 2 vols. (Chicago: Washington Intercollegiate Club, 1927, 1929), 1:183; St. Clair Drake and Horace R. Cayton, *Black Metropolis: A Study of Negro Life in a Northern City* (hereinafter referred to as *BM*) (New York: Harcourt, Brace and World, 1945), 436, obviously influenced by the preceding contemporary accounts; and Sterling D. Spero and Abram L. Harris, *The Black Worker: The Negro and the Labor Movement* (1931; repr., New York: Atheneum, 1969), 466, which contains an incisive criticism of the impossible actualization of the Black Metropolis concept .

10. *CT*, January 10, 1929, 22.

11. Quoted from a reproduction of Frederick Douglass's speech given on Colored American day, August 25, 1893, in Christopher Robert Reed, "All The World Is Here!" *The Black Presence at White City* (Bloomington: Indiana University Press, 2000), 194.

12. For the 1915 Half-Century Exposition, see "Mayor's Night at Half Century Exposition," *Chicago Defender* (hereinafter referred to as *CD*), September 11, 1915, 1; "Mayor at Lincoln Jubilee, 22,000 Cheer Him," *CD*, September 18, 1915, 4; for the 1940 American Negro Exposition, see "American Negro Exposition" and Report of the Afra-American Emancipation Exposition to the Governor and General Assembly of the State of Illinois, 1938, Irene McCoy Gaines Papers, Chicago History Museum.

13. Chicago Commission on Race Relations (hereinafter referred to as CCRR), *The Negro in Chicago* (Chicago: University of Chicago Press, 1922), 403.

14. James N. Simms, comp., *Simms' Blue Book and National Negro Business and Professional Directory* (Chicago: James N. Simms, 1923; repr. 1977).

15. Binder, *Chicago and the New Negro*, 11, 12.

16. Juliet E. K. Walker, ed., *Encyclopedia of African American Business History* (Westport, CT: Greenwood Press, 1999), xxiii. Allan H. Spear wrote of Harlem/Black Manhattan in his preface to *Black Manhattan* (New York: Atheneum, 1969), observing, "its businesses [were] small and underfinanced" (xiv). For their part, Drake and Cayton noted the intensity of intercity rivalry as to which African American business group excelled over the others (*BM*, 438). Objectivity dictated acceptance of the fact of black business achievement. Just as the popular dictum holds that necessity is the mother of invention, dreams and entrepreneurial risk are the handmaidens of future generational business successes.

17. Drake and Cayton, *BM*, 434.

18. Scrapbook, 1930, Julius Rosenwald Papers (hereafter referred to as JR Papers), Regenstein Library, University of Chicago.

19. The logic of Drake and Cayton on the unreasonableness of black thinking that racial-owned businesses and mass, buy-black purchasing could propel blacks as a group forward economically was based on both Great Depression distress and failure and World War II–era lack of recognition of positive aspects of the status quo. See also Oscar L. Handlin, "The Goals of Integration," in "The Negro American-2," *Daedalus* 95 (Winter 1966): 272, commenting on scholarly treatment on the period after 1865. Handlin states "there has been a tendency to underestimate the extent of his [the Negro's] achievements even in the fifty years after emancipation, under conditions immensely more difficult than those of the present."

Scholarship from the University of Chicago probably played its part. Contemporarily, Frederick H. H. Robb wrote that the African American "is still a mighty insignificant factor in the economic whirl of Chicago. . . . [T]he Negro does not employ 5% of the 200,000 men of color in the city, the banks do not hold 1/12 of his wealth" (*NIC*, 2:200). Spero and Harris in *The Black Worker* took a dim view of the attempts to create separate economies (466). Political scientist Harold F. Gosnell in *Negro Politicians: The Rise of Negro Politics in Chicago* (Chicago: University of Chicago Press, 1935) rendered a similar verdict ten years before the publication of *Black Metropolis*: "In the Negro community there were no great industrial and financial leaders who were concerned with exercising influence upon local politics. There were no utility companies, no great contracting concerns, and no banks in the financial center of the city that were run by Negroes. Relatively speaking, the Negro is weak in economic power" (106).

Drake made a return appearance to Chicago from California on November 6, 1981, as part of a series on "Chicago's Black History in the Making" held at the University of Chicago. He asserted that Black Metropolis was indeed a period piece and would be in need of revision as the years progressed (notes from "How We Wrote Black Metropolis"). In fact, his revised sociological analyses of 1961 and 1969 had already accompanied reprints of *Black Metropolis* in the years after its initial publication.

For reflections on Black Metropolis successes, see the interview with Jacoby Dickens in Timuel D. Black Jr., *Bridges of Memory: Chicago's First Wave of Black Migration* (Evanston, IL: Northwestern University Press, 2003), 328–29. Also, see the example of Reginald Lewis, http://www.africanamericanculture.org/museum_reglewis.html (accessed August 25, 2010). The cases of Reginald Lewis in industry, Robert Johnson in communications, and Chicagoan Oprah Winfrey in electronic entertainment confirm that success is possible and real. See Derek Dingle, "Reginald Lewis: The Deal Heard 'round the World: His $985 Million Buyout of TLC Beatrice Set the Bar for the Next Generation," *Black Enterprise* (June, 2005).

20. For a powerful centrist argument in this vein, see Abram L. Harris, *The Negro as Capitalist: A Study of Banking and Business among American Negroes* (New York: American Academy of Arts and Sciences, 1936; repr., Gloucester, MA: Peter Smith, 1968), 168–79.

21. "Union League Goes Calling in Black Belt: Sees Homes, Enterprises of Chicago Negroes," *CT*, July 23, 1926, 23.

22. *CCRR*, 495–97.

23. Binder, "Chicago and the New Negro," 7, 8.

24. Invitation to invest, Abel Davis to Robert S. Abbott, January 30, 1929; February 27, 1929; May 17, 1929; and June 20, 1929; Robert S. Abbott File, 1–12; and, memorandum,

Rufus C. Dawes, February 29, 1928, and Peabody to Binga, August 20, 1928, Jesse Binga File, 1–1737, all items in "A Century of Progress" papers.

25. See Robb, *NIC*, 2:55. The extent to which black business played a minor role in the city's economy is explored in "The Negro's Place in Business," Robb, *NIC*, 2:200.

26. Carroll, "Chicago and the New Negro," 13. Abbott biographer Roi Ottley wrote in 1955 that by the 1920s Abbott had become "an authentic millionaire" based on his actual wealth; Roi Ottley, *The Lonely Warrior: The Life and Times of Robert S. Abbott* (Chicago: Henry Regnery, 1955), 219.

27. Arnett G. Lindsay, "The Negro in Banking," *Journal of Negro History* 14 (April 1929): 192–93; "Objective reality" from Drake and Cayton, *BM*, 433; "sterling" and Chicago Clearing House Association status from John A. Carroll, "The Great American Bank Bubble and Why It Burst," *Real America* (April 1935): 19–20.

28. Lindsay, "The Negro in Banking," 192–93.

29. Harris, *The Negro as Capitalist*, 154–63; James O'Donnell Bennett, "Plans, Work, Binga's Secret For Success," *Chicago Sunday Tribune*, May 8, 1927, 1; "Binga State Bank," *Messenger* (January 1925): 5 ; Tribune coverage from *Chicago Sunday Tribune*, May 8, 1927, 1, 20; Spingarn and Harmon awards from photo page of the *Chicago Tribune*, June 4, 1927, 32.

30. Robb, *NIC*, 2:96; letter, Jesse Binga to Anthony Binga Jr., Richmond, Virginia, January 30, 1930, Binga file.

31. "Survey of the Month," *Opportunity* 5 (July 1927): 216; "Make 13 Awards to Negroes in Arts, Sciences," *CT*, January 9, 1928, 23; "White and Colored Pastors to Join in Tribute to Lincoln," *CT*, February 9, 1928, 15; and Binder, *Chicago and the New Negro*, 12.

32. The image of the Black Metropolis through print is the story of a changing landscape, one that goes from vitality to distress. *Black Metropolis* provides an excellent exposition of business between 1860 through 1937 through statistical and illustrative presentations on pp. 434–35. The major contemporary sources are W. E. B. Du Bois, "Chicago," *Crisis* (September 1915); Johnson, "These 'Colored United States,'" 928; Carroll Binder, in *Chicago and the New Negro*, 11, says "banking and insurance are the two outstanding developments in the business life of Chicago Negroes"; Frazier, "Chicago: A Cross-Section of Negro Life," 70–73.

33. See vol. 1 of Christopher Robert Reed, *Black Chicago's First Century, 1833–1900* (Columbia: University of Missouri, 2005). Drake and Cayton position this *increasing* consciousness in the twentieth century, linked to the massive population movement associated with the Great Migration (*BM*, 434).

34. Preface to Isaac C. Harris, *Colored Men's Professional and Business Directory* (Chicago: I. C. Harris, 1885) and Robert E. Weems Jr., *Black Business in the Metropolis: The Chicago Metropolitan Assurance Company, 1925–1985* (Bloomington: Indiana University Press, 1996), xiv.

35. Robb, *NIC*, 1:183; Robert C. Puth, "Supreme Life: The History of a Negro Life Insurance Company, 1919–1962," *Business History Review* 43 (Spring 1969): 3; Drake and Cayton, *BM*, 436.

36. Carl F. Osthaus, "The Rise and Fall of Jesse Binga, Black Financier," *Journal of Negro History* 58 (January 1973): 43.

37. Baldwin, *Chicago's New Negroes;* Jacqueline Najuma Stewart, *Migrating to the Movies: Cinema and Black Urban Modernity* (Berkeley: University of California Press, 2005).

38. Roi Ottley, "'Red Dick' Recalls Blazing Negro Rialto," *CT*, August 1, 1954, SW_A9.

39. For Durham, see E. Franklin Frazier, "Durham: Capital of the Black Middle Class,"

in Alain Locke, ed., *The New Negro* (New York: Albert and Charles Boni, 1925), 333–40; for Durham and Tulsa, see John Silbey Butler, *Entrepreneurship and Self-Help among Black Americans* (Albany: State University of New York Press, 2005), 175–206, 214–29, and 232–37.

40. Harris, *The Negro as Capitalist*, 163.

41. Harris, *The Negro as Capitalist*, 163; Lindsay, "The Negro in Banking," 192–93.

42. W. E. B. Du Bois, "Postscript," *Crisis* (December 1930): 425; "A Negro Bank Closes Its Doors," *Opportunity* 8 (September 1930): 264; Carroll, "The Great American Bank Bubble," 20; Christopher R. Reed to Anthony J. Binga, December 17, 1981, Binga file.

43. Drake and Cayton, *BM*, 549, 550.

44. This lack of knowledge of general business practices plagued both men as they routinely made personal decisions as to their operations, expansions, and investments. This was a constant assessment by former businessman and legal mind Earl B. Dickerson. (Interview with attorney Earl B. Dickerson on July 11, 1968, in Chicago.)

45. Julius Rosenwald to George [Woodruff], June 11, 1930, notebooks, JR Papers. See also Harris, *The Negro as Capitalist*, 163.

46. Johnson, "These 'Colored United States,'" 928.

47. Drake and Cayton, *BM*, 82, 83.

48. Binder, *Chicago and the New Negro*, 7, 8.

49. "Binga State Bank," *Messenger* (January 1925): 5.

50. Claude A. Barnett, "We Win a Place in Industry," *Opportunity* 6 (March 1929): 84.

51. Interview with attorney Earl B. Dickerson on July 11, 1968, in Chicago.

52. "Liberty Life Insurance Company of Illinois," *CD*, January 3, 1920, 8.

53. Drake and Cayton, *BM*, 437–53. See also Christopher Robert Reed, "Manifestations of Black Nationalism in 1920s Chicago," MA thesis, Roosevelt University, 1968, 33–35.

54. *CD*, April 24, 1920, 13.

55. *CD*, January 8, 1921, 8.

56. Osthaus, "The Rise and Fall of Jesse Binga," 43.

57. "Binga State Bank," *Messenger* (January 1925): 5.

58. "Who's Who: A Leading Negro Banker," *Messenger* (August–September 1923): 884; "Binga State Bank," *Messenger* (January 1925): 5.

59. Lindsay, "The Negro in Banking," 192–93. Drake and Cayton (*BM*, 465) indicated a variance with Lindsey's 1929 figures with $1,465,266.62 shown in deposits.

60. Lindsay, "The Negro in Banking," 192.

61. See Harris, *The Negro as Capitalist*, 163; Lindsay, "The Negro in Banking," 192; "Draft of Landmark Designation Report on Home Trust and Trust Company Building," December 1, 2006, City of Chicago, Department of Planning and Development, for white banking links to their communities.

62. "Black Belts Cause Chicago's Bank Failures," *CD*, August 23, 1930, 13.

63. "Binga Bank Had Only 2 Accounts of Over $10,000," *CD*, October 31, 1931, 1.

64. "Binga State Bank," *Messenger* 7(January 1925): 5.

65. Inez V. Cantey, "Jesse Binga," *Crisis* (December 1927): 352.

66. Bennett, "Plans, Work, Binga's Secret for Success," *CT*, May 8, 1927, 20.

67. Ottley, *The Lonely Warrior*, 226.

68. "Trio of Imposing Buildings for Neighborhood Centers," *CT*, May 20, 1928, B1. To a well-respected clergy on the present-day South Side, it was remembered as "a beautiful building." See interview with Bishop Arthur Brazier in Black, *Bridges of Memory*, 550.

69. Drake and Cayton, *BM*, 465.

70. Rosenwald to George [Woodruff], June 11, 1930, Notebooks, "Bank for Negroes," JR Papers; Du Bois, "Postscript," 425.

71. Madrue Chavers-Wright, *The Guarantee: P. W. Chavers, Banker, Entrepreneur, Philanthropist in Chicago's Black Belt of the Twenties* (New York: Wright-Amstead, 1985), 341.

72. Chavers-Wright, *The Guarantee*, 51.

73. Chavers-Wright, *The Guarantee*, 52, 355.

74. Chavers-Wright, *The Guarantee*, 76–78; "R. W. Woodfolk & Co. Bank's Mission," *CD*, June 14, 1919, 14; Harris, *The Negro as Capitalist*, 144.

75. "Negro Bank Chartered," *New York Times*, April 28, 1921.

76. "Negro Bank Chartered," *New York Times*, April 28, 1921.

77. Chavers-Wright, *The Guarantee*, xvi, 164–69.

78. Anthony Overton was fictionalized by the biographer as Mr. Owens in Chavers-Wright, *The Guarantee.*

79. Chavers-Wright, *The Guarantee*, 135; Lindsay, "The Negro in Banking," 194.

80. Chavers-Wright, *The Guarantee*, 132.

81. Chavers-Wright, *The Guarantee*, 155–58.

82. Chavers-Wright, *The Guarantee*, 161.

83. Chavers-Wright, *The Guarantee*, 340–41.

84. Harris, *The Negro as Capitalist*, 59.

85. Robert Howard, "Black Banking in Chicago," MA thesis, Roosevelt University, 2002; Rosenwald to George [Woodruff], June 11, 1930, Notebooks, "Bank for Negroes" JR Papers; Du Bois, "Postscript," 425.

86. "A Negro Bank Closes Its Doors," *Opportunity* (September 1930): 264.

87. Harris, *The Negro as Capitalist*, 161.

88. Simms, *Simms Blue Book and Directory*, 78.

89. For inefficiency, see Harris, *The Negro as Capitalist*, 147; Arthur J. Wilson, "The Douglass National Bank of Chicago," in Robb, *NIC*, 2:213; "The National Baptist Convention and Its Leader," *Half-Century Magazine* (July–August 1923): 8.

90. *Half-Century Magazine*, May–June, 1924, 17. Also see Drake and Cayton, "Insurance," *BM*, 461.

91. Puth, "Supreme Life," 1–20.

92. Binder, "Chicago and the New Negro," 8.

93. Interview with Earl B. Dickerson on July 11, 1968.

94. Interview with Earl B. Dickerson on July 11, 1968.

95. Lloyd G. Wheeler III was a future president of the company as well as linked to Old Chicago as the grandson of Lloyd G. Wheeler I, the son-in-law of John Jones and subsequent owner of merchant-tailor business of nineteenth-century renown. When Wheeler III slowly ventured into Chicago society, he was surprised to learn that the memory of his grandfather as a civic spokesman and social leader of the elite still elicited respect from the Old Settler element. Interviews with Lloyd G. Wheeler III on February 26, 1997, and July 3, 1998, in Chicago.

96. *CD*, January 22, 1921, 9.

97. Johnson, "These 'Colored United States,'" 928.

98. Binder, *Chicago and the New Negro*, 12.

99. Puth, "Supreme Life," 6.

100. Puth, "Supreme Life," 9.

101. Binder, *Chicago and the New Negro*, 12.

102. "Anthony Overton, Born Entrepreneur," *Issues and Views* (Spring 1977), *http://www.issues-views.com/index.php/sect/1000/article/1006 (accessed August 25, 2010).*

103. Weems, *Black Business in the Black Metropolis*, xii.

104. Robb, *NIC*, 1:190.

105. Robb, NIC, 2:210–11, 241. As to his residence, Williams resided outside of the Black Metropolis at 5504 Everett Avenue in the Hyde Park community. Simms, *Simms' Blue Book and Business Directory*, 92, 99.

106. "Lincoln Saved the Union," *Messenger* 7 (January 1925): 10.

107. Binder, *Chicago and the New Negro*, 6. See Homer Hoyt, *One Hundred Years of Land Value in Chicago, 1830–1933* (Chicago: University of Chicago Press, 1933).

108. Simms, *Simms' Blue Book and Business* Directory, 82; "T. W. Champion Realty Agency & Loan Company," *Messenger* 7 (January 1925): 66. Also, see program booklet of the Original Forty Club, 1964.

109. Osthaus, "The Rise and Fall of Jesse Binga," 42–43.

110. Juliet E. K. Walker, *The History of Black Business in America: Capitalism, Race, Entrepreneurship* (New York, Twayne, 1998), 192.

111. *Half Century Magazine*, (January–February, 1924): 8.

112. Binder, *Chicago and the New Negro*, 6.

113. Harris, *The Negro as Capitalist*, 163.

114. Hugh Gardner, "The Rise and Fall of Jesse Binga," *Chicago Defender*, July 1, 1950, 13; "Binga State Bank," *Messenger* (January 1925): 5; Osthaus, "The Rise and Fall of Jesse Binga," 45.

115. Drake and Cayton, *BM*, 434.

116. Binder, *Chicago and the New Negro*, 11; Robb, *NIC*, 1:206.

117. Robb, *NIC*, 1:114.

118. Binder, *Chicago and the New Negro*, 12.

119. Binder, *Chicago and the New Negro*, 6, 7.

120. Binder, *Chicago and the New Negro*, 7.

121. "Black Belts Cause Chicago's Bank Failures," *CD*, August 23, 1930, 13.

122. "The Critic," *Messenger* 7 (May 1925): 204, 206.

123. "New Hotel," *Messenger* 7 (February 1925): 83.

124. Robb, *NIC*, 1:211.

125. Ottley, "'Red Dick' Recalls Blazing Negro Rialto."

126. "Thousands See Corner Stone Laid in Masonic Temple," *CD*, October 25, 1924, 3.

127. Robb, *NIC*, 1:198. Also, interview with Mrs. Rosalia Holt on August 15, 2007, in Chicago.

128. "Architecture's Forgotten Pioneer," *Culture* (Chicago, Illinois), Summer 2003, 22. For further comments on Walter T. Bailey, see Lee Bey, "Black Influence in Architecture," *Chicago Sun-Times*, May 2, 1998, 18.

129. "A Modernistic Bit for South State," *CT*, October 27, 1929, B9; see also www.cr.nps.gov/NR/twhp/wwwlps/lessons/53black/53visuals5.htm.

130. "Survey of the Month," *Opportunity* 6 (September 1928): 280.

131. "Survey of the Month," 280. Twenty-five years later, the truth of the matter was shown. The loss on bad rentals was a low three-tenths of 1 percent of collections. See Roi

Ottley, "Many Negroes Owe Happy Homes to R. R. Taylor," *Chicago Daily Tribune*, May 21, 1955, 5.

132. Interview with Jones's grandson, Mr. James Hudson, during summer 1998 in Chicago.

133. Electronic correspondence with Mrs. Barbara Taylor Bowman, daughter of Taylor, on December 5, 2007. See source of the discrepancy, Roi Ottley, "Many Negroes Owe Happy Homes to R. R. Taylor," *Chicago Daily Tribune*, May 21, 1955, 5.

134. F. B. Ransom, "Manufacturing Toilet Articles: A Big Negro Business," *Messenger* 5, (August-September 1923): 937.

135. For "leading producer, see Walker, *Encyclopedia of African American Business History*, 629; for Bradstreet rating, see "Anthony Overton, Born Entrepreneur" Issues & Views (Spring 1977), available at http://www.issues-views.com/index.php/sect/1000/article/1006 (accessed August 25, 2010).

136. Simms, *Simms' Blue Book and Business Directory*, 81.

137. For "High Brown Cosmetics," see http://www.blackseek.com/bh/2001/49_AOverton.htm (accessed August 25, 2010); for Turnbo-Malone, see Walker, *Encyclopedia of African American Business History*, 629.

138. Robb, *NIC*, I: 187. Of all the businesses of the decade, the name most recognized today in the twenty-first century is that of the Parker House Sausage Company, still located on South State Street but under threat of demise as the character of the thoroughfare changes back to residential.

139. Company brochure address: 5305 South State Street.

140. Binder, *Chicago and the New Negro*, 11.

141. Reed, *Black Chicago's First Century*, 1:74.

142. Camille Cohen-Jones, "Your Cab Company," *Crisis* (March 1927): 5, 6.

143. Robb, *NIC*, 2:222.

144. "To Open Motor Salesroom in Chicago," *CD*, January 19, 1929, 2.

145. Robb, *NIC*, 1:99.

146. Binder, *Chicago and the New Negro*," 11. See also Robb, *NIC*, 1:124, "Race Publications in Chicago."

147. "The Realization of a Dream: An Epic of Negro Business," *Messenger* 5 (August-September 1923): 871–73; also, Robb, *NIC*, 1: 90–91.

148. Robb, *NIC*, 1:91; also, Johnson, "These 'Colored United States,'" 928.

149. Simms, *Simms' Blue Book and Business Directory*, 79. See also Ford S. Black, comp., *Black's Blue Book, 1923–24* (Chicago: Douglass National Bank, 1923), 43.

150. Ottley, *The Lonely Warrior*, 194, 301.

151. Carter G. Woodson, "Personal [Remarks]," *Journal of Negro History* 25 (January 1940): 262.

152. William E. Berry, "Robert S. Abbott," in *Encyclopedia of African American Business History*, ed. Juliet E. K. Walker (Westport, CT: Greenwood Press, 1999), 2.

153. Robb, *NIC*, 1:90. See chapters 7 and 8 with Pullman columns.

154. Lincoln Cemetery, where Abbott is buried, is located immediately southwest of the Chicago city limits in Alsip, Illinois, and has been the final resting place for black Chicagoans since the early twentieth century.

155. Telephone interview with Mrs. Goldie Bibb (the widow of Joseph B. Bibb) of Chicago, Illinois, on January 25, 1978. The interview was conducted form the home of Mrs.

Lovelynn Evans, who for ten years served as the women's editor of the *Chicago Whip*. See Robb, *NIC*, 2:233, 247. A fourth founder is listed as W. C. Linton, Robb, *NIC*, 1:122. The paper is incorrectly described as "socialist-leaning" and "anti-capitalist" in Cohen, *Making a New Deal*, 148, 154.

156. Robb, *NIC*, 2:233; Simms, *Simms' Blue Book*, 115; Oliver Cromwell Cox, "The Origins of Direct-Action Protest among Negroes," unpublished manuscript, c. 1932, 1933 (microfiche copy), 13, Kent State University Libraries.

157. Telephone interview with Mrs. Goldie Bibb.

158. Cox, "The Origins of Direct-Action Protest," 13; John McKinley, "Leaders Endorse the *Chicago Whip's* New Economic Program," cited in Robb, *NIC*, 2:233.

159. "A Reply to Joe D. 'Blibb,' 'Idiot-or' of the Chicago 'Flip,' Misnamed the Whip,'" *Messenger* (December 1925): 379; Chandler Owen, "The Neglected Truth," *Messenger* 8 (January 1926): 5.

160. "Anthony Overton, Born Entrepreneur," *Issues & Views* (Spring 1977), 2, available at http://www.issues-views.com/index.php/sect/1000/article/1006 (accessed August 25, 2010).

161. Robb, *NIC*, 2:214–15; Ralph Nelson Davis, "The Negro Newspaper in Chicago," MA thesis, University of Chicago, 1939, 128; "A Modernistic Bit for South State," *CT*, October 27, 1929, 3:9, 10; Cox, "Origins of Direct-Action Protest."

162. "Race Riots and the Press," *Half-Century Magazine* (August 1919): 18.

163. "The *Chicago World* Fulfills an Ideal," in Robb, *NIC*, 2:238.

164. Simms, *Simms' Blue Book and Business Directory*, 77.

165. Simms, *Simms' Blue Book and Business Directory*, ad on p. 82.

166. Robb, *NIC*, 2:237.

167. This claim of a link to the world of antiquity carried on a tradition extending from Bishop Henry McNeal Turner's pronouncement during the Columbian World's Exposition of 1893 that "God Is Black" to former diplomat and attorney George Washington Ellis's assertion in 1914 about black roots that predated the Christian era (see Reed, *Black Chicago's First Century*, 2:127). In his mature years, Robb traveled the world, established a teaching center known as The House of Knowledge, and adopted the name Hammurabi.

168. Robb, *NIC*, 1:206.

169. Drake and Cayton, *BM*, pp. 437, 448, 456–57

170. Binder, *Chicago and the New Negro*, 11.

171. Drake and Cayton, *BM*, 457.

172. Simms, *Simms' Blue Book and Business Directory*, 101.

173. Simms, *Simms' Blue Book and Business Directory*, 65–66.

174. A'Lelia, Bundles, *On Her Own Ground: The Life and Times of Madam C. J. Walker* (New York: Scribner, 2001), 280.

175. Weems, *Black Business in the Black Metropolis*, 21.

176. Robb, *NIC*, 2:205.

177. "Monarch Tailors Furnish Men with the Best," in Robb, *NIC*, 2:255.

178. "Mr. Edward T. Lee-One of Chicago's Leading Merchants," *Messenger* 8 (January 1926): 10.

179. Robb, *NIC*, 1:98–99; "A Colored Electrician," *Crisis* (May 1927): 77–78, 98–99; Binder, *Chicago and the New Negro*, 12, 13.

180. "Firms Fear End of Chicago Set-Asides," *CT*, December 31, 2003, Business sec., 1, 4.

181. Chavers-Wright, *The Guarantee*, 39.

182. Chavers-Wright, *The Guarantee*, 58–71.

183. Interview with Ida M. Cress in Black, *Bridges of Memory*, 82.

184. "Business Club in New Program," *CD*, January 12, 1924, 4; "Jesse Binga Gives Points on Real Estate to A.B.C.," February 16, 1924, 4; "Holsey Is Guest at A.B.C.," *CD*, February 23, 1924, 4. The founding of the ABC represented a collaborative effort rather than a one-man endeavor. See Wallace D. Best, *Passionately Human, No Less Divine: Religion and Culture in Black Chicago, 1915–1952* (Princeton: Princeton University Press, 2005), 85, for an attribution solely to Robert S. Abbott.

185. "The Negro Sanhedrin," *Half-Century Magazine* (March–April 1924), 8, 10.

186. "Sanhedrin Aftermath," *CD*, March 8, 1924, 2:12.

187. Black, *Black's Blue Book, 1923–24* (Chicago: Douglass National Bank, 1923).

188. Simms, *Simms' Blue Book and Directory*, 130. Its other officers included vice president, L. P. Johnson, real estate broker and general contractor, 151 N. Peoria; treasurer David McGowen, undertaker, 3515 Indiana Avenue; executive secretary, W. D. Alimono, Alimono & Co., Certified Public Accountants; and recording secretary, R. W. Lewis, industrial engineer, 3456 Michigan Avenue.

189. "Business Club Hears Talk by Mr. Gillespie," *CD*, February 9, 1924, 4.

190. See "Holsey Is Guest at A.B.C.," *CD*, February 23, 1924, 4; "Business Men Back from Goodwill Tour in South," *CD*, May 3, 1924, 4; "Trip through South Discussed at A.B.C.," *CD*, May 10, 1924, 11; "Mrs. Ethel Minor Gavin Leaves for California," *CD*, July 17, 1926, 5.

191. "Prince Kojo Pays Visit to Chicago," *CD*, October 11, 1924, 3. See also Ottley, *The Lonely Warrior*, 289–90.

192. Reed, *All the World Is Here!*, chap. 8, "Continental Africa at the Fair: Dahomey Village."

193. For trusts, see "Holsey Is Guest at A.B.C.," *CD*, February 23, 1924, 4; for real estate, see "Jesse Binga Gives Points on Real Estate to A.B.C.," February 16, 1924, 4.

194. "Give Cards to Members of Associated Business Club," *CD*, March 1, 1924, 3; "Visitors Give Business Club High Praises," *CD*, March 8, 1924, 2; "'Cooperation' Theme of Talk to A.B.C. Men," *CD*, March 22, 1924, 2.

195. "Give Cards to Members," *CD*, 3. When researchers for the *Black Metropolis* (1945) project logged the complaints of black customers doing business with African American storekeepers during the 1930s and 1940s, the very problems the ABC meant to be addressed seemed to have been never been overcome sufficiently. See Drake and Cayton, *BM*, 439–53.

196. Kelly Miller, "Before the Negro Becomes One with the Rest of the American People, He Must Become One with Himself," in *Black Nationalism in America*, ed. John H. Bracey Jr., August Meier, and Elliott Rudwick (Indianapolis: Bobbs-Merrill, 1970), 350–51. Also, see "Purpose of the Sanhedrin," *CD*, January 5, 1924, A1.

197. *CD*, March 8, 1924, A12; Editorial: Dean Miller and the Sanhedrin, *Messenger* 6 (March 1924): 106.

198. Tony Martin, *Race First: The Ideological and Organizational Struggles of Marcus Garvey and the Universal Negro Improvement Association* (Dover, MA: Majority Press, 1976), 245.

199. Robb, *NIC*, 2:55, 57–58.

200. Christopher Robert Reed, "A Reinterpretation of Black Strategies for Change at the Chicago World's Fair, 1933–1934," *Illinois Historical Journal* 81 (Spring 1988): 2–12.

201. For 35th Street, see "South Side to Have 15 Story Colored Club," *CT*, August 19,

1923, A11; for proposed entertainment complex, see "Huge Cinema and Ballroom at 47th-Grand," *CT*, August 29, 1926, B1; Cox, "The Origins of Direct-Action Protest."

202. Clovis Semmes, *The Regal Theater and Black Chicago Culture* (New York: Palgrave MacMillan, 2006), 15.

203. Semmes, *The Regal Theater*, 11.

204. Semmes, *The Regal Theater*, 11.

205. Gardner, The Rise and Fall of Jesse Binga."

206. Brown, "Binga Downfall Ends Spectacular Career," *CD*.

Chapter 4. Labor

1. Gareth Canaan, "Part of the Loaf: Economic Conditions of Chicago's African-American Working Class during the 1920s," *Journal of Social History* 35 (Fall 2001): 147–74.

2. Chicago Commission on Race Relations [Charles S. Johnson] (hereinafter referred to as CCRR), *The Negro in Chicago* (Chicago: University of Chicago Press, 1920), 401.

3. Christopher Robert Reed, "A Study of Black Politics and Protest in Depression-Decade Chicago, 1930–1939." PhD diss., Kent State University, May 1982.

4. See Sterling D. Spero and Abram L. Harris, *The Black Worker: The Negro and the Labor Movement* (1931; Repr., New York: Atheneum, 1969); Brailsford R. Brazeal, *The Brotherhood of Sleeping Car Porters: Its Origin and Development* (New York: Harper and Bros., 1946); William H. Harris, *Keeping the Faith: A Philip Randolph, Milton P. Webster, and the Brotherhood of Sleeping Car Porters, 1925–1937* (Urbana: University of Illinois Press, 1977); Beth Tomkins Bates, *Pullman Porters and the Rise of Protest Politics in Black America, 1925–1945* (Chapel Hill: University of North Carolina Press, 2001); Larry Tye, *Rising from the Rails: Pullman Porters and the Making of the Black Middle Class* (New York: Henry Holt, 2004).

5. Randi Storch, *Red Chicago: American Communism at Its Grassroots, 1928–35* (Urbana: University of Illinois, 2007), 150.

6. Charles S. Johnson, "The New Frontage on American Life," in *The New Negro*, ed. Alain Locke, 289–90 (New York: Albert and Charles Boni, 1925).

7. For Chicago Urban League, see CCRR, 401–2; for South's labor shortage, see "Getting Their Eyes Open," *Chicago Defender* (hereinafter referred to as *CD*), April 3, 1920, 16.

8. Interview with an unidentified person #3 on July 23, 1968, in Washington Park, Chicago.

9. *CD*, March 12, 1921, 2.

10. Arvarh E. Strickland, *History of the Chicago Urban League* (Urbana: University of Illinois Press, 1967), 58.

11. Alma Herbst, *The Negro in the Slaughtering and Meat-Packing Industry in Chicago* (Boston Houston Mifflin, 1932; repr., New York: Arno Press, 1971), xxii.

12. Johnson, "The New Frontage on American Life," 289–90.

13. Frederick H. H. Robb, *The Negro in Chicago* (hereinafter referred to as NIC), 2 vols. (Chicago: Washington Intercollegiate Club, 1927, 1929), 1:99.

14. Claude A. Barnett, "We Win a Place in Industry," *Opportunity* 6 (March 1929): 83.

15. Carroll Binder, *Chicago and the New Negro* (Chicago: Chicago Daily News, 1927), 9.

16. Roger Horowitz, *"Negro and White, Unite and Fight": A Social History of Industrial Unionism in Meatpacking, 1930–1990* (Urbana: University of Illinois Press, 1997), 12–13, 19; Rick Halpern and Roger Horowitz, *Meatpackers: An Oral History of Black*

Packinghouse Workers and Their Struggle for Racial and Economic Equality (New York: Twayne, 1996), 6.

17. Horowitz, "*Negro and White, Unite and Fight*," 33.

18. "Labor Union Movement," *CD*, April 3, 1920, 16.

19. Herbst, *The Negro in the Slaughtering and Meat-Packing Industry in Chicago*, 61–62.

20. Herbst, *The Negro in the Slaughtering and Meat-Packing Industry in Chicago*, 60–62.

21. Herbst, *The Negro in the Slaughtering and Meat-Packing Industry in Chicago*, 56–57.

22. Herbst, *The Negro in the Slaughtering and Meat-Packing Industry in Chicago*, 64–65.

23. Spero and Harris, *The Black Worker*, 279–80.

24. Spero and Harris, *The Black Worker*, 281.

25. Interview with Patricia Walker Bearden on November 2 and 9, 2007, in Chicago; unpublished manuscript on the life of Alex W. and Julia Walker. See also interview in http://atlanta.creativeloafing.com/gyrobase/PrintFriendly?oid=oid%#A125219. For Alex W. Walker's involvement in the 1906 event, see Mark Bauerlein, *Negrophobia: A Race Riot in Atlanta, 1906* (San Francisco: Encounter Books, 2001), 246–49. Leon F. Litwack, *Trouble in Mind: Black Southerners in the Age of Jim Crow* (New York: Alfred A. Knopf, 1998), 315–19, covers the episode in its broader context.

26. Interview with Wayman Hancock in Timuel D. Black Jr., *Bridges of Memory: Chicago's First Wave of Black Migration-An Oral History* (Evanston, IL: Northwestern University Press, 2001), 143.

27. Herbst, *The Negro in the Slaughtering and Meat-Packing Industry in Chicago*, xxii.

28. Spero and Harris, *The Black Worker*, 281.

29. "The Strike at the Yards," *CD*, December 17, 1921, 15.

30. For Big Four, see Spero and. Harris, *The Black Worker*, 283; for 1930, see Horowitz, "*Negro and White, Unite and Fight*," 63.

31. Johnson, "The New Frontage on American Life," 289–90.

32. See Julius Rosenwald to E. J. Buffington, president, Illinois Steel Company, September 1, 1922, Chicago Urban League File, JR Papers; and chapter 2 of this book describing the support mechanism of Provident Hospital that acted as a major community preserver of life. Under the shrewd guidance of Dr. George Cleveland Hall, and with the generosity of Julius Rosenwald, it managed to keep its doors open. The big meatpackers contributed heavily also during this period, notably Swift, Armour, Wilson, and Libby, as well as Carson, Pirie, Scott, Company and Illinois Steel. See also Lizabeth Cohen, *Making a New Deal: Industrial Workers in Chicago* (Cambridge: Cambridge University Press, 1990), 176–83.

33. CCRR, 364; the story begins on 385.

34. Spero and Harris, *The Black Worker*, 263.

35. Barnett, "We Win a Place in Industry," 83.

36. Lloyd A[ugustus] Hall, "Opportunities in [the] Chemical Industry," *Opportunity* 6 (July 1929): 221–22, 229.

37. Harris, *Keeping the Faith*, xi.

38. Brazeal, *The Brotherhood of Sleeping Car Porters*, 25.

39. Brazeal, *The Brotherhood of Sleeping Car Porters*, 25.

40. Brazeal, *The Brotherhood of Sleeping Car Porters*, 125.

41. Bates, *Pullman Porters and the Rise of Protest Politics*, 63–64.

42. Spero and Harris, *The Black Worker*, 431; Brazeal, *The Brotherhood of Sleeping Car Porters*, 21.

43. Brazeal, *The Brotherhood of Sleeping Car Porters*, 47–48, 50–54; Roi Ottley, *The*

Lonely Warrior: The Life and Times of Robert S. Abbott (Chicago: Henry Regnery, 1955), 264; Strickland, *History of the Chicago Urban League*, 33–34; Harris, *Keeping the Faith*, xi, xii; Bates, *Pullman Porters and the Rise of Protest Politics in Black America*, 63–64.

44. Strickland, *History of the Chicago Urban League*, 72–73.

45. Brazeal, *The Brotherhood of Sleeping Car Porters*, 40, 44.

46. Joseph H. Logsdon, "The Rev. Archibald J. Carey and the Negro in Chicago Politics" unpublished master's thesis, University of Chicago, 1961, 79–80; "Bishop Carey," *Messenger* 6 (March 1924): 137. Also see Bates, *Pullman Porters and the Rise of Protest Politics in Black America*, 45–46, 55–57.

47. Spero and Harris, *The Black Worker*, 435.

48. Ottley, *Lonely Warrior*, 265–66.

49. For influence of finances, see "Speak Up Mr. Abbott," *Messenger* (January 1926): 16–17; Brazeal, *The Brotherhood of Sleeping Car Porters*, 53; Harris, *Keeping the Faith*, 47, 129–33; and Ottley, *Lonely Warrior*, 259–60, 265–66.

50. Brazeal, *The Brotherhood of Sleeping Car Porters*, 51–52; Harris, *Keeping the Faith*, 46; Bates, *Pullman Porters and the Rise of Protest Politics*, 75, 209–10, n. 78.

51. Harold F. Gosnell, *Negro Politicians: The Rise of Negro Politics in Chicago* (Chicago: University of Chicago Press, 1935), 320.

52. Brazeal, *The Brotherhood of Sleeping Car Porters*, 23, 38; "A Reply to Joe D. 'Blibb,' 'Idiot-or' of the Chicago 'Flip,' Misnamed the Whip,'" *Messenger* 7(December 1925): 379; Chandler Owen, "The Neglected Truth," *Messenger* 8(January 1926): 5.

53. See Brazeal, *The Brotherhood of Sleeping Car Porters*, 51.

54. Bates, *Pullman Porters and the Rise of Protest Politics*, 4, 32, 33.

55. Spero and Harris, *The Black Worker*, 455. See also Harris, *Keeping the Faith*, 114–15.

56. Spero and Harris, *The Black Worker*, 436; Brazeal, *The Brotherhood of Sleeping Car Porters*, 22.

57. For parochialism, see E. Franklin Frazier, "Chicago: A Cross-Section of Negro Life," *Opportunity* 7 (March 1929): 70; for New Yorker, see Jervis Anderson, *A. Philip Randolph: A Biographical Portrait* (New York: Harcourt Brace Jovanovich, 1972), 170.

58. Anderson, *A. Philip Randolph*, 75, 173–74.

59. Anderson, *A. Philip Randolph*, 173; Brazeal, *The Brotherhood of Sleeping Car Porters*, 21, n. 25; Harris, *Keeping the Faith*, xi, 39–40, 76.

60. See Fenton Johnson, "Personal Reminiscences of [the] Eighth Regiment: Col. John R. Marshall," Box 23, Folder 1, p. 2, Illinois Writers Project.

61. Brazeal, *The Brotherhood of Sleeping Car Porters*, 9–10.

62. Brazeal, *The Brotherhood of Sleeping Car Porters*, 20–21; Tye, *Rising from the Rails*, 143.

63. Anderson, *A. Philip Randolph*, 170. See also Harris, *Keeping the Faith*, 76–79.

64. Harris, *Keeping The Faith*, 117–18; also 106, 126, 143–44, 151.

65. Robb, *NIC*, 2:197.

66. Bates, *Pullman Porters and the Rise of Protest Politics*, 17, epigraph, citing Du Bois's *Darkwater*; Brazeal, *The Brotherhood of Sleeping Car Porters*, 35.

67. Bates, *Pullman Porters and the Rise of Protest Politics*, 4, 5; Brazeal, *The Brotherhood of Sleeping Car Porters*, 40.

68. Bates, *Pullman Porters and the Rise of Protest Politics*, 1, 5; Harris, *Keeping the Faith*, 3.

69. Brazeal, *The Brotherhood of Sleeping Car Porters*, 43.

70. A. Philip Randolph, "A New Day Dawns for Race Workers," *CD*, July 20, 1929, 10. See Ida B. Wells, *The Reason Why the Colored American Is Not in the World's Columbian Exposition* (Chicago: World's Fair, 1893).

71. Ida Giddings, *A Sword among Lions: Ida B. Wells and the Campaign against Lynching* (New York: Harper Collins, 2008), 639; Harris, *Keeping the Faith*, xi.

72. See Brazeal, *The Brotherhood of Sleeping Car Porters*, 61; Bates, *Pullman Porters and the Rise of Protest Politics*, 65.

73. See Bates, *Pullman Porters and the Rise of Protest Politics*, 72 and supporting n. 56 on 208; also, 73, 85. Compare to Giddings, *A Sword among Lions*, chap. 26.

74. Bates, *Pullman Porters and the Rise of Protest Politics*, 78–79.

75. Gosnell, *Negro Politicians*, 110.

76. Bates, *Pullman Porters and the Rise of Protest Politics*, 64, 77. Bates identified Rev. L. K. Williams as being pro-Pullman, which is a logical conclusion to draw because of his close association with his congregant, banker Anthony Overton. Yet, his previous pro-labor stance made his shunning of the BSCP an issue of puzzlement. See pp. 77 and 210, n.89.

77. Giddings, *A Sword among Lions*, 639.

78. Brazeal, *The Brotherhood of Sleeping Car Porters*, 46.

79. For loyalty, see photographic caption, *CD*, November 27, 1926, 4 (national edition available of CD on ProQuest). For Binga, Bates cited the local edition that carried a comment from Jesse Binga that was pro-Pullman and was cited in the same dated newspaper, 53, 84.

80. Harold F. Gosnell, *Machine Politics* (Chicago: University of Chicago Press, 1939), 221; Spero and Harris, *The Black Worker*, 468. Bates in *Pullman Porters and the Rise of Protest Politics* (55–57) posits the view that AME Bishop Archibald J. Carey Sr. played an inordinately influential role over the politics of the Black Metropolis in contrast to the evidence presented here of Wright's and DePriest's control since the turn of the century. Harris, *Keeping the Faith*, 40, refers to DePriest as the city's leading black politician.

81. Bates, *Pullman Porters and the Rise of Protest Politics*, 58; Giddings, *A Sword among Lions*, 640–41.

82. Harris, *Keeping the Faith*, 151.

83. Lorenzo J. Greene and Carter G. Woodson, *The Negro Wage Earner* (Washington, DC: Association for the Study of Negro Life and History, 1930), 350.

84. Greene and Woodson, *The Negro Wage Earner*, 351. New York followed in second place with 225 members and third-place Oakland, California, claimed 182. See also Spero and Harris, *The Black Worker*, 455.

85. Spero and Harris, *The Black Worker*, 459–60. Writing in 1930 and publishing in 1931 on a contemporary basis, these authors expected the BSCP to collapse. The advantage of historical hindsight lets us know it did not.

86. Henry W. McGee, *Autobiography of Henry McGee: Chicago's First Black Postmaster* (Chicago: n.p., August 1994), 8.

87. Spero and Harris, *The Black Worker*, 122.

88. McGee, *Autobiography of Henry McGee*, 7.

89. Richard Wright, *American Hunger* (New York: Harper and Row, 1944), 26–27. Also, see Richard Wright, *Lawd Today* (New York: Walker, 1963).

90. Spero and Harris, *The Black Worker*, 122.

91. George F. Robinson Jr., "The Negro in Politics in Chicago," *Journal of Negro* History 17 (April 1932): 186–87.

92. Robinson, "The Negro in Politics in Chicago," 228.

93. Robinson, "The Negro in Politics in Chicago," 196.

94. Political cartoon, *CD*, April 23, 1927, 1.

95. Robinson, "The Negro in Politics in Chicago," 190.

96. Gosnell, *Negro Politicians*, 234.

97. Robinson, "The Negro in Politics in Chicago," 190.

98. Harold F. Gosnell, "The Chicago 'Black Belt' as a Political Battleground," *American Journal of Sociology* 38 (December 1933): 331, n. 4 citing the fifteenth U.S. Census.

99. Barnett, "We Win a Place in Industry," 83.

100. Robb, *NIC*, 1:99.

101. *Opportunity* (February 1926): 52.

102. Frazier, "Occupational Classes of Negroes in Cities," 732–33.

103. *Black's Blue Book, 1923–24* (Chicago: Douglass National Bank, 1923), 15.

104. Binder, *Chicago and the New Negro*, 13. For a description of policy during the 1930s and 1940s, see St. Clair Drake and Horace R. Cayton, *Black Metropolis: A Study of Negro Life in a Northern City* (New York: Harcourt, Brace and World, 1945), 470–94.

105. Binder, *Chicago and the New Negro*, 14.

106. Binder, *Chicago and the New Negro*, 13–15.

107. Frazier, "Chicago: A Cross-Section of Negro Life," 72.

108. See Barnett in "We Win a Place in Industry," 82–86; Frazier, "Chicago: A Cross-Section of Negro Life," 72, both in the March 1929 issue of *Opportunity*.

109. Frazier, "Chicago: A Cross-Section of Negro Life," 72.

110. "Binga Bank Is Ordered Closed for State Audit," *Chicago Tribune*, August 1930, 6.

111. *CD*, March 5, 1927, pt. 1, p. 11. The *CD* issue of July 27, 1928, pt. 2, p. 11 refers to troubling economic signs in 1926. See also Jane Addams to Mrs. Blaine, January 20, 1928, Anita McCormick Blaine Papers, State Historical Society of Wisconsin, Madison.

112. *Tenth Annual Report for the Chicago Urban League, 1925-1926*, p. 11, Levinson Papers.

113. *Eleventh Annual Report for the Chicago Urban League, 1926–1927*, 7, ACOP; and *Twelfth Annual Report for the Chicago Urban League*, n.p., Levinson Papers. See also Thyra J. Edwards, "Attitudes of Negro Families on Relief," *Opportunity* 14 (July 1936): 213.

114. Strickland, *Chicago Urban League*, 92.

115. A. L. Foster, "Twenty Years of Interracial Goodwill through Social Service," in *Two Decades of Service: 1916-1936* (Chicago: Chicago Urban League, 1936), Race Relations Committee Report File, 151, n.p., Chicago Woman's Aid Papers, University of Illinois, Chicago Circle Campus (hereafter referred to as Woman's Aid Papers).

116. *CD*, January 1, 1927, 1:11.

117. *CD*, March 5, 1927, 1:11.

118. *CD*, January 29, 1927, 1:3.

119. Frank L. Hayes, "Chicago's Rent Riot," *Survey* (September 15, 1931), 548.

120. Stephen Breszka, "And Lo! It Worked," *Opportunity* 11 (November 1933), 344. Also, note 47.

121. *CD*, December 22, 1928, 1:9.

122. *Twelfth Annual Report of the Chicago Urban League*, n.p., Levinson Papers.

123. Ralph Nelson Davis, "The Negro Newspaper in Chicago," MA thesis, University of Chicago, 1939, 122.

124. Cox, "The Origins of Direct Action," 16–21.

125. This is a counter thesis to that posited by Bates, *Pullman Porters and the Rise of Protest Politics in Black America*. See Oliver Cromwell Cox, "The Origins of Direct-Action Protest among Negroes," unpublished manuscript, c. 1932, 1933 (microfiche copy), Kent State University Libraries.

126. Interviews with Mrs. Goldie Bibb and Mrs. Lovelynn Evans, January 17, 1978, in Chicago.

127. Storch, *Red Chicago*, 27.

128. Storch, *Red Chicago*, 27–28.

129. "The Plot To Make Our Blacks Red," *Literary Digest*, 21 November 1925, 13.

130. *CD*, October 31, 1925, 1:4.

131. Harris, *Keeping the Faith*, 24.

132. Wilson Record, *The Negro and the Communist Party* (Chapel Hill: University of North Carolina Press, 1951; Atheneum, 1971), 51.

133. Brazel, *The Brotherhood of Sleeping Car Porters*, 130–31.

134. Harris, *Keeping the Faith*, 25; David Levering Lewis, *W. E. B. Du Bois: The Fight for Equality and the American Century, 1919–1963, vol. 2* (New York: Henry Holt, 2000), 196, 255–56.

135. *Women Building Chicago, 1790–1990: A Biographical Dictionary*, ed. Ruma Lunin Schultz and Adele Hast (Bloomington: Indiana University Press, 2001), 239.

136. Eugene K. Jones to Horace Bridges, July 23, 1925, Chicago Urban League File, JR Papers.

137. St. Clair Drake, Churches and Voluntary Associations in the Chicago Negro Community (Chicago: Work Projects Administration, 1940), 258.

138. Record, *The Negro and the Communist Party*, 53.

Chapter 5. The Struggle for Control over Black Politics and Protest

1. Memorandum, To the Conference, June 22, 1927, Branch Files, Papers of the National Association for the Advancement of Colored People (hereinafter referred to as NAACP Papers).

2. See Christopher Robert Reed, "A Study of Black Politics and Protest in Depression-Decade Chicago, 1930–1939," PhD diss., Kent State University, May 1982. Although the primary focus of this study centered on the 1930s, it was during the preceding decade that the foundation was forged for pursuit of a dual agenda of struggling to secure wider employment opportunities and the attainment of citizenship rights. Concomitantly, the divergent aims of political parties and protest groups guaranteed their clash with greater and greater frequency.

3. The fruition of the pursuit of a dual agenda to meet the myriad needs of African Americans is explored in Dona Cooper Hamilton and Charles V. Hamilton, *The Dual Agenda: The African-American Struggle for Civil and Economic Equality* (New York; Columbia University Press, 1997).

4. Politically savvy contemporaries such as Ralph J. Bunche, George F. Robinson Jr., and Harold F. Gosnell perceived the submachine as effective in extracting the maximum amount of benefits from the Chicago political scene in terms of patronage and racial rec-

ognition. See Ralph Johnson Bunche, "The Negro in Chicago Politics," *National Municipal Review* 17 (May 1928): 261–64; George F. Robinson Jr., "The Negro in Politics in Chicago," *Journal of Negro History* 17 (Winter 1933): 180–229; Harold F. Gosnell, *Negro Politicians: The Rise of Negro Politics in Chicago* (Chicago: University of Chicago Press, 1935). Social commentators of the decade witnessed the same phenomenon. See Charles S. Johnson, "These 'Colored United States,' VIII-Illinois: Mecca of the Migrant Mob," *Messenger* 5 (December 1923): 926–28, 933; Carroll Binder, *Chicago and the New Negro* (Chicago: Chicago Daily News, 1927), 2–24; and E. Franklin Frazier, "Chicago: A Cross-Section of Negro Life," *Opportunity* 7 (March 1929): 70–73. A generation later, Martin L. Kilson agreed with these assessments in "Political Change in the Negro Ghetto, 1900–1940s," in *Key Issues in the Afro-American Experience*, vol. 2, ed. Nathan I. Huggins, Martin L. Kilson, and Daniel M. Fox (New York: Harcourt, Brace Jovanovich, 1971), 167–92. More modern observers differ. See in particular Diane H. Pinderhughes, *Race and Ethnicity in Chicago Politics: A Re-examination of Pluralist Theory* (Urbana: University of Illinois Press, 1987) as to the failure of black politics to meet the needs of black people. The bigger question is: To what extent did any ethnic group ever get its full due from having its ethnic leadership aligned with a dominant group?

5. Joseph Bibb, "Achievements of Ten Years," cited in Frederick H. H. Robb, *The Negro in Chicago* (hereinafter referred to as *NIC*), 2 vols. (Chicago: Washington Intercollegiate Club, 1927, 1929), 2:96.

6. Oscar Hewitt, "Chicago Bets over Billion on Its Future," *Chicago Tribune* (hereinafter referred to as *CT*), June 14, 1924, 1.

7. The office of ward committeeman is, and was, one of the most important and powerful in Chicago politics since it was the committeeman as a chief party functionary and not the alderman who controlled the ward's patronage. Although the committeeman received no salary for holding his post, he usually held a salaried position elsewhere in city government. Besides his power over patronage, he lorded over slate making for local judicial and legislative posts, and membership in the real governing body of the county and city, the Cook County Central Committee. See C. B. Rourke, "Why the Scramble for the Office of Ward Committeeman," *Woman's City Club Bulletin* 19 (April 1930): 269-71, in the Woman's City Club Papers, the University of Illinois at Chicago; Cora A. Graham, "Woman Explains Duties of Chicago Ward Committeeman," *CD*, April 5,1930, 5.

8. See Gosnell, *Negro Politicians*; Claude A. Barnett, "We Win a Place in Industry," *Opportunity* 6 (March 1929); Robinson, "The Negro in Politics in Chicago"; Binder, *Chicago and the New Negro*.

9. Ralph Johnson Bunche, "The Negro in Chicago Politics," *National Municipal Review* 17 (May 1928): 261–64.

10. Gosnell, *Negro Politicians*, 52-54, 71, 74.

11. Harold F. Gosnell, *Machine Politics* (Chicago: University of Chicago Press, 1937; Phoenix Books, 1968), 221. See Beth Tomkins Bates, *Pullman Porters and the Rise of Protest Politics in Black America, 1925–1945* (Chapel Hill: University of North Carolina Press, 2001), 77–78, for the influence of patronage as it undermined individual and community independence.

12. Gosnell, *Negro Politicians*, 319.

13. Gosnell, *Negro Politicians*, 36, 41 (see appendix 16), 374. Also, see Robert M. Lovett, "Chicago, the Phenomenal City," *Current History* 31 (November 1929): 331. When Allan F. Spear talks of Harlem/Black Manhattan in his preface to *Black Manhattan: The Mak-*

ing of a Negro Ghetto, 1890–1920 (New York: Atheneum, 1969), he sees that "its political organizations [were] unresponsive to the needs of the people" (xiv).

14. *Chicago Defender* (hereinafter referred to as *CD*), October 21, 1939, 1.

15. Gosnell, *Negro Politicians*, 61.

16. Kirk H. Porter and Donald Bruce Johnson, comps., *National Party Platforms: 1840-1960* (Urbana: University of Illinois Press, 1961), 236, 265, and 290. The Republican national platforms for 1920, 1924, and 1928 all contained specific planks regarding the rights of Negroes. The plank in 1920 condemned and called for an end to lynching; in 1924, the plank called for an end to lynching but in a watered-down form; and, in 1928, the plank condemned lynching as strongly as the 1920 plank had. The *Chicago Defender* reflected the views of many blacks in regard to the party's place in their lives as its pages often carried complimentary as well as condemnatory items. See the issue of June 25, 1927, 2:12, for an example in an article carrying the former sentiment, and October 9, 1926, 1:1 for an example of the latter feeling.

17. A. N. Fields, "Eventful History of Early Chicago: R. R. Jackson Born in the Windy City in 1870, Start His Career as a Postal Employee," *CD*, January 28, 1933, 10.

18. Gosnell, *Negro Politicians*, 158.

19. Interviews with attorney Earl B. Dickerson on July 11, 1968, in Chicago and with Dr. Arthur G. Falls on May 3, 1977, in Chicago.

20. Chicago Commission on Race Relations (Charles S. Johnson), *The Negro in Chicago* (Chicago: University of Chicago Press, 1920), 3 (hereinafter referred to as CCRR); Ralph J. Bunche, "The Thompson-Negro Alliance," *Opportunity* 7 (March 1929): 78-80.

21. Dempsey J. Travis, *An Autobiography of Black Politics* (Chicago: Urban Research Institute, 1987), 74–75.

22. Gosnell, *Machine Politicians*, 61–63. Also, see Madrue Chavers-Wright, *The Guarantee: P. W. Chavers, Banker, Entrepreneur, Philanthropist in Chicago's Black Belt of the Twenties* (New York: Wright-Amstead, 1985), 325.

23. Deton J. Brooks Jr., "From Buffalo Bill Aide to Mayor's Floor Leader," *CD*, February 27, 1943, 13.

24. "Increased Pay for City Employees," *CD*, April 3, 1920, 16.

25. A.N. Fields, "Political Survey of Early Chicago: Ald. Louis B. Anderson Is First Member of Race to Serve on City Finance Committee," *CD*, January 7, 1933, 11.

26. Martin L. Kilson, "Political Change in the Negro Ghetto," 2:185-88.

27. *CD*, February 26, 1926, 1: 1.

28. Morris Lewis to Walter White, December 27, 1922, Branch Files, NAACP Papers.

29. Gosnell, *Negro Politicians*, 64.

30. Gosnell, *Negro Politicians*, 150-51.

31. Gosnell, *Negro Politicians*, 63.

32. *CT*, April 4, 1923, 1,2,5; Johnson, "These 'Colored United States,'" 928; and Gerald D. Suttles, *The Man-Made City: The Land-Use Confidence Game in Chicago* (Chicago: University of Chicago, 1990), 188. Sociologist Suttles locates the next independent action in 1972 with the defeat of the Democratic Cook County state attorney Edward Hanrahan, Mayor Richard J. Daley's Harvard-trained, hand-picked successor, whom the Democratic organization had reslated for this prosecutor's office. The election of Harold Washington as Chicago's first African American mayor in 1983 opened the next major phase of political independence.

33. Gosnell, *Negro Politicians*, 159. In 1924, at the time of Albert B. George's election as

the city's (and nation's) first black municipal judge, the Second Ward was described as "the most highly organized, politically, in the city, where the political power of the Negro has won preferment for many of his brothers." ("The First Negro Elected Judge," *Literary Digest*, November 29, 1924, 12.)

34. Dempsey J. Travis, *The Victory Monument: The Beacon of Chicago's Bronzeville* (Chicago: Urban Research Institute, 1999), 41.

35. Interviews with Earl B. Dickerson on June 13, 1977, January 23, 1978, and March 21, 1984, in Chicago at the offices of Supreme Life Insurance Company.

36. A. N. Fields, "The Body Politic of Early Chicago: Edward H. Wright Reaches Zenith of His Power," *CD*, December 31, 1932, 11; Gosnell, *Negro Politicians*, 158.

37. Edward T. Clayton, *The Negro Politician: His Success and Failure* (Chicago: Johnson, 1964), 48.

38. See Douglas Bukowski, *Big Bill Thompson, Chicago, and the Image of Politics* (Urbana: University of Illinois Press, 1998), 178, who says incorrectly that Hall was first.

39. Librarian [Carl D. Roden] to O[G]. E[C]. Hall, March 17, 1926; Librarian [Carl D. Roden] to E. H. Hart, February 16, 1927; and N. Hymen to Andrew J. Kolar, February 24, 1927; all in Carl D. Roden Papers, Special Collections Division, Harold Washington Library Center, Chicago Public Library (hereafter referred to as Roden Papers).

40. "New Library to Be Used by All Races: Dr. Hall Resents Hint of Segregation," *CD*, June 1, 1929, 10. Hall's efforts in behalf of this civic project, along with his support for and leadership roles on the Chicago Commission on Race Relations, the Chicago NAACP, and the Chicago Urban League served to bring into question the historical portrayal of Hall as a civic and social pretender based on the early twentieth-century squabble at Provident Hospital with Dr. Daniel Hale Williams. See chapter 8.

41. G. C. Hall to C[arl B.] Roden, September 3, 1929, and Librarian [Carl B. Roden] to Hall, September 5, 1929, in Roden Papers.

42. Some works on Chicago have made reference to an appointment before Dr. Midian O. Bousfield's selection in 1946, but they are inaccurate. See, for example, Clifton O. Dummett and Lois Doyle Dummett, *Charles Edwin Bentley: A Model for All Times* (St. Paul, MN: North Central, 1982), 155, citing Mary White Ovington.

43. See "Defender's Fight Wins '8th' Glory," *CD*, March 27, 1926; Gosnell, *Negro Politicians*, 159; Christopher R. Reed, "The Manifestations of Nationalism in the Black Belt of Chicago, 1920–1929," master's thesis, Roosevelt University, September, 1968, 29; see Travis, *The Victory Monument*, which uses the monument as a pivot from which flows the story of the Black Metropolis.

44. U.S. Congress, Senate Committee on Privileges and Elections, Special Committee Investigating Expenditures in Senatorial and General Elections, 69th Cong., 1st sess., Chicago (Reed) Hearings, July 26 to August 5, 1926, 2:1678 (Testimony of Edward H. Wright).

45. Carroll Hill Wooddy, *The Chicago Primary of 1926: A Study in Election Methods* (1927; repr. New York: Arno Press, 1974). 187.

46. Interview with attorney Earl B. Dickerson on July 11, 1968, in Chicago.

47. *CD*, February 26, 1927, 1; Robert J. Blakely, *Earl B. Dickerson: A Voice for Freedom and Equality* (Evanston, IL: Northwestern University Press, 2006), 62.

48. "Thompson Is Given City's Biggest Vote," *CD*, February 26, 1927, 1.

49. A. N. Fields, "Chicagoans Make Political History: E. H. Wright, Peer of Politicians," *CD*, December 24, 1932, 11. See also Fields, "Political Survey of Early Chicago," 11.

50. Fields, "Chicagoans Make Political History."

51. Interview with attorney Earl B. Dickerson on July 11, 1968, in Chicago; Pinderhughes, *Race and Ethnicity in Chicago Politics.*

52. Fields, "Chicagoans Make Political History"; Fields, "The Body Politic of Early Chicago," 11. Gosnell, *Negro Politicians*, 160–61; *NIC*, 2:103; interview with attorney Earl B. Dickerson on July 11, 1968, in Chicago.

53. For ailing Wright, see "Dan Jackson Given State Official Post," *CD*, September 1, 1928, 1; for Anderson, see Fields, "Political Survey of Early Chicago," 11; "DePriest Backs Dawson for Alderman of Second Ward," *CD*, February 25, 1933, 3.

54. Chavers-Wright, *The Guarantee*, 292.

55. *CT*, April 15, 1926, 2; *CD*, April 24, 1926, 2. Chavers-Wright, in *The Guarantee* (295), incorrectly claimed Chavers received 6,000 out of 20,000 cast votes.

56. Gosnell, *Negro Politicians*, 75.

57. "Colored Voters Urged to Stage Revolt at the Polls," *CT*, November 4, 1928, 3.

58. "More Business Men Rally to Judge Swanson," *CT*, September 10, 1928, 11. See Gosnell, *Negro Politicians*, 107, for this inaccuracy.

59. "Hubbub Halts Mayor Talk at Negro Rally," *CT*, April 5, 1928, 1; "Negroes Turning against Mayor, Observers Find," *CT*, April 5, 1928, 4; "Mayor Promises Negroes 150,000 Jobs for Votes," *CT*, April 9, 1928, 5; "How We Will Vote and Why," *CD*, April 7, 1928, A2.

60. Gosnell, *Negro Politicians*, 79; "Memorial Services of William L. Dawson," 92nd Congress, 2nd sess., November 1, 1970 (Washington, DC: U. S. Government Printing Office, 1971).

61. "Wm. L. Dawson Would Succeed Dan Jackson," *CD*, July 6, 1929, 2.

62. Gosnell, *Negro Politicians*, 80.

63. "DePriest Wins Congress Seat by Slim Margin," *CT*, November 8, 1928, 14.

64. For triumph, see Maurine Christopher, *America's Black Congressmen* (New York: Thomas Y. Crowell, 1971), 170; for a national figure, see Gosnell, *Negro Politicians*, 183; for eyes of supporters, see Frances Williams McLemore, "The Role of the Negroes in Chicago in the Senatorial Election, 1930," master's thesis, University of Chicago, 1931, 50; for "he fought segregation," see *CD*, February 13, 1932, 2; for "kick down a door," see interview with Mr. Earl Thomas Sr. in Chicago on June 21, 1977; for "always could be counted on," see interview with Dr. Arthur G. Falls in Chicago on May 3, 1977.

65. Gosnell, *Negro Politicians*, 193.

66. Fields, "The Body Politic of Early Chicago," 11.

67. Oliver Cromwell Cox, "The Origins of Direct Action among Negroes," unpublished manuscript written at the University of Chicago, 1932-1933 and revised in 1973 (microfiche available at the Kent State University Libraries), 140.

68. *Eleventh Annual Report of the Chicago Urban League, 1926–1927*, 7, "A Century of Progress" papers, Chicago Urban League File, the University of Illinois in Chicago (hereafter referred to as the ACOP).

69. Lewis to Robert W. Bagnall, 30 March 1923, Branch Files, NAACP Papers; White to Lillian Proctor, 14 January 1925 and press release, 30 January 1925, both in Adm. File, Theater Discrimination Cases, NAACP Papers.

70. *CD*, November 28, 1925, 2:10.

71. Ida Giddings, *A Sword among Lions: Ida B. Wells and the Campaign against Lynching* (New York: HarperCollins, 2008), 648–49.

72. For donation, see *CD*, November 28, 1925, pt. 2, 10; for DePriest's service, see Report

of the Chicago NAACP for 1927, n.p., NAACP; for membership, see *The Light* newspaper file, February 26, 1927, NAACP Papers.

73. Morris Lewis to Bagnall, March 30, 1923; Lewis to James Weldon Johnson, March 30, 1923; Lewis to Bagnall, April 14, 1923, all in Branch Files, NAACP Papers. Also, *CD*, March 24, 1923, 6.

74. Morris Lewis to Bagnall, March 30, 1923; Lewis to James Weldon Johnson, March 30, 1923; and Lewis to Bagnall, April 14, 1923, NAACP Papers. Also see *CD*, March 24, 1923, 6.

75. Blacks contributed 10 percent of monies raised in 1926-1927; W. C. Graves to Julius Rosenwald, 23 November 1917, Chicago Urban League file, Julius Rosenwald papers (hereinafter referred to as JR Papers). They contributed 18 percent of the budget or $4,900.00 in 1922; T. Arnold Hill to W. C. Graves, February 21, 1922, Chicago Urban League file, JR Papers. By 1924, a plan was proposed to raise $10,000.00 from blacks, see Hill to Salmon O. Levinson, March 7, 1924, Chicago Urban League file, Levinson papers. By 1927, Robert S. Abbott contributed $1,500.00 as part of a three-year personal pledge; *CD*, January 14, 1928, 2:1.

76. Arvarh E. Strickland, *History of the Chicago Urban League* (Urbana: University of Illinois Press, 1967) 81.

77. Strickland, *History of the Chicago Urban League*, 81–82.

78. Strickland, *History of the Chicago Urban League*, 80.

79. Strickland, *History of the Chicago Urban League*, 79.

80. See material in the Anti-Thompson Campaign File, box 39, JR Papers; note 34; and *CD*, March 2, 1929, 1:1.

81. Telegram, Harry D. Oppenheimer to (Salmon) Sol Levinson, 8 February 1923, Chicago Urban League file, Levinson Papers, the University of Chicago (hereafter referred to as Levinson Papers).

82. Frazier, "Chicago: A Cross-Section of Negro Life," 72.

83. *CD*, March 3, 1923, 1:1.

84. Julius Rosenwald to E. J. Buffington, president, Illinois Steel Company, September 1, 1922, Chicago Urban League file, JR Papers. See profile on Hill in Nancy J. Weiss, *The National Urban League: 1910-1940* (New York: Oxford University Press, 1974), 183.

85. Edwin R. Embree to Julius Rosenwald, January 17, 1929, Chicago Urban League File, JR Papers.

86. *Chicago Whip*, May 9, 1931, n.p., in the Arthur W. Mitchell papers, Chicago History Museum.

87. Alfred K. Stern to Rosenwald, 15 October 1929, Chicago Urban League file, JR Papers. Interviews with Walter L. Lowe in Chicago on May 3, 1977, and Howard Gould on June 11, 1977. Also, see Horace J. Bridges to (Julius) Rosenwald, 30 October 1930, Chicago Urban League file, JR Papers.

88. Robert W. Bagnall to Archie Weaver, 14 April 1932, Branch Files, NAACP Papers.

89. Rosenwald's close association with the conservative Booker T. Washington and his equally conservative racial ideology is noted in such secondary works as Spear's *Black Chicago*, 170, 173; and Charles Flint Kellogg's *NAACP* (Baltimore: John Hopkins Press, 1967), 124–25. See also Charles E. Bentley to Professor (Joel) Spingarn, March 29, 1915, Joel Spingarn papers, Box 95-1, Moorland-Spingarn Collection, Howard University, Washington, DC. Also, interview with Dr. Arthur G. Falls on May 3, 1977, in Chicago, Illinois.

90. Arthur I. Waskow, *From Race Riot to Sit-In, 1919 and the 1960's: A Study in the Con-*

nections between Conflict and Violence (Garden City, NY: Doubleday, 1966; Anchor ed., 1967), 46.

91. Morris Lewis to Bagnall, 15 January 1923, NAACP Papers.

92. Bagnall to Daisy E. Lampkin, 18 September 1930, Adm. File, Spec. Corres.: Bagnall, NAACP Papers.

93. Charles E. Bentley to James W. Johnson, January 16, 1923; Johnson to Bentley, January 20, 1923; Bagnall to Dr. Carl Roberts, March 31, 1925; Walter White to Archie Weaver, July 27, 1929, all in NAACP Papers.

94. Harold L. Ickes to Bagnall, May 24, 1924, NAACP file, Ickes papers, Library of Congress, Washington, DC.

95. Lewis to Bagnall, March 15, 1923, Branch files, NAACP. Also, Ickes' rather conservative views on race are contained in his *The Secret Diary of Harold L. Ickes: The First Thousand Days, 1933–1936* (New York: Simon and Schuster, 1953), 2:115.

96. *CD*, October 3, 1925, 1:3.

97. Mary McDowell was well thought of by black Chicagoans and laudatory comments about her were often seen in the pages of the *Chicago Defender* as it reported on events that were held to honor her. See *Chicago Defender* issues of October 10, 1925, 1:13; June 25, 1927, 1:1; and July 2, 1927, 2:2.

98. James W. Johnson to Morris Lewis, February 6, 1925, Branch Files, NAACP Papers.

99. Johnson to Lewis, February 30, 1925, Branch Files, NAACP Papers.

100. Lewis to Johnson, 11 December 1924, Branch Files, NAACP Papers.

101. Bagnall to Carl G. Roberts, 31 March 1925, Branch Files, NAACP Papers.

102. Lewis to Walter White, 5 December 1925, Branch Files, NAACP Papers.

103. Weaver to Bagnall, 13 June 1926, Branch Files, NAACP Papers.

104. Several examples occurred once the period of black hegemony began in 1925. See William H. Haynes to White, January 12, 1925, Adm. File, Subject File: Tivoli Discrimination Case, NAACP Papers; and in the *CD*, June 11, 1927, 1:2; May 26, 1928, 1:8; and, July 20, 1929, 1:1.

105. *Crisis* (May 1926): 24.

106. Bagnall to Weaver, July 12, 1926, Branch Files, NAACP Papers.

107. *CD*, December 10, 1927, 2:12 (torn page).

108. *CD*, 19 October 1929, 8.

109. As early as 1912, politics was considered a detrimental influence among Chicago NAACP supporters. Specifically, Jane Addams's endorsement of Theodore Roosevelt's candidacy on the Progressive Party ticket was the cause of consternation among her friends and fellow NAACPers, who felt that this partisan political involvement would damage the association's image. See Charles E. Bentley to Joel Spingarn, August 13, 1912, Box 95-1, Joel Spingarn papers, Moorland-Spingarn Library, Howard University. .

110. Lewis to Bagnall, September 9, 1922, Branch Files, NAACP Papers.

111. Lewis to Bagnall, March 30, 1923; Bagnall to Lewis, April 3, 1923; and Lewis to Bagnall, April 6, 1923, all in Branch Files, NAACP Papers.

112. Charles E. Bentley to Bagnall, March 13, 1922, Branch Files, NAACP Papers.

113. Lewis to Johnson, November 25, 1923, Branch Files, NAACP Papers.

114. William T. Andrews to Lewis, May 2, 1928; and second letter, October 3, 1928, Branch Files, NAACP Papers.

115. Gosnell, *Negro Politicians*, 313. Larry Tye, *Rising from the Rails: Pullman Porters and the Making of the Black Middle Class* (New York: Henry Holt, 2004).

116. Randi Storch, *Red Chicago: American Communism at Its Grassroots, 1928–35* (Urbana: University of Illinois Press, 2007), 139.

117. St. Clair Drake, *Churches and Voluntary Associations in the Chicago Negro Community* (hereinafter referred to as CVA) (Chicago: Work Projects Administration, 1940), 257.

118. Gosnell, *Negro Politicians*, 326.

119. CCRR, 61.

120. *CT*, June 21, 1921, 1.

121. Newspaper accounts report that nine men were arrested for their part in the "Abyssinian incident" and no mention was made of anything other than small crowds of observers at their meetings.

122. *Chicago Daily Journal*, June 21, 1920, 3.

123. *CD*, July 3, 1920, 1.

124. *CT*, June 23, 1920, 5.

125. David L. Lewis, *W. E. B Du Bois: Biography of a Race* (New York: Henry Holt, 1993), 456, 459–62. Du Bois served as stage director in several productions of "The Star of Ethiopia," presented nationally between 1913 through 1925.

126. *CT*, June 21, 1920, 2.

127. CCRR, 59.

128. *Chicago Whip*, June 26, 1920, 1. The *New York Times* had information initially on the incident with subsequent issues ignoring it.

129. E. Franklin Frazier, "Garvey: A Mass Leader," *Nation*, August 18, 1926, 147; Martin, *Race First*, 13, 15.

130. Frazier, "Garvey: A Mass Leader," 147.

131. Martin, *Race First*, 13.

132. Roi Ottley, *The Lonely Warrior: The Life and Times of Robert S. Abbott* (Chicago: Henry Regnery, 1955), 212.

133. *Chicago Whip*, June 26, 1920, 2.

134. St. Clair Drake and Horace R. Cayton, *Black Metropolis: A Study of Negro Life in a Northern City* (hereafter referred to as *BM)* (New York: Harcourt, Brace and World, 1945), 752.

135. *Chicago Whip*, November 5, 1921, 8.

136. Martin, *Race First*, 322–24; David E. Cronon, *Black Moses: The Story of Marcus Garvey and the Universal Negro Improvement Association* (Madison: University of Wisconsin Press, 1955), 188–90.

137. Arna Bontemps and Jack Conroy, *They Seek a City* (Garden City, NJ: Doubleday, Doran, 1945), 171.

138. Cronon, *Black Moses*, 206.

139. Drake and Cayton, *BM*, 752. Interviews with Mr. J. J. Peters in July 1968 in Chicago and Mrs. Vernon Ford Sr. in May 1988 in Chicago. The former was a high-ranking official in the UNIA and the latter was a child of a UNIA member who, along with others, witnessed the organization's activities on Chicago's West Side.

140. Chavers-Wright, *The Guarantee*, 284, 286.

141. Alfreda F. Duster, *Crusade for Justice: The Autobiography of Ida B. Wells* (Chicago: University of Chicago Press, 1967), 380–82.

142. Interview with Everett Renfroe on July 11, 1968, in Chicago. See also Frazier, "Garvey: A Mass Leader," 147.

143. Martin, *Race First*, 121, chap. 7, "Africa." Garvey's widow stated in 1963 that the "Back to Africa" phase of the UNIA program was exploited by enemies of her late husband in an effort to discredit his organization. See Amy Jacques Garvey, *Garvey and Garveyism* (Kingston, Jamaica: United Printers, 1963), 127. Also, Truman H. Talley, "Garvey's Empire of Ethiopia," *World's Work* 41 (January 1921): 268. This attack was very effective as evidenced by the literature of the time and by the statements of the vast majority of the author's interviewees in 1968.

144. Storch, *Red Chicago*, 96.

Chapter 6. Transformed Religion and a Proliferation of Churches

1. Harold F. Gosnell, *Negro Politicians: The Rise of Negro Politics in Chicago* (Chicago: University of Chicago Press, 1935), 97–100.

2. Gosnell, *Negro Politicians*, 99.

3. E. Franklin Frazier, "Chicago: A Cross-Section of Negro Life," *Opportunity* 7 (March 1929): 71.

4. Rev. L. K. Williams, "The Urbanization of Negroes: [The] Effect on Their Religious Life," *Chicago Tribune* (hereinafter referred to as *CT*), January 13, 1929, 12. See also "2,000 Southern Negroes Arrive in Last Two Days," *CT*, March 4, 1917, 1.

5. Wallace D. Best, *Passionately Human, No Less Divine: Religion and Culture in Black Chicago, 1915–1952* (Princeton, NJ: Princeton University Press, 2005), 130–31.

6. Best, *Passionately Human, No Less Divine*, 128, 129.

7. "Colorful Career of Church and Civic Leader Ended," *Chicago Defender* (hereinafter referred to as *CD*), March 28, 1931, 1.

8. "Archibald J. Carey," *CD*, March 28, 1931, 14.

9. Z. Withers, "Bethel Church," *Half-Century Magazine*, July, 1918, 8.

10. Harold M. Kingsley, "The Negro Goes to Church," *Opportunity* (March 1929): 90; "114th Anniversary Souvenir Book," *Bethel African Methodist Episcopal Church* (Chicago: Bethel A.M.E. Church, 2006), n.p; Susan Perry, Commission on Chicago Landmarks, "Preliminary Summary of Information on the Metropolitan Apostolic Community Church" (typewritten copy, December 2006), 19, 20. Also, "Rev. William D. Cook Dies," *CD*, July 12, 1930, 1, 4. Funerary ceremonies are sometimes excellent indicators of an individual's impact on a society, and the list of honorary pallbearers, along with the thousands who attended who attended his services, attested to Rev. Cook's prominence in the Black Metropolis. Best, *Passionately Human, No Less Divine*, 134–35, attributes the split to AME bureaucracy in rotating his ministerial duties away from Chicago.

11. "114th Anniversary Souvenir Book," n.p.

12. "113th Anniversary Souvenir Book of Saint Stephen African Methodist Episcopal Church," Chicago, 1985, n.p.; Rev. M. C. Wright Quits A.M.E. Fold; Will Start New Church," *CD*, October 4, 1931, 10; "Ministers' Conference in Annual Election of Officers," *CD*, October 25, 1930, 12.

13. Kingsley, "The Negro Goes to Church," 90.

14. Beth Tomkins Bates, *Pullman Porters and the Rise of Protest Politics in Black America, 1925–1945* (Chapel Hill: University of North Carolina Press, 2001), 45–46, 55–57.

15. "Archibald J. Carey," *CD*, March 28, 1931, 14.

16. *Black's Blue Book, 1923–24* (Chicago: Douglass National Bank, 1923), 41.

17. "The National Baptist Convention and Its Leader," *Half-Century Magazine* (July–August 1923):8; Kingsley, "The Negro Goes to Church," 90; "Clergy in Politics, *CD*, February 19, 1916, 8.

18. Best, *Passionately Human, No Less Divine*, 77.

19. "Says Pastor Would Make Him Beggar," *CD*, January 10, 1925, A1.

20. "65th Anniversary Souvenir Book of the Pilgrim Baptist Church," Chicago, 1982, n.p. See photographs of the interior before the disastrous fire of January 2006 at www.gryjhnsn.tripod.com/chicagohistory/pilgrimage.html. Because of its architectural grandeur, it is currently considered both a city and national landmark.

21. Oscar C. Brown Sr., *By a Thread* (New York: Vantage Press, 1983), 51–52.

22. "100th Anniversary Souvenir Book of the Greater Bethesda Missionary Baptist Church: A Century with Christ, 1882–1982," Chicago, 1982, n.p.

23. "Berean's 100th Anniversary Souvenir Booklet" (Chicago: Berean Baptist Church, 2001).

24. Mildred J. Armstrong, *The Miracle on Fifty-Seventh Street: The History of the Church of the Good Shepherd* [Congregational] (Chicago: Church of the Good Shepherd, c. 2003), 4–6, 8, 12–15; also Kingsley, "The Negro Goes to Church," 91.

25. Kingsley, "The Negro Goes to Church," 91.

26. Interview with Mrs. Pauline Lewis Williams conducted by Professor Suellen Hoy in Evanston, Illinois, on January 22, 2001, 2.

27. St. Monica's Catholic Church, box 18, folder 36, Illinois Writers Project.

28. Interview with Mrs. Pauline Lewis Williams conducted by Professor Suellen Hoy in Evanston, Illinois, on January 22, 2001, 3.

29. Frazier, "Chicago: A Cross-Section of Negro Life," 71. See Best, *Passionately Human, No Less Divine*, xvii, who describes the southern linkages in a modern day Washington, D.C., church that explains the same linkages as they existed in black Chicago's religious past.

30. Best, *Passionately Human, No Less Divine*, xv.

31. "Bailiff Ike Weil Busts Trusty Gavel," *CT*, November 3, 1925, 1.

32. Olivia Mahoney, *Douglas/Grand Boulevard: A Chicago Neighborhood* (Chicago: Arcadia, 2001), 82.

33. http://www.firstchurchofdeliverance.org/Our_Church.htm (accessed August 30, 2010).

34. Best, *Passionately Human, No Less Divine*, 41.

35. Inscription, Chicago Commission on Landmarks Plaque, implanted 1994, at 4341 South Wabash Avenue.

36. Best, *Passionately Human, No Less Divine*, 147.

37. http:/findarticles.com/p/articles/mi_mOSOR /is_nl-v54/ai_13976708/pg_10.

38. Best, *Passionately Human, No Less Divine*, 149.

39. Arna Bontemps and Jack Conroy, *They Seek a City* (Garden City, NY: Doubleday, Doran, 1945), 175.

40. Arthur H. Fauset, *Black Gods of the Metropolis* (Philadelphia: Philadelphia Anthropological Society, 1944), 42.

41. Interview with Mrs. Lucine Walker on May 25, 1968, in Chicago.

42. *Constitution*, Moorish Science Temple of America, n.p.

43. *CD*, October 20, 1928, 1:2.

44. *CD*, March 23, 1929, 1;1; interview with Sister C. Price Bey on June 22, 1968, in Chicago.

45. *CD*, March 16, 1929, 1:1 and March 23, 1929, 2:2. See also E. U. Essien-Udom, *Black Nationalism* (Chicago: University of Chicago, 1962), 48.

Chapter 7. Cultural and Aesthetic Expressions

1. See Carroll Binder, *Chicago and the New Negro* (Chicago: Chicago Daily News, 1927), 22, who describes the city's landscape and the status and activities of African Americans therein. The historical dimensions to this claim of a budding literary tradition are discussed by Jack Conroy in three successive drafts in "African American Literature in Illinois, 1861–1941" Box 46, folders 1, 2, 3, Illinois Writers Project, Work Projects Administration, 1941 (hereafter IWP). Informatively, this essay is indebted to the publication of the monumental and comprehensive *Call and Response: The Riverside Anthology of the African American Literary Tradition*, ed. Patricia Liggins Hill et al. (Boston: Houghton Mifflin, 1998) that posits the influence of a Black Aesthetic as the centerpiece of any dialogue on African American art. Chicago's early pre-jazz and -blues musical development is explored contemporaneously in volume 2 of *The Negro in Chicago*, 2 vols., ed. Frederick H. H. Robb (Chicago: Washington Intercollegiate Wonder Book, 1927 and 1929), cited throughout as Robb, *NIC*. Importantly, a more comprehensive treatment of the issue of black creativity is under review by the University of Illinois Press under the cover of *The Black Chicago Renaissance: An Anthology*.

2. Arna Bontemps, "Famous WPA Authors," *Negro Digest* (June 1950): 47.

3. See Kevin K. Gaines, *Uplifting the Race: Black Leadership, Politics, and Culture in the Twentieth Century* (Chapel Hill: University of North Carolina Press, 1996). Perhaps Gaines's chapter 6, entitled "Urban Pathology and the Limits of Social Research," holds the answer to how eager, young researchers (in the mold of a young Du Bois) could so easily reach the unfavorable conclusions they did about any particular African American population they were observing. Perhaps they conformed to some academically rooted racial personality overlooked in Charles S. Johnson, "Some Racial Types," *Opportunity* 5 (January 1927): 4, or acutely overanalyzed in E. Franklin Frazier, "The Mind of the American Negro," *Opportunity* 6 (September 1928): 264–66, 284.

4. Carroll Binder, "Chicago and the New Negro," 22.

5. John Hope Franklin and Alfred M. Moss Jr., *From Slavery to Freedom: A History of African Americans*, 7th ed. (New York: McGraw-Hill, 1998), 376.

6. Harriet G. Warkel, "Image and Identity: The Art of William E. Scott, John W. Hardrick, and Hale G. Woodruff," 18, in *A Shared Heritage: Art by Four African Americans*, ed. William E. Taylor and Harriet G. Warkel (Indianapolis: Indianapolis Museum of Art, 1996).

7. "Wm. E. Scott, Noted Painter, Dies at Age 80," *Chicago Tribune*, May 17, 1964, E8.

8. Alain Locke, "The New Negro," in *The New Negro*, ed. Alain Locke (1925; repr., New York: Atheneum, 1992), 2–3.

9. Allan H. Spear, *Black Chicago: The Making of a Negro Ghetto, 1890–1920* (New York: Atheneum, 1969), 26.

10. Harry Schuchmacher, "Best of the Best of American Music: Louis Armstrong, Changing the World," *American Mix* (May–June 2001): 4; Howard Reich, "A Wail of a Town-Hotter near the Lake" Chicago Tribune Magazine, September 5, 1993, 14. Reich wrote that the economic diversity was such that "mobsters, musicians, socialites and working people danced past dawn to rhythms of America's only original art form"; and

see the interview with L[ewis A. H.] Caldwell in Timuel D. Black Jr., *Bridges of Memory: Chicago's First Wave of Black Migration-An Oral History* (Evanston, IL: Northwestern University Press, 2003), 262.

11. Roi Ottley, *The Lonely Warrior: The Life and Times of Robert S. Abbott* (Chicago: Henry Regnery, 1955), 224. Abbott bridged the two worlds of culture. His stroll along his thoroughfare was an affirmation that he had not lost touch with the common person, upon whom he depended for both business and ego support.

12. For the jazz landscape, see http://www.lib.uchicago.edu/e/su/cja/jazzmaps/listalph.htm (accessed August 30, 2010). For a description and analysis of the activities and changes at the Regal Theater, see Clovis E. Semmes, *The Regal Theater and Black Culture* (New York: Palgrave MacMillan, 2006); also, see Dempsey J. Travis, "Cab Calloway," in *An Autobiography of Black Jazz* (Chicago: Urban Research Press, 1983), 230–31.

13. David Levering Lewis, *When Harlem Was in Vogue* (New York: Oxford University Press, 1981), 171–72. See also interview with Jimmy Ellis in Black, *Bridges of Memory*, 160; William Howland Kenney, *Chicago Jazz: A Cultural History, 1904–1930* (New York: Oxford University Press, 1993), 53, 54; and Gaines, *Uplifting the Race*, 184. Moreover, the pressure to please white audiences, whether patrons, publishers, or readers, is well accepted as fact. See its exposition in both novel and scholarly forms in Wallace Thurmond, *Infants of the Spring*, and Gaines, *Uplifting the Race*, 184.

14. Travis, "Bud Freeman," in *An Autobiography of Black Jazz* (Chicago: Urban Research Press, 1983), 324. Likewise, the great clarinetist Jimmy Noone is credited with teaching Benny Goodman his level of proficiency; see Reich, "A Wail of a Town," 18.

15. Kenney, *Chicago Jazz*, 120–46

16. Quoted in James R. Grossman, *Land of Hope: Chicago, Black Southerners, and the Great Migration* (Chicago: University of Chicago Press, 1989), 154.

17. William Barlow, "Black Music on Radio during the Jazz Age," *North American Review* (Summer 1995), online at http://www.findarticles.com/p/articles/mi_m2838/is_n2_v29/ai_17534809/pg_3 (accessed August 30, 2010).

18. Lawrence W. Levine, *High Culture/Low Culture: The Emergence of Cultural Hierarchy in America* (Cambridge: Harvard University Press, 1988).

19. Carroll Binder, *Chicago and the New Negro*, 4. In contrast, Langston Hughes said of Harlem: "Harlem nights became show nights for the Nordics." Certain writers were also affected and wrote to amuse white people. See Langston Hughes, *The Big Sea: An Autobiography* (New York: 1940; repr., New York: Hill and Wang, 1963), 226–28.

20. Clifton O. Dummett and Lois Doyle Dummett, *Charles Edwin Bentley: A Model for All Times* (St. Paul, MN: North Central, 1982), 190, 201–2.

21. See "Greater Poets in Chicago," in Robb, *NIC*, 1:86–87.

22. Binder, "Chicago and the New Negro," 11. See also Robb, *NIC*, 1:124, "Race Publications in Chicago."

23. See Christopher Robert Reed, *Black Chicago's First Century*, vol. 1, *1833–1900* (Columbia: University of Missouri Press, 2005), 155, 430.

24. Robb, *NIC*, 1:87. Also, 1:156 and 199.

25. "African American Life in Illinois," Box 46, Folder 1, 25, Illinois Writers Project, 803.

26. Michel Fabre, *The Unfinished Quest of Richard Wright* (New York: William Morrow, 1973), 79–80.

27. Hughes, *The Big Sea*, 226. Also, see 309–10.

28. E. Franklin Frazier, "Chicago: A Cross-Section of Negro Life," *Opportunity* 7 (March 1929): 73; Robb, *NIC*, 1:223.
29. Warkel, "Image and Identity," 27.
30. Locke, *The Negro in Art*, 135.
31. "*Defender's* Fight Wins '8th' Glory," *Chicago Defender*, March 27, 1926, 1.

Conclusion and Legacy

1. See Christopher Robert Reed, "Black Chicago Political Realignment during the Depression and New Deal," *Illinois Historical Journal* 78 (Winter 1985): 242–56.
2. See Wright's experiences with his fellow black comrades in his *American Hunger* (New York: Harper and Row, 1944), 37–41, 77, 94.

SELECTED BIBLIOGRAPHY

Collections and Papers

CHICAGO HISTORY MUSEUM (FORMERLY THE CHICAGO HISTORICAL SOCIETY)

Claude A. Barnett Papers
Irene McCoy Gaines Papers
Harold F. Gosnell Papers
Arthur W. Mitchell Papers

CHICAGO PUBLIC LIBRARY, HAROLD WASHINGTON LIBRARY CENTER

Carl B. Roden Papers
Westside Neighborhood History

CHICAGO PUBLIC LIBRARY, CARTER G. WOODSON REGIONAL LIBRARY CENTER

Illinois Writers Project (IWP). "The Negro in Illinois." Vivian G. Harsh Collection on Afro-American History and Literature

LIBRARY OF CONGRESS, WASHINGTON, D.C.

Papers of the National Association for the Advancement of Colored People

NEWBERRY LIBRARY, CHICAGO

George M. Pullman Papers

ROOSEVELT UNIVERSITY, CHICAGO

Papers of Christopher Robert Reed

UNIVERSITY OF CHICAGO

Ida B. Wells Barnett Papers
Julius Rosenwald Papers

UNIVERSITY OF ILLINOIS AT CHICAGO

A Century of Progress Papers
Chicago Urban League
Lawrence J. Gutter Collection on Chicagoana

PRIVATE HOLDINGS OF THE AUTHOR

Anthony Binga Jr. Family File, Richmond, Virginia
Henry and Josephine Peay Slaughter Family File
Ephemera, including Albert Brooks, "Orphans of the Storm [Substitute Postal Employees]," typewritten copy of autobiographical sketch, c. 1985

Government Documents

City of Chicago, Chicago Planning Commission. *Residential Chicago*. Vol. 1, *Chicago Land Use Survey*. Chicago: Chicago Planning Commission and Work Projects Administration, 1942.

City of Chicago, Department of Planning and Development. "*Black Metropolis Historic District*," March 7, 1984 (rev. December 1994).

City of Chicago, Department of Planning and Development. *Chicago Historic Resources Survey* (Chicago: Chicago Department of Planning and Development, 1996).

"Giles-Calumet District." Preliminary Summary of Information, Commission on Chicago Landmarks, July 2008.

U.S. Congress. Memorial Services for the Late Rep. William L. Dawson (Illinois), 91st Cong., 2nd sess. (Washington, DC: U.S. Government Printing Office, 1971), 1–74.

U.S. National Advisory Commission on Civil Disorders, Report (New York: Bantam Books, 1968).

U.S. Senate Committee on Privileges and Elections. Special Committee Investigating Expenditures in Senatorial and General Elections, 69th Cong., 1st sess., Chicago hearings, July 26 to August 5, 1926, 2: 1676–1686 [Testimony of Edward H. Wright].

Newspapers and Journals

Chicago Daily News
Chicago Defender (CD)
Chicago Tribune
Crisis
Half-Century Magazine
Messenger
Opportunity

Books and Articles

Anderson, Jervis. *A. Philip Randolph: A Biographical Portrait*. New York: Harcourt Brace Jovanovich, 1972.

"Are We Ashamed of Our Lineage?" *Half-Century Magazine* (January 1920): 1.

Armstrong, Mildred J. *The Miracle on Fifty-Seventh Street: The History of the Church of the Good Shepherd* [Congregational]. Chicago: Church of the Good Shepherd, c. 2003.

Ascoli, Peter M. *Julius Rosenwald: The Man Who Built Sears, Roebuck and Advanced the Cause of Black Education in the American South*. Bloomington: Indiana University Press, 2006.

Baldwin, Davarian L. *Chicago's New Negroes: Modernity, the Great Migration and Black Urban Life*. Chapel Hill: University of North Carolina Press, 2007.

Barnett, Claude A. "We Win a Place in Industry." *Opportunity* 6 (March 1929): 82–86.

Bates, Beth Tompkins. *Pullman Porters and the Rise of Protest Politics in Black America, 1925–1945*. Chapel Hill: University of North Carolina Press, 2001.

Beisel, Courtney Leigh. "Celebrating the Legacy of Charles Pierce." *X-Links* [alumni magazine of the Illinois Institute of Technology] (Fall 2007): 4–7.

"Berean's 100th Anniversary" Souvenir Booklet. Chicago: Berean Baptist Church, 2001.

Best, Wallace D. *Passionately Human, No Less Divine: Religion and Culture in Black Chicago, 1915–1952*. Princeton: Princeton University Press, 2005.

Binder, Carroll. *Chicago and the New Negro*. Chicago: Chicago Daily News, 1927.

Black, Ford S., comp. *Black's Blue Book: Business and Professional Direct Compilation of Names, Addresses and Telephones of Chicago's Colored Business and Professional People*. Chicago: F. S. Black, 1927.

Black, Timuel D., Jr., comp. *Bridges of Memory: Chicago's First Wave of Black Migration-An Oral History*. Evanston, IL: Northwestern University Press, 2003.

Black's Blue Book, 1923–24. Chicago: Douglass National Bank, 1923.

Blakely, Robert J. *Earl B. Dickerson: A Voice for Freedom and Equality*. Evanston, IL: Northwestern University Press, 2006.

Bontemps, Arna, and Jack Conroy. *They Seek a City*. Garden City, NY: Doubleday, Doran, 1945.

Boris, Joseph I., ed. *Who's Who in Colored America*. New York: Who's Who in Colored America, 1929.

Bracey, John H., Jr., August Meier, and Elliott Rudwick, eds. *Black Nationalism in America*. Indianapolis: Bobbs-Merrill, 1970.

Bracey, John H., Jr., and Manisha Sinha, eds. *African American Mosaic: A Documentary History from the Slave Trade to the Twenty-First Century*, vol. 2: *From 1865 to the Present*. Upper Saddle Valley, NJ: Pearson Education, 2004.

Branham, Charles R. "The Transformation of Black Political Leadership in Chicago, 1865–1942." Ph.D. diss, University of Chicago, 1981.

Brazeal, Brailsford R. *The Brotherhood of Sleeping Car Porters: Its Origin and Development*. New York: Harper and Bros., 1946.

Brodie, James M. *Created Equal: The Lives and Ideas of Black American Innovators*. New York: W. Morrow, 1993.

Brooks, Gwendolyn. *Report from Part One*. Detroit: Broadside Press, 1972.

Brown, Oscar C. *By a Thread*. New York: Vantage, 1982.

Buckler, Helen. *Daniel Hale Williams: Negro Surgeon*. New York: Pittman, 1968.

Bukowski, Douglas. *Big Bill Thompson, Chicago, and the Image of Politics*. Urbana: University of Illinois Press, 1998.

Bulmer, Martin. "Charles S. Johnson, Robert E. Park and the Research Methods of the Chicago Commission on Race Relations, 1919–1922: An Early Experiment in Applied Social Research." *Ethnic and Racial Studies* 4 (July 3, 1981): 289–306.

Bunche, Ralph Johnson. "The Negro in Chicago Politics," *National Municipal Review* 17 (May 1928): 261–64.

———. "The Thompson-Negro Alliance." *Opportunity* 7 (March 1929): 78-80.

Bundles, A'Lelia. *On Her Own Ground: The Life and Times of Madam C. J. Walker*. New York: Scribner, 2001.

Caldwell, Louis A. H. "Chicago's Policy Kings." MA thesis, Northwestern University, 1939.

Canaan, Gareth. "Part of the Loaf: Economic Conditions of Chicago's African-American Working Class during the 1920s." *Journal of Social History* 35 (Fall 2001): 147–74.

Carmichael, Stokley (aka Kwame Ture), and Charles V. Hamilton. *Black Politics: The Politics of Liberation in America* (New York: Random House, 1967).

Carroll, John A. "The Great American Bank Bubble and Why It Burst." *Real America* (April, 1935): 16–20.

Cayton, Horace R. *Long Old Road: An Autobiography*. Seattle: University of Washington Press, 1963.

Cederholm, Theresa Dickason, comp. *Afro-American Artists: A Bio-Bibliographical Directory*, 249–50. Boston: Boston Public Library, 1973.

Chavers-Wright, Madrue. *The Guarantee: P. W. Chavers-Banker, Entrepreneur, Philanthropist in Chicago's Black Belt of the Twenties*. New York: Wright-Amstead, 1985.

Chicago Commission on Race Relations [Charles S. Johnson]. *The Negro in Chicago*. Chicago: University of Chicago Press, 1922.

Christopher, Maurine. *America's Black Congressmen*. New York: Thomas Y. Crowell, 1971.

Clayton, Edward T. *The Negro Politician: His Success and Failure*. Chicago: Johnson, 1964.

Cohen, Lizabeth. *Making a New Deal: Industrial Workers in Chicago, 1919–1939*. Cambridge: Cambridge University Press, 1990.

Courage, Richard. *The Muse of Bronzeville: African American Creative Expression in Chicago, 1942–1950*. New Brunswick, NJ: Rutgers University Press, 2011.

Cox, Oliver Cromwell. "The Origins of Direct-Action Protest among Negroes." Unpublished manuscript, c. 1932, 1933 (microfiche copy). Kent State University Libraries.

Cronon, David E. *Black Moses: The Story of Marcus Garvey and the Universal Negro Improvement Association* (Madison: University of Wisconsin Press, 1955).

Davis, Corneal A. "Corneal A. Davis Memoir." Vols. 1 and 2. Illinois General Assembly Oral History Program, Legislative Studies Center. Springfield: Sangamon State University 1984.

Davis, Ralph Nelson. "The Negro Newspaper in Chicago." MA thesis, University of Chicago, 1939.

Detweiler, Frederick G. *The Negro Press in the U.S.* Chicago: University of Chicago Press, 1922.

Dickerson, Dennis C. *African American Preachers and Politics: The Careys of Chicago*. Jackson: University Press of Mississippi, 2010.

Dingle, Derek. "Reginald Lewis: The Deal Heard 'round the World: His $985 Million Buyout of TLC Beatrice Set the Bar for the Next Generation," *Black Enterprise* (June, 2005)

Drake, St. Clair. *Churches and Voluntary Associations in the Chicago Negro Community*. Chicago: Works Progress Administration, 1940.

Drake, St. Clair, and Horace R. Cayton. *Black Metropolis: A Study of Negro Life in a Northern City*. New York: Harcourt, Brace and World, 1945.

Driskell, Claude Evans. *The History of Chicago Dental Professionals*. Chicago: Claude E. Driskell, 1982.

Du Bois, W. E. B. "Colored Chicago." *Crisis* 4 (September 1915): 230–36.

Dummett, Clifton O., and Lois Doyle Dummett. *Charles Edwin Bentley: A Model for All Times*. St. Paul, MN: North Central, 1982.

Duster, Alfreda F. *Crusade for Justice: The Autobiography of Ida B. Wells*. Chicago: University of Chicago Press, 1967.

Edwards, Thyra J. "Attitudes of Negro Families on Relief." *Opportunity* 14 (July 1936): 213.

Elias, Sarah Davis. *Recalling Longview: An Account of the Longview Riot*. Baltimore: C.H. Fairfax, 2004.

Essien-Udom, E. U. *Black Nationalism*. Chicago: University of Chicago, 1962.

Evans, Linda J. "Claude A. Barnett and the Associated Negro Press." *Chicago History* 12 (Spring 1983): 44–56.

Fabre, Michel. *The Unfinished Quest of Richard Wright*. New York: William Morrow, 1973.

Fauset, Arthur H. *Black Gods of the Metropolis*. Philadelphia: Philadelphia Anthropological Society, 1944.

Fields, A. N. "Chicagoans Make Political History: E. H. Wright, Peer of Politicians." *Chicago Defender*, December 24, 1932, 11.

———. "Eventful History of Early Chicago: R. R. Jackson Born in the Windy City in 1870, Start His Career as a Postal Employee," *Chicago Defender*, January 28, 1933, 10.

Fisher, Miles Mark. "The History of Olivet Baptist Church." MA thesis, University of Chicago, June 1922.

Floyd,Samuel A., Jr. *The Power of Black Music: Interpreting Its History from Africa to the United States*. New York: Oxford University Press, 1995.

Flug, Michael L. "Vivian Gordon Harsh." In *Women Building Chicago, 1790–1990: A Biographical Dictionary*, ed. Ruma Lunin Schultz and Adele Hast, 359–61. Bloomington: Indiana University Press, 2001.

Foster, A. L. "Twenty Years of Interracial Goodwill through Social Service." In *Two Decades of Service: 1916-1936*. Chicago: Chicago Urban League, 1936.

Franklin, John Hope, and Alfred M. Moss. *From Slavery to Freedom*, 6th ed. New York: Alfred A. Knopf, 1988.

Frazier, E. Franklin. "Chicago: A Cross-Section of Negro Life." *Opportunity* 7 (March 1929): 70–73.

———. *The Negro Family in Chicago*. Chicago: University of Chicago Press, 1932.

———. *The Negro Family in the United States*. Chicago: University of Chicago, 1939.

———. "Occupational Classes of Negroes in Cities." *American Journal of Sociology* 35 (March 1930): 718–38.

Gatewood, Willard B., Jr. *Aristocrats of Color: The Black Elite, 1880–1920*. Bloomington: University of Indiana Press, 1990.

Garvey, Amy Jacques. *Garvey and Garveyism*. Kingston, Jamaica: United Printers, 1963.

Garvey, Marcus M. "Who and What Is a Negro?" In *The Philosophy and Opinions of Marcus Garvey*, 2 vols., ed. Amy Jacques Garvey. New York: Atheneum, 1970. Repr., New York: n.p., 1923.

Giddings, Paula J. *Ida: A Sword among Lions: Ida B. Wells and the Campaign against Lynching*. New York: HarperCollins, 2008.

Gold, Howard R., and Byron K. Armstrong. *A Preliminary Study of Inter-Racial Conditions in Chicago*. New York: Home Missions Council, 1920.

Gosnell, Harold F. "The Chicago 'Black Belt' as a Political Battleground." *American Journal of Sociology* 38 (December 1933): 329–41.

———. *Machine Politics*. Chicago: University of Chicago Press, 1939.

———. *Negro Politicians: The Rise of Negro Politics in Chicago*. Chicago: University of Chicago Press, 1935.

Greene, Lorenzo J., and Carter G. Woodson. *The Negro Wage Earner*. Washington, DC: Association for the Study of Negro Life and History, 1930.

Grossman, James R. *Land of Hope: Chicago, Black Southerners, and the Great Migration*. Chicago: University of Chicago Press, 1989.

Grossman, James R., Ann Durkin Keating, and Janice L. Reiff, eds. *The Encyclopedia of Chicago*. Chicago: University of Chicago Press, 2004.

Gruenberg, Robert. "Dawson of Illinois: What Price Moderation?" *Nation* 183 (September 18, 1956): 196

Gutman, Herbert G. *The Black Family in Slavery and Freedom, 1750–1925*. New York: Pantheon Books, 1976.

Haller, Mark H. "Policy Gambling, Entertainment and the Emergence of Black Politics: Chicago from 1900 to 1940." *Journal of Social History* 24 (Summer 1991): 719–39.

Halpern, Rick, and Roger Horowitz. *Meatpackers: An Oral History of Black Packinghouse Workers and Their Struggle for Racial and Economic Equality*. New York: Twayne, 1996.

Hamilton, Charles V. *The Black Preacher in America*. New York: William Morrow, 1972.

Hamilton, Dona Cooper, and Charles V. Hamilton. *The Dual Agenda: The African-American Struggle for Civil and Economic Equality*. New York: Columbia University Press, 1997.

Harris, Abram L. *The Negro as Capitalist: A Study of Banking and Business among American Negroes*. 1936. Reprint, Gloucester, MA: Peter Smith, 1968.

Harris, Isaac C. *Colored Men's Professional and Business Directory*. Chicago: Harris, 1885.

Harris, William H. *Keeping the Faith: A Philip Randolph, Milton P. Webster, and the Brotherhood of Sleeping Car Porters, 1925–1937*. Urbana: University of Illinois Press, 1977.

———. *The Harder We Run: Black Workers since the Civil War*. New York: Oxford University Press, 1982.

Hartfield, Ronne. *Another Way Home*. Chicago: University of Chicago Press, 2004.

Herbst, Alma. 1932. *The Negro in the Slaughtering and Meat-Packing Industry in Chicago*. Boston: Houghton Mifflin Company. Repr., New York: Arno Press, 1971.

Hine, Darlene Clark, ed., *Black Women in America: A Historical Encyclopedia*. Brooklyn: Carlson, 1993.

———. *Speak Truth to Power: Black Professional Class in United States History*. Brooklyn: Carlson, 1996.

Hine, Darlene Clark, and Kathleen Thompson. *A Shining Thread of Hope: The History of Black Women in America*. New York: Broadway Books, 1998.

Horowitz, Roger. *"Negro and White, Unite and Fight": A Social History of Industrial Unionism in Meatpacking, 1930–1990*. Urbana: University of Illinois Press, 1997.

Howard, Robert. "Black Banking in Chicago." MA thesis, Roosevelt University, 2002.

Hoyt, Homer. *One Hundred Years of Land Values in Chicago, 1833–1933*. Chicago: University of Chicago Press, 1933; repr., New York, 1970.

Hughes, Langston. *The Big Sea: An Autobiography*. New York: 1940. Repr., New York: Hill and Wang, 1963.

———. *Not without Laughter*. New York: Alfred A. Knopf, 1930. Repr., 1968.

Hunter, Albert. *Symbolic Communities: The Persistence and Change of Chicago's Local Communities*. Chicago: University of Chicago Press, 1974.

Ickes, Harold L. *The Secret Diary of Harold L. Ickes: The First Thousand Days, 1933–1936*. New York: Simon and Schuster, 1953.

Johnson, Charles S. "The New Frontage on American Life." In *The New Negro*, ed. Alain Locke, 278–98. New York: Boni, 1925.

———. "These 'Colored United States,' 8-Illinois: Mecca of the Migrant Mob." *Messenger* 5 (December 1923): 926–28, 933.

Johnson, James Weldon. *Black Manhattan*. New York: Atheneum, 1968.

Johnson, John H. *Succeeding against the Odds: The Inspiring Autobiography of One of America's Wealthiest Entrepreneurs*. New York: Warner Books, 1989.

Jones, Dewey R. "Chicago Claims Supremacy-Jesse Binga." *Opportunity* 6 (March 1929): 92.

Kellogg, Charles Flint. *NAACP*. Baltimore: John Hopkins Press, 1967.

Kenney, William H. *Chicago Jazz: A Cultural History*. New York: Oxford University Press, 1963.

Kent, George E. *A Life of Gwendolyn Brooks*. Lexington: University Press of Kentucky, 1990.

Kilson, Martin L. "Political Change in the Negro Ghetto, 1900–1940s." In *Key Issues in the Afro-American Experience*, vol. 2, ed. Nathan I. Huggins, Martin L. Kilson, and Daniel M. Fox, 167–92. New York: Harcourt, Brace Jovanovich, 1971.

Kiser, Clyde Vernon. *Sea Island to City: A Study of St. Helena Islanders in Harlem and Other Urban Centers*. New York: Columbia University Press, 1932. Repr., New York: Atheneum, 1969.

Krieg, Richard M., and Judith A. Cooksey, comps. *Provident Hospital: A Living Legacy*. Chicago: Provident Foundation, c.1997.

Landesco, John. *Illinois Crime Survey: Organized Crime in Chicago*. Chicago: University of Chicago Press, 1929.

Langer, Adam. "Black Metropolis." *Reader* [Chicago's Free Weekly], April 9, 1993, 1, 13–18.

Lasswell, Harold D., and Dorothy Blumenstock. *World Revolutionary Propaganda: A Chicago Study*. Chicago: Alfred A. Knopf, 1939.

Levine, Lawrence W. *High Culture/Low Culture: The Emergence of Cultural Hierarchy in America*. Cambridge: Harvard University Press, 1988.

Lewis, David L. *When Harlem Was in Vogue*. New York: Oxford University Press, 1981.

———. *W. E. B. Du Bois: Biography of a Race*. Vol. 1. New York: Henry Holt, 1993.

———. *W. E. B. Du Bois: The Fight for Equality and the American Century, 1919–1963*. Vol. 2 New York: Henry Holt, 2000.

Lindsay, Arnett G. "The Negro in Banking." *Journal of Negro History* 14 (April 1929): 156–201.

Litwack, Leon F. *Trouble in Mind: Black Southerners in the Age of Jim Crow*. New York: Alfred A. Knopf, 1998.

Locke, Alain. "The New Negro." In *The New Negro*, ed. Alain Locke, 3–4. New York: Albert and Charles Boni, 1925.

Logsdon, Joseph H. "The Rev. Archibald J. Carey and the Negro in Chicago Politics." MA thesis, University of Chicago, 1961.

Long, Herman H., and Charles S. Johnson. *People vs. Property*. Nashville: Fisk University Press, 1947.

Lovett, Robert M. "Chicago, the Phenomenal City." *Current History* 31 (November 1929): 331.

Lyon, Jeff. "Generations: A Quiet Quest to Honor a Family's Legacy." *Chicago Tribune*, February 23, 1992, 12–14.

Mahoney, Olivia. *Douglas/Grand Boulevard: A Chicago Neighborhood*. Chicago: Arcadia, 2001.

Major, Gerri, and Doris Saunders. *Black Society*. Chicago: Johnson, 1976.

Manning, Christopher. *William L. Dawson and the Limits of Black Electoral Leadership*. DeKalb: Northern Illinois Press, 2009.

Marquis, A. N. *Who's Who in Chicago and Vicinity, 1926*. Chicago: A. N. Marquis, 1926.

———. *Who's Who in Chicago and Vicinity, 1931*. Chicago: A. N. Marquis, 1931.

Martin, Tony. *Race First: The Ideological and Organizational Struggles of Marcus Garvey and the Universal Negro Improvement Association*. Dover, MA: Majority Press, 1976.

Materson, Lisa Gail. "Respectable Partisans: African American Women in Electoral Politics: 1877 to 1936." PhD diss., University of California at Los Angeles, 2000.

Mayer, Harold M., and Richard C. Wade. *Chicago: Growth of a Metropolis*. Chicago: University of Chicago Press, 1969.

McGee, Henry W. "Autobiography of Henry McGee: Chicago's First Black Postmaster." Chicago: n.p., August 1994.

McKissick, Patricia, and Frederick McKissick. *A Long Hard Journey: The Story of the Pullman Porter*. New York: Walker, 1989.

McLemore, Frances Williams. "The Role of the Negroes in Chicago in the Senatorial Election, 1930," master's thesis, University of Chicago, 1931.

Meier, August. *Negro Thought in America, 1880–1915: Racial Ideologies in the Age of Booker T. Washington*. Ann Arbor: University of Michigan Press, 1963.

Meyerowitz, Joanne J. *Women Adrift: Independent Wage Earners in Chicago, 1880–1930*. Chicago: University of Chicago Press, 1988.

Moore, R[ichard] E. *History of Bethel A.M.E. Church*. Chicago: Bethel A.M.E. Church, 1915. Repr., 1988.

Nichols, J. L., and William H. Crogman, comps. *New Progress of a Race*. Naperville, IL: J. L. Nichols, 1925.

"90th Anniversary Booklet, West Point Missionary Baptist Church." Chicago: West Point Missionary Baptist Church, 2007.

"Noted Men and Women in Illinois." *Negro History Bulletin* 5 (May 1942): 179, 182–83, 191.

O'Donnell, Sandra M. "'The Right to Work Is the Right to Live': The Social Work and Political and Civic Activism of Irene McCoy Gaines." *Social Service Review* 75 (September 2001).

"100th Anniversary Souvenir Book of the Grace Presbyterian Church." Chicago: 1988.

"100th Anniversary Souvenir Book of the Greater Bethesda Missionary Baptist Church: A Century with Christ, 1882–1982." Chicago: 1982.

"100th Anniversary Souvenir Book of the Original Providence Baptist Church." Chicago: 1963.

"108th Homecoming Celebration of [the] Friendship Baptist Church of Chicago." Chicago: July, 2005.

"113th Anniversary Souvenir Book of Saint Stephen African Methodist Episcopal Church." Chicago: 1985.

"114th Anniversary Souvenir Book of Bethel African Methodist Episcopal Church." Chicago: Bethel A.M.E. Church, 2006.

"The Original Forty Club of Chicago: 50th Anniversary Record." Program booklet. Chicago: Forty Club, 1966.

Osofsky, Gilbert. *Harlem: The Making of a Ghetto: Negro New York, 1890–1930*. New York: Harper Torchbooks, 1963.

Osthaus, Carl F. "The Rise and Fall of Jesse Binga, Black Financier." *Journal of Negro History* 58 (1973): 39–60.

Otis, Philo A. *The First Presbyterian Church, 1833–1913*. 2nd, rev. ed. Chicago: Fleming H. Revill, 1913

Ottley, Roi. *The Lonely Warrior: The Life and Times of Robert S. Abbott*. Chicago: Henry Regnery, 1955.

Pacyga, Dominic A., and Ellen Skerrett. *Chicago: City of Neighborhoods*. Chicago: Loyola University Press, 1986.

Perata, David D. *Those Pullman Blues: An Oral History of the Africa American Railroad Attendant*. New York: Twayne, 1996.

Poinsett, Alex. *Common Folk in an Uncommon Cause*. Chicago: Lakeside Press, 1962.

Pinderhughes, Diane H. *Race and Ethnicity in Chicago Politics: A Re-examination of Pluralist Theory*. Urbana: University of Illinois Press, 1987.

Platt, Anthony M. *E. Franklin Frazier Reconsidered*. New Brunswick, NJ: Rutgers University Press, 1991.

Puth, Robert C. "Supreme Life: The History of a Negro Life Insurance Company, 1919–1962." *Business History Review* 43 (Spring 1969): 1–20.

Record, Wilson. *The Negro and the Communist Party*. Chapel Hill: University of North Carolina Press, 1951. Repr., Atheneum, 1971.

———. *Race and Radicalism*. Ithaca: Cornell University Press, 1964.

Reed, Christopher Robert. "All the World Is Here!" *The Black Presence at White City*, 107–10. Bloomington: Indiana University Press, 2000.

———. "Beyond Chicago's Black Metropolis: A History of the West Side's First Century, 1837–1940. 92 *Journal of the Illinois State Historical Society* 92 [special Issue: African Americans in Illinois] (Summer 1999): 119–49.

———. "Black Chicago Civic Organization before 1935." *Journal of Ethnic Studies* 14 (Winter 1987): 65–77.

———. "Black Chicago Political Realignment during the Depression and New Deal." *Illinois Historical Journal* 78 (Winter 1985): 242–56.

———. *Black Chicago's First Century*, vol 1, *1833–1900*. Columbia: University of Missouri Press, 2005.

———. *The Chicago NAACP and the Rise of Black Professional Leadership, 1910–1966*. Bloomington: Indiana University Press, 1997.

———. "A Reinterpretation of Black Strategies for Change at the Chicago World's Fair, 1933–1934." *Illinois Historical Journal* 81 (Spring 1988): 2–12.

———. "A Study of Black Politics and Protest in Depression-Decade Chicago, 1930–1939." PhD diss., Kent State University, May 1982.

Reich, Howard. "A Wail of a Town." *Chicago Tribune Magazine*, September 5, 1993, 12–14, 16, 18, 24.

Ribowsky, Mark. *A Complete History of the Negro Leagues: 1884–1955*. New York: Birch Lane Press, 1995.

Robb, Frederick H. H. *The Negro in Chicago*, 2 vols. Chicago: Washington Intercollegiate Club, 1927, 1929.

Robinson, George F., Jr. "The Negro in Politics in Chicago." *Journal of Negro History* 17 (April 1932): 180–229.

Santino, Jack. *Miles of Smiles, Years of Struggle: Stories of Black Pullman Porters*. Urbana: University of Illinois Press, 1989.

Semmes, Clovis. *The Regal Theater and Black Chicago Culture*. New York: Palgrave MacMillan, 2006.

"75th Anniversary History of the Friendship Baptist Church." Chicago; n.p., 1972.

Simms, James N., comp. *Simms's Blue Book and National Negro Business and Professional Directory*. Chicago: James N. Simms, 1923. Repr., 1977.

"65th Anniversary Souvenir Book of the Pilgrim Baptist Church." Chicago: 1982.

Smith, J. Clay, *Emancipation: The Making of a Black Lawyer, 1844–1944*. Philadelphia: University of Pennsylvania Press, 1993.

Spear, Allan H. *Black Chicago: The Making of a Negro Ghetto, 1890–1920*. New York: Atheneum, 1969.

Spero, Sterling D., and Abram L. Harris. *The Black Worker: The Negro and the Labor Movement*. New York: Atheneum, 1969. Repr., 1931.

Stackhouse, Perry J. *Chicago and the Baptists: A Century of Progress*. Chicago: University of Chicago Press, 1933.

Stephens, Ronald J. *Idlewild: The Black Eden of Michigan*. Chicago: Arcadia, 2001.

Stewart, Jacqueline Najuma. *Migrating to the Movies: Cinema and Black Urban Modernity*. Berkeley: University of California Press, 2005.

Storch, Randi. *Red Chicago: American Communism at Its Grassroots, 1928–35*. Urbana: University of Illinois Press, 2007.

Strickland, Arvarh E. *History of the Chicago Urban League*. Urbana: University of Illinois Press, 1967.

Sutherland, Robert Lee. "An Analysis of Negro Churches in Chicago." PhD diss., University of Chicago, June 1930.

Suttles, Gerald D. *The Man-Made City: The Land-Use Confidence Game in Chicago*. Chicago: University of Chicago, 1990.

———. *The Social Structure of Communities*. Chicago: University of Chicago, 1972.

Taylor, William E., and Harriet G. Warkel, eds. *A Shared Heritage: Art by Four African Americans*. Indianapolis: Indianapolis Museum of Art, 1996.

Travis, Dempsey J. *An Autobiography of Black Chicago*. Chicago: Urban Research Institute, 1981.

———. *An Autobiography of Black Politics*. Chicago: Urban Research Institute, 1987.

———. *An Autobiography of Black Jazz*. Chicago: Urban Research Institute, 1983.

Tye, Larry. *Rising from the Rails: Pullman Porters and the Making of the Black Middle Class*. New York: Henry Holt, 2004.

Walker, Helen Edith. "The Negro in the Medical Profession." MA thesis, University of Virginia, 1949.

Walker, Juliet E. K. *The History of Black Business in America: Capitalism, Race, Entrepreneurship*. New York, Twayne, 1998.

———, ed., *Encyclopedia of African American Business History*. Westport, CN: Greenwood Press, 1999.

Walker, Margaret. *Richard Wright, Daemonic Genius: A Portrait of the Man, a Critical Look at His Work*. New York: Warner Books, 1988.

Warkel, Harriet G. "Image and Identity: The Art of William E. Scott, John W. Hardrick, and Hale G. Woodruff." In *A Shared Heritage: Art by Four African Americans*, ed. William E. Taylor and Harriet G. Warkel, 18. Indianapolis: Indianapolis Museum of Art, 1996.

Warner, W. Lloyd, et al. *Color and Human Nature: Negro Personality Development in a Northern City*. Washington, DC: American Council on Education, 1941.

Waskow, Arthur I. *From Race Riot to Sit-In, 1919 and the 1960s: A Study in the Connections between Conflict and Violence*. Garden City, NY: Doubleday, 1966. Originally published by Anchor, 1907.

Weems, Robert E., Jr. *Black Business in the Black Metropolis: The Chicago Metropolitan Assurance Company, 1925–1985*. Bloomington: Indiana University Press, 1996.

Wesley, James H. "Carter G. Woodson-as a Scholar." *Journal of Negro History* 36 (January 1951): 10.

Withers, Z. "Bethel Church." *Half-Century Magazine* (July 1918): 8.

Wooddy, Carroll Hill. *The Chicago Primary of 1926: A Study in Election Methods*. Chicago: University of Chicago Press, 1927. Repr., New York: Arno Press, 1974.

Woodson, Carter G. *The Negro Professional Man and the Community, with Special Emphasis on the Physician and the Lawyer*. Washington, DC: Association for the Study of Negro Life and History, 1934. Repr., New York: Negro Universities Press, 1969.

Wright, Richard. *American Hunger*. New York: Harper & Row, 1944.

———. *Lawd Today*. New York: Walker, 1963.

Wright, Richard R. Jr. *87 Years behind the Black Curtain: An Autobiography*. Philadelphia: Rare Book Company, 1965.

Interviews and Personal Communication

Bearden, Patricia Walker. Interview, Chicago, November 2 and 9, 2007.

Bey, Sister C. Price. Interview, Chicago, June 22, 1968.

Bibb, Goldie. Telephone interview, Chicago, January 25, 1978.

Dickerson, Earl B. Interview, Chicago, July 11, 1968; March 21, 1984

Dickerson, Spencer C. Interview, Chicago.

Evans, Lovelynn. Interview, Chicago, December 6, 1984.

Falls, Dr. Arthur G. Interview, Chicago, March 10, 1978.

Falls, Dr. Arthur G. and Mrs. Lillian Proctor Falls. Interview, Chicago, November 4, 1983.

Holt, Rosalia. Interview, Chicago, August 15, 2007.

Jones, Jean Boger. Telephone interview, Grand Rapids, Michigan, October 25, 2007.

Renfroe, Everett. Interview, Chicago, July 11, 1968.

Rhodes, Josephine Reed. Interview, Chicago, July 21, 1968

Topps, Libby Davis. Interview, Chicago, July 13, 2007.

Walker, Lucine. Interview, Chicago, May 25, 1968.

Wheeler, Lloyd G., III. Interviews, Chicago, February 26, 1997; September 3, 1998; and March 18, 2001.

Williams, Pauline Lewis. Interview, Evanston, Illinois, January 22, 2001, conducted by Professor Suellen Hoy.

Unpublished manuscript on the life of Alex W. and Julia Walker

Websites

"The Life of The Pullman Porter," http://www.scsra.org/library/porter.html, p. 6 of 10.

INDEX

ABBREVIATIONS

ABC	Associated Business Clubs
AMCBW	Amalgamated Meat Cutter and Butcher Workmen (AMCBW)
BSCP	Brotherhood of Sleeping Car Porters
CPUSA	Communist Party of the USA
NAACP	National Association for the Advancement of Colored People

CHRISTOPHER ROBERT REED is a professor emeritus of history at Roosevelt University and the author of *"All the World Is Here": The Black Presence at White City* and *The Chicago NAACP and the Rise of Black Professional Leadership, 1910–1966.*

THE NEW BLACK STUDIES SERIES

Beyond Bondage: Free Women of Color in the Americas *Edited by David Barry Gaspar and Darlene Clark Hine*

The Early Black History Movement, Carter G. Woodson, and Lorenzo Johnston Greene *Pero Gaglo Dagbovie*

"Baad Bitches" and Sassy Supermamas: Black Power Action Films *Stephane Dunn*

Black Maverick: T. R. M. Howard's Fight for Civil Rights and Economic Power *David T. Beito and Linda Royster Beito*

Beyond the Black Lady: Sexuality and the New African American Middle Class *Lisa B. Thompson*

Extending the Diaspora: New Histories of Black People *Dawne Y. Curry, Eric D. Duke, and Marshanda A. Smith*

Activist Sentiments: Reading Black Women in the Nineteenth Century *P. Gabrielle Foreman*

Black Europe and the African Diaspora *Edited by Darlene Clark Hine, Trica Danielle Keaton, and Stephen Small*

Freeing Charles: The Struggle to Free a Slave on the Eve of the Civil War *Scott Christianson*

African American History Reconsidered *Pero Gaglo Dagbovie*

Freud Upside Down: African American Literature and Psychoanalytic Culture *Badia Sahar Ahad*

A. Philip Randolph and the Struggle for Civil Rights *Cornelius L. Bynum*

Queer Pollen: White Seduction, Black Male Homosexuality, and the Cinematic *David A. Gerstner*

The Rise of Chicago's Black Metropolis, 1920–1929 *Christopher Robert Reed*

The University of Illinois Press
is a founding member of the
Association of American University Presses.

Composed in 10.5/13 Minion Pro
with Minion Pro display
by Celia Shapland
at the University of Illinois Press
Manufactured by Sheridan Books, Inc.

University of Illinois Press
1325 South Oak Street
Champaign, IL 61820-6903
www.press.uillinois.edu